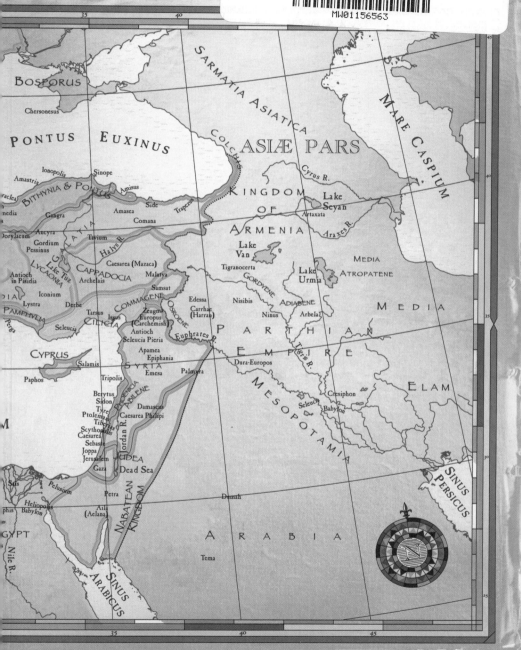

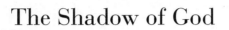

The Shadow of God

# The Shadow of God

*Stories from Early Judaism*

Leo Duprée Sandgren

Printed in the United States of America

*First Printing — August 2003*


**Library of Congress Cataloging-in-Publication Data**


Sandgren, Leo Duprée.
    The shadow of God : stories from early Judaism /
  Leo Duprée Sandgren.
        p. cm.
    Includes bibliographical references.
    ISBN 1-56563-605-8
    1. Jews—History—586 B.C. to 70 A.D—Fiction. I. Title.
    PS3619.A536S53 2003
    813′.6—dc21
                                    2003013536

# CONTENTS

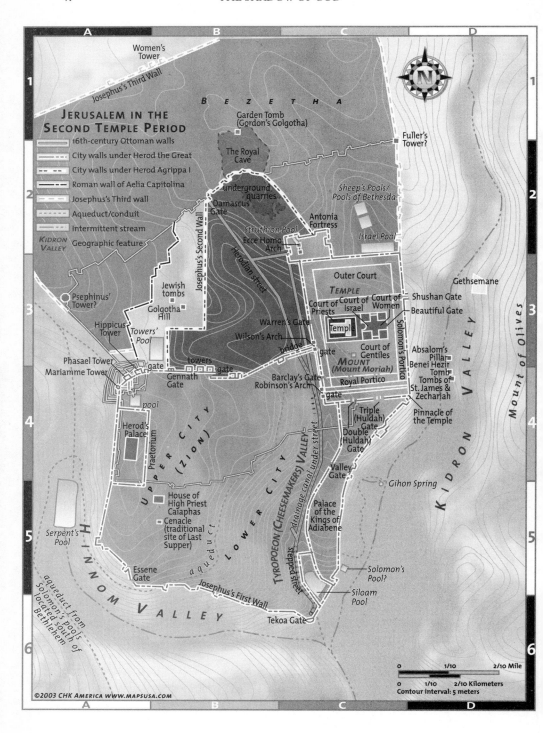

Jerusalem in the Second Temple Period

# Prologue

Because there is far more to Jewish history than may be discovered from the reputations of its illustrious dramatis personæ, I, Leontius, scribe and librarian by training, make bold to narrate the stories of men and women who have been left out of the magnum opus, namely, the Jewish Antiquities, which my employer Flavius Josephus is near to completing, now in the twelfth year of the reign of Domitian, emperor of Rome. Josephus, in his great undertaking, retells the story of God and his people, us the Jews, though he is careful to call us Jews only after the destruction of Jerusalem by the king of Babylon; for during our exile in Egypt Jacob's descendants were named the children of Israel, and out of our exile in Babylon did the children of Israel become known as Jews. When writing of us in distant antiquity, as paraphrasing biblical history, Josephus calls us Hebrews and follows judiciously the sacred tale now elevated to the status of canon. At times he follows the Hebrew text, but more often the Greek text, entitled the Septuagint on account of the miraculous way in which the books of Moses were translated from the Hebrew by seventy, or some say seventy-two, scholars, each working independently yet producing an identical and divinely inspired translation, perfect in every way. Still, there is room for improvement, or else, why retell it?

Josephus began this work in the tradition of the Book of the Chronicles, that magnificent history of Israel whose anonymous and humble author inspired the Jews of his day to see the rule of God sustained through the priesthood of the temple in Jerusalem and the kingship of Persia. Josephus intends the same for our day, that is, he writes to convince Jews across the empire that Providence has set the scepter of its sovereignty over Italy, but he would also persuade the Greeks and Romans that the Jews are an ancient and virtuous race that contributes to the welfare of the empire. Josephus will extol our ancestors, their faith and nobility. He will compose eloquent speeches for the players in the divine drama.

For so momentous a task, Josephus required a detachment of scribes to do his bidding, which he was able to hire thanks to the largess of his patrons from the Flavian household, and others like the generous Epaphroditus, who placed at our disposal his library of 30,000 books. We scribes collected obscure sources, and read them thoroughly, while Josephus read the histories of Thucydides and Polybius, Nicolaus of Damascus, but most importantly the twenty books of Dionysius Halicarnassus entitled Roman Antiquities, on which the master has modeled his own work. My task has been to search the many and varied writings of the Jewish people. These books of the Jews written over six centuries, in Hebrew, Aramaic, and Greek, are no small number, and they occupied me for most of the fifteen years I have labored for Josephus. I wrote down in chronological order the significant events and principal players in the history of the Jews since our exile in Babylon, and presented digests, or epitomes, to Josephus. On occasion I suggested the story of a lesser person, this one or that, was worthy of inclusion in his history. The master, however, invariably declined to include them. Although Josephus is a good historian, having a gifted mind—quite the child prodigy, to hear him tell of it—his vision for greatness blinds him to the voices that do not exhibit lives favorable to his vision, or for some other reason complicate his history.

How many were there who played a telling rôle, but for reasons known only to the tellers of the tale, received no place in the scheme of things? We cannot listen to them all, nor replay their stories with the same detail as they originally played themselves out. We must be selective, and economical with parchment and ink. We cannot retell life itself, not even the waking hours, leaping over the dreams of night. All that transpires in the minds and mouths of each person is a story only God can tell, and then only in the timelessness of eternity, if we are to follow each thread and make sense of it all, to say nothing of ultimate justice. But we can let the voices speak unhindered, and very nearly uninterrupted, for the spirit that lives, lives on in us. Must there not be something of the spirit that survives from generation to generation, just as there is something of the seed that is passed on from parent to child, as every genealogy proves? If I am fully authorized to speak on behalf of my father, and he of his, and so on backward from generation to past generation, may we not all speak of the lives of our progenitors and those with whom they made merry? Though our full authority be reduced to a hundredth, or a six-hundredth, of an ancestor of the past, still, it is a piece of authority. Each of us may, in some small way, speak for Adam and Eve, and partake of their words and deeds, and even the consequences.

Now, there are two schools of thought concerning the art of story-telling, as indeed, there are two philosophies of history, or two different goals of the historian. The one speaks *to* the present, the other *of* the past; the one persuades men to virtue, the other exposes truth. Here we will incline toward the latter, and let the Heliconian Muses, offspring of Zeus they say, persuade to virtue as best they can. Having admitted a place for the Muses, whether they amuse one or bemuse another, I also confess that I take up this task principally for my own relief and pleasure, as if I alone sit among the tiered stone seats of the theater. Relief that these ever-present spirits will have their voice and leave me alone, and pleasure that I shall be the first to hear them. To anyone who may join me, I whisper a welcome, and I move along the stone bench of our theater to give room.

I, of course, must narrate. I shall lay down appropriate genealogy and string a backdrop behind the voices, to set their text in its context, describing the whence and the whither that give meaning to each day. Just as no one demands of Adam an explanation as to why he woke up one morning from the deep sleep of oblivion, nor of Eve when she woke up beside Adam after his second sleep, it is not fitting that the players of the drama, whether great or small, should have to explain why they are on the stage—that would be an unforgivable humiliation—they are there, that is all, and that is that. I shall play my part as narrator then, and any deficiencies therein must not be laid to their account. Under the same canopy of justice, I assume no responsibility for what they say. In particular, I shall refrain from pronouncing the Name, יהוה, using only the customary tetragram YHWH, which a reverent Jew now pronounces as Adonai, the Lord. But it was not always so, and our voices may speak according to their custom in calling amiably on YHWH by name. And even as God himself on occasion invokes the first person plural, we too, may invoke the communal voice as it suits our fancy—their story is, after all, ours, and our story, God's.

# 1

## Figurines of Clay

As for you, O house of Israel, thus says the Lord GOD: Go serve every one of you his idols, now and hereafter, if you will not listen to me; but my holy name you shall no more profane with your gifts and your idols.

Ezekiel ben Buzi

Are we figurines of sun-baked clay who dwell throughout the ages sheltered within a niche of ancient walls, to be grasped and carried away on the back of a desert ass and set within a niche of another ancient wall? We are not! We breathe the breath of life. We cannot stand long without roots sinking themselves into the earth, seeking what nourishment may be found. Even our sandals send their thongs downward. And when roots take hold, do not branches and leaves shoot forth? And the soil, does not its nourishment, when softened by heaven's rain, determine the nature of our limbs and the very sap of our veins?

Exile became our home. Yes, home in a fertile land between the rivers Tigris and Euphrates, a land not far from legendary Eden, but a home without the throne of David, for Jehoiachin, king of Judah, was imprisoned in Babylon; home without the throne of Yahweh our god, for his house too, had fallen amid the ruins of Jerusalem. To those of us who arrived in the first deportation from Judah, King Nebuchadrezzar gave land along the Chebar canal, a day's journey from the ancient and sacred city of Nippur.[1] "Dwell here in this land," they said to us. "Build homes, till the earth, reap and give tribute to the king of kings. Sing songs of joy and mirth." We sang, but only the lament of the exiles: *By the waters of Babylon, there we sat down and wept, when we remembered Zion.*[2] There we sat down and wept tears like almonds shaken from bowed and laden trees; but when our tear sacks dried up, we rubbed the shriveled skins beneath our eyes and we built homes in the settlement of Tel-aviv and six others, Tel-melah, Keruv, Kassifia, Addan, Immer, and Tel-harsha—the seven settlements of the exile.[3]

We built homes of clay brick. We worked the fields, we carried goods on our backs and on the backs of our beasts of burden, and in all ways served our new masters by the sweat of our brows. We worked and we waited with glistening foreheads and listening ears cocked toward the west winds for tidings from Judah. Perchance Zedekiah, viceroy of Judah, would negotiate our return. Vainly we waited. Zedekiah proved himself unfaithful to the king of kings. He rejected the counsel of the prophet Jeremiah, and he sought alliance with Egypt.[4] Nebuchadrezzar went up against Judah the second time. He laid waste to all the villages of the land, he besieged Jerusalem, and destroyed the temple of Yahweh 470 years after King Solomon built it, in the twelfth year of the captivity of Jehoiachin.[5] Thus was Judah exiled from his land.[6]

The first generation of exiles, who had begun to prosper in Babylon, sold their homes to these late-comers of the second deportation, who were the poorer of the land, and the more accustomed to simple dwellings. The first exiles then built larger homes, even villas, on the settlement perimeters. In the older portion of Tel-aviv, the homes expanded like a pomegranate, rooms attached themselves to exterior walls, and roofs became floors.

For a span of three decades the settlement had grown. Children were born, families allied themselves in marriage, parents were buried. Young men sought their fortunes in the wealth of Babylon. Few of the first streets in Tel-aviv remained straight, and behind every complex of dwellings, crooked alleys found their ways hither and thither. Did not one alley lead to the home of Eliakim the potter and his wife Marah?

Protected by the high walls of a small courtyard, Eliakim stripped to his loincloth for the slaughter. He grasped the chicken by the neck and draped its nervous brown and white feathered body over his arm. His hands were firm, his fingers smoothed and calloused, the color of clay, the reddish clay of Babylon, but his arms had taken on the yellowish pallor of age. His rounded shoulders and back, stooped from years of bending over the potter's wheel, relaxed as he raised his face to the heavens and recited the blessing. When he had blessed his god, he lowered his face and his gray beard brushed against his drooping chest. Eliakim held the knife in his right hand, and with his left hand forefinger he brushed open the neck feathers. He slit the neck of the chicken. The bird fluttered in its death throes; its feet ran swiftly in the air, but no sound escaped. He held the bird at arm's length as the blood spurted to the beating of the wings and drained onto the dusty ground. Later, Marah would scoop up the blood stained dust and sprinkle it in the soil of her potted plants, which she nurtured under a thatch shelter.

Eliakim took the limp bird, now quite dead, and plucked it clean and cut it into five pieces. These he placed into a clay bowl and brought them to Marah. "Take this offering, my wife," he intoned, "and make a meal for us and our son. Let us eat and remember the blessings of Abraham our father. Let us honor the sabbath of Yahweh, and hasten the day of our return."

Marah took the bowl from his hands, and bowed her head in recognition of his lordship and his lordly sorrow. Eliakim, in the sixth decade of his life, acquainted with the life-sorrows of aged and wrinkled men, still chanted the lament of the exiles and longed for the day when he might return to the land of the promise, and if not he, then his seed, his son Hattil, and if not Hattil, then the son of his son. But return they must, to rebuild the temple, and resume the divine promise given to Abraham, Isaac, Jacob, and the throne to David, and the priesthood to Zadok.[7] For Marah, Tel-aviv was home, and she lived only for the day.

Eliakim washed himself and went off to the house of an elder where he would join old men in afternoon prayers, a custom begun in exile.[8] Marah rose and salted the meat to remove any blood from the bird that they should not in the least disobey the law of Yahweh against the eating of blood.[9] She placed the bloodless and salt-shriveled meat into a pot of steaming water set upon the hearth.

Marah knelt down on a mat of reeds in the corner of the one room dwelling. The Babylonian sun, well past its zenith, shone through the open doorway and illumined the clay walls. Each object in the chamber cast its own shadow; a low table and two stools, a jug of water on the table, and a chest of acacia wood against the opposite wall, which protected all things valuable to her, and which no one but herself opened. Upon the chest sat a copper lampstand brought from Judah. Beside the door to their courtyard lay a large woven basket filled with cracked and misshapen earthenware vessels, those which Eliakim discarded from his potter's wheel and kiln. Soon he would take the vessels to market to sell as scrapers, spoons, or shards to write upon.

Marah pulled a lump of dough from the batch in her clay bowl and pressed it into the center of a small wooden tray and patted it into a circle. She tossed the thin loaf into the domed brick oven. The flat bread would bake quickly. Marah tossed a second lump and prepared a third. While the loaves baked, she glanced again about the house. She had swept the clay floor and sprinkled water to give it a dustless sheen in preparation for the entrance of the sabbath. Their wool bed mat lay folded against the wall, covered with a new multicolored striped blanket and three wool-filled cushions. Her leafy greens and onions lay nearby in a shallow basket, ready for the stew. All these preparations she would perform for every sabbath, as her husband desired, but on this occasion she made ready in greater anticipation, for her only son, Hattil, would join them. Many months, many sabbaths had passed since Hattil, an officer in the king's service, had come home.

Marah, which meant "bitterness," was born in a bitter year, the year that the great King Josiah perished in battle against Pharaoh Necho on the hills of Meggido.[10] She entered the consciousness of memory in the village of Nob, not far from Jerusalem. Her father betrothed her to Eliakim, a potter and the son of a potter, in the town of Anathoth. At fourteen she became the wife of Eliakim. Marah scarcely recalled the years of childhood, so much turmoil lay between the past and the present. And what did it matter? A girl child came into the world only to sustain the people, to mature quickly, to take a man and the seed of a man, and to give birth to the next generation. Marah had fulfilled her destiny, but only as rags fulfill the need for clothing. She first gave birth to a stillborn, without a name of remembrance, and Marah herself nearly perished. When she recovered, her older sister Bilah gave Marah a small idol of Astarte to hide and keep with her that she might again be fertile. Marah hid the small clay statuette under her mattress, and when Eliakim came again to impregnate her, she conceived and gave birth to a son, a male heir to carry on his name, and thus she settled the heart of her husband. She conceived again and gave birth to a girl, but the child died from disease within a few months, during the siege of Jerusalem.

Eliakim and Marah came to Babylon among the second deportation, after the temple was destroyed and half the city razed. They were the residue of the land, the remnant of the exiles, yet many, such as Eliakim, were from long established families whose heritage and reputation reached back to the days of David the king. They came with one heavily laden donkey and their infant son. In crossing the desert, her womb dried up and her breasts grew limp.

When the loaves had baked, and their aroma filled the dwelling, Marah placed them on her wood platter and covered them with a cloth. She took the last bit of dough and rolled it lightly into a fat elongated lump. From her apron she withdrew a small mold of Astarte, or Ishtar, as the Queen of Heaven had long been known in Babylon.[11] Marah pressed it into the lump of dough, and tossed the dedicated loaf bearing the likeness of Astarte into the dying coals beneath the oven. Marah took her oven stick and brushed ashes over the Astarte cake until it hardened. She withdrew the cake and blew upon it with quick short breaths. Quietly and reverently she murmured: "O Ishtar, merciful goddess, I have come to you, I have prepared for you an offering, a pure cake baked in ashes; I have poured out libations for you. Hear me and act favorably toward me!"[12]

Just then, Marah heard the footsteps of Eliakim returning. She hid the statuette back into her chest of belongings and placed the cake in her apron. Should her husband know of this, he would declare the sabbath meal defiled, and he would surely take a round stone from his potter's kiln and pound the statuette into dust. But Marah kept her devotion to Astarte hidden from Eliakim. All the wives of Tel-aviv who appealed to Astarte kept their devotion hidden. Certainly, all the settlement knew that some women worshiped Astarte, as women of Israel and Judah had always done, and some men allowed their wives to demonstrate quietly their devotion, but most did not, and the elders forbade it. Most husbands chose not to suspect their wives so that they might denounce the practice with a clear conscience, and by mutual consent no man openly accused another man's wife. Such a man was Eliakim. Marah did her best to protect his reputation, but she had conceived with the help of Astarte, and she sought prosperity and protection for her son by the hand of the goddess.

Hattil came with the long shadows. He wore a long yellow tunic, pleated below the waist and held firmly to his body by a heavy leather belt and a silver clasp. He trimmed, curled, oiled, and perfumed his dark beard after the manner of Babylon. His own shadow stretched across the street and onto the walls of the closely packed dwellings. Ahead, he saw the shadows beside the street bowing to his shadow. "Shalom Hattil ben Eliakim, soldier of the king," they greeted him. This was right and proper, for he carried a military insignia around his neck. It pleased Hattil to see the shadows bowing before him. No longer were the sons of Israel prisoners and outcasts. Many entered into the service of the king of Babylon, and a few rose to important positions among his advisors. The sons of Judah demonstrated their superior skills in the service of the great king, and he welcomed them. A few sons of the exile, the gifted Daniel and Mishael, rose to the king's council, eating at the king's table.[13] Others followed close behind. Hattil nodded to the community. The further he penetrated into Tel-aviv, the more imposing his shadow became. "Shalom Hattil ben Eliakim, soldier of the king."

At the home of his youth, Hattil paused. So pathetic, the walls. Unlike the settlement walls where shadows bowed, he now stood at the compound of his impoverished origins, and like the ruins of Jerusalem, their cracked sun-baked clay mocked him: *Thou knowest thou art but clay and dust.* Hattil frowned. He had grown accustomed to the enameled walls of his barracks in Babylon, and already he longed to return, but he came to pay his respects to his family before departing on his next mission. He flared his nostrils, drew a deep breath, and approached the open door. His shadow crossed the threshold, announcing his presence. Marah rose from her mat and hurried to greet her son.

Hattil let his mother embrace him, and responded stiffly, "Shalom, mother."

"Shalom," Marah sighed. She let her arms fall and looked briefly into his face. "Come," she said softly, "come and greet your father." Marah took the stiff hand of her son, ever the soldier, and drew him into the chamber. Hattil stooped slightly beneath the low slung lintel and entered the dwelling. Eliakim sat cross-legged on the folded wool mattress, resting amid cushions against the wall. His simple brown cloak hung loosely over his shoulders and arms, and opened wide at his chest to let the cool of the evening penetrate his white robe beneath. Eliakim remained motionless, awaiting the homage of his son. Hattil bowed low. Filial piety was a far-reaching law of every land and people. The heart might scorn, the mind wander, but the head must bow. "Peace be with you, father."

"My son," Eliakim intoned, and gestured to the cushions beside him. "Come, sit at my right hand, rest and refresh yourself and welcome the sabbath with me."

Hattil took a place on the couch. He leaned his elbow upon a cushion while Marah removed his sandals and washed his feet. She brought cups of water, sweetened with honey and a dash of wine, and placed before them a bowl of dates and almonds. Marah tended her stew, adding the onions, leafy greens, and herbs, and when satisfied with all her preparations, she drew near upon the mat.

The conversation began, as it did in any village, with minor affairs—the comings and goings of village folk—affairs important enough to them, but much less momentous to others, and in terms of the cosmos, minor indeed. Marah spoke and Hattil occasionally asked further after so-and-so, and he nodded his blessings upon them all. Soon, visitors arrived, boyhood friends of Hattil, and Menachem, a member of the council of elders, and his sons. Marah withdrew as the guests crowded around upon the matt. She added dates and almonds to the bowl, and the men thanked her and blessed her home.

Hattil received their salutations, for it was right and proper they should come. They came to learn of the news in Babylon, and the impending military expedition against Egypt, where, as all the world knew, the over-reaching general Amasis had slain Pharaoh Hophra, and tribute to Babylon had dried up. He responded to their queries with a guarded authority, and imparted to them such information as an officer in the king's army might know and, of course, be permitted to speak. If Hattil hesitated at a request, the questioner placed his hand before his mouth, and raised his eyebrows, the wiser for knowing there were things afoot forbidden to the common man.

Hattil told them of the coming military campaign. The king would indeed march upon Egypt to restore tribute. Preparations were indeed underway across the land. Hattil lowered his voice. "In three days time I and my men are to go and levy a tribute of horses from the nobles of Ur, powerful horses bred and trained for chariots." Hattil grew animated and vigorous. During times of war, officers rose swiftly in rank, both for their many heroic deeds and the loss of their companions in arms. Glory lay at his fingertips. "Our king Nebuchadrezzar will again crush the Egyptians." He clenched his fist as if crushing a rock, and scattered the imaginary grains on the floor. "The armies of the slothful and repugnant Egyptians are as dung beetles beneath his feet. Egypt will bow down to the great king, just as the Ibis-headed gods are servants of Marduk the all powerful."

At the name of Marduk, the company caught its collective breath. Although it was not sacrilege to utter the names of the gods of Babylon, there was a time and a place and a protocol. In the streets of Babylon, Nippur, and Ur, one might sing the hymns of Marduk, who ruled before the great flood, and whose absence caused the great flood, and who chose to dwell in Babylon. And because Babylon is the center of the universe, and Marduk is the god of Babylon, the gods of other cities must now pay homage to the great god of the universe, and to his son Nabu. Upon such a parcel of presumption, a son of Judah might agree with a son of Babylon, for the sake of the price of grain or a jar of olives, but within the town of Tel-aviv, and behind the cloistered walls of an Israelite home, well, one was expected to leave the gods of other peoples outside the door. Eliakim, who never let spill the name of Marduk from his lips, raised his hand. "Do not honor the gods of Babylon in this house my son, strength of my right arm, for we are the seed of Abraham, and of the stock of Jacob. Our god is Yahweh."

Hattil dutifully let his shoulders sag in submission. "Forgive," he mumbled.

Eliakim said simply, "Did I not raise you in worship of Yahweh?"

Hattil responded, "Thus you raised me, father, and from my earliest recollection. But worship is one thing and life is another. We must distinguish between words and deeds, and choose gods who by their victory are worthy of worship."

Eliakim replied, "Our god Yahweh punished us. He was not defeated. For our sins Yahweh sent the army of Babylon against us."

Hattil lowered his voice in derision. "The fathers have eaten sour grapes, and the children's teeth are set on edge."[14] The young men who grew up with Hattil grunted in agreement with the ancient proverb. Hattil continued, "What shall my mouth reply, O elders of Judah? In innocence I came into exile. We are as slaves, unless we rise up by our own strength, as I have done."

Eliakim opened his mouth, but closed it and shook his head. Whereupon, Menachem snatched up Eliakim's voice and made it his own. "Have we said that you should not rise up?" Menachem replied. "It is right and proper that our sons seek the favor of king Nebuchadrezzar, and serve him diligently. Do we not pray for the welfare of this land, as the prophet Jeremiah admonished us, for in its welfare will we not find our own welfare?[15] But as your father said, we must not forget who we are. We are not sons of Babylon, but sons of Judah, and Jacob, Isaac, and Abraham."

"May my offensiveness not offend, but I choose to be a son of Babylon. Nor do I accept that Yahweh sent Babylon to punish us. The great king came against us because we did not pay tribute to his greatness, and Marduk—forgive me—whose strength is like the rising sun, gave Judah into his hand, and Yahweh—forgive me—whose strength is like the setting sun, surrendered us to him."

Eliakim ignored Hattil's second offense. "Because, because" he repeated laboriously, "we broke covenant with Yahweh, we did not observe the sabbath, Yahweh rejected us on that day, and despised even his own altar."[16]

Marah listened intently, for of her past life that day alone stood emblazoned in her memory, the day fire laid waste the temple. She remembered not the crumbling walls of Jerusalem, rather the rigid face of her husband. As the fires of the temple rose into the sky, cracking the stones and scorching their faces, Eliakim stood gazing at the smoke and cinders like a pillar of disbelief. Could it be that Marduk, the god of Babylon, defeated Yahweh, the god of Judah? The prophet Jeremiah had already given answer. Jeremiah used to stand beneath the Benjamin Gate and cry out: "Hear the word of the Lord. Take heed for the sake of your lives, and do not bear a burden on the sabbath day or bring it in by the gates of Jerusalem. But if you do not listen to me, to keep the sabbath day holy, and not to bear a burden and enter by the gates of Jerusalem on the sabbath day, then I will kindle a fire in its gates, and it shall devour the palaces of Jerusalem and shall not be quenched."[17] Thus it came to pass, and Eliakim repeated the answer each step of the long trek to Babylon. The words of the prophet were repeated so that the memory of a few was preserved to become the memory of all. And the sabbath was hallowed within the seven settlements of the exile.

Menachem the elder attempted to smooth over the awkwardness of the moment by confirming that the great king would certainly bring order to the throngs of Egyptians and Ethiopians, and the conversation resumed on the tactics of imperial government, and the plight of the Judahites in Egypt.[18] When the sun settled behind the sand hills of the Euphrates, and the shadows dissolved into twilight, the visitors excused themselves with blessings upon the house of Eliakim the potter, and the good fortunes of war for Hattil his son.

Marah rose to prepare the lamps. The flames of the large copper lamp and two small clay lamps transformed the mud-brick walls from twilight gray to lamp-light yellow. The silence of the street carried the muffled songs of neighbors as the sabbath settled upon them. Marah set the food before them, the bread, the stew in a bowl, and the chicken upon a platter. Eliakim offered up the blessing. While they ate, the appropriate comments upon the food were offered to Marah, but the tension of Hattil's breech of protocol by which he dishonored his home and heritage lingered over them, and Eliakim admonished his son.

"Son of my loins," said Eliakim, "do not reject your blood. Do not reject your heritage. Do not anger the elders of your people." They ate in silence for some moments, until Hattil again found his voice.

"Yahweh has no temple, father, and his priests are without tasks to perform. Is there a more useless thing than a priest without a temple?"

Eliakim chewed his food, unperturbed by his lack of good teeth, or by the vigor of his son's contempt for the heritage of Judah. "Our priests," he said, as he swallowed, "must share in the sabbath of the land. They must rest and not work. But they shall return to Zion, for the temple will be rebuilt. And if not they, then their sons, and if not their sons, then the sons of their sons." Eliakim paused to rest beneath the weight of his hope. He murmured, "And I must have a son to reclaim my portion of the land."

Hattil leaned toward his father. "Who whispers in your ear that the temple in Jerusalem will be rebuilt?"

"Ezekiel the prophet," replied Eliakim. "And tomorrow we will join the company who visit the prophet on the sabbath of each new moon. Perhaps he will have a word concerning the invasion of Egypt."

Hattil grew somber. Marah watched her son. She could see that he hesitated before the name of Ezekiel. And who did not? Prophets are unpredictable. To visit a prophet is to prod a nest of bees in search of the honey. The question lingers, will they fly away and leave you the honey, or attack and leave you in agony?

"Eat your chicken," Marah said to them, "for it grows cold." She looked upon her handsome son, and touched the Astarte votive cake hidden in her apron. Once, in speaking of Marduk, Hattil nearly spoke the name of Ishtar, but his eye caught hers and he refrained.

The house of Ezekiel ben Buzi stood near the center of the town, alongside the market square. Ezekiel, a priest and the son of priests, descended from Jerusalem into the exile among the first deportation, with the priests and nobles and the king and his retinue.[19] In the fifth year of King Jehoiachin's exile, Ezekiel began to prophesy woe upon the exiles and those who remained in Judah, and even upon the nations at the borders of Babylon. In the ninth year of his exile, the prophet foretold the destruction of Jerusalem and the temple of YHWH.[20] Soon after, YHWH took Ezekiel's wife, and commanded him not to mourn or to remove his shoes or eat the bread of weeping, as a sign that YHWH Elohim would profane his sanctuary and many who were left in the land of Judah would fall to the sword. When that came to pass, the exiles were not to eat the bread of mourning, for this was their punishment at the hand of their god.[21] The people revered the prophet Ezekiel, and honored him for remaining among the poorer of the land, in the old center of the settlement. Elders of Tel-aviv and the other settlements came to him seeking a word from YHWH on matters of law. How shall we observe the laws of our god outside the land, and without the temple?

Now, in the thirtieth year of the exile, Ezekiel adopted the customs of an elder priest and sage, and he comforted the common folk with words of solace and visions of the return to Judah. On the first sabbath of every new moon he invited all to come and seek his counsel. Eliakim led Hattil into the assembly seated on mats in the market square outside the home of the prophet. The men respectfully gave them room, as the presence of a soldier of the king summoned forth murmurs of heightened anticipation. Marah, along with other women, lingered at the edge of the circle of men.

The old prophet sat in a wicker chair, in the shaded threshold of his doorway, watching through the overhang of his white-ripened eyebrows. At either side of the doorway stood a disciple, young priests devoted to him, his teachings, and attentive to his needs. For a double hour Ezekiel taught the crowd, reciting portions of the book of law, the ancient scroll discovered in the temple chambers during the reign of Josiah the king.[22] He commented upon the laws, and explained their significance to the covenant people and the necessity of obedience to the law as the foundation of their salvation, just as disobedience to the law became the foundation of their destruction. At times he repeated, in cadenced monotone and perfect meter, oracles long ago received from YHWH that promised the renewal of Israel.[23] And when he had delivered of himself, with open palms draped over the armrests of his wicker chair, he rested his aged body. A young girl brought a cup of water to Ezekiel. He ruffled the hair of her head, and he drank.

Amid the murmurings, a man raised his voice. "Prophet of Yahweh, have you a word from Yahweh concerning the land of Egypt? Will Nebuchadrezzar be victorious?"

"I have no word from Yahweh save that already spoken. Nebuchadrezzar got nothing, neither he nor his army, from his siege of Tyre; therefore, the Lord Yahweh has given him Egypt as compensation, and he shall carry off its wealth as wages to his army."[24]

Hattil straightened himself and grimaced disdain. This prophecy did not require a seer to see that the great king would be victorious—did not all the astrologers see the same?—but if Yahweh continued to bestow riches upon Nebuchadrezzar and promise good wages to the army, only an ingrate would complain.

Another man asked, "And what will be the lot of the sons of Judah in Egypt?"

The prophet frowned deeply. "As Jeremiah prophesied, the Judahites in Egypt are an abomination to the Lord. They reject Yahweh, and play the harlot, and worship the Queen of Heaven.[25] The Lord will destroy them and scatter them, and he will not bring them again to Judah, as he once brought Israel out of the land Egypt, as he swore to the house of Jacob."

"Prophet of Yahweh," a younger man spoke out. "When will the Lord deliver us to return us to the land of our fathers? When shall obedience bring vindication? When shall we return to Zion?" Many nodded at the words, and murmured their assent. That the question had been asked for thirty years, and always got the same answer, troubled them not at all.

Ezekiel replied, "Behold, did not the Lord Yahweh command us to cast away the idols of Egypt? In the wilderness of Sinai, did he not give us his sabbaths as a sign, and his statutes and ordinances by which we are to live? When the people is purified and the land is rested, then will the Lord, for the sanctification of his name, rebuild his holy dwelling, high and lifted up upon the holy mountain."

"But," the young man objected, "we have given birth to a new generation. How many generations until we return?"

"When the disobedience that caused our exile is wiped out and the people is pure, then shall the Almighty act according to his own pleasure."

Hattil chaffed and constrained himself no longer. He called out with sufficient strength for all to hear: "Did I transgress the sabbath that I should be sent into exile? The fathers have eaten sour grapes and the children's teeth are set on edge!"

Ezekiel looked in the direction of the voice. "Nay, say not this proverb from Israel. The Lord has declared: If a man is righteous and does what is lawful, and does not lift up his eyes to idols, or defile his neighbor's wife, or oppress the poor, but withholds his hand from iniquity and observes my statutes, he shall surely live. And if a man begets a son who walks in the way of the wicked, the Lord will not punish the father. If a son, seeing the wickedness of his father, nevertheless walks in the path of righteousness, he will not be punished for the sins of his father."[26]

Hattil replied, "Yet we are punished for the sins of our fathers. Have we not been instructed from our youth that Yahweh visits the iniquity of the fathers upon the children to the third and fourth generation?"[27]

Ezekiel seized a staff leaning against the door post, and drew himself up. His tunic, frayed and threadbare of many years, thinly covered the frame of his body. Though he never openly mourned the death of his wife in the ninth year of their captivity, for twenty years he refused a new garment, perhaps in mute defiance of the Lord's command not to mourn. Ezekiel surveyed the crowd of people and in turn all eyes rested upon the aged and tormented face couched behind the veil of his white silken beard. "No longer," he called out, "no longer will the Lord visit the iniquity of the fathers upon the children. Thus says the Lord: Behold, all souls are mine, the soul of the father as well as the soul of the son. The soul that sins shall die."[28]

"Yet I am alive!" shouted Hattil. He stood up, forgetting all respect and decorum of the moment. "I worship Marduk, and I am alive and I am strong."

Ezekiel began to tremble, whether from age or from dread, one could not tell. He stepped forward. The men squatting closest to him shuffled backwards upon the feet of others to give the prophet room. "Do I not know you, Hattil ben Eliakim, soldier of the king? Does not your pride reach out before you, whither you walk? Do you not lift yourself up to the heavenly heights?" Leaning on his staff, Ezekiel stepped forward in the direction of Hattil. Young boys jumped up in terror and scrambled from the crowd. But Hattil knew his moment had come. Time to throw off this shroud of ancient fear.

"You are an old man," he said bravely, "a relic of a defeated people and a defeated god. I say Nebuchadrezzar destroyed Jerusalem because we failed to send tribute to the great king." He pulled from beneath the neck of his tunic a clay figurine of the god-king Nebuchadrezzar as Marduk suspended by a bronze chain and held it before him.[29] "I say Marduk is greater than Yahweh. I say the temple of Yahweh was burned to the ground because we no longer offered libations to Ishtar, the Queen of Heaven."

Eliakim bowed his head in shame. Not a soul stirred. At the perimeter, Marah recoiled and contracted in terror. She knew Ezekiel despised all gods but Yahweh, and forbade the worship of any lesser god. But the protection of Astarte sustained and comforted her. The men of Israel dealt with the chief gods, who concerned themselves with war and the movement of nations. If Yahweh and Marduk were in conflict, that was no concern of women. If women were incapable of understanding the disputation of men, how much more the disputes of the gods. The Queen of Heaven cared for women and their responsibilities to give life, to nourish, and to sustain. That was the nature of things, the way of heaven and earth. Marah backed away from the far-reaching gaze of the prophet.

Ezekiel shouted, "Long ago the Lord told me that not all the house of Israel would listen to me. You are of a hard forehead and of a stubborn heart. Whether you hear or refuse to hear, I speak for Yahweh."[30]

Hattil stood his ground, as if facing the army of Egypt. "There is a proverb long known in this land, 'Man is the shadow of a god, and a slave is the shadow of a man; but, the king is the mirror of a god'.[31] Jehoiachim, our king of impotent Judah, remains in house arrest under the foot of Marduk and his reflection, King Nebuchadrezzar. Only a fool would say Yahweh is greater than Marduk. I have gained strength from the king, and I will no longer suffer beneath the whip of a vengeful and impotent god!"

Ezekiel clung heavily on his staff, grasping it as if his legs could no longer bear him. His pale thin lips moved to speak, but only spittle ran from the corners of his aged mouth. He gazed above the heads of the men with such intensity that many looked over their shoulders in fear, expecting to see angels or demons poised to grasp them by the hairs of their heads, but they saw only the women and the walls that were equally still. They turned back to the old man, and remembered the symbolic behavior of his prophetic past. Would he again shave off his hair and beard and destroy three piles of hair differently, or lay down in the street for months on one side, or dig a whole in his wall, or cook his food over cattle dung?[32] So long ago the prophet acted out his prophecies that most had forgotten his strangeness. But now something was happening; the spirit again stirred. They saw movement. The thin stalks of the prophet's legs grew rigid, and his back strengthened. Ezekiel let go of the staff and it fell to the earth. He extended his right arm, and from it sprang a gnarled finger pointed directly at Hattil. The finger wavered erratically, like a branch in the wind. And the wind appeared to rush into the withered old frame of the prophet, filling the dried billows of his aged lungs and bulging his eyes so that the lids stretched wide to bursting. A voice deep from within, or far beyond, cried out: "Stubborn and rebellious son!"

Gasps echoed back upon Ezekiel. Eliakim stared at the prophet in abject despair. He knew well enough the ancient law. If a son would not listen to his parents, they were to bring him to the elders at the city gate and declare him a stubborn and rebellious son. And all the men of the city were to stone him to death.[33]

"The soul that sins shall die," Ezekiel commanded. "Take this son to the gate outside Tel-aviv and stone him as the law of Moses requires."

Still no one moved. Eliakim looked helplessly at Menachem, and the elder rose and spoke for all the elders. "If it please you to listen to us, prophet of Yahweh, he is a soldier of the king. We cannot stone him."

"Thus says Yahweh. You shall purge this evil from your midst."

"If it please you," Menachem stammered, "we will censure him."

The crowd awaited some response from Ezekiel, some measure of compromise, some hint that he did not mean literally the words he spoke, that he understood their predicament, that he was a reasonable man after all. At length Ezekiel emerged from his trance and focused again on the people. He waved his arm over them, as if casting a net from which none might escape. In measured cadence, yet with a vigor sufficient to penetrate the most deafened ears, the prophet spoke: "As I live, says Yahweh Elohim, with a mighty hand and an outstretched arm, and with wrath poured out, I will be king over you. I will bring you into the wilderness of the peoples, and there I will judge you face to face, as I entered into judgment with your fathers in the wilderness of the land of Egypt. I will make you pass under the rod, and I will let you go in by number. I will purge out the rebels from among you, and those who transgress against me. O house of Israel, go serve every one of you his idols, but do not profane my holy name."[34] Then, as with a final breath he rasped, "The soul that sins shall die!" For a moment he surveyed the hushed crowd. Not a soul stirred, not a parted lip quivered, not a mouth whispered. Ezekiel sighed, bent down, and grasped his staff, and clinging again to it with both arms, he returned to his house. His disciples closed the door behind him.

Hattil preserved the sneer that had fastened upon his face, a waxen face, pale and wan. He looked about him at the faces of his own people. After all, what could they do? They were powerless between the claims of the gods, and beneath the strong arm of the king. He turned his back to the doorway and the prophet's words. He walked through the crowd, which parted before him. With eyes cast down, they let him pass. His military insignia and the figurine of Marduk-Nebuchadrezzar swung to and fro across his chest. When he had left the market square and walked alone toward the gate, a few young men came up to escort Hattil and congratulate him for his bold speech. This was a new land, a new era, and new gods. They all knew the truth of it, but for the god of their fathers to die, their fathers must die first.

In the month of Tammuz, on the fourteenth day of the month, an officer of the king's army entered Tel-aviv seeking the house of Eliakim the potter. Certain elders showed him the way and Menachem accompanied him to the door of Eliakim. Marah greeted them, and the countenance of the elders bespoke the weight of the moment. She turned and called to Eliakim. Together they stood before the officer and the elders.

"Word has come from Nippur," the officer said solemnly. "The detachment of the royal army which came up from Ur with the king's horses was attacked by nomads. The king's horses were taken, and his men destroyed." The officer paused and grew more rigid. "Your son has been invited by the gods," he said, using an ancient euphemism.[35]

Perplexed, Mara simply gazed at the face of the officer.

Menachem said softly, "Hattil has gone down to Sheol.[36] He is swallowed up in the land of shades. Your son is dead." The officer handed Eliakim the belt of his son, and the military medallion, and a broken figurine on a bronze chain.

Marah stood transfixed, mouth agape. The fluids drained from her bowels and her heart shrank. Eliakim dropped the possessions of his son at his feet. "Hattil, my son," whispered Eliakim. He rent his garment from the neck to his navel and bowed his head. Gone was his promise of return to the land. Gone was the promise of Abraham. His part in the promise had dried up. His life had come to an end.

Marah covered her face with her shawl and wept. Amid her tears, she turned to the chest of her secrets and removed the statuette of Astarte. Her hands trembled. She took the statuette to the courtyard, to the work-wheel of Eliakim. Kneeling down, she grasped a rock and smashed the idol into fine powder.

# 2

# Uriah's Dilemma

The land which you are entering, to take possession of it, is a land unclean with the pollutions of the peoples of the lands, with their abominations which have filled it from end to end with their uncleanness. Therefore give not your daughters to their sons, neither take their daughters for your sons, and never seek their peace or prosperity, that you may be strong, and eat the good of the land, and leave it for an inheritance to your children for ever.

Ezra the Scribe

Forty-nine years after the destruction of the temple in Jerusalem, in the first year of Cyrus, king of Persia, the Lord stirred up the spirit of Cyrus so that he proclaimed throughout all his kingdom, and put into writing, saying: "Yahweh, the god of heaven, has given me all the kingdoms of the earth, and has charged me to build him a house at Jerusalem, which is in Judah. Whoever is among you of all his people, may his god be with him, and let him go up." Thus spoke the conqueror of the Babylonian dynasty of Nebuchadrezzar, the anointed one of the Lord, in the sixtieth year of the captivity of Judah.[1]

Upon the word of Cyrus, the elders in exile arose, the heads of the fathers' houses of Judah and Benjamin, priests and the Levites, and everyone whose spirit the Lord stirred up to go and build the house of the Lord, a number approaching, from one direction or the other, forty thousand. We shall not, from the comfort and piety of hindsight, question too deeply the motivation of those who stayed in Babylon, nor those whose spirit was "stirred up," except to note that only a portion of the elect were stirred, and the Deity surely had his reasons. But among the stirred ones, a certain Mattaniah, numbered as a Bethlehemite, sought to reclaim his heritage in the vicinity of Bethlehem.[2] He came with his wife, sons, and unmarried daughters. Mattaniah found his ancestral farm land, in part occupied and in part abandoned, just as all the returning exiles found their homes and fields either in ruins or inhabited by Israelites who had never left the land, or Edomites, Moabites, and Ammonites who had come to take possession of the ruins. Under the authority of Sheshbazzar and his imperial directive,[3] Mattaniah fought for his heritage; through the courts, he secured some of the former boundary markers, and for the rest, he came to a purchase agreement. His sons repaired their ancestral home, stone by stone, and added rooms for themselves and their wives, and for three generations a descendant repaired the terrace walls, stone by stone, of the fields along the hills east of Bethlehem.

The first return from Babylon was, alas, a faltering and dismal beginning, or as tradition recalls it, "a day of small things."[4] True, the returned Exiles laid a foundation for the temple, but at the dedication ceremony, those few aged men and women who remembered from their youth the magnificent temple of Solomon could only hang their heads and weep at the sight of this paltry footing.[5] Upon so inauspicious a layer of stone nothing more was added for nearly fifteen years. Only after the second return of Exiles under Zerubbabel and Jeshua the priest, and with the prophets Haggai and Zechariah haranguing one and all, did we complete the mediocre temple on its mediocre foundation. Mattaniah died before we rebuilt the temple, but his sons helped to lay the stones, and his grandsons, even to the fourth generation, spread his heritage across the land of Judah, so that the promise to Abraham might endure.

Mattaniah's ancestral home outside of Bethlehem came, in the appointed course of years, to his seed and descendant, Uriah ben Hodiah, ben Pelah, ben Azariah, ben Mattaniah. Uriah shouldered the long heritage and vowed to honor his portion in the story of Israel.

Uriah took his two youthful sons to their terraced fields outside of Bethlehem. Together they worked to repair a wall around his olive grove; that is to say, his sons worked after their own fashion, and Uriah directed their labor. Amos and Iddo carried the stones from a pile where they had been gathered and placed them at the base of the stone wall. Amos, the elder, carried the larger stones, while Iddo, a lad of four years, followed his protruding belly wherever it went and carried the smaller stones that would provide the chinks for the stones to rest firmly in place. Uriah watched them. So quickly, like weeds, his sons grew. In Amos, nigh twelve years of sprouting, and the boyish frame had begun to show breadth in the shoulders, as one, perhaps two pubic hairs, pushed through as the sign of manhood.[6] Amos had the likeness of Uriah, fair of complexion, sturdy of limb. Iddo, yet like a girl, wore long dark curls of hair; indeed, he bore the olive-skinned likeness of his mother Orpah, but his greatest joy was to be in the fields with his father, and not tagging along with his sisters at home, where Orpah found it increasingly difficult to find manly tasks for his undomesticated abilities. When the boys had carried sufficient stones to resume the building, Amos lifted a large stone and set in on the half-height wall, while Iddo pressed in a stone shard between the cracks.

"Tsk," Uriah caught their attention. "Not so, but so, my little Iddo" he said, and inverted his hand in order to demonstrate what he meant. Iddo turned the stone one way, and Amos cuffed him on the ear with his elbow, indicating that Iddo should flip it over. The lad quickly obeyed. "Good," Uriah nodded, "always flat to flat, edge to round. Now, push it in a little more. Yes. Thus and so and onward, my sons. This wall must be finished while the earth is damp from autumn rains, and these stones become a wall before the evening falls. Your father rests only to give you a chance to prove your skill and cunning, to show that without your father you can build a wall, and even plant a field."

Amos paused. "Why would we build a wall without you, father? And where would we build it?"

"Have I given you a riddle, Amos, my strong one? When you are a full man, with a full growth, upper and lower and not one hair, perhaps two, as a sign and promise of manhood, it may be that you will have fields of your own with walls of their own, or you will have to repair these, and teach your sons to do likewise, and even do better, since here we are learning, and not building as if it were the wall of Jerusalem. In due course, your father will go the way of all the earth, dust to dust, as his father before him, and thus and so. Walls crumble, and need repair, for that is the way of the earth and the works of men."

Iddo opened wide his long-lashed eyes, and asked, "Why must we build walls?"

"Why? Why indeed?" Uriah nodded gravely, to encourage Iddo's inquisitive nature, and imitation of the older brother. "Well, do we not build walls to protect the land they surround?"

Amos laughed, "but a wolf can easily jump over this wall, and the locusts can still reach our olive trees."

"Yes, Amos, you are right; despite our walls, harm befalls us. But the walls also contain the soil when the heavens open its gates to wash the earth. And we build walls to define our land, our inheritance, to tell others that they may come this far and no further, unless we invite them and they accept our domain. Inside the walls, we live according to our ways; outside men may do as they please. Walls and fences are the guardians of our heritage."

"A worm," squealed Iddo, and he pulled at the writhing centipede crawling beneath a stone. Iddo pushed away the stone, grasped the centipede and placed it on his arm. "See, father," he boasted, while the centipede crawled up his arm, "I am not afraid."

"You are the brave one," Uriah smiled. "But now, let it return to its home, and you to your labor."

Amos brushed the centipede off Iddo's arm. "We must work, little raven," he said in his deepest voice, "and not peck here and there for crawling things." The boys picked up new stones and resumed their manly labor.

The sons of Uriah, each circumcised on the eighth day, held their heads upright whenever he recounted to them their national stories, intertwined peoples from his own side and their mother's side. They followed with him whenever they visited the temple in Jerusalem, but they also attended to the *matsevot,* the sacred stone pillars of Kemosh the god of Moab, when they visited the land of their mother, Orpah, who was not a daughter of Israel, but a daughter of Moab.[7] Such marriages were not uncommon, for the desires of the flesh and the bartering of goods lead hither and yon. Uriah's father, Hodiah, sought to purchase a large field outside Bethlehem on which sat nine ancient olive trees. The rightful owner, Hadid the Moabite, himself born in Bethlehem, had departed to the land of his forefathers as the Judahites became more numerous and encroached from all sides.

Uriah journeyed three days with his father, crossing the Jordan River at the ford near the northern rim of the Dead Sea, to the town of Ataroth in the land of Moab. Hadid received his former neighbor with all the rigors of their legendary hospitality, which both Moabite and Israelite knew had been grievously undermined when Moses led the children of Israel out of Egypt. The Israelites, seeking bread and water from the king of Moab, had been refused. On an ethnic level, the Jews still bore a grudge and the Moabites remained defensive, but rarely on the individual level did anyone bring it to mind, and never at the expense of a business affair. Hodiah and Uriah sat upon the cushioned tapestry in the house of Hadid and conversed about the health and wealth of their respective domains, the droughts and locusts and Persian politics, and what marriages and other alliances had altered the boundaries of Bethlehem.

It came about during this hospitality feast, served by Hadid's wife and his last and least daughter, Orpah, that Uriah's gaze lingered, and more than lingered, upon the bronze-tinted virgin who quietly and reverently served them. In the past, Hadid had suggested the name of a maiden of Bethlehem, with whose father he might enter into negotiation on his behalf, but Uriah had felt little urgency and therefore shown little interest. Now, urgency, like a spring shower, fell headlong upon him.

The sale of the field and the olives trees, when the two men should come to speak of it, was agreeable, and the purchase price was a matter of common understanding of its worth, both for the near term and for perpetuity. But Hadid, upon seeing the yearning, withersoever gaze of Uriah, altered the conditions of the sale to his advantage, so that when they took themselves to sit out under the acacia tree and got down to business, Hadid offered his daughter Orpah in marriage to Uriah, with the field as pledge for her dowry, and half of the produce of oil to be paid to him. In this way Hadid both rid himself of his least and last daughter while securing a steady, if measly, return from the field, as well as the surety that the field would remain his should death or divorce end the blissful bond of kinship. Hodiah, clapped his hands together and bowed his head, for he found the notion much to his liking, but could in no wise give up half the produce. But a sixth were possible, as behooves a liberal arrangement among kin. For an hour, with wine cups raised, tipped, depleted, and refilled, the fathers thus bargained, and in the end secured the betrothal: the field, olives trees, and a fourth of the produce, along with an unblemished lamb or kid as a token of good will.

A scribe was summoned and the betrothal and dowry were recorded. It was agreed upon, and so recorded, that the share of the field and its produce which belonged to Hadid, was the inheritance of Orpah forever, and should Uriah son of Hodiah the Jew, divorce Orpah, daughter of Hadid the Moabite, the field would be sold and the money be returned to Orpah. But no one seriously considered divorce, for the reputation of Moabite women was well-known, in beauty, loyalty, and fertility. And if Orpah was not so terribly beautiful, nevertheless she was pleasing enough in appearance beneath the veil, with her tiny waist and strong childbearing hips, and what she lacked in oriental beauty, she made up for in warmth and womanly care. So it came about by means of all the proper rituals, both Israelite and Moabite, that Uriah took Orpah to wife in the land of Moab, and brought her, as we say, "into his tent" in Judah. He laid his shoulder to the plow, and his member to her thighs; he sowed his seed in the earth and in Orpah.

"Ayieee!" Iddo's wail shattered the afternoon stillness. Nearby ravens pecking in the soil took flight. Uriah looked over to see Amos pulling a large rock off the hand of Iddo. Uriah sprang toward his sons.

"I did not see his hand," Amos defended himself, and attempted to reach for the hand of Iddo, but his little brother kept shaking his arm. "Ayieee! Ayieee!"

Uriah picked the lad up. "Courage, my little soldier." Iddo whimpered and clenched his teeth. "Give me your hand," said Uriah. Two fingers were bruised and bleeding. "Come, we will take you to *Imma* and she will kiss away your pain, and place sweetness in your mouth. Courage, now."

"I did not see his hand," Amos repeated.

"Of course you did not," Uriah replied sternly. "Are you Cain, to slay your brother? Even so, you were careless, and not without fault. Now, finish with the large stones, and bring the adze when you return."

Uriah lifted his son onto his shoulders, so that Iddo could rest upon his head, and carried him along the path that wound through the hills east of Bethlehem, until they reached their four-room house of unhewn stone just outside the town. Orpah came to the door with their youngest daughter, Zevia, on her hip. At the sight of Iddo, she gave Zevia to Rachel, the oldest daughter, and took little Iddo who, having suffered bravely, gave up his manliness and began to sob. Uriah's two middle daughters, Yael and Esther, gathered round Iddo caressing him with sufficient sympathy to bathe away the deepest grief and pain. Orpah daubed ointment on the wounded fingers and swathed them with a strip of old cloth kept for just such injuries. She dipped her little finger in the honey pot and gave it to Iddo. He sucked her finger clean, and then buried his head in her breasts and she caressed him until the pain had gone.

Amos returned at dusk, later than required, partly out of penance and partly out of shame, but the family quietly drew him into the meal, around the common pot, and he helped the wounded Iddo with his food.

For Uriah and Orpah, so gentle a life—gentle even in accounting, as we must, for the daily hardships that beset us—might have passed from the fourth to the fifth generation of Mattaniah, and onward, even to this day. But the land still lacked a certain discipline, the communal procession along clearly marked paths and guided by a rod of authority. There lingered much of the ancient egalitarian feeling that every man might do what was right in his own eyes. Kinglessness has that air about it. The chief priests, to whom the clans of Judah and Benjamin looked for guidance, had little of the zeal and wisdom ascribed to Moses, or even to their forefather, Zadok. We should not, therefore, be surprised that the Deity again felt obliged to "stir up" the children of Israel.

It came about, in the seventh year of Artazerxes the king, that Ezra, priest and scribe of the law of the god of heaven, came from Babylon up to Jerusalem bearing a letter from the king. In it, Artaxerxes opened his treasuries that Ezra might fulfill all the requirements of temple worship in Jerusalem. The letter further decreed: "And you, Ezra, according to the wisdom of your god which is in your hand, appoint magistrates and judges who may judge all the people in the province Beyond the River,[8] all such as know the laws of your god; and those who do not know them, you shall teach. Whoever will not obey the law of your god and the law of the king, let judgment be strictly executed upon him, whether for death or for banishment or for confiscation of his goods or for imprisonment."[9]

Ezra came, leading a group of prominent exiles, families who had established themselves in Babylon over five generations. They brought their wealth to infuse life into the land of Judah. Ezra handed over the vessels of silver and gold from the king's treasury, and offered up numerous bulls, rams, lambs, and goats as a burnt offering. He then delivered the king's commission to the governors of the two provinces Beyond the River.

On the first day of Tishri, the seventh month according to the Babylonian calendar, the heads of the families of Israel gathered at the Water Gate of the temple in Jerusalem to receive the scribe and envoy of the great king.[10] Ezra, by nature a man of somber countenance, mounted a high wood platform constructed from planks and beams for the occasion. As prominent elders flanked him like a sentry of archangels upon the dais, his stature grew beneath his white robe, and when they handed him the scroll of the book of the law of Moses, brought from Babylon, Ezra the scribe rose up like a colossus holding on his shoulder a pillar of the heavens. His dark oiled hair and Persian beard glistened under the fresh rays of the morning sun. All in all, the council appeared divine, the likes of which had never been seen in Jerusalem. Ezra opened the scroll of the book of the law in the sight of all the people, and two elders stood by to hold it. Immediately the assembly rose and stood before him. Ezra blessed the Lord, and all the people answered "Amen, Amen," and together they lifted up their hands and bowed their faces to the ground. Then Ezra, in a clear and penetrating tenor voice, read from the book of the law until midday. Certain elders and Levites interpreted the ancient Hebrew into Aramaic so all the people understood.

Uriah, with Elam, a friend and elder of Bethlehem, beside him, stood shoulder to shoulder among the men of Judah. He listened intently to the words of the law of the god of heaven, given to Moses. His heart swelled with gratitude and contracted in pain. The book gave stability to his soul, as if Moses himself were again standing before the assembled multitude at Sinai; and yet, the statutes and ordinances of the Lord had not been obeyed, nor the festivals celebrated. Many of the men and women around him were weeping. But for disobedience to the laws, the kingdom of David would never have perished. The temple would never have been destroyed. Israel would never have been exiled. By eventide on the temple mount, they agreed, then and there, that the laws of God must be heard and obeyed so that the blessings of the Lord should not cease. Thereafter, the congregation of Judah dispersed to their homes, only to return the following day for more reading of the law.

The second day found Uriah and Elam again in position amidst a far larger throng, to which Amos and Iddo added their number. Ezra read the law, and it was found that God had commanded that the people of Israel should dwell in huts during the feast of the seventh month. And as it was now the seventh month, and the full moon was but thirteen days hence, all agreed that Israel should perform this feast of the Lord. They dismissed the assembly to fulfill the commandment. Amos and Iddo could not contain their excitement to begin building their hut, and Amos announced he would fetch the olive and palm branches.

"Elam, my friend," said Uriah, as they worked their way along the rocky path down from Jerusalem to Bethlehem, "you are older than I, and far wiser, so tell me, I pray, how can it be that our fathers remained so long in ignorance of the laws of Moses? How can it be that we have never properly celebrated the feast of booths? Where have these laws and traditions got lost?"

Elam shook his head. "The exile in Babylon? I do not know. Have not farmers dwelt in makeshift huts during the grape harvest to protect the vines, and when the threshing floor is filled? Some say our fathers used to build huts to dwell in when they came up to Jerusalem for the Feast of Ingathering, but building huts in commemoration of our wandering in the wilderness, this I have never heard."[11]

"And that we are to make huts using the branches of olive, oil tree, myrtle, palm?"

"Father, what is the oil tree?" Amos asked.

Uriah threw open his hands and clucked, "Tsk, I know not, but we must find one."

"The oil tree is any resinous pine," replied Elam, "though you must seek it in the hills north of Jerusalem. Perhaps you can trade olive and palm for myrtle and pine. Surely there will be a market for all these branches."[12]

"And have I understood correctly," Uriah continued, "that we are to make these huts not in our fields, but on our roofs?"

"That is how they interpreted the commandment."

Uriah shrugged. "The purpose of it all is lost to me. A hut on a roof is like a bowl of water at the bottom of a well."

"The reason, my friend, it seems to me, is that to perform an unnecessary act bespeaks the ritual of memorial all the more."

"Even so, that my father's father knew nothing of this tradition troubles me."

"It troubles me also," Elam replied. "But let not your sons say the same."

The Feast of Booths became an occasion for great festivity as homes throughout the villages of Judah sprouted little green caps, and the people piously dwelt for seven days in their freshly constructed huts. Uriah's daughters proudly served meals, which they carried up the ladder in their shawls, such that Orpah herself reclined and received of their labor. Amos and Iddo insisted on sleeping in their makeshift house, and took care to repair it as the leaves began to wither and openings appeared where there had been shade. Elam and his wife came to eat in their hut, and in turn, Uriah took his family to eat in theirs. Each day, many who lived close to Jerusalem came up for the reading of the law, and spent some time in the large communal huts built around the temple courts, and at the Water Gate on the east wall of Jerusalem, near the Gihon spring. The festival concluded on the eighth day with another solemn assembly.

On the twenty-fourth day of the month, the chief priests declared a day of fasting and repentance, in which only native Israelites were to participate.[13] Uriah thought it good to bring his sons, that they might see the congregation of Israel in public confession of sin. Ezra prayed, recounting a history of stubbornness, disobedience, acting presumptuously, and of rejecting the prophets and saviors sent by the Lord. Amos tried to follow the prayer, but he could not understand most of it, and Iddo fidgeted throughout the convocation. They returned home feeling weary but forgiven, and Uriah praised his sons for their endurance.

In due course, certain officials came to Ezra on a delicate matter. "The people of Israel," they declared, "have not separated themselves from the peoples of the lands. For they have taken their daughters as wives, for themselves and their sons, so that the holy race has mixed itself with the peoples of the lands."[14] The delicate matter was particularly egregious among the priests and Levites, but applied to every Israelite, and as such, the "holy race," that is, the "seed" of Abraham was in danger of diluting the consistency of its singularity into the idolatrous flux of humankind. This blanket accusation was far from newly woven; the debate had long festered among the men of Judah, the Abrahamic faction against the Adamic faction. The arguments—and we may note without fear of contradiction that among the descendants of Shem, the Jewish reputation for argument was already secure—went something as follows:

On the one hand, who can count the number of Canaanite, Ammonite, Moabite, and even Egyptian women who have entered into the bloodline of Abraham, and formed its progeny, its kings, in their wombs? Was not Asenath, daughter of an Egyptian priest, the mother of the half-tribes of Manasseh and Ephraim? Was not Tamar the Baal worshiper, daughter-in-law and wife of Judah, the womb of all past and future Davidic kings? Did not Moses himself take a Midianite wife, and also a Cushite?[15] And Solomon . . . where shall we begin? We must not press this "seed" matter too far, for enticing and fertile wombs are often wanting. And if we must count seeds, we are all descendants of Adam, even of Shem, even of Abraham's father Terah, when it comes to Ammonites and Moabites.

On the other hand, never mind that blood kinship is always possible to demonstrate if one goes back far enough. Never mind that the great grandmother of David was a Moabitess.[16] Never mind that Solomon married women from each of these people, as well as—if his reputation for 700 wives is not merely centuries of accumulated hyperbole—from every race under the sun.[17] Never mind all that. These times are not those times. Former times led to the exile, the forsaking by God of his own house, his own people. These times lie not on the far side of the exile, but on the near side, and are given for reparation, not repetition, of past errors, as if the second act of the divine drama were to be no different than the first. God called Abraham *from out of* Ur, and promised to make his seed a great nation. We are the Remnant, the seed from which a new people shall spring. A holy people occupying a holy land in worship of Yahweh alone, the foundation of Abraham's call and blessing, was again in danger of dissolution.

Such words, with raised and growling voices, no doubt accompanied by the emphasis of hand flourishes, often passed between those who had married gentile women and those who had not. But now the festering sore had come to the attention of Ezra, who carried with him the authority of Artaxerxes the king to enforce the "laws of YHWH." They informed Ezra that half the children of mixed and unholy marriages spoke not in the language of Judah, but in their own languages.[18] "Our heritage is soon forgotten," they said, "and where our heritage flees, worship follows swiftly on her heels." And they assured Ezra that many of these foreign women openly or secretly revered their ancestral gods and taught their children the same reverence. It could only have been such import that caused Ezra to rend his tunic and his mantle, to pull hair from his head and his beard, and in all ways, ritual and genuine, to demonstrate his grief and shame before the Lord. The wrath of an angry God would surely fall upon this fledgling remnant and wipe it out forever; but that his wrath had not yet fallen meant there was yet time to repent.

A proclamation went out to all returned exiles in Jerusalem and all Judah, that they should assemble at Jerusalem. If anyone did not come within three days, by order of the officials and the elders, all his property should be forfeited, and he himself should be banned from the congregation of the exiles.[19] The proclamation stirred up the heart of Uriah. He brooded alone, but in the afternoon before the appointed day, he sought the counsel of his friend concerning the mixed marriages. Elam found himself unable to calm the troubled waters.

The next morning, on the twentieth day of the ninth month, Uriah and Elam joined the men of Bethlehem and all of Judah and Benjamin who dutifully came to Jerusalem and assembled in the courtyard of the temple. A turbulent winter sky preceded them, and even as the men assembled a cold rain had begun. When the gates were clear and the reluctant congregation huddled around him, Ezra stood upon the platform and preached against the mixed marriages. "You have trespassed," he accused in his high and penetrating voice, "and increased the guilt of Israel." He rehearsed the verdict of Yahweh on the past assimilation that sprang from mixed marriages, from the Israelite slain by Phinehas for taking a Midianite into his tent, to the folly of Solomon himself. The wrath of God waited at the gate. Then Ezra addressed the Almighty: "And now, O our God, what shall we say after this? For we have forsaken your commandments, which you commanded by your servants the prophets, saying, 'The land which you are entering, to take possession of it, is a land unclean with the pollutions of the peoples of the lands, with their abominations which have filled it from end to end with their uncleanness.' Therefore give not your daughters to their sons, neither take their daughters for your sons, and never seek their peace or prosperity, that you may be strong, and eat the good of the land, and leave it for an inheritance to your children for ever."[20] Ezra demanded that all true Israel put away foreign wives, along with their children. He might have gone on at great length, as scribes and preachers are accustomed to do, but the rain made everyone miserable, and the voice of Ezra could scarcely be heard, so he retreated to the council chamber with the elders. Elam, as an elder of Bethlehem, joined them.

Most of the men in the temple court departed for shelter in Jerusalem or made haste to return to their villages nearby. Uriah sought the half shelter of a portico and awaited Elam. There he sat down and pondered the higher and darker affairs of the Lord. By late afternoon, when the rain had abated into a chilly drizzle, the elders came out. Elam came to Uriah, and they descended toward Bethlehem. Uriah kept silent while Elam searched the landscape for words and phrases.

"My heart is heavy," Elam began. "My heart is heavy because the voice of the majority has spoken. The elders have voted that a census be made of all mixed marriages. Jonathan ben Asahel and Jahzeiah ben Tikvah vigorously opposed the decision, and others supported them, but those who demand purity of blood line, with the support of Ezra, have won the debate."[21]

"And what follows when the census has been completed?" asked Uriah.

"When the count is made, each man must divorce his wife and send her and his children away, out of the land of Judah."

"The law is harsh that demands wives become widows and children become fatherless."

Elam nodded. "Verily it is. But the harsh rule of Yahweh has fallen on us before."

"Where do you stand on the matter?"

Elam frowned in deep reflection as they walked along the road. Their sandals were coated in mud, and steam had begun to rise from their sodden garments. The dreary hills were but shades of gray and everywhere weeping. At length Uriah repeated his question. "Where do you stand on the matter?"

"During the debate I spoke but once," Elam replied. "I called on them to evaluate each case on its own merits, and I spoke of your wife and your own children, and sons circumcised on the eighth day."

Uriah interrupted, "Have we not lived among the descendants of Haran since the beginning of time? Are not the children of Moab, unsavory though it may be, the children of Lot by his eldest daughter?"[22]

"They are, and you well know the arguments concerning the Moabites. But Ezra opened the scroll and read a decree of which I have never heard, yet written it was in the book of Moses, for I saw it with my own eyes. According to the decree: *No Ammonite or Moabite shall enter the assembly of Yahweh; even to the tenth generation none belonging to them shall enter the assembly of Yahweh for ever; because they did not meet you with bread and with water on the way, when you came forth out of Egypt, and because they hired against you Balaam the son of Be'or from Pethor of Mesopotamia, to curse you.*[23]

Uriah set his jaw and stopped, incredulous. "This unknown decree from the book of Moses is a grudge so ancient, even twenty generations past, that it cannot sustain itself on bread and water, but requires salt and vinegar to be preserved."

"Even so, Ezra declares it valid."

Uriah shouted, "This is madness and unjust."

Elam nodded. "Unjust, perhaps. Another elder proposed that oaths of fidelity to our laws and customs be taken by all gentiles who choose to remain. But they said that exceptions cannot be made, or there will be no end of it, and soon oaths will have no meaning."

"Are we not taught that Yahweh is god of heaven and earth? If Yahweh is lord of all, how then shall we reject the Moabites from this land and this people?"

"Ezra's concern," replied Elam, "is for the purity of Israel, not the rejection of the Moabites. No one has said they may not worship Yahweh."

"Orpah is devout before Yahweh, and prepares food as carefully as any woman in Judah. Neither swine's flesh nor forbidden fowl enter my house, and she reveres the sabbath rest even as your wife does."

"Uriah," Elam said softly, "speak to me as you speak to your own heart and hide nothing from me. Does not Orpah worship the god of her fathers, Kemosh the god of Moab, at the high places in Moab? Does she not take offerings to the stone pillars with her when she visits her kin in Ataroth?"

"It is the custom which she performs out of respect to her heritage."

"Even so, it may lead your children astray, and all the land return to idolatry."

Uriah's shoulders slumped. "What will Jerusalem do to those who refuse to obey the decree?"

"I do not know. Ezra has authority to confiscate all possessions, to imprison, and to banish. Whether or not he is willing to take matters that far, you will at least be excommunicated from the fellowship, your produce will be banned for sale to all Israel, and your temple offerings refused. You will be in exile in your own land. Even I would have difficulty in speaking with you in public."

Uriah returned to his home by evening. Orpah awaited him at the gate and his children gathered round him. He entered his warm dwelling. Rachel and Yael helped remove his wet cloak. He heard them playfully chiding each other in the courtyard as they twisted his cloak to wring out the rain, and then watched them stretch it out to dry near the hearth. Uriah donned a dry woolen tunic and quietly ate his meal of lentils and fresh bread, bidding the children to tell him of their day, and what they had accomplished, both for work and for play. Amos assured his father that the goats had rain water in the trough, and he fed them in their stalls. "When shall we begin the sowing of barley?" he asked.

"The earth is soft," Uriah agreed. "Soon, soon."

Orpah produced the weaving Rachel had begun under her watchful eye. Uriah praised her workmanship, and Rachel said, "I shall make you a cloak when I am able."

"Good, good," Uriah murmured. "I need a new cloak."

Though Orpah knew of the decree, the children as yet were ignorant. She waited for the moment when the children were asleep on their mats before she approached Uriah, who sat upon his stool by the hearth of their oven. Kneeling down beside him, she began, "Uriah, my husband of sixteen years, tell to your wife the outcome of the assembly and the burden of your heart."

Uriah recounted the day's events, the decree of the council, and the passage from the book of Moses. He rubbed his eyes with his open palms, and sighed. "I will be required to divorce you and send you and the children back to your father's house."

Orpah looked him in the eyes. "If so, let it be so."

"No, I will not let it be so. Surely there are many who will rise up against this unjust decree and refuse to obey it. If the numbers are sufficient. . . ."

"And if they are not?"

"I will sell the land and go with you to Moab, or to Egypt."

"But your heritage is more than fields and trees."

"Orpah," Uriah said weakly, "do I not know this?"

She laid her head upon his knee. "My husband," she whispered, "act as your heart speaks, and know that we will abide by your decision."

On the first day of the tenth month, a temple official came to Bethlehem to take a census of all those in the vicinity who had married foreign wives. He dispatched Elam to bring Uriah ben Hodiah. Elam came to Uriah's house. Orpah greeted him at the door. "Welcome, Elam, friend and friend of my family."

"My heart is heavy, Orpah," said Elam, eyes cast down.

"It is a time for heavy hearts," she said. "Uriah is in the fields."

Elam walked out to the fields near the ancient olive grove. He found Uriah on a ladder, sickle in hand, pruning small branches from his revered trees, many hundreds of years old. A few dwarfed olives on the uppermost branches lingered, clinging tightly amid the dark green leaves and the cold winter nights. Farther down the hill Amos and Iddo were lifting stones and fitting them just so into the stone wall.

"Uriah, Shalom." Uriah reached for another branch, drew it near and cut off the end. Elam continued, "The temple priest has come to take the census. They have asked that I bring you. Will you come with me?"

Uriah dropped his arms and rested—a rest summoned by a furrowed brow, not weariness of shoulders, though his shoulders naturally took their portion of rest, for the body finds rest in the briefest of moments, but the soul has a much harder time of it. He gazed down at Elam, and then looked beyond him into the southern hills of the Judaean wilderness. "See the heavens?" he said faintly. "The winter will be hard."

"The cycle of seasons has come again. There will perhaps be snow even in Bethlehem."

"When did we last see snow in Bethlehem?"

Elam pondered a moment. "Five or six years now, I believe."

"The wall will soon be repaired," said Uriah, waving his sickle toward his sons.

"Amos and Iddo are stalwart sons," Elam nodded.

"But to what end, sons and walls?" murmured Uriah.

Elam sighed, but said nothing.

"I must yet sow my barley and . . ." Uriah looked for more branches in need of pruning.

Elam asked again, "Uriah, will you come?"

# 3

# Great is Yah of Elephantiné

Memorandum from Bagavahia and Delaiah. They said to me:
Be instructed to you in Egypt that you may say to Arsames the
satrap concerning the altar-house of the God of Heaven, which
was formerly built in Yeb the fortress, before the reign of
Cambyses, which Vidranga, that reprobate, destroyed in the
fourteenth year of Darius the king: let it be rebuilt in its place as
it was before, and let them offer the meal-offering and incense
upon that altar as formerly was done.

Jedaniah of Elephantiné

Since the days that our ancestors rejected Jeremiah the prophet, we
have begun to cling more faithfully to Yahweh, or Yah or Yahu, as we
called him by the ancient forms in Egypt.[1] Here and there, like scrub
brush and scattered palms beyond the oasis, some Jews still paid tribute
and offerings to ancient goddesses of Canaan, and to Anathyahu, consort
of Yahu, but after six generations we quietly conceded that Yahu has no
consort, and that the jealous attachment of Yah for his people may be
laid to the isolation, even loneliness, of our wifeless god.[2]

No one remembers when Jews first settled on the island in the
upper Nile at the first cataract, five hundred miles south of the Delta.
The island measures over a mile and a half in length, and a quarter of a
mile in breadth at its widest point. Because of the great ivory trade, already in ancient times the elephant became the symbol identified with
the great rock splitting the Nile, which they called Elephant Island, Abu
in Egyptian, Yeb in Aramaic, and Elephantiné in Greek. The island garrison formed the sentry of the southern gate of Egypt. Before Persia conquered Egypt and Ethiopia, soldiers of Elephantiné defended Egypt
against the southern kingdoms of Ethiopia, the land of the burnt faces.
They guarded caravans, oversaw quarry workers, and performed other
tasks that preserve order.

The fortress town of Elephantiné, like its sister city Syene on the east bank of the Nile, was stocked with a strange variety of the human race: Babylonians, Bactrians, Caspians, Khwarezmians, Ionians, and Aramaeans. The small and crowded homes of sun-dried Nile mud brick stood shoulder to shoulder in ethnic clusters, like conscripts mustering at dawn.[3] The streets were narrow, mere passageways really, not proper streets at all, except the Streets of the King, which were the public thoroughfares that surrounded the temple district and lead to various clusters of homes. The ethnic quarters were not entirely pure, for Egyptians and Jews might be found side by side, and sometimes joined in marriage. The entire fortress used the same market and sat under the same fan palms, which grew in clusters of three and four and even five.

The vital center of Elephantiné was the temple to Khnum, chief god of the first cataract. This granite sanctuary was equal in its grandeur to the temples of Amun-Re at Karnak, Ptah at Memphis, and Re-Harakhte at Heliopolis. And great it should be. He who controls the Nile flood controls Egypt, for the Nile is Egypt, a long, serpentine land of verdant fertility between desert and endless desert. Near the temple of Khnum lay the ancient Nilometer, a square stone pit into which the river flowed and rose unperturbed by current and eddies. Two scales marked the sandstone walls, one to measure the rise of the river, and the other to calibrate its height above the arable land. During the flood season, which begins at the summer solstice and continues for one hundred days, priests recorded daily the height of the Nile and sent the information by swift couriers to the cities along the Nile, where others coordinated the measure with a second Nilometer at Memphis and a third in the Delta. In this manner all Egypt knew how great would be the seminal spill of the swollen river, how wide the flood plane, and how vast the arable land, and crops and tribute and life.

The community of Jews at Elephantiné distinguished itself from the other Jewish communities in Egypt by its temple to Yahu. Though far smaller than the temple of Khnum, the early Jewish settlers built their temple with gray and pink granite cut from the quarries of Syene. They built the sanctuary roof and five gates of cedar wood brought from distant Lebanon and suspended the gates by large hinges of beaten bronze. They commissioned basins of fine gold and silver and bronze, and priests offered up incense and meal-offering and burnt-offering. Jews from the lower Nile used to come on pilgrimages to worship Yahu and participate in the sacrifices, and each year they commemorated the festival of Passover. We speak of the temple as past, because it no longer is.

In the fourteenth year of Darius the king, while Arsames, the governor of Egypt, reported to the king in Persia, the priests of the god

Khnum gave silver to Vidranga, the chief of Elephantiné. Vidranga accepted their bribe and wrote to Naphaina his son, who commanded the garrison at the fortress in Syene, saying: "Let them demolish the temple of Yahu which is in Yeb the fortress." Naphaina led the Egyptians bearing their weapons and they broke into the Temple and razed it to the ground.[4]

Rami, daughter of Osea, sister of Natan, hurried down the rawboned ridge of sandstone along the east bank of the Nile. The raging waters of the cataract sounded in her ears. Rami came hobbling as fast as she could, but the wooden block strapped to her clubfoot slipped on the pebbles in the pathway, despite its leather sole. With one arm she balanced herself, with the other she held her breasts, which bounced up and down as she hurried; for while the Lord had withheld stature from her left leg, he had bestowed abundantly in her bosom. Her linen robe, home spun from field flax and dyed a deep ochre, fluttered around her like a pillar of flame rising from the reddish brown sandstone earth. A faded white shawl had slipped off her head, so that the numerous tight braids of brown hair bounded and rebounded off her shoulders and shimmered beneath the late summer sun. She hurried, limping along, impatient to tell her brother Natan that the priest Jedaniah had called an assembly of the Jews and that she wanted to attend the assembly. Upon hearing of the news in Elephantiné earlier that morning, she immediately ferried over to Syene and took the south road beside the agitated Nile to where her brother and his master, Hor, repaired longboats. She saw them at work farther along the bank.

Natan apprenticed to Hor the boat builder. For seven years he had so labored. Natan stood taller than most Egyptian youths his age, not that others mistook him for an Egyptian, despite his Egyptian clothing, the tell-tale apron, and his hair cut trim at the shoulders. The fair complexion and sand colored hair identified his lineage as Hebrew, or Aramaean, and his name, the diminutive of Yehonatan, "Yahu will provide," marked him as a Jew, a member of "the other ones," a foreigner, not Egyptian. Nevertheless, his shoulders had begun to square like the figures on an Egyptian wall painting, as muscles wove themselves along his lanky arms, which now worked rhythmically, wielding the iron faced mallet against the sycamore planks and bronze nails of a cargo longboat. The mast of the vessel rose into the air, on which a sail would carry the boat

up river pushed by the north wind. Below the deck lay three small openings on each side for oars by which men guided it down river with the
current. The high lotus prow now hung over the shore, but the hull,
built of aged sycamore, rested lightly in the river, slowly shifting between two anchor ropes.

Rami slowed her gait, for it did not become a woman to approach
men at work breathless and bouncing. She recalled one day, years ago
before the destruction of their temple, early into the apprenticeship of
Natan, he had returned from work and posed a question. "Why do the
river boats have bronze nails on the outside and iron nails on the inside?" he asked her. Rami thought a bit, shrugged, and replied, "The
bronze are more beautiful?"

"No, my sister," Natan replied gravely, "although you answer well.
Iron is stronger than bronze and must be used inside to keep the boat
frame firmly together, whereas bronze does not rust and is suitable to
the hull in the water, but also, as you say, more beautiful on the deck."

"Oh, how wise you are, my brother," Rami had replied, and she
reached up to him, to be held by so wise an older brother.

Natan gave Rami her first jewelry, copper bracelets. He repaired a
fisherman's boat, a bit of labor not negotiated by Hor, and the fisherman
gave him a Nile perch, which he sold and bought the bracelets for her.

Rami entered the world with a shortened left leg and a deformed
foot. The birth was difficult, they said, and the proof was the death of
her mother soon after. They said that Yahu had punished them for sins,
whether her own or that of her parents, she did not know, but thereafter, she came to believe that Yahu, having punished her, now loved
her, and she reached out to embrace Yahu and be embraced by him.
Nor did she waver when her father perished while defending their
temple against the Egyptian mob. That could not be for sin, but for a
higher purpose, something that lay beyond her understanding, but lay
there just the same.

Upon the death of her father three years before, Rami came under
the authority of her brother Natan, elder by four years and the last of her
family. Natan had attempted to arrange a marriage for her, but many
Jews had departed the island in search of some livelihood outside the
military, and since the destruction of their temple, other families moved
to Thebes or still closer to the Delta, and Rami's club foot made the
finding of a husband all the more difficult. Then, by chance a merchant
from Thebes who desired a second wife, sought a betrothal. Rami protested, she did not wish to be the second wife-slave of a merchant from
Thebes, and Natan had withdrawn from the arrangement. Though he
wished to provide for her, he had not the stamina to do so against her

desires. Rami was content to wait; indeed, she thought of herself as consecrated to Yahu.

Natan and Hor had repaired boats for many days along the banks of the Nile above the cataract, where workers unloaded longboats and barges bearing ivory, ebony, incense, spices, skins, slaves, and gold, and hundreds of porters hauled and carted the baggage down to the docks of Syene, to be loaded on Egyptian barks and barges for all Egypt, and from Egypt to all the world. Egypt likewise sent its bounty to the south, and kept boatmen constantly loading and unloading their wares. During flood tide of the Nile, skilled "boatmen of rough waters" could navigate small boats down the cataract, but large boats were towed and guided by scores of men from the shore, and even then, they dashed against the rocks and boat-wrights stood by rubbing their hands gleefully.[5] Hor and Natan carted the tools, bronze and iron nails, boards, buckets of pitch, and arsenic from Syene.[6] They slept in a tent at night to avoid making the journey morning and evening back to the island of Elephantiné, and to keep a watchful eye on their materials.

Hor inspected the deck repairs of the longboat while Natan chiseled at the edges of a gashed hole in the side, a cubit and a span in length. The crew had removed the cargo, amphorae of balm and rare spices, and gone down to Syene to drown themselves in Egyptian beer and to proposition a whore of any race. Only one crewman stayed with the boat, a young man perhaps Natan's age of seventeen years, but taller and burnt-skinned from the land of the desert. The Ethiopian, who called himself Hekhamet, spoke a basic Aramaic, the lingua franca of Persia, or sang it, to be more precise, with an exaggerated hum whenever his lips vibrated around a vowel. Over the two days that Natan repaired his boat, they had struck up conversation and a certain amicable bond.

Hekhamet leaned upon the balustrade at the front of the boat. "A wommann commes," he sang.

Natan looked up and saw Rami. "My sister," he replied in surprise. "What brings her to me at this time?"

"Your sister?" asked Hekhamet with equal surprise. "Is your sister married?"

"I tried to find her a husband," Natan shrugged, "but what I found she does not want."

"Ahn," Hekhamet smiled, with apparent sympathy.

Hor rose from inspecting the deck. "She is a young woman with a young woman's duties," he said. "It is not hers to want or not want."

Natan cast his eyes down. "Even so, master," he murmured, "she does not want."

Hor walked to the gateway of the balustrade and descended a narrow plank to the shore, shrugging his narrow shoulders repeatedly and mumbling, "She wants, she does not want." His hairless torso resembled a pear, from which a darkened belly hung ripe over a tight belt that kept his apron from slipping off deprived buttocks. "Women . . ." he pronounced authoritatively, "they all want and don't want, and if once you give a want to them, there is no end. You sooner fill a bottomless bucket. Are there no men in all Yeb and Syene?"

"There are men everywhere," said Natan, "but Jews are few. My sister is devoted to Yahu. She does not want to be under the authority of a man who does not acknowledge our god."

Hekhamet asked quietly, "Your sister is devoted to Yah?"

"Yes," replied Natan. "Her name Rami is only the half of Ramiah, 'Great is Yah,' and she has always shown great devotion to Yahu."

"Devotion to the gods is good," said Hekhamet.

"She wants, she does not want," said Hor. "You Jews and your one god. But you also swear by Sati, wife of Khnum, in all contracts of marriage and business. Do not Egyptians give their sons and daughters to Jews and Aramaeans, and take their sons and daughters in return?"[7]

Natan sought some words to help him retreat from an argument with Hor. Assuredly Jews used the oaths required in the law court of Yeb, that was the custom of the land. Assuredly they honored the customs of the land because the land put food in their bellies. It were folly to do otherwise, but offering such wisdom in the form of exposing folly to his employer would bring no reward, and Natan opted for neutral silence.

Rami had halted a dozen paces away, awaiting a summons to approach. Natan clicked his tongue, and with a toss of his head, motioned her to come closer. Rami pulled her shawl back over her head, and lay a corner over her shoulder to hide her nose and mouth. She lifted her robe slightly and limped toward them. Soon she could smell the potent odor of pitch, arsenic, and wax that clung to boat builders. Her eyes beamed with hopeful expectation. Natan wore his slightly apologetic mien naturally, and on behalf of their departed mother, he had instructed Rami in the art of servility that had long been the secret defense of minorities and all women, but to no avail. Innocent and without guile, she could be none other than true. Natan asked, "What tidings, my sister, do you bring?"

Rami took a deep breath and spoke as if reciting a proclamation of the king: "A messenger has come from Jerusalem bearing a response from the governors of Judah and Samaria concerning our request to rebuild the temple of Yahu. Our high priest Jedaniah has called all the heads of families to assemble in the temple precinct."

"Important news," Natan responded gravely. "I am eager to hear the answer." Rami, too, wished to know, for the survival of the entire Jewish community seemed to rest on a favorable decision that their temple to Yahu be rebuilt.

Hor frowned. "Well then, will the Jews resume their offensive sacrifices?"

"We belong to Yahu," said Rami, "and we must obey him."

"You belong to Yahu," replied Hor, "and you are called Jews because you come from the land of Judah. Your god Yahu is the god of the land of Judah, but this is the land of Amun and Khnum."

Rami spread open her palms. "Yahu is god of heaven, the Most High. Whither can we go to escape the heavens?"

"Amun-Re then, the sun and Lord of the Sun, or Baal Shamaim of the Aramaeans, who, like Apis, takes the form of the bull. That is all well and good to worship one god above others, but we must respect all gods in all their manifestations. Boat builders ignore Ptah at their peril."

"It is explained to us," Natan began softly, lest he further offend his offended Egyptian master, who as Egyptian was offended by the ritual sacrifice of lambs and rams, and as master, was offended by the impertinence of an apprentice. "It is explained to us that Yahu, the god of heaven, is so greater than that which might represent him, that nothing is better than anything."

"That is a fine jest," said Hor, and shook his head to indicate that in fact it was quite other, such as childish, or demented. "Khnum, chief god of the first cataract, is a ram-headed god, just as Bastet in the land of Delta is a cat, Heket a frog-goddess, and Thoth an ibis or an ape. Both god and animal are sacred in each other, for how will we see the god if not in the beast?"

Natan said, "I meant only that the god of heaven can have no image, for the earth cannot contain an image greater than itself. So it has been explained."[8]

"I heard what your mouth says, for as you understand so you speak, and not a beetle's weight better. If you are pleased by an invisible god, without form or likeness, a god of air in the heavens above, then shall you not find comfort in a house of air for your god? What need have you of a temple when all the earth is too small and insignificant?"

Natan kept his gaze lowered as he thought. Then the voice of Rami troubled the stillness.

"We have need for our sake," she said. "Yahu, Lord of heaven, is pleased to dwell among us, and when he smells the sweet savor of his offerings, he hears our prayers and will bless us."

"Well then," said Hor, rubbing his shaven chin with irritated gravity, "you choose your own husband and you declare how the gods reason." Hor turned to Natan. "Why did you not confess that your sister is a priestess? No man is worthy of her. No, she belongs among the oracular shrines of the Sibyls."

Rami glowed. "May Yahu find me a worthy mouth for his wisdom."

"All well and fine, balm and spices," said Hor, "wisdom from the suckled and the suckler. But you Jews do not stop with the incomprehensible, you march slapdash into the reprehensible, which leads to strife in the land."

Natan replied, "Not the Jews and Aramaeans destroyed the temple of Khnum, but the Egyptian troops destroyed our temple of Yahu, and stole our costly vessels."

"I favor not desecration of any sacred shrine," replied Hor, as he raised himself up in a defensive posture, for he knew their father had perished at the hands of the Egyptian mob. "Nature brings troubles enough that we need not offend the gods too. But you know right well the slaughter of lambs at your festival called Passover is an offense to us, odious indeed, and very like a desecration of the dignity of Khnum. I do not say that such an offense alone accounts for the base actions of base men, for as the saying goes, if you want to beat the dog, you can always find a stick—but it was the justification for their anger, and the priests of Khnum will not permit such desecration."[9]

Rami said, "The offended god was Yahu, and he brought justice upon Vidranga."

"Vidranga is brought low, this we have seen with our own eyes. But beware, for where one falls, others may follow."[10] With this admonition, Hor walked over to a pile of wood and began searching for a piece to mend the hull.

Rami looked to Natan. "Will you come, my brother, and take me to the assembly?"

"Yes, we will go listen to the elders. But I must finish this," he said, pointing to the gaping hole in the longboat's hull, "and introduce my friend Hekhamet to my sister." Natan took Rami by the shoulder and drew her over to Hekhamet. "My sister, Rami."

Rami stood wide-eyed and open-faced in curiosity, for her shawl had fallen away from her mouth and she did not know the tall and handsome man who lingered upon the longboat balustrade was a friend of her brother.

"Great is Yah," said Hekhamet with a smile, revealing even rows of ivory colored teeth.

"Great indeed," she replied, immodestly searching his dark eyes with her own that shone from her round moon face.

Hekhamet nodded knowingly. "In my land along the lesser river, there are people who worship Yah. Among them are clans who claim descent from a king called Shlomo, by the womb of a queen of Ethiopia."[11]

"Solomon?" said Natan. "It may be. We are told he married many wives."

"Ahn. Many wives is good. Great wealth, many children, much happiness."

Hekhamet pondered his picture of great wealth and many wives for a spell.

Rami put her hands on her hips. "Are you a worshiper of Yah?" she asked quite pointedly, with a tone of "or not?"

"I worship all gods," replied Hekhamet in surprise. "Where I find myself, there I worship as I ought. But your god Yah," Hekhamet said, "is different from other gods. They say he is . . . what is the word . . . ?"

"Jealous?" suggested Natan.

"Ahn. He gives you no quarter to worship the gods of other lands, even when you live in the lands of other gods."

Rami said, "We do not offend the gods of other lands, only we do not seek their help."

"As you like," said he. "There are advantages to having but one god. Like one master, one captain of the ship."

Hor returned with a suitable piece of sycamore plank and held it up to the hull. He marked it while Natan resumed his pounding and finished chiseling away the rough edges of the hole in the hull. Hor cut the wood to fit the hole, applied pitch to the edges of the hole and the wood patch. They pressed it in, tapping lightly with wood mallets.

While they worked, Hekhamet asked Rami, "How long have people of Yah lived along the Nile?"

"Many years, past counting," she replied.

Natan added, "We are told many Jews joined the army of Pharaoh Psammtik and helped defeat Ethiopia."[12] He looked up and smiled, "May peace now rest between you and me."

Hekhamet laughed. "Ahn, Egypt and Ethiopia have always fought, and Egypt has always required foreigners to help defeat Ethiopia. But many soldiers from Egypt deserted the army of Pharaoh Psammtik, because he did not pay them. Now thousands live in the Land of the Deserters."[13]

Hor grumbled, "We are now all under the thumb of Darius and Arsames, but we will throw off their yoke and place an Egyptian on the Sun-Throne. Then let Ethiopians and Jews bow down to Khnum and beware."

"We will never bow down to Khnum," said Rami.

Hor glanced at her, and said to Natan, "Muzzle your lame cow."

Rami ignored Hor. "From where do you come?" she asked Hekhamet.

"Beyond Meroë," said the Ethiopian.

"Beyond Meroë?" Rami's eyes widened. In her understanding of geography, Meroë lay at the southern end of the earth.[14]

"Ahn, far beyond," he said, waving his arm toward the distance, "in the mountains above Meroë, along the blue waters of the Nile. Three months to Meroë, and four months to my land along the blue waters of the lesser Nile."

"Will you return?" she asked.

"Ahn. In two, maybe three seasons." Hekhamet straightened up and folded his long slender arms across his chest. "When I have wealth I will take a wife."

Hor scraped the excess pitch from around the seam of the patch. "Secure it from within," he said to Natan.

Natan took strips of beaten iron and nails up to the boat. Hekhamet left the balustrade and followed Natan down beneath the foredeck. The Ethiopian, or Cushite, as they had long been known in Hebrew and Egyptian tradition, was tall indeed, a full head above Natan, and he bent his head the lower to watch.[15] Natan found the new wood patch and began pounding the iron strips across the joints.

"How came you to be a boat builder?" said Hekhamet. "I ask because I have no skills with boats, only to lift cargo on and off, and skilled craftsmen gain wealth before lifters."

"My father apprenticed me." Natan shrugged. "I have worked seven years for Hor, but soon I will be a master and work for myself."

"A skilled craftsman in boats can find work anywhere."

"Only where there is water."

"Ahn," Hekhamet laughed.

Natan dropped an iron band he had placed against the hull. Hekhamet bent down to retrieve it. "Thank you," said Natan

"Your sister," Hekhamet ventured hesitantly, "she is a lively one."

Natan shook his head in imitation of Hor. "She wants, she does not want."

"It is good to want and not want," he replied. "Such a woman understands the difference between tasty food and bland food."

"Yes, Rami is a good cook," Natan confirmed, patting his stomach. From the corner of his eye he saw Hekhamet nodding in satisfaction.

"She wants a man devoted to Yah?"

"She wants to be free to worship Yah," Natan replied. "A husband devoted to Yah is twice wanted."

"Ahn," Hekhament murmured.

Natan finished securing the iron supports, and they returned to the river's edge. Rami had taken off her sandal and wood block, and swished her feet in the water. Natan stepped into the river and scooped water over his head and back. Hekhamet waded in. "In my land we wash to music," he said, and began beating the river like a drum. The water jumped up high in handfuls which he then caught on his head. Delighted, Rami swayed to its rhythm and shook her copper bracelets.

When Natan had dried himself and donned a light cloak, he said to Hor, "I will leave for Yeb now, and return tomorrow."

"Go then," Hor waved him off, "and temper your people concerning the temple of Yahu."

Natan said to Hekhamet, "In three day's time, the pitch will harden and the boat will be ready to sail. But we will inspect it again."

"That is good," Hekhamet said. "The crocodiles in the upper Nile are three times larger than here."

"Truth?" asked Rami.

"Ahn," Hekhamet grinned.

The sun hovered above the western dunes, casting shadows over Elephantiné, painting the stone dwellings with varied hues of copper and bronze. The towering palms rustled in the evening breeze, and seagulls wheeled along the bank of the Nile where fishermen unloaded their catch. Across the Nile's east branch, the dense dwellings of Syene glowed against the backdrop of the granite quarry. Natan and Rami reached the temple precinct with but an hour of light remaining. Natan had donned a short-sleeved tunic and over it he lay a symbolic mantle of sackcloth, a shawl of goat's hair that suitably irritated his neck and shoulders, and left room at his chest for beating. Sackcloth became their communal act of mourning the loss of their temple.[16] Some Jews wore sackcloth all the time, but all men and women wore it when they assembled in the temple precinct. The smooth stone floor of the former temple remained the meetinghouse for the community of Jews.[17] They had constructed a roof of beams, reed mats, and dried palm branches to give shade over a third of the area, and under it the priests and elders had gathered. The rest of the men settled down on the pavement and women stood by at the perimeters, and spilled into the Street of the King. Natan stopped among the women so that Rami might remain by his side.[18]

Jedaniah, the chief priest, sat in a modest ebony cathedra, inlaid with chips of ivory, his priestly armchair from which he ruled the community. He listened to several bearded men nearby. Each one gesticulated energetically as he spoke to those who listened. Jedaniah looked up, and seeing the great numbers of the community, he rose. A hush fell upon the men closest to him and gradually settled across the assembly, until only the women at the perimeter could be heard whispering and, finally, they too ceased.

He began in his grave priestly voice, "Bagavahia, the satrap of Samaria, and Delaiah, the satrap of Judah, have granted our request to petition Arsames to rebuild the temple of Yahu." The women burst into dance and shrieked in joy with high-pitched ululations normally reserved for marriages and burials. The men rumbled their applause. "Great is Yah! Ramiah, Ramiah!" As it was not possible to quiet the assembly by adding another voice to the acclamation, Jedaniah stood silent until they hushed of their own accord. "We are instructed to petition Arsames to rebuild it on the same foundation, and to offer up meal-offering and burn incense as we have done formerly."

"Hallelu-Yah, Ramiah!" came the voice of the multitude. Jedaniah remained standing, impassive, and clearly unfinished. When quiet returned, Jedaniah said, "The high priest of Jerusalem, Johanan, has declared that sacrifices may only be performed in the Temple of Yahu in Jerusalem. We are forbidden to offer up burnt sacrifices in the temple of Yahu in Yeb."[19]

At this proclamation, the hush lingered. Micaiah, a captain in the army, and a highly respected man of the community rose to speak. "By what authority," he said calmly, "do they prevent us from sacrificing?"

Jedaniah replied, "The high priest of Jerusalem says it is so written in the Torah of Moses: *But you shall seek the place which Yahweh your god will choose out of all your tribes to put his name and make his habitation there; thither you shall go, and thither you shall bring your burnt offerings and your sacrifices, your tithes and the offering that you present, your votive offerings, your freewill offerings, and the firstlings of your herd and of your flock.*"[20]

Natan felt Rami's grip on his arm grow tight. He glanced down and saw her face alight. She tilted her head now this way, now that, as if gleaning inspiration from the echo of their words.

Another man responded, "My father journeyed twice to Judah, and he knew of this injunction brought to Judah by Ezra, but he always believed, and so passed on to me, that the restriction applies only to the land of Judah, not to the ends of the earth."

Said Jedaniah, "Whether we agree or do not agree on what Moses meant by his words, Darius the king listens to his satraps and the high priest of Jerusalem. Our satrap, Arsames, listens to the king."

Micaiah said, "They are casting their rod of authority over our heads once again. Since the days of Ezra, Jerusalem has sought to rule all Jews everywhere. The high priest presumes to govern in Egypt. You know well that Khnum is against us since Hananiah arrived to tell us when and how to celebrate Passover, on the set day of the fourteenth of Nisan, instead of our ancient practice at the time we put the sickle to the grain.[21]

Emboldened by Micaiah, another man spoke out. "Our fathers built the temple of Yahu before they rebuilt the temple of Jerusalem. We have sacrificed in Egypt for more than two centuries."[22]

One of the elder priests next to Jedaniah rose to speak. "Men of Yeb, we know that Johanan the high priest would prevent us even from meal-offerings and burning incense. The high priest, if he truly ruled us, would not allow us to rebuild the temple at all, but only houses of prayer, like in Susa and throughout Persia, for he too, is jealous of his domain. And we do not know whether Arsames will listen to us. All we have been granted is permission to ask. The priests of Khnum will send their own delegation to Arsames to speak against us, but if it is known that we will no longer sacrifice rams upon the altar, the major offense in their eyes is removed, and we have a greater hope of rebuilding our temple. A little is better than nothing, and we must not reach too far in the land of Khnum."

At his words, small conclaves of discussion broke out across the assembled Jews. Rami stood rigid beside Natan, still clutching his arm. This decision of Jerusalem concerning the worship of Yahu must be acceptable to the god of heaven, and the god of all the earth. To gainsay Yahu was, according to Rami's simple insight, the height of folly. Suddenly Rami cried out, "No. Yahu has spoken through his priest of Jerusalem. The sacrifice and sweet savor in Jerusalem is accepted by Yahu for us all. One temple for the one god."

The women nearby shrank away from her breach of silence. The men turned their heads and scowled. Natan himself stared into her earnest face.

"Who speaks for Yahu?" Jedaniah called out.

"I heard his voice," Rami replied. "Yahu has spoken from Zion. He said to me: From beyond the rivers of Egypt, from beyond the rivers of Ethiopia, my suppliants shall sing my praise and they shall bring my offerings to my house in Zion."[23]

"Away with you!" shouted one of the elders. "Will Yahu speak to you and not to us? This is unheard of, impossible, and cannot be believed. Natan, take charge of your sibyl!"

Natan obeyed, and taking Rami's hand he led her out of the assembly. They walked along the Street of the King, the thump of her wood block beat a ponderous gait, for she labored beneath the weight of the thoughts in her head. Natan, though he believed Rami thought she had heard the voice of Yahu, himself knew not what to make of it, or, for that matter, of the temple decision, good and bad, day and night. What is a temple to Yahu without burnt-offerings? Could they raise the funds to rebuild a temple where sacrifices were not allowed. Would Jews from lower Egypt come to worship at such a temple?

Divining his thoughts, Rami said, "My brother, must this not be a sign that Yahu will extend his people under the heavens? One temple, one sacrifice for all the earth, else Yahu would instruct his high priest in Jerusalem to permit sacrifice in Yeb."

"I cannot deny it," he said, bowing to her prescient eyes.

Rami held more tightly to his arm. "If you deny it not, then deny me not a request."

"Speak."

"Let us leave Yeb, you and I."

"But Yeb is our home."

"It is only an island in the Nile, my brother," replied Rami.

"But where shall we go?"

"To the lands of the south, my brother; even Egypt let us leave behind. Has not Yahu provided the long boat and a guide?"

He shrugged in resignation to the will of Rami, who seemed to know better than he the will of Yahu. "I will think upon your words, but let not your eyes or mouth betray me until a decision is made."

When Natan returned the next morning to the boats above the cataract, he found the tidings of the temple of Yahu had swept across the river. Syene, like all of Elephantiné, was abuzz with verdicts and opinions of every shade and color. Even without the ram sacrifices, worshipers of Khnum resented the rival temple of the Jews. And the Jews resented the authority of Jerusalem and the priests of Khnum. The council of elders agreed to seek financial contributions from wealthy Jews, and when they had secured proof of their ability to rebuild the temple, they would request permission from Arsames, Satrap of Egypt.[24] Natan quietly let Hor speak his mind, the content of which is already well known to us, in essence if not in entirety. Natan pondered the desire of his sister, and as she took hold of his imagination, the troubles of the cataract towns grew faint and his thoughts the more animated. He could find work in Ethiopia, and they would find other worshipers of Yahu, and find Rami a husband, if she had not already found him. He could teach Hekhamet how to repair boats. Cloaked in his servile demeanor, Natan inspected the repairs. He found Hekhamet, and just between the two of them, revealed his desire to accompany Hekhamet to his home on the lesser Nile and to bring his sister Rami.

Amid the comings and goings along the Nile, plans were made and permission secured. The longboat captain agreed to take Natan and his sister as passengers to Meroë, provided that Natan traveled as crew, a refurbisher of the boat here and there.

It came about days later, in the cool of the morning-night, Rami gathered up a small bundle of clothes and toiletries, possessions that might have been, and might yet be, part of a dowry. With a shawl wrapped around her shoulders, she slipped out of Elephantiné. Natan helped her into a small ferry boat, one of many that anyone used to cross between the island and the east bank, and he guided the little bark up river to the southernmost landing of Syene. From there, while a faint darkness lingered, they walked up through the low ridges around the cataract until they reached the longboat on which the Ethiopian awaited, a shadow against the early light of dawn.

"Welcome," Hekhamet beckoned them.

Natan took her bundle and walked up the plank, Rami grasped his sash and limped behind. He wore a head-cloth, bound by a black cord, with wings falling upon his shoulders. Rami draped her white shawl over her braided hair for protection from the tireless sun and for modesty's sake. The crew leaned into their poles to push the longboat back into the river and turned its prow up current. They continued to guide their longboat through the rocks until they reached the open flow. They unfurled and raised the sail. Natan and Rami stood on the foredeck, careful to avoid the laboring crew. As the morning north wind caught the sail, the longboat began its slow journey up the Nile.

Hekhamet came and stood beside them. "Long ago, they say, the foaming waters of the cataract gushed up from a bottomless pit of the netherworld, half the water flowed north to Egypt, and half flowed south toward Ethiopia."[25]

Rami looked back at the disappearing rapids. She said, "Long ago, perhaps it was so. But now it flows from farther south, does it not?"

"Ahn," smiled Hekhamet. "The turbulent waters continue for over seven hundred furlongs between the mountain cliffs," he said, with the calm assurance of seasoned sailor, "but we will come to a smooth and level plain."

"Yahu will go before us," said Rami with equal assurance.

"Yahu, god of the wanderers?" he said, with apparent interest.

"Yahu, god of heaven," Rami said. She stood on the foredeck, one hand on the balustrade, the other shading her eyes that beamed like stars from her round moon face in the light of the rising sun. Rami searched the horizons, east and west, the endless desert, and therefore the ends of the earth, as if to test the hypothesis and conviction that the god of heaven may be found anywhere on earth. She peered along the winding river, ever southward toward a land where she would merge her life blood with the greater house of Israel, in the land of the burnt faces.

# 4

## The Foresight of Tobiah

So Alexander came into Syria, and took Damascus, and when he had obtained Sidon, he besieged Tyre, when he sent an epistle to the Jewish high priest, to send him some auxiliaries, and to supply his army with provisions; and that what presents he formerly sent to Darius he would now send to him, and choose the friendship of the Macedonians, and that he should never repent of so doing; but the high priest answered the messengers, that he had given his oath to Darius not to bear arms against him and he said that he would not transgress this while Darius was in the land of the living. Upon hearing this answer, Alexander was very angry; and though he determined not to leave Tyre, which was just ready to be taken, yet, as soon as he had taken it, he threatened that he would make an expedition against the Jewish high priest, and through him teach all men to whom they must keep their oaths.

Flavius Josephus

Hindsight is the ability to evaluate correctly events and their consequences. Foresight is the ability to anticipate events and consequences; that is to say, foresight is hindsight when it is most needed. Prophets are called seers because they foresee events and their consequences, but shrewd and successful men of trade are able to anticipate the future with an accuracy to make augurs hang their heads in shame. And if such seers use their gifts of anticipation and wit for the good of God's people, are they not prophets in their own right?

The Tobiads were perhaps the wealthiest clan of Jews in the world.[1] Members of the clan had successfully anticipated the rise of

Nebuchadrezzar, and within two generations, likewise the dominion of Cyrus. They ordered their affairs accordingly. A contingent of the "sons of Tobiah" duly returned from exile to reclaim pasture lands in Ammon, Moab, and Judah, only to find their ancestral right of return questioned. It seems their marriages were often business affairs, mergers and acquisitions, arrangements to keep the wealth "in the family," and inevitably the stock of Abraham was fortified by the wider commonwealth of humanity.[2] Tradition tells us that sons of priests who could not verify their genealogies were excluded from the priesthood as unclean "until there should be a priest to consult Urim and Thummim"; in other words, when the sun stands still.[3] But the Tobiads answered the challenge by simply dominating the landscape and distributing their wealth as necessary. Others of the clan had long since established themselves in Arabia and Persia. More than likely, they themselves did not know the extent of their wealth, nor even the extent of their clan, though all would claim descent from an obscure ancestor remembered simply as Tob-el, meaning "god is good." During the intermittent religious reforms of Israel, the family name changed to Tob-Yah, the more ethnically correct name of the god of the Israelites.[4] Hence sundry men bore the name Tobiah, or So-and-So ben Tobiah, and to be a member of the Tobiads was to wield a certain degree of repute and notoriety.

Our Tobiah was the eldest son of Simeon ben Tobiah, a descendant of the "sons of Tobiah" who returned from the exile. Tobiah was a stout man, even rotund, corpulent, if you like, in a dignified sort of way, wrapped as he was like a plump olive in fine Egyptian linen, but he always walked upright and wore a munificent blue turban that lent him what his ancestors had withheld; namely, height. An extravagantly large sapphire set within a gold clasp kept his turban in place and announced his well-to-do stature. He comported himself as such: manicured, coiffed, oiled, and perfumed at all hours. And he expected to be heard, for beneath his dark countenance Tobiah was a devout and industrious man of no particular nonsense. He contributed to the Temple upkeep through tithes and offerings, bestowed gifts upon the priesthood as occasion arose, prayed twice daily, and most reasonably expected God to keep his part of the bargain: that virtue is rewarded and vice punished—*in this life!* Such a prescript provided for the harmonious interplay between heaven and earth, a long-term relationship one could bank on.

Like his forefathers, Tobiah added wealth to wealth. Should we be surprised? Does not cream rise to the top of a jar of milk? Does it matter if the milk is from cow, goat, camel, or sheep? Jews had proven themselves no less capable in affairs of commerce than Persians, or, for that matter, Greeks, Cypriots, Egyptians, or Romans. Tobiah inherited lands and pastures, and by the blessings of heaven, he built up his wealth with vast herds and flocks, massive granaries, immense spice groves, and endless caravans, such that we may accuse him of being among the original culprits that gave rise to the whispered slanders of envy against us.[5] Tobiah's principal estate was in Ammon, across the Jordan River, where his family resided and his sons oversaw the fields, flocks, and herds, but he kept a white stone villa outside Nehemiah's wall around Jerusalem, a palatial apartment in Damascus, and a seaside residence in Joppa, each staffed with servants. While his caravans traded with the east, Tobiah kept a wetted finger to the breezes, which he found steadily increasing from the west. He hired a tutor to ensure that his Greek, if not rhetorically polished, was competent. Thus, we may be certain Tobiah enjoyed the gift of foresight.

It came about during the brief reign of Arses, king of Persia, that Tobiah sailed from Joppa to Athens in search of business opportunities such as occur when a city-state of towering culture falls victim to war and must recover.[6] The year before, Philip of Macedon had declared himself ruler of the Greeks. The city-states demurred, for they did not consider the Macedonians to carry Greek blood, and the citizen army of Thebes and Athens engaged the mountain bred stalwarts of Philip in the battle of Chaeronea. The true Greeks were swiftly defeated and forthwith payed meek obeisance to Macedonia. Philip then prepared his allied army of the Greeks for an invasion of Persia.

In Athens, Tobiah sought the services of a scribe, one fluent in Mediterranean dialects and the common Aramaic of Persia. He happened upon an educated steward outside a notary public, who stood about as a day laborer seeking employment. Tobiah learned that not only could the steward read and write Aramaic—the classical form taught in Athens, uninfluenced by Jewish idiom—he also had a gift for numbers. The steward, Theokeles by name, was a man whom Nature had gifted and Fortune had chastened. While yet a youth in the gymnasium, his father had fallen into debt, and in order to maintain the family honor, Theokeles sold himself into indentured servitude to a wealthy landowner of Athens. After serving thirteen years, his master perished in the battle against Philip, and the estate could no longer afford his service.

Theokeles was a long, angular man, with a high and lightly wrinkled forehead that betrayed power of thought and was flanked by ears that deftly held a stylus or two. Beneath his thinly drawn eyebrows, which he maintained by plucking, his intense brown eyes looked down a prominent beak of a nose, the nostrils of which flared conspicuously when he

breathed in silent meditation. He kept his curly light brown hair cropped short, and he preferred a clean chin to any style of beard. In other
words, he knew the classic appearance of the learned clerk in a plain
white tunic and scrupulously maintained it.

Tobiah found the steward *cum* scribe entirely capable of leading him
through the rigors of Athenian commerce, as well as providing him with
guided tours of the historic art and classical architecture housing the
birth of civilized culture, or so Theokeles explained. When the summer
solstice had passed, Tobiah prepared to depart. He offered Theokeles a
comfortable, even generous, term of service, by which, should Theokeles
meet the high expectations, he might venture into business affairs as
commissioned partner. Theokeles bowed stoically in recognition of
Fortune's long overdue smile and returned with Tobiah to Judah. Let it
be known the two painted a fine and envious picture within the upper
circles of Judah: the lanky, wide-eared Hellenistic steward hovering with
intense gaze and tablet in hand above the blue-turbaned and corpulently
successful Tobiah.

Tobiah set Theokeles to work in Joppa, in a small office room within
his polished stone residence near the central market and overlooking the
sea. Tobiah summoned a scribe to show Theokeles the lists, records,
transactions, a host of garbled shorthand on papyrus and potsherds that
would interest no one but those who expected a profit. When Theokeles
had demonstrated his mastery of the system, Tobiah introduced him to
various ship's captains and traders, and instructed his steward to begin
seeking shares in the more profitable trade ventures with Cyprus, from
where they would extend their reach to Carthage and Greece. Satisfied
with Theokeles' grasp of affairs, Tobiah departed for Jerusalem, but before he reached the gates of the holy city, tidings from Greece caught
him from behind. During a final celebration in the theater of Aigai, filled
with pomp and the immaculately carved images of the Greek pantheon,
Philip of Macedon had been assassinated by one of his bodyguard.
Tobiah hurried back to Joppa where he hoped Theokeles might read the
signs of the times. He found his steward on a stool, in his room
overlooking the sea, diligently poised over a wax tablet.

"Judgment of the gods," Theokeles murmured, as he perched a stylus above his ear.

"Think you?" said Tobiah.

"Merely a turn of phrase, master," Theokeles replied. "Surely the
gods do favor the punishment of barbarians."

"Well they may," said Tobiah, "but I have more concern for who will
rule next and how this will affect trade." He added judiciously, "So your
concern should be."

Theokeles arched his ever-preened eyebrows. "As the Macedonians are barbarians, and vote by clashing their spears rather than raising their hands, the customary blood feuds among their overlords will follow. When the dead are buried, I expect Philip's son Alexander will succeed him, should he survive the bloodletting. Alexander is known to be the most capable of Philip's sons, born of Olympias, his true wife and rightful queen, with the added distinction of some tutoring under the learned Aristotle. Then," Theokeles shrugged, "Alexander will slay all other claimants, and the Macedonian conquest will resume."

Tobiah frowned. "War is a dirty business, and results are subject to greater whims than weather."

"Then we must weather the whims of war."

"We Jews have long fared poorly in war."

"One only need side with the victor, master Tobiah."

"Ah, to be sure. Have you many such pearls of Greek wisdom?"

"A lesson, I fear, many a Greek has failed to learn."

"Help me see to it, then, and your partnership in trade is secured."

Theokeles bowed slightly, and his stylus fell from his ear.

"An ill omen," said Tobiah, as Theokeles picked it up off the marble floor.

"Not at all, master. You see, I am already at work."

Within three months, while Jerusalem solemnly observed the high holy days of autumn, reports from Greece announced that Alexander had secured the throne. Tobiah clasped his hands together, well pleased with the prediction of Theokeles, and ordered his steward to keep him apprized of Macedonian affairs. Soon Theokeles sent word that Alexander had visited the oracle at Delphi, which bequeathed upon him a favorable omen, and he had resumed the conquest. First Alexander avenged his father on the Thracian tribes, who had wounded Philip and stolen war booty that he had brought from the banks of the Danube. Alexander marched north, crossed the Danube in fishing boats and rafts of sewn tent skins stuffed with straw. The natives fled before him, and the faraway Celts, whose greatest fear was that the sky would fall on their heads, sued for peace. With Europe's restless tribes subdued and loyal, Alexander returned to a rebellious Thebes, which he quickly destroyed.

But the submission of Greek cities and ignorant tribes beyond the Danube sparked little concern in distant Judah. Of far greater significance was the death of Arses of Persia, and the rise of a new king, Darius, being the third of that name in the now feet-of-clay dynasty of Cyrus the Great.[7] Darius ruled all the lands west of the Indus River and east of the Great Sea even to Egypt and Anatolia, a vast empire that had endured for two hundred years—and the provinces sent ambassadors to renew their oaths of loyalty. Thus, when Alexander of Macedon crossed the Hellespont and led a swift victory over a Persian force at the river Granicus, advisers to Jaddua, high priest of Jerusalem, explained that the Macedonians momentarily outnumbered the Persians fifty thousand to thirty-five thousand. When the cities of Anatolia submitted one after the other to Alexander, they explained that many of the cities were filled with democracy loving Greeks, and welcomed this freedom from Persia. When Alexander's cavalry of the Companions routed the troops of Darius in the battle of Issus, wagers still favored the odds that Alexander would pursue Darius as far as Babylon and Susa, where the regrouped myriads of Persia would crush the Greeks upon the steppes of Asia; for it was one thing for Spartans to have turned back Xerxes at the narrow pass of Thermopylae, and quite another for a handful of Macedonians to defeat the monarch of 120 satrapies in his own garden. But when Alexander let Darius flee to Babylon while he proceeded to march on Tyre, a wave of perplexed consternation swept over the land of Judah. The high priest Jaddua summoned yet another council of the leading men of Judah to discuss the "what if" possibilities. Tobiah dutifully attended the council, which hemmed and hawed and came to naught. Thereafter, Tobiah dispatched Theokeles to the encampment of the Macedonians so that he might assess the peril and propose a proper course of action.

The island city of Tyre had never been truly conquered during the two thousand and four hundred years of its celebrity, though various rulers had been given the crown of submission.[8] There was, of course, the much larger city of Old Tyre, on the mainland, separated by a half mile of shallow sea. Various conquerors had occupied Old Tyre, but in times of trouble, the populace found refuge behind the impregnable walls of New Tyre, and when they spoke of Tyre, they meant the impossible-to-conquer island city of Tyre. The prophet Ezekiel had predicted that Nebuchadrezzar would destroy Tyre, but after thirteen years of siege, Nebuchadrezzar gave up the futile effort. We may quote the assessment of the Almighty himself: "Son of man, Nebuchadrezzar king of Babylon made his army labor hard against Tyre; every head was made bald and every shoulder was rubbed bare; yet neither he nor his army got anything from Tyre to pay for the labor that he had performed against it."[9] In the minds of Jews, therefore, Tyre was indeed unconquerable.

Alexander found the old city of Tyre vacated, save for waifs and strays, and straightway organized a portion of his foot soldiers, buttressed with day laborers from across the land, to begin tearing down the old city. He then sent an envoy to Jerusalem, asking for assistance and supplies for his army, and the gifts that were formerly sent as tribute to Darius, urging the high priest to choose "the friendship of the Macedonians."

The high priest Jaddua blanched and trembled at the request and bade the envoy accept the hospitality of the high priestly villa, or enjoy themselves in the hot springs of Jericho, or the therapeutic waters of Lake Asphaltitis. The Macedonians curtly replied that they would accept the high priest's hospitality for the one night, perhaps two, but the conqueror of the world was impatient to fulfill his destiny. Jaddua hastily summoned his council of seventy advisors. Tobiah arrived breathless in the temple chamber, a large rectangular room with stone benches in rising tiers along the walls. Upon the dais at the far end of the chamber, Jaddua sat in his exalted bronze and silver cathedra. Behind him hung Persian draperies of finely woven wool in intricate patterns of blues, reds, and purples, giving all the appearance of an assembly of the heavenly hosts in oriental garb. Only a drone of anxious voices in the air belied the human condition of uncertainty.

Jaddua rose from his cathedra and recounted the demand of Alexander. He spoke briefly on the dangers of renouncing their allegiance to Darius, then gave leave for the council to speak.

"To begin with, the city of Tyre will never be taken," the elders of Jerusalem agreed in nodding unison. "By the time the Macedonians realize the futility of their engagement, Darius will be upon them."

Tobiah stood and declared his presence: "Anything may be taken if one's grasp is sufficient."

"Tobiah," said one, with belabored ennui, "the walls of Tyre are 150 feet high, and as thick as required to sustain them.[10] To think they can be breached while standing on water is but the dream of youth."

"Minor victories have made Alexander drunk," said Amasias, the captain of the priests. "He imagines he can reach to the heavens."

"And how do we know the heavens will not reach down to him?" demanded Tobiah.

"Surely, Tobiah, that is putting things too much in his favor."

"Did not Yahweh, may his name be praised, give Jericho to Joshua?"

"He did, but that was to Joshua, not an uncircumcised heathen."

"Did not Yahweh, blessed be he, give Jerusalem into the hands of Nebuchadrezzar?"

"In the days of our fathers," replied Amasias, "he spoke to us by his prophets, and although we did not heed the voice of Jeremiah, we might have. Unless a prophet arise, who will tell us the will of heaven in our days?"

"I will tell you," said Tobiah. "It is clear enough that if our god had intended that Darius defend us from Macedon, he would have done so at his earliest convenience and given Darius a victory at Issus. That Yahweh, may his name be revered, did not, is sufficient a prophecy for me."

"One cannot read the plans of the Almighty from the way the winds blow."

"We can determine that a storm threatens by the blowing of the wind, and it is well known that the Almighty, when dealing with uncircumcised heathens, sides with the stronger."

"But you seem to have forgotten that Alexander did not pursue Darius. Perhaps it was because he knew that defeat in Persia was certain, or perhaps our god filled his heart with fear and will yet bring him into the bowels of disrepute."

Menachem, a respected man of an ancient family, and always a voice of moderation, attempted to calm them. "My brethren," he said feebly, "we are now caught between the wrath of Alexander and the wrath of Darius, and whichever way we turn, we shall have to answer for it if we err. Let us provide the best possible case for choicelessness to Alexander as a reply."

"Choicelessness?" echoed Tobiah, rising from his seat. "Choicelessness?!" he croaked in dismay. "My understanding stands still and I accuse my ears of not hearing aright. When the city of Tyre is destroyed, then we shall face choicelessness." And Tobiah proceeded to argue his case with all the power of his vocabulary, limited only by the strength of his lungs. "It is," he allowed, "a grave matter to change our loyalty from the empire into which the Lord gave us to another. But let us remember that Darius himself may be called usurper, and for this reason alone I say the Lord has determined to give the scepter to another, a more worthy king."[11] He concluded, "As for me and my house, we side with the west."

It must be admitted that Tobiah's reasoning roused the elders. They wavered and whispered among themselves, but Jaddua raised his hands, and the council grew silent. "Brethren," he called out in his now phlegmatic voice, "Tobiah will do as Tobiah sees fit, this we know, but we must act for the sake of the nation, and give answer to the embassy of Alexander.

Menachem spoke for all. "Let us tell Alexander that we are bound by oath to Darius not to take up arms against him, and while Darius lives, we cannot break our oath." The phrase "while Darius lives" was, of course, key and diplomatic code for "as soon as Alexander defeats Darius, we will swear allegiance to the conqueror."

The council affirmed the precise wording, using the more poetic "while Darius is in the land of the living," and Jaddua, bolstered by their confidence, informed the envoy of Alexander that he had given his oath to Darius, and so forth. Within a fortnight, a solitary messenger returned to Jerusalem with the words of Alexander, who, in his anger, threatened that when he was done with Tyre, he would march against the high priest and "teach the world to whom they must keep oaths." Still, a calm and calculated ambience lingered in Jerusalem: let Alexander kick against the walls of Tyre as would-be conquerors had done from the dawn of time.

Tobiah, to make good upon his word, dispatched Theokeles with a large gift of silver for the campaign of Alexander and jars of perfumed balm for his officers, with the promise of a thousand head of sheep—that is to say, a large flock difficult to number—to help feed his army. Theokeles found the ambassador of Alexander who had come to Jerusalem and made the gifts of his master Tobiah known, along with apologies for Jerusalem. In Jerusalem the elders voted a formal censure of Tobiah for his treasonous act, but otherwise shrugged their shoulders. He would have to make his own defense to Darius, the king of kings, when the time came, and he should not count on them to come to his aid. A few were pleased that Tobiah sided with the vanquished, and they secretly contemplated how they might divide up his possessions.

Reports came daily from sources close to the battle. Because Alexander had no fleet of ships, he began using the rubble of Old Tyre to build a mole from the shore to the island. The causeway quickly extended across the shallow waters near the shore, but as the water grew deeper, to its full depth of some twenty feet, his army of engineers drove massive piles into the sea bed two hundred feet apart and filled it in with stones, earth, and wood.[12] For their part, the Tyrians built catapults on their walls and showered the workers with stones and arrows. Alexander responded by building towers filled with archers which he advanced along the front of the causeway. The Tyrians then loaded an old horse transport ship with twigs and bitumen and all manner of flammable materials, the mast and yard arms hung with cauldrons of sulfur and oil. They towed the ship close to the causeway and let the wind carry it ashore next to the towers. Men aboard set the ship alight and swam back to the island. Meanwhile, the catapults on the walls of Tyre pelted the Macedonians as they tried to extinguish the burning towers. Other ships came at the Macedonians from the side, and the towers were completely destroyed, and the end of the causeway cracked and fell away under the waves. Within an hour of conflagration, the work of two months had been destroyed.[13]

News of the "defeat of Alexander" reached Jerusalem with the swiftness of falcons. In the aristocratic circles, as the elders mingled about the corridors of power, there was, beneath arched brows and knowing frowns, an agreeably sly sense of "vanity, vanity, all is vanity." Tobiah weighed the collective appraisal of their predicament and began to doubt the wisdom of his engagement with the Macedonian. When he had taken all the elderly consolation in the form of disdain and grave concern that his otherwise robust constitution could stomach, he went to the temple court, offered up prayers on behalf of Alexander, and departed again for Joppa, that he might assess the nature of their predicament with the aid of his steward.

"I have offered to pay you well for sound judgment," said Tobiah rather sternly, "but what shall I pay for dubious judgment? As I have tied my fortune to Alexander, so is yours tied, and things are not going aright."

Theokeles remained squatting on his settle so that Tobiah could lord it over him without having to look upward. From his lowly seat by the window overlooking the sea, Theokeles listened with a grave façade and stylus tilting precariously from his ear. When given leave to speak, he murmured, "Xerxes, ill-fated, led the war; Xerxes, ill-fated, leads no more."

"What's that?" asked Tobiah.

"A line from *The Persians*," replied Theokeles. "Aeschylus."

Tobiah stood open-mouthed, trying to make sense of his steward. "Pray explain yourself, while you still have a tongue," he managed.

"May I share a brief anecdote concerning Alexander?"

"If you must."

"While King Philip yet lived," Theokeles said, "there circulated a story of the brash young Alexander. Philip wished to buy a splendid steed called Bucephalus for thirteen talents. They brought the horse to Philip, but Bucephalus would not be mounted, nor would he listen to the king's attendants. Philip ordered them to take it away, when Alexander came and said, 'What an excellent horse do they lose for want of address and boldness to manage him!' Philip chastised his son for supposing himself better than his elders, but Alexander replied, 'I could manage this horse better than they.' To which Philip said, 'And if you do not, what will you forfeit for your rashness?' Alexander answered, 'I will pay the whole price of the horse.' At this the whole company fell a-laughing; and as soon as the wager was settled amongst them, Alexander immediately ran to the horse, and taking hold of the bridle, turned him directly toward the sun, having, it seems, observed that he was disturbed at the motion of his own shadow. And coaxing Bucephalus gently, he led him about until he had gained the confidence of the horse. At length he mounted Bucephalus to the acclaim of all."[14] Theokeles pointed north. "This very horse will be found near Tyre, in a stable tent of his own, well fed and content."

Tobiah said, "And therefore, on the strength of a rumor about his equestrian abilities you remain confident that he will capture Tyre and defeat Darius?"

"The moral of the story," replied Theokeles, "is that Alexander and his engineers will find a way. With him, nothing can be safely called impossible. Will the loss of two towers discourage Alexander? Nay, it will not, for he is incapable of retreat. Send him rather more silver and promise of aid."

"More silver?!" cried Tobiah. "A thousand sheep have I lost."

"Eight hundred and seventy-three, master. And they are not lost, but invested."

"But now the investment is truly a wager, is it not?"

"If so, the gods have given you a chance to raise the stakes, and therefore, the rewards. In time of need, master, gifts are the more valued." Tobiah grasped his beard in contemplation, and granted him a certain shrewd logic. Theokeles continued, "His gratitude for loyalty is already legendary. Such a small venture will reap interest a hundredfold. Go and see for yourself."

Tobiah straightened with resolve. "Indeed I shall. I must see the investment with my own eyes."

"Then let us go to the outskirts of Tyre," said Theokeles, as he rose to make the arrangements.

Tobiah retrieved additional bags of silver from creditors, loaded twenty mules with costly provisions, and, with a handful of servants, he journeyed north. Tobiah set himself up in a widespread tent worthy of his mission on a hill outside the old city of Tyre, while Theokeles renewed his contacts among the Macedonians. The officers accepted the invitation of Tobiah to dine under his awning, and delivered the bags of silver to the treasury of Alexander. For his part, Tobiah spent freely on hosting them and learned a great deal more about the intentions of their captain and king, though he never got close enough to lay eyes on the legend himself.

It was now early spring, and Alexander had set his corps of engineers and machinists to rebuilding the causeway, both wider and at an angle more favorable to withstanding the pounding waves. He traveled to Sidon and enlisted the aid of the kings of Aradus and Byblus. They, who had formerly served the Persian navy, sensed the expectation in the air and now placed their fleets, upwards of eighty ships, at the disposal of Alexander. Rhodes followed suit with a small fleet to join in the battle, and shortly thereafter, Cyprus sent one hundred and twenty ships to Alexander. Tobiah saw the odds shifting again in his favor. Throughout the ruins of Old Tyre, Alexander's engineers built a vast number of catapults, and brought others in from Cyrpus and to the north. They equipped ships with towers and drawbridges to be thrown against the walls of Tyre. Such knowledge and science, such technology and master builders, and with such zeal and attention to detail did Alexander drive his men on, that Tobiah grew faint of heart in awe and for a moment suspected he was in danger of committing idolatry. He paid homage, if not worship, to this master overseer of multitudes, and he returned to Jerusalem breathing rather more freely, with a smug Theokeles by his side.

In Jerusalem, belabored breath and worried airs returned. Darius had sent his own envoy with promises of reduced tribute should Jerusalem hold the western front and undermine Alexander of Macedon. Shortly, the king of kings would come with an army of a hundred thousand and rid them of this foreign threat. Jaddua, with the blessings of his council, renewed his oath of allegiance to Persia. At the same time, they later learned, Darius had sued for peace with Alexander, offering ten thousand talents for the release of his family hostages, his daughter Statira in marriage, and all the land west of the Euphrates. According to the report, Parmenio, one of Alexander's Companions, advised: "If I were Alexander, I would accept." Alexander is reputed to have replied: "So would I, if I were Parmenio."[15] We mention this exchange only because legend has bequeathed it to us, and it sounds very much like the legendary Alexander. Whatever answer Alexander sent to Darius, he refused, and Jerusalem could only learn from the Jews in Babylon that Darius had begun amassing the largest army ever assembled in Asia.

When the causeway had reached to within a few yards of the island, Alexander began attacking with catapult ships at all sides of the besieged city, seeking weaknesses in the walls. Toward midsummer the Macedonian fleet broke through both harbors, and Alexander breached the south wall with his catapult ships. He brought in two bridge ships and threw the bridges onto the broken walls. His Shield Bearers led the assault and once they had taken the wall, Alexander followed and relentlessly advanced to the royal citadel. From both harbors the soldiers erected ladders and poured like frothing waves over the walls. Though the Tyrians fought bravely, they were overwhelmed, and great was the slaughter. The enraged soldiers, more savage than half-bestial Centaurs, slew eight thousand Tyrians, and two thousand were later nailed to gibbets on the seashore. Alexander counted his slain at four hundred, among them twenty of his elite Shield Bearers. What the king of kings, Nebuchadrezzar, failed to achieve in thirteen years, Alexander and his engineers accomplished in seven months.

Out of his great respect for all gods and goddesses, Alexander pardoned those who had taken refuge in the temple of Heracles but sold the remaining Tyrians and mercenary troops, some thirty thousand, into slavery. He held a festival with gymnastic sports, paraded his soldiers before the temple gates, and offered sacrifices and dedications to Heracles. Then, when his men had rested and made merry, he set his gaze on Egypt.

All Syria had fallen to the Macedonian. Only Jerusalem and Gaza had not sent emissaries with tokens of submission. In Gaza, the Persian governor Batis remained loyal to Darius and believed he could withstand Alexander until Darius came with a new army to rid them of this pestilent adventurer. Batis had stocked the city with food and water for a year-long siege, and the city stood atop an earth mound sixty feet high with marsh land all the way to the sea. Because ships would not avail Alexander nor catapults reach the walls, Alexander raised an earth ramp to meet the height of Gaza's south wall, until his siege engines could hurl their missiles over the walls, and simultaneously sappers dug tunnels under the walls which sat upon the ruins of the more ancient city. Within two months Gaza fell, quite literally, to the Macedonians. Alexander ordered all the men slaughtered, all the women enslaved. Although twice wounded, Alexander, in imitation of his ancestor Achilles and the vanquished Hector, tied Batis to his chariot and dragged him by the heels around the crumbling city walls.

Jerusalem now stood alone. The elders who once declared that Tyre could not be taken, had never counseled their leader so poorly. Now they awaited white faced, as if the slaughter of Tyre had drained the blood from each of them. Amasias resigned from the council in disgrace and fled to Babylon, while many in the council who retained strong ties with Babylon hastily sent their families eastward. The question that hung over Jerusalem and all Judah was directed to the mystery of heaven. Had the Lord of heaven again given up his people to a battle between gentile kings, or was he in control and fought on the side of the Macedonian? If only the Lord would send a prophet like Jeremiah to make known his will for all Israel. But the will of heaven often lay hidden behind the clouds. Jaddua sent privately for Tobiah.

The diminutive merchant and his hovering steward hurried along the streets of Jerusalem to the temple precinct. The people bowed respectfully and gave way. Although they were not privy to all the council's wisdom, the common folk, from whom we get the notion of common sense, could see plainly enough that the time to change sides was past due. Although they wistfully yearned for the blessings of the Most High upon the transfer of power, they could no longer wait for king Darius to depart the "land of the living."

"Our time has come," Tobiah said. "A great deal rests on our words and actions today and tomorrow."

"For this you have prepared, master."

"You excel in confident hyperbole, my faithful Theokeles. No, I have prepared only for my own fortune with the west. I have not prepared to act as mediator between an angry conqueror and a people ruled by a jealous god."

"I can help you with Alexander," Theokeles shrugged, "but your god . . ."

"What will Alexander require?"

"You will find Alexander ever ready to accept peaceful submission. Only when he pays for submission by the blood of his friends does he require tribute in blood."

"A bow and arrows as tokens of submission?"

"And your tribute," Theokeles added.

"Yes, yes," replied Tobiah. "But we cannot acknowledge the gods of Greece or sacrifice to them. Persia has never required us to worship Marduk."

"There, the king of Macedon has the advantage over you," said Theokeles, "for he is free to pay homage to any god who sustains his mastery over the earth."

"It is a disadvantage we have lived with a long time," said Tobiah. "On the other hand, we are free to acknowledge that our god has raised up any conqueror to do his bidding. Just as Cyrus became the Lord's anointed, so now he has raised up Alexander."[16]

"Well spoken, master," said Theokeles. "Mutual recognition between two conquering and unconquerable rulers. Such a declaration Alexander is bound to accept. Now, can you place these words in the mouth of your high priest?"

"Jaddua is a practical man. But the people require divine sanction."

"Have you no oracle?" asked Theokeles.

"Long ago we had the Urim and Thummim," said Tobiah, "but it is no longer consulted."

"How do you consult your god?"

"In former times we had prophets, but they too have ceased."

"So, Jews are left to their own devices?"

"Yes and no," Tobiah frowned. "There are ancient prophecies awaiting prophetic interpreters, and some claim the Deity speaks to us in
dreams, but on balance, we are reduced to wisdom and wit."

They reached the house of Jaddua. Out of respect to the high priest's
sanctity, Theokeles waited outside the gate, that he not defile the chambers of the priestly abode. "Gird up your wit and wisdom," Theokeles
encouraged his master, "for if you are not successful, there may soon be
an uncircumcised Macedonian in the Holy of Holies."

The following morning, Jaddua assembled the remaining council
and revealed to them that in the night the Most High had told him in a
dream to fear not, but to offer the golden crown of submission to the
Macedonian. With the sign of divine approval set forth, Jaddua prepared
to approach the king of Macedon, and it was understood—thanks be to
God—that Tobiah, "Friend of Alexander," would lead the delegation.
Tobiah, content that his hour of greatness had come, sent Theokeles
ahead to Gaza, where he would make the arrangements with the staff of
Alexander for the embassy from Jerusalem. Tribute came from every
quarter, silver and gold coins—a full year's tribute, not the half tribute
Darius had promised should they hold against Macedon—and a hundred wagons filled with the finest produce of Judah: large jars of olives,
amphorae of olive oil and skins of wine, flour ready for the baking, baskets of melons, figs, citrons, raisins, and pomegranates. Behind the caravan, herds and flocks followed, bleating in the dust of the way. On a calm
and cool autumn afternoon, a great procession wound its way out of the
Judaean hills bearing a peace offering to the new king of kings.

Tobiah rode upon his ass at the head of the caravan, appropriately
flanked by other notables of the land who had also privately favored
Alexander, though not as generously. The sea breeze washed over them
as they reached the fallen city of Gaza, and helped dissipate the stench of
death. Rubble from the collapsed walls, once thought unreachable,
spilled down the embankment. Theokeles awaited at the gate. The city
itself had not suffered greatly, and Alexander had taken up a brief residence in the palace of Darius's governor. While the other notables delivered the bounty and tribute, a Macedonian officer escorted Tobiah and
his steward into the palace courtyard. There beneath a large yellow awning that fluttered gently in the breeze sat a group of soldiers. The escort
led them into the shade and announced the presence of a friend of

Macedonia, Tobiah the Jew. The military entourage, a half-dozen sea-soned soldiers and a youth of smooth chin, rose and turned to their guest. Each was clothed in similar tunics of finely spun wool and cotton, none more distinguished than the other.

Theokeles whispered to Tobiah, "The shortest is Alexander." [17]

"Of course the smallest is the greatest," replied Tobiah under his breath.

The mighty Macedonian, from the crown of his head to the soles of his boots, stood no taller than a medium sized lad after a morning stretch. At age twenty-four Alexander yet appeared like a servant to one of his herculean generals. It was divine, thought Tobiah, that such en-ergy and aura should be bundled in so small a frame—but a frame very nearly divine, a handsome youth by any reckoning, long curls of hair, bright penetrating eyes, a straight nose, a smooth chin, and impulsive lips. Yes, very nearly divine, a suitable model for Greek gods and all con-querors to come. Tobiah bowed low to the shortest man among them.

Alexander acknowledged the respect and beckoned Tobiah forward. "I receive my benefactor among the Jews at last." Alexander seemed de-lighted that he could look Tobiah in the eye without raising his head.

"My lord, the king," said Tobiah, keeping himself slightly bent so as not to rise above Alexander, "we Jews, as a body, are your loyal subjects."

"My companions call me Alexander, and I desire that my friends do the same."

"By your leave, my lord Alexander, the high priest of Jerusalem is eager to receive you into the city, tomorrow, the day after, or when you return victorious from Egypt."

Alexander said, "How do you know I will be victorious?"

"Our high priest received a divine oracle in a dream that we are to submit to you. I can only assume that means you will rule all Persia and therefore Egypt."

"A timely oracle," he said. "And an oracle that takes its time." His en-tourage laughed at the sharp humor. "Very well, I shall pay my respects to your high priest when I return . . . victorious." He reached out to Tobiah. "But it is to you that I owe my immediate gratitude. After all, Alexander cannot accept timely aid without granting something in re-turn. Have you a son who might accompany me to Egypt? There are many Jews in Egypt with whom I shall have to come to terms. And the wealth of the Nile lies at our fingertips."

"I do have sons, lord Alexander, but they are unprepared for such a venture. I shall have them ready on your return, for they are well ac-quainted with Babylon, and we have kinsmen there who can facilitate your administration of the Jews in these vast lands."

"Excellent. Will you then, accompany me to Egypt?"

"My lord is too gracious. It would be a momentous honor to follow in your company, but your servant can do greater service by remaining here in preparation for your return. If it please you, I will send my steward, Theokeles of Athens." Tobiah gestured toward his steward hovering behind him. Theokeles bowed.

Alexander looked him over. "An Athenian, no less, in your employ?"

"A most excellent judge of providence, my lord. I have relied on his counsel."

"If so," Alexander said to Theokeles, "where were you when Athens refused my father his due?"

"Your servant was indentured at the time to an Athenian with obviously depraved eyes and ears," replied Theokeles.

Alexander smiled. "You have fared far better with your new master, I see." And addressing himself again to Tobiah, he said, "So be it. He will act on your behalf and reap your reward, which shall be great." He waved his hand toward the palace and the baths. "But tonight, you will partake of a feast in honor of friendship between the Greeks and the Jews?"

"Your servant will be indeed honored, my lord Alexander."

Thus, and in this manner, Tobiah sent Theokeles down to Egypt, the land of miracles and mud, in the retinue of Alexander.[18] There, by the strength of his steward's ears and lightly wrinkled brow, Tobiah added wealth upon wealth, and was greatly blessed by the Lord, both he and all Israel.

# 5

# The Lawless Ones

In those days lawless men came forth from Israel, and misled many, saying, "Let us go and make a covenant with the Gentiles round about us, for since we separated from them many evils have come upon us." This proposal pleased them, and some of the people eagerly went to the king. He authorized them to observe the ordinances of the Gentiles. So they built a gymnasium in Jerusalem, according to Gentile custom, and removed the marks of circumcision, and abandoned the holy covenant. They joined with the Gentiles and sold themselves to do evil.

First Book of the Maccabees

Legend assures us that Alexander wept when Anaxarchus gave a lecture on the possibility of an infinite number of worlds. They asked him why he wept. "So many worlds," said he, "and we have not yet conquered one."[1] Weep not, Alexander. Weep not. Your mantle of Hellenism continues to conquer. It has fallen heavily upon the land of Judah.

Our civil war began in Jerusalem among the high and mighty, the chief priests and the aristocracy. Some say it was a struggle among claimants to the high priesthood; the intrigues of power and prestige that lie tantalizing within sight. Others say it was a matter of allegiance to our Gentile overlords, and that just as our fathers had to choose between Darius and Alexander, so now we must choose between Ptolemy in Egypt or Antiochus in Syria. But as life often overwhelms itself and leaves yesterday buried, the cause was neither here nor there and soon forgotten beneath the dust of acrimony.

After the death of Alexander the Great, his successors, the Diadochi, fought for control of the vast conquered territory, culminating in the battle of Ipsus. Two of his generals divided up the eastern kingdom between them: Ptolemy took Egypt and Arabia; Seleucus kept

Mesopotamia and Syria. The council of victors awarded the province of Judah to Seleucus, but Ptolemy had occupied the area and refused to concede the land. Whether Ptolemy's claim was just or unjust, the Jews thrived under the Ptolemaic Dynasty. Ptolemy II Philadephus commissioned seventy elders from Jerusalem to translate the Torah of Moses into the Greek tongue, that it might become known to all the earth.[2] Under the dominion of Ptolemaic kings, a long lineage of high priests governed the Jews of Palestine for over a hundred years. In the last years of the high priest, Simon the Just, the Seleucid Dynasty of Syria wrested Judaea and Palestine away from the Ptolemies.[3] During the high priesthood of his grandson, Onias the third, our strife began.

Enemies falsely accused Onias of supporting the pro-Ptolemaic faction of Jews, and the Seleucid king Antiochus summoned him to answer the charges. While Onias went to Antioch, his brother Jason, in imitation of the envy of Cain, bribed King Antiochus, and got the high priesthood for himself. Straightway, Jason, on behalf of the many Jewish Hellenists, asked Antiochus to make Jerusalem a self-governing *polis,* like the Greek city-states. Antiochus, lauded as Epiphanes, "the god manifest," approved the request. The Hellenists declared the city Antioch-at-Jerusalem, or Antiochia, and registered themselves as citizens, Antiochenes. They established an *ephebeion* within Jerusalem, a school for young men and women to prepare for citizenship, and a *gymnasion* where the youths discipline their bodies and engage in athletic contests of the javelin, the discus, grappling, and the race.

In the fifth year of his reign, Antiochus invaded Egypt, that he might rule both kingdoms. Meanwhile, Menelaus, brother of Simon of Antioch who was the captain of the temple, offered Antiochus a greater sum for the office of high priest, and thereby deposed Jason. While Antiochus campaigned in Egypt, Jason came with an armed force financed by Hyrcanus the Tobiad to take back Jerusalem from Menelaus and cut off the supply line to Egypt. Jason failed. And when Antiochus returned, on this pretext, as well as claiming tribute in arrears, he came to Jerusalem, and with Menelaus by his side he entered the temple sanctuary and took the golden altar and many golden utensils for his own treasury. Antiochus established his military garrison in Jerusalem, in a walled city within a city, called the Akra, below the southern end of the temple mount. He stocked the fortress with Syrian soldiers and Jews loyal to the king. The Syrian soldiers demanded an altar in the temple at which they might worship Baal Shamem, Lord of Heaven, whom the Greeks call Zeus. Antiochus authorized, and the priests sanctioned, an altar upon the altar of YHWH, the Lord of heaven, and they dedicated the temple to Zeus Olympius, as Lord of the Heavens in his own right, though in deference to the Jews, they did not place a statue of Zeus in the temple. Menelaus, to consolidate his power, arranged the murder of Onias, and the people in turn tore the brother of Menelaus, the innocent Lysimachus, guilty only of blood kinship, limb from limb.

If your eyes have glazed over at the names, the who, why, and wherefore, worry not yourself; clearly law and order had gone astray. Fratricide, the second most ancient sin, was alive and well. And we know what happened next, for the tradition is quite clear, as indeed the feast of dedication annually reminds us. Antiochus banned the central rites of the Jews—sabbath worship and circumcision—and he required sacrifices to Zeus. Mattathias, a priest of Modein, refused to sacrifice on an altar to Zeus, and when a fellow Jew stood up to perform the rite of loyalty, Mattathias burned with ancient zeal and slew the apostate Jew upon the altar. The five sons of Mattathias quickly killed the king's men and tore down the altar. Thus, in the one hundred and forty-sixth year of the Seleucids, the priest of Modein and his sons rose up, gathered the "devout" around them, and sallied forth from their wilderness caves to attack the Hellenists in the countryside. As tradition tells us, "they struck down sinners in their anger and lawless men in their wrath."[4] When Mattathias died, his son Judah, surnamed Maccabaeus, the Hammerer, became leader of the struggle.[5] After three years of renowned victories, they took Jerusalem and rededicated the altar of the temple. But the official tradition in the books of the Maccabees is inexcusably one-sided, as histories written by victors invariably are, and it is our task to balance the tradition.

The sides of the conflict may be described as the Hellenists and the Hebrews. If you hailed from the former, Cosmopolitans and Provincials. If you bound yourself to the latter, the Lawless and the Pious. The one side sought to bring the Jews fully into the universal culture of the Hellenes, Greek philosophy, science, and art, and in the process of reform, to relieve Jews of certain timeworn and embarrassing "marks of Jewishness." The other side sought to preserve the ancient identity laid upon Abraham, both marked and fenced round by the laws of Moses.

The storm of civil strife swirled relentlessly above the head of Hannah, daughter of Annaeus of Modein, and handmaid to Glaphyra, wife of Rhodocus. She came into their service at age eight, the very year that her master Rhodocus wed, and brought her mistress Glaphyra into his home in the city of Lydda, seven miles west of the village of Modein. Hannah's father gave her in service to Rhodocus for six years as repayment of a loan to buy an ox. At age twelve her father betrothed her to Jacob, son of Gadi, a simple shepherd of Modein, and when her six years of service ended, she was to have wed, but the turmoil delayed her wedding and Hannah remained in the service of Rhodocus for payment. Glaphyra even expressed hope that Hannah might remain in her service when she married, and Rhodocus once suggested that her betrothed, whom he hired as a day laborer from time to time during the ingathering of his orchards, could also come into their employ and settle on his large estate outside Lydda. But that occurred before the war, before her betrothed, the stalwart young shepherd in peasant garb, cast his lot with the pious ones and fled to the hills.

Jacob came to her one afternoon, perspiring, dirty and disheveled, and in great haste. "The king's men came and set up an altar in Modein," Jacob began in hushed gasps. "The priest Mattathias forbade any man to perform such an abomination in the village of Modein. But when the captain threatened to destroy the village, your uncle Nicomedes stepped forward to offer the sacrifice so that no evil would fall on us. Then Mattathias came to Nicomedes, grasped the knife from his hand as if to sacrifice, but he slew Nicomedes upon the altar. Immediately the sons of Mattathias rushed upon the king's men, slew many, and sent the others in flight." Hannah gasped and began to weep. "Many of the villagers fled with Mattathias," Jacob told her. "Your father fled for fear of revenge, and he sends word that you must remain in the protection of Rhodocus." When Jacob had delivered his message, he joined the opposition and fell into disfavor with Rhodocus.

Hannah busied herself over the meal preparations in the moderate white stone villa with glazed tile floors, hardwood doors, and a beautiful mosaic design in the atrium. The evening sun broke below the lintel of the open door of the kitchen, its rays swirling on the wings of the west wind that swept across the plain of Sharon from the Great Sea. The autumn air cooled the land more quickly and even left a slight chill in the night. Only days before, an army from Antioch, sixty thousand strong, marched south along the road outside Lydda, and the anticipation of a decisive battle spread across the region. Two prominent men from Jerusalem were to arrive this day on their way to Strato's Tower, one of whom was a brother of Glaphyra, the other a priest. Her master invited two neighbors from Lydda to come and share the meal and hear the tidings of Jerusalem. Already the neighbors joined Rhodocus in the courtyard, where they awaited the guests from Jerusalem.

Glaphyra sniffed, "No, Hannah, place the figs on the outside, line them with apricots, and bunch the raisins in the center. The art of dining requires color and a sense of symmetry." Glaphyra went round to the other preparations. The meal itself was simple: sauces simmered and loaves of bread had just come out of the oven; and her only meat, roast peacock, lay sheltered beneath stalks of leeks and onions. "Alas," the mistress sighed. But the guests would understand, for times were hard and uncertain.

Hannah arranged the dried fruit in shallow ornamental baskets. Glaphyra was the mistress of her domain. She had an eye for the finest detail and energetically attended to every aspect of her domestic affairs, upstairs and down, from the atrium to the kitchen. The only exception was the wine cellar, which she treated as a crypt, for the odors upset her digestion. But many a woman in Lydda envied her household, and the wives of important men often came to her for advice on how to run a villa. And the Creator, in his wisdom, had granted Glaphyra an aristocratic face: oval shape, high forehead and prominent cheeks, a slender nose that sniffed just so, and a receding chin sufficient only to prop up lips that could speak volumes in complete silence. And she had delicate hands. Glaphyra sought beauty, though she rarely found it among the *hoi polloi*. She obtained works of art, preferably from the west, though she had a jade bowl from Bactria. She prized a statue of Pan, two cubits in height, which came from Antioch and now stood prominently on a pedestal in the atrium. Of course she spoke Greek, and read it as well. But beneath the airs, the mistress cared for Hannah like a mother hen. Glaphyra had done her duty: she gave her husband two sons, Timotheus and Philip, and no longer wished to give birth. She absently considered Hannah her own daughter.

Hannah, when she gazed into a bronze mirror, saw only a peasant's face, uncolored and slightly adorned with bronze earrings; too round, with lips too large, and nose too fleshy—thoroughly commonplace. Only her hazel eyes, she allowed, as Glaphyra often reminded her, were beautiful. She came from humble stock, a humility that included plainness of thought and a simple faith, one that believed whatever seemed pleasing to heaven, that heaven's blessings might continue, and in good years, perhaps increase a little. Piety, the observance of laws and customs, must find its place among the weeds and thistles of life. As her father often said: piety is no cause to starve. Hannah now held fast to her security in the house of Rhodocus.

The two Jerusalemites arrived: Aristides, brother of Glaphyra, and the priest Alcimus, who had served as captain of the priests under the high priest Menelaus. Rhodocus ushered them in with the customary greetings and oriental kiss. Rhodocus himself cut a highborn figure, clean shaven and hair cropped short, a high forehead on a head perhaps a bit too large for his slender body, but finely dressed in a white woolen tunic embroidered by Grecian frets. The guests, too, were all of the sort one finds among the upper class. They gave their cloaks to the steward and each took his turn in an ornamental chair of mahogany while Hannah washed their feet and Timotheus, off to one side, held a towel and basin for their hands. Ablutions performed, the company reclined on low couches arranged around three sides of a table cut from a single slab of pink marble and set upon legs of bronze. The couches were of the finest Greek design, constructed from thin oak slats, strong yet very light, with small, silver, lion-paw feet. Even the cylindrical cushions took their pattern from the west.

At a nod of Glaphyra's head, servants brought in the food. Hannah set the trays of legumes, bread, and sauces on the table, and placed a portion of roast peacock near each guest. The steward filled their silver wine cups, polished to perfection, one-third wine, two-thirds water. Glaphyra introduced the meal with the appropriate apologies for its simplicity— due to the war—and hopes were expressed all around that better times lay ahead. She and Hannah withdrew to the archway and stood just off the dining room, ready to replenish a bowl or plate. Hannah knew that one neighbor, Memnon, was the descendant of a Macedonian soldier who married a Samaritan woman and settled in Samaria after the conquest of Alexander. The other, Silas, was a Jew from Damascus who had come to Lydda since Antiochus took control of Palestine. Rhodocus proclaimed a brief blessing in gratitude to the Deity, and invited the guests to partake of the food.

"Tell us, then, Aristides, what tidings of the war," said Rhodocus, when each man had at least tasted of the meal. "We know the Vice-Regent marched south."

Aristides nodded. "Lysias lays siege to the fortress of Beth-Zur with an army of sixty thousand picked soldiers and five thousand cavalry."

"To what end?"

"To secure an open approach to Jerusalem, a wide passage in the territory of Idumaea that will not allow Judah to trap him as happened to the battalion of Gorgias. Thereafter, he will secure Jerusalem." Aristides sipped from his goblet, and shook his head sadly. "Friends, Jerusalem is a wasteland. The Akra remains in our hands, but dogs come and go as they please. A forest of weeds grows in the rubble and from the cracks in the walls."

"Ah, what Jerusalem might have been," Rhodocus lamented. "A beautiful city set on a hill, with a temple to the universal god of heaven, and a gymnasium for the perfecting of mind and body. A true rival to Corinth or Pergamum."

"Our golden Jerusalem may yet come to pass," said Alcimus. "We have only to make peace between the factions and hammer out some constitution that allows traditional culture and universal culture to coexist."

"Only?" Glaphyra whispered to Hannah. "Hmph, has he ever tried mixing oil and water?"

Hannah smiled at the homespun analogy. Her mistress held an authoritative opinion on any topic be it a recipe or affair of the kingdom. She would never embarrass her husband by setting things aright in the presence of guests, but she kept her household staff well informed on all her verdicts. Glaphyra made them feel as if they belonged to the elite class, because they were privy to its manner of thought and way of life. But Hannah remembered her betrothal to Jacob, who now sided with the traditionalists, and though she prayed for peaceful reconciliation, the day of decision would surely come; oil and water mix poorly.

". . . Judged as rebels whether or not they took up arms?" Hannah caught the end of a question posed by her master.

"I have it on good authority," said Alcimus, "that Menelaus has written a petition to the king, asking that a general amnesty be granted for Judah and all the Jews who wish to follow our ancestral customs to the letter."[6]

"But will Judah and his rustic rebels allow us to follow our customs in spirit only?"

"Even they keep oaths, Rhodocus. A new constitution for Jerusalem will serve as the law of the land within the Seleucid Empire, such that the thousands of Greeks can live in harmony with the ten thousands of Jews. We will establish a proper balance between the law of Moses and the laws of Antiochus."

"Then let us hope such a solution will bring peace to the land," said Rhodocus. "Let every man sit under his own vine and fig tree and observe the customs of our fathers as seems good in his own eyes. I rest on the sabbath, but if my rest takes me to the gymnasium, of what concern is that to a law that forbids work?"

Alcimus fingered his roast peacock, and shrugged. "The council will have to decide some definition of work, what is permitted and forbidden, but that is what councils do," he replied. "The Hasidaeans have shown themselves reasonable and willing to alter the statutes."[7]

"Indeed," Silas laughed. "At least we may now defend ourselves on a sabbath without tarnishing our piety. Can you fathom the Syrians not fighting one day in seven? Did not Joshua and his hosts march around Jericho on a sabbath?"

Hannah could not but recall the first great slaughter of the people who fled to the wilderness. Even now tears came to her eyes. Mattathias called on all who revered the law to rise up, and many peasants, whole families, including hers, answered his call and fled to the hills where they hid in caves. The king's soldiers pursued them, and cornered a large group on the sabbath. They urged them to surrender and obey the king. But the people would neither surrender, nor in their simple faithfulness would they take up arms and defend themselves on the sabbath. The soldiers slaughtered the whole company—a thousand souls. When reports of this great calamity reached Mattathias, he decreed then and there that all Jews must wage defensive war on the sabbath.[8] Many months passed before Hannah learned that her father and mother numbered among those who perished on that sabbath. Did her father resolutely refuse to fight on the sabbath or had a majority, or even just the strong men of the company, constrained him to perish? She supposed he would have fought, but she would never know.

"But you will agree, will you not," Aristides was saying, "that forbidding public worship on the sabbath is equally unjust and impossible to enforce?"

"Antiochus the king cares not a barley straw about our sabbath rituals. Do not the Samaritans in Shechem continue to study Torah and observe the sabbath? Has the king imposed a ban on our coreligionists in the Transjordan? The prohibition is meant for Jerusalem, to ensure the freedom of the city and all Antiochenes who dwell there."[9]

"How do you account for the ban on study of Torah and circumcision of our sons?"

"Bad advice from the king's Jewish counselors," Rhodocus replied. "See here, Aristides, all sides commit excesses in their zeal. You know the law of conflagration: action, reaction, and overreaction. Zealots against the law summon zealots for the law. We wish to expand our view of the Most High God of Israel to be truly universal, they respond by refusing even to pronounce his name. I do not care what the Hasidaeans do or how they choose to demonstrate their piety. I do not care if they interpret the ancient injunction to 'bind the words of the law upon your forehead' literally and strap a leather amulet stuffed with laws writ on papyrus to their foreheads, so long as I may read the injunction as our fathers read it, a poetic reminder to heed and remember the law.[10] My god! Some of them interpret the quaint prohibition against boiling a kid in its mother's milk to mean that we may not eat any meat boiled in any milk.[11] Where will this end? If I choose to attend a theater on the sabbath, that is how I choose to rest—as I am not an actor it can hardly be called work. If I dispense with literal circumcision, in favor of symbolic or allegorical, that is my affair." He turned to his neighbor. "Not so, Silas?"

Silas nodded. "I believe Scripture contains a phrase somewhere that allows us to opt for the allegorical meaning of circumcision; that is, of the circumcision of the heart, meaning control of excessive passions, or in a word, moderation.[12] Even the Greeks will applaud such striving toward such virtue. Not so, Memnon?"

"Quite so," Memnon replied, and applauded softly for emphasis.

Rhodocus added, "Perhaps these practices served a useful purpose, some secret sign of identification back in the nomadic days of our forefathers, but surely there are more civilized and universally appreciated ways of declaring one's ethnic origin." He turned to the priest Alcimus. "Are my sons no longer Jews because they wear a foreskin?"

Alcimus inclined his head. "They are Jews . . . but it is a delicate matter. . . ."

"So to speak," Memnon cajoled.

"So to speak," smiled Alcimus. "Some propose a symbolic snippet of foreskin as fulfilling the law.[13]

"Well then, my sons may decide when they reach the age of majority, whether a snippet or the whole."

"It only seems fair," Aristides chided. "Give the lads a chance to think about it. Circumcision is far less traumatic than epispasm, not so Rhodocus?"[14]

Rhodocus grimaced in mock anguish. "God, yes!"

Glaphyra shook her head and turned back into the kitchen. "I do wish they would not make issue of privy matters at table. It is bad enough that his sons are seen as impious, and this reflects on us all."

At the dedication of the gymnasium in Jerusalem, Rhodocus had proudly worn the broad-brimmed hat of Greek athletes.[15] And in order to display his Grecian form like a statue for all eyes to gaze upon when he threw the discus, he employed a Greek surgeon to cover his male member and thus remove the nakedness of circumcision, that he not appear as one whose arm had lost its hand, or even a finger. So much for precocious vanity; for soon enough he had recourse to regret the operation. When he married his wife Glaphyra, the extended skin, while it passed for a foreskin in the gymnasium, nevertheless caused him pain in the act of lovemaking, and after two years of the mixed blessing, such honey and vinegar, he again employed a surgeon to cut away the awkward foreskin. Glaphyra confided this to Hannah shortly after the operation, when the master hobbled about the house as if a great stone were tied to his privy part and dangled between his legs. "It is his just desert," she said. "Besides, his performance with the discus was abysmal."

Rhodocus lifted his goblet in a toast. "Let me be a Hellene and a Jew. Why should Jews remain in the backwater marshes like the Egyptian fellaheen? See how the Jews in Alexandria prosper by adopting the ways of the Hellenes, while the Egyptians remain inbred slaves.

Did not Joseph son of Tobiah become King Ptolemy's chief of tributes, even as his father, Tobiah, prince of the Land of Tobiah, before him? The fact that the offspring of Joseph are not of the same fiber as their ancestors does not detract from the eminence of the Tobiad clan in the corridors of power and prestige."[16]

"They have risen high, 'tis true," said Alcimus, "but at some cost to their heritage. They eat forbidden meat as occasion serves."

"So would I, at the king's table," replied Rodocus with a sneer of disdain. "It is a small price to pay, and I will not be called provincial."

"Let it be so," they said, raising their cups.

"Permit a Greek to offer an opinion, esteemed Rhodocus," said Memnon. "If there is but one god over the world, as Jews maintain, does it not follow that we all worship that god? The Greeks call him Zeus and the Romans call him Jupiter, and Jews call him by another name, which, out of respect to all, I shall refrain from mispronouncing.[17] That we Greeks use different names, and worship other gods besides, need not detract from our common worship of a supreme god. I ask then, to you Aristides, and you Alcimus, what harm is there in letting Syrians worship Baal Shamem, their lord of the heavens, in the temple to the Jewish lord of heaven? Let each be revered within the pantheon of names."

"I side with you, noble Memnon," replied Aristides. "If Greeks allow Jews to live at peace and worship as they like in Antioch, shall we not give such freedom in Jerusalem? We are all part of Coele-Syria. I favor such freedom of worship for the Syrians and for you as well. Mind you," Aristides smiled, "although I think the lesser gods are but whisperings of the muses, be it far from me to prevent a man from offering incense to his imagination."

"You are indeed gracious," replied Memnon. "And be it far from me to prevent a man from mutilating his most precious member."

Amid the laughter, Rhodocus said, "There you have it, my friends. This freedom of worship our Jewish brethren cherish in Alexandria and Antioch. Why should we in Judaea be deprived of it?"

Philip tugged on the robe of Hannah and led her back to the kitchen, where Galphyra said, "It is time for the sweet meats, and"— she rolled her eyes—"more wine for this symposium." When she had surveyed the trays, she half complained, "Oh, my dear Hannah, how my husband goes on about our heritage and all. Most of our rituals are not a burden, and if they allow us to live in peace with the peasants, they are a small price to pay." Hannah gave her a frown of sympathy. "Men, besides being stiff-necked can be so, so . . . thick headed. Especially counselors, who imagine themselves as veritable sages, or even as wise as matrons!"

Hannah laughed. How might the land prosper if women ruled? Tradition recalled many heroines, but only one queen, Athaliah, who ruled briefly when her husband and son had perished, but she herself was slain in the court rivalries of Jerusalem.[18] Esther and Judith used their beauty and wisdom to save the people, and all agreed that such women would have ruled wisely. Hannah was confident that Glaphyra would find a way to settle any dispute. Of course they should worship their god as they had always done, that there might be food on the table, and milk in the mother's breasts. Yet, Hannah also saw the reason in the arguments of Rhodocus. The west brought wealth and culture, new machines and ideas, and enhanced life with the arts. Jews had every right to this culture. But for all that, women did not rule, and wisdom knew the truth of it—that life, real day-to-day life was very confusing, and she only wished the war would end, that she might give birth to her own children, and have wherewith to feed and clothe them.

A clap of hand from her master interrupted Hannah's thoughts. "Timotheus," called Rhodocus, "come, my son, and recite a portion of what you committed to memory. Let us challenge the learning of our guests." Hannah beckoned Timotheus and guided him by the shoulder into the atrium. Rhodocus proudly introduced his son to them, and said, "Recite only that portion, a favorite of mine, on the twelve springs which you learned most recently."

The lad, still very much a figure of youth, a small Rhodocus, but with his mother's chin, stood before the assembled guests, and in his bright tenor voice recited the verse in iambic pentameter:

> Take note, most noble Moses, of this place
> which we have found near yonder airy glen.
> 'Tis over there, where you, too, now may see.
> From thence a lustrous light now flashes forth,
> by night, a sign, like to a fiery pillar.
> And there we found a meadow shaded o'er
> and splashing streams: a place profuse and rich,
> which draws from out one rocky ledge twelve springs;
> the trunks of fruitful palms rise like a hedge,
> threescore and ten, with water flowing round,
> and tender grass yield pasture for the flocks.

Timotheus stopped and awaited a response. The men burst into applause. "Bravo! Well done, Timotheus. Your father rightly boasts of you."

"Wait," said Rhodocus, "can anyone here tell us whence the passage?"

"Were the name of Moses not given," Memnon ventured, "I might have supposed some obscure work of Euripides, but now I confess my ignorance."

Aristides said, "Can it be other than Ezekiel the Tragedian?"[19]

"Even so," replied Rhodocus. "Have you seen his play *Exagoge?* I believe the Jerusalem theater first performed it, what, five years past?"

"I have not, but may we look forward to another performance in the future."

"Aye," replied Memnon, "and may we hope that a few poets of repute might arise from our own midst, even such as young Timotheus, who quotes them authoritatively."

"Hear, hear," they chorused, as Rhodocus proudly dismissed his son. Thereafter, the conversation did turn to the practical elements of bringing a lasting peace in the land of Judah, one that would somewhat satisfy all, the cosmopolitan Jews, the parochial Jews, and the many Gentiles in the land. Hannah brought in her baskets of delicately arranged fruit, and the steward refilled their goblets.

Dire tidings reached Lydda. The rebels defeated the Seleucid general Lysias. The ten thousand rebels led by Judah slew five thousand, some said ten thousand, of the sixty thousand strong Seleucid army. Lysias retreated to Damascus. Now Jerusalem lay at the mercy of Judah, with only the Akra fortress still under the control of the king's forces.

Some days later, Hannah, carrying a jar of water, returned from a well near the city gate when she felt a hand on her shoulder from behind. She turned to face a man whose face lay shadowed behind a hooded wrap, and only when he spoke her name did she know it was her betrothed, Jacob.

"Hannah," he said, and led her down a narrow side street. She set her jar of water on the ground as Jacob removed the cloth from his face. His dark beard was much fuller, his eyes were red and worn, and his youthful face aged and weathered. "Hannah, I must warn you of things to come. Great events have occurred and the Lord will give us victory over our foes." Hannah felt her shoulders tighten. Jacob was no longer the humble peasant shepherd, who cared more about the shearing and the milking of his flock than the rules of sabbath rest. She saw a new fire lit in his dark eyes. Jacob continued, "On the march to Beth-Zur, while Judah and his men departed Jerusalem, a horseman appeared at their head, an angel of the Lord, they said, clothed in white, brandishing weapons of gold. The hosts of Judah followed and wrought victory over our foes. Magnificent the slaughter. Magnificent! Never has the Lord wrought so great a victory in this land—like the days of old, when Gideon stood before the angel of the Lord, when the chosen few defeated the many.[20] Now, the army of Israel hurled themselves like lions against the enemy and slew thousands of them and horsemen by the hundreds. They forced all the rest to flee, most were stripped and wounded, and Lysias himself escaped by disgraceful flight."[21] Jacob gazed about him, suddenly aware his voice had risen. Seeing no suspicious eyes, he grabbed Hannah by her shoulders. "Hannah," he said, "come with me now."

Hannah remained silent, dumbfounded. "Where would I live?" she asked.

"Live in Modein," Jacob replied. "Your father's house still stands, empty and ransacked, but not destroyed. When Jerusalem is securely in our hands, then I will come and take you to myself and we will wed."

"But I am now safe under the protection of Rhodocus, as my father instructed."

"Rhodocus is the enemy of God."

"Master Rhodocus always treated you well, Jacob."

Jacob grunted, "He paid me a day's wages for a day's labor, nothing more."

"But he also would give you employment on his estate."

"Only so that Glaphyra might keep you as her maidservant."

"Jacob, I dare not leave now."

"Hannah, your father is dead, or I would go to him. But our betrothal is valid and may be enforced. I keep the document safely hidden."

"So long ago, Jacob, we were betrothed. The land is not the same. You are not the same."

"A great truth, my Hannah. I now understand the meaning of zeal for God." Jacob covered his face again. "You must flee this villa," Jacob warned her. "Jerusalem is taken. The temple will be restored and the laws of God will be enforced. Listen to me, and obey my words." He lifted her water jug, handed it to her, and departed.

Within a fortnight, eight men in ragged mud-spattered cloaks stormed the villa.

"Rhodocus!" a voice called out, "Rhodocus!"

Rhodocus came out to the atrium holding a lamp, wearing naught but a loin cloth. "Who are you, and by what authority do you enter my home?" he demanded.

"We are soldiers of the Lord God, and we enter by the authority of Torah, or by the strength of arms, whichever you revere."

"I grant you the strength of arms." He squinted in the lamplight and recognized one of the men. "And you, Jacob, are you the informant and guide to my door?"

Jacob grinned. "You cannot hide from the Lord, master Rhodocus."

"What do you want?" Rhodocus asked them.

The leader growled, "Bring us your sons!"

"Whether you demand by Torah or by strength, I will not surrender my sons."

"Apostate! We asked in a *civilized manner*," he mimicked, "only to avoid bloodshed."

Rhodocus screamed out, "Help! Help against the rebels." One man grabbed the lamp from his hand, and two others held his arms and put a knife to his throat. "No help from the heathen," one laughed.

Glaphyra now came, with Hannah following close behind. Seeing the men and shadows of men in her home, Glaphyra pleaded calmly, "Do us no harm."

The leader sternly acknowledged her. His bearded face was that of the common peasant, but his brow was fashioned of conviction. "Bring us your sons," he commanded.

She hastened to bring them in. Timotheus and Philip stood mute and terrified at the sight.

"Prepare ointment and bandages," the man ordered.

"For what need?" Glaphyra demanded.

"We come to redeem your sons."

"Redeem?" Rhodocus shouted. "You mean butcher."

"So little you remember of your heritage, Rhodocus, and still call yourself a Jew?"

"This land is mine as much as yours. Yes, I call myself a Jew. But if it means identifying with you, I will reconsider."

"What do you know of the heritage of Abraham and Moses?"

"Fools! You fight for freedom of worship, yet you deny me that freedom."

"You are wrong, Rhodocus. You are very wrong. We do not fight for freedom of worship, we fight for the laws of the Lord God in the land of our God. The only freedom to be had is from pagan rule and lawless Jews. God be praised, this is now within our power."[22]

Without further explanation or apology, they stripped the boys naked. One man knelt on the floor and told Timotheus to sit on his knees. The lad obeyed. The man reached over his shoulders and spread open Timotheus's legs. An older man, their circumciser, bent down and deftly pulled the foreskin of Timotheus. He determined the amount of skin to be removed, and clamped a small metal yoke around it as a shield to the member. He lifted up his face and prayed in a loud voice: "Blessed is the Lord of heaven. Reclaim your own, and restore this land." He grasped a small bronze knife and swiftly sliced off the foreskin. Timotheus grimaced but said not a word as the tight wad of flesh fell to the floor. The old man had no doubt circumcised an army of infant males into the world. He removed the clamp, pulled back the remaining skin and let it bleed.[23]

Glaphyra returned with a jar of ointment and cloth, and seeing the droplets of blood, she hurried to her son. "Do you mean to bleed him to death?" she barked.

The circumciser grinned, and wiped away the blood. "May this be the only blood your son be required to shed."

Glaphyra applied ground cumin to the wound. Hannah took the cloth and tore a thin stip, which she handed to Glaphyra and she bound up the member for healing.

When the ritual was completed, they stood Timotheus in their midst and lay their hands upon him. The men chanted, "Blessed be the Lord God who hallows us by your commandments and commands us concerning circumcision."

The leader turned to Rhodocus. "Now recite your portion."

Rhodocus shouted, "Barbarians! Swine! Accursed Egyptians!"

The leader shrugged. "Then I will recite your portion." He placed his hands on Timotheus's head. "Blessed be the Lord God, King of the Universe, who has sanctified us with your commandments and has commanded us to lead him into the covenant of our father Abraham."[24]

They took Philip. The lad began to cry, though he tried to be brave like Timotheus. Glaphyra turned away, and Hannah whispered to him, "Be courageous, son of the covenant."

Again the old man performed the prayer and the rite and the benediction. Philip whimpered and Glaphyra came again with the ointment. Hannah was at hand with the cloth. When they had bound up his slightly smaller, but no less painful wound, Glaphyra drew him up to her breast and soothed him.

Rhodocus struggled with his captors, as their leader again faced Rhodocus. "Listen to us, Hellene and son of Belial.[25] Have not the sages said: 'Children will blame an ungodly father, for they suffer reproach because of him. Woe to you, ungodly men, who have forsaken the law of the Most High God! When you are born, you are born to a curse; and when you die, a curse is your lot.'[26] The temple will soon be restored. Even now we are cleansing it. When the altar is rededicated, bring your sacrifice and offering. It may be that God will have mercy on you and on our land. If not, we will cut you down like ripened wheat and burn your home like chaff."

"Your god is not my god," said Rhodocus bitterly.

"Yet there is but one god. *Shema, Israel, the Lord our God, the Lord is one.*"[27] He signaled his men let go of Rhodocus. "Remember, Rhodocus, there is but one Israel and one god of Israel. One law. Obey or perish."

Jacob came to Hannah. "Come with us."

Hannah shook her head. "I cannot."

"You are my betrothed, Hannah. The document is valid and binding under the law."

"Leave her alone," Rhodocus said "Annul the betrothal and go your way. Have you not caused enough pain?"

"I will reclaim what is mine," said Jacob.

Glaphyra said, "Go with Jacob, Hannah, and remember us for good."

Hannah sighed. Women did not rule the land, and wisdom knew the truth of it. She drew near to Glaphyra and kissed her mistress. "May we abide together," she whispered. Hannah gathered a bundle of her belongings and followed Jacob into the night.

# 6

## The Pious Ones

Nineveh is laid waste; who shall grieve over her? Whence
shall I seek comforters for you? Interpreted, this concerns those
who seek smooth things, whose counsel shall perish and whose
congregation shall be dispersed. They shall lead the assembly
astray no more, and the simple shall support their counsel no
more.

Pesher Nahum

Not since the days of King David and Solomon had Israel been a
united kingdom reaching from Dan to Beer-sheva. The Hasmonaeans, therefore, are remembered by their admirers with misty eyes in
eulogy and song. Did not old Mattathias, on his death bed, rally the
faithful with his immortal words: "Remember the deeds of the fathers,
which they did in their generations; and receive great honor and an everlasting name."[1]

Judas and a small band of pious men, beat down the enemy relentlessly, and they called him Maccabaeus, "the Hammerer." His brother
Eleazar, ran sword in hand beneath an elephant of the army of the
Seleucids and split open the belly of the great beast so that it fell upon
him and he died for the glory of Israel; they called him Auran, "the
Borer." A third brother, John, was murdered in ambush by Nabataeans;
they called him Gaddis, and no one remembers why.[2] After Judas fell in
battle, his brother Jonathan took up the sword and the scepter. Jonathan
made himself high priest and led the pious for eighteen years, waging
war against the kings of Syria, until he was treacherously murdered by
the Antiochene general Tryphon. Immediately, Simon, the last of the
brothers, stood in his place. Under Simon, "the yoke of the Gentiles was
removed from Israel," and the people began to date their documents: "In
the first year of Simon the great high priest and commander and leader
of the Jews."[3] Simon ruled Israel for eighteen years, until one night,

while feasting he became drunk, and Ptolemy, governor of Jericho, slew him in the banquet hall. Then his son, John Hyrcanus ruled over Israel.

Now in those days there arose factions in Israel, each determined to direct the way in which Israel should walk.[4] The more Israel threw off the yoke of the Gentiles, the more we revived the ancient rule of God over Israel, and opinions on how God should rule multiplied. All this occurred despite the Hasmonaean offspring, who, being born into the upper echelons of society, came to mimic, for better or worse, Hellenistic rulers throughout the world. A faction known as Zadokites, or the Sadducees, comprised of the priesthood and other elite, supported the trappings and excesses of the Hasmonaeans, while jealously guarding their control of the lucrative temple cult and the calendar. A second faction separated themselves from the masses, and received the name *Perushim,* "Separated Ones," or Pharisees. They were more numerous because they came from the ranks of artisans and small landowners, and by their great learning and ingenious interpretations of Torah, they retained the greatest influence on the common people. A third faction were known as Essenes, because they claimed to be the true "Doers" of the Torah.[5] They held that God ordained a solar, not a lunar, calendar; therefore, they issued a pox on both of their rival factions, and no longer attended the temple festivals determined by the moon, lest sacred days be profaned.[6] Essenes became famous for the gift of prophecy and knew the secrets of the end times. But above all, they held to a higher standard of purity in all they ate and touched, and they withdrew yet further from the congregation of Israel.[7]

Seth walked hastily over the scrubby soil into the hills outside the town of Beth-shean. Beads of perspiration congealed on his smooth forehead, glistening in the breezeless heat, and trickled down his cheeks into his light reddish-brown beard. Nature called impatiently. Seth reached a slight depression in the hill and walked down to a clump of bushes. A startled turtledove took flight from the ground before him, the whistle of its wings disappearing over the hill. A rock badger huddled beside its burrow and a large lizard on a rock outcrop watched, its head moving slightly to and fro. Seth slipped the cubit long mattock from his girdle and dug a small trench in the earth to the depth of the mattock. He gathered up the hem of his threadbare tunic and arranged it around him modestly as he squatted, that he not offend the divine rays of the sun.[8] The badger had gone elsewhere, but the lizard still moved to and fro. When certain he had cleansed his bowels, Seth rose, and after briefly inspecting his excrement, satisfied that his constitution was in order, he clawed the soil back into the hole with his mattock. He breathed deeply, massaged his abdomen, and returned to the encampment, which lay a half mile from the outskirts of Beth-shean.

Born into a priestly family, his father betrothed him at age twelve to a girl age six, the daughter of another priestly family. He was expected to marry his betrothed in her fourteenth year, so that eight years of his life were written on parchment and he had only to follow its directives. His father enrolled him in training as a scribe, to read Torah and write documents. With a sharp mind and a gift for script and phrases, Seth became a promising temple scribe, perhaps even a temple jurist, a credit to the Sadducees. But he found, as the years molded him, that he could not wait for his betrothed, nor was she likely to please him at all. He frequented the prostitutes in Jerusalem and its environs, for which he was reprimanded; but in a debased moment while visiting Jericho, he committed an abomination. To add insult to abomination, the boy was a Greek, with no sense of discretion. The priests might have stoned Seth, but for the sake of his family honor and the priestly reputation they banished him from Jerusalem. The breech of betrothal contract required a face-saving solution. Word spread that Seth had dedicated himself to a life of abnegation, and strange though it appeared to those who knew him, such a calling was nonetheless honorable. Thus, he came to the Essene community with a fat purse—a portion of his inheritance—which he handed over to them, and his talents, such as they were, in search of a place where the base desires of the flesh, from lust to gluttony to frivolity, would atrophy in the sober solitude of a sparse and strictly-ordered life.

At the stone gate of the community, they questioned him. Why did he want to become one of them? To know the truth, he replied, and his earnestness satisfied them. Why else would a priest of Jerusalem seek to dwell in the poverty of the Essenes and hand them a small fortune in silver coin? They presented him with a mattock, a linen loin cloth, and a white tunic. For one year he dwelt in a small goatskin hut, furnished with a reed mat, a wool blanket, a stool, a water jug, and a clay cup. In the winter his wool blanket became his cloak. He worked the fields farmed by the small community, or assisted their craftsmen; he labored as instructed and never spoke to a member save when addressed.

After the year of probation, they again questioned him, and finding him firm of resolve, they brought him further into the community to share in more teachings and to purify himself in their holy bath. During his second year, they treated him with greater respect, but still he never spoke unless spoken to. Because he was trained as a scribe, they gave him documents to copy and then books of Holy Writ. When the double year of initiation had passed, the brethren gathered around him, as the husk of a pomegranate, and adjured him by powerful oaths, lest his soul be consigned to eternal perdition and his body to the pit, to observe their rules, to fight for justice, to preserve their books and the names of the angels, and to transmit the teachings of the community exactly as he received them.[9]

Having come that far, Seth never looked back. The removal of temptation revealed a will to righteousness as strong as had been his inclination toward evil. The simplicity of his abode, and the severity of his regimen hardened his frame, both limb and sap. Spilling one's seed was taboo, copulation, out of the question. Continence was possible, and with sufficient discipline, even licentious thoughts evaporated into thoughtless oblivion. If, in his sleep, by chance an emission occurred, he would remove himself to the goatskin tent for three days, immerse in the ritual bath, and rejoin the community.

The community let Seth open a scribal booth outside the gate of Beth-shean, by which he turned over to the elders a regular income every market day. On other days he copied texts or composed missives to other groups of Essenes. Peacefulness surrounded him, at work and at rest; the heart of each Essene beat to the rhythm and revolution of the heavens. Human turmoil began at the edge of town and built up step by step as town became city where tempters lurked and demons crouched, and city swelled into districts, and districts into the land of Judah, and from there across the troubled and evil inhabitable lands.

During Seth's sojourn with the Essenes, King Jannaeus died, and his queen Alexandra Salome, unwilling to yield power to either of her sons, Hyrcanus or Aristobulus, kept the scepter for herself. She had now ruled the land for nine years. She brought the Pharisees back into power, which they had not held for two generations, and they took vengeance upon the Sadducees and Essenes who had opposed them and hounded them since King John Hyrcanus expelled them from his court. But the queen was old and must soon die. Already Aristobulus gathered his supporters, all opponents of the Pharisees. Hyrcanus, the high priest, gathered his supporters, the Pharisees. The Essenes peeked out from their cloistered lairs and sought to read the future in the clouds amid the rumors of war.

Seth passed the brothers in silence and went directly to his room in the stone complex of their community. Begun in a single house, they added rooms as the community grew over the years from a handful to their present number of seventy-eight, so that now the appearance was like a villa in size and like a honeycomb in structure. The brethren slept two and three to a small chamber. He took off his tunic, and wrapped his loins in the linen cloth that served him these eleven years. Walking across the courtyard to their covered cistern, he removed his sandals at the entrance and crouched through a low opening. The chamber was cool and pleasant. He removed the linen cloth and hung it on a peg, walked down the steps along the right side, dipped himself completely in the cold water, and came out by the left steps, purified and ready for the evening meal.[10]

At the appointed hour, the brethren glided silently into their refectory. The elders had discussed the construction of a larger dining hall, but the community might also split and begin a colony outside another town in the lower Galilee. For now they sat in two circles, one inside the other, according to their seniority, with the inner circle being the more senior and revered. Those appointed as stewards and caretakers of guests brought in cups of water and earthenware bowls with the simple meal they had prepared. Each cup passed from hand to hand along the two circles, beginning from both sides, and plates followed. When all the food lay before them, the elder selected to give thanks did so. "Amen, amen," the voices rose together in unison, and swelled the chamber with song so that it could not but escape through the doorway and small windows. Children came to listen, and a traveler might pause to enjoy the melodious songs.

Few spoke during the meal, which each man ate slowly. But if one did speak, he spoke undisturbed, for interruption of another's words heaped shame upon the heads of all. The elders of the inner circle finished their meal and the bowls were collected and removed. Then Ananias, the wizened old leader, rose and addressed the assembly.

"Tomorrow a Guardian will visit us," Ananias informed them.[11] He paused to let the solemnity of his voice settle upon them. Seth recalled the first occasion during his eleven years with the brotherhood that a Guardian visited them, just when King Alexander Jannaeus died and his queen Alexandra Salome began to rule. With every change of ruler, the Essenes came together to formulate praise for the new king, or for the first time in the Hasmonaean Dynasty, the queen, and express their guidelines for a blessed rule. The elders and Guardians expressed cautious fears at the rule of a woman, fears soon realized. The Pharisees managed to delude the poor woman into siding with them. By her authority they recalled men in exile and freed prisoners, and took vengeance on those who had urged Jannaeus to crucify the eight hundred.[12] The elder confirmed his thoughts. "The Pharisees, those Seekers of

Smooth Things, have long prevailed upon Salome, and all manner of error in the land has followed swiftly on her heels. But she is now gravely ill, and we must unite with our brethren. This is the task of the Covenanters."[13]

Seth awoke in the dark, as he did every morning. The distant cry of a cock heralded the new day, but cocks were notoriously competitive, so he lay still until he discerned the faint square of the window, the first sure sign of dawn's advance. His companions lay beside him until he stirred. They donned their tunics and joined the great awakening. Singly and silently they spread themselves out across the hillside. Facing east, they began, at their own pace and fervor, to pray, soliciting the sun to rise and mount the heavenly dome, and direct this day out of its charge of three hundred and sixty-four. They blessed the Holy One whose grandeur the sun was but a lowly symbol, yet by itself gave warmth to the earth, light to the eyes, and life to all living creatures.[14] They continued reciting prayers received from their forefathers until the ruling disk broke from the Peraean hills east of the Jordan River and began its mount upon the blue dome. Then they went each to his own task and occupation.

As it was the fifth day of the week, a market day, Seth took his three-legged stool, his scribe's board, and his pouch of inks and quills to the market outside the east gate of Beth-shean. The city, also known by the Greek name of Scythopolis, was settled by Macedonians after Alexander's conquest, and remained a Greek city until it surrendered to John Hyrcanus. For three generations Jews repopulated it, though many Greeks remained. Seth impartially wrote contracts for Jews or Greeks, so long as neither touched him. Though not the only scribe, he invariably arrived first; and being esteemed by the community for impartiality in disputes, his knowledge of legal terms, and his beautiful script, he was usually busy. Most documents were in Aramaic, but on occasion Hebrew was requested. Seth carefully crafted each letter so that his words were not subject to a wide range of conjecture: his *resh* (ר) was distinct from a *dalet* (ד), and his *heh* (ה) from a *khet* (ח). He did not, as did some scribes, write at a speed which sacrifices form and clarity, on the prideful presumption that any intelligent reader will immediately know what the misshapen letter must be for the word to be what it is within the context of the phrase. Clearly, such scribes felt inferior to even the humble illiterate, bolstering their esteem at every occasion.

Betrothals and divorces, bills retained in fear or joy, required fine parchment, which he kept in various sizes. Promissary notes, a minor business transaction, could be on anything. Poor people often brought some item to serve as a legal document, a flat piece of wood or a pottery chink. He kept different inks and quills for each surface, and all his ink contained oil of vitriol to keep flies away from the freshly written letters which might alter their appearance. Thus he sat upon his stool near the gate, placed the writing board upon his knees, and wrote as the customer dictated, or put into a legal tongue what the customer wished to say, spelling the words correctly and occasionally suggesting a different turn of phrase. Fascinated, they watched their voice and will take shape in fixed and eternal form. What he would not write, and was rarely asked, were curses or incantations. Nor did he allow his customers to touch him, and the people, impressed by his art and his sanctity, kept their respectful distance. Once he completed the document to the satisfaction of all, he held up his writing broad and let the customer take it, and deposit the payment in a small pouch at his side.

The fifth hour approached. Seth packed his instruments, picked up his board, and returned to the settlement. He left his stool indicating his intention to return, that they might await him instead of seeking a different, and much inferior, scribe. After purifying himself in the *mikveh,* he joined the brethren to break their fast upon a single loaf of bread, a boiled egg, and six olives. The brethren spoke among themselves concerning their work, whatever might interest another, so that each member had a general sense of the welfare of the community. The meal began and ended with a blessing. Then Seth returned to his scribal stool and worked until the tenth hour.

The Covenanter, Guardian Joshaphat, arrived at the Essene house. The chief elders hovered around him in the refectory while the brethren entered and took their places, not in circles as for a meal, but in rows according to their rank and position, least at the left. The Guardian was a tall man, strikingly gaunt in appearance, perhaps fifty. Beneath an utterly bald and polished dome, thin ivory brows overshadowed deep sockets whence his eyes assessed the men before him. From his lean-fleshed face a scraggy sheet of beard, like faded yellowed linen, clung tenaciously and drooped down his chest. He had never been a hairy man, thought Seth.

Brother Ananias spoke to the assembly briefly, explaining the developments in the court of Salome, and the mission of the Guardians, to whom they now owed their rapt attention. Guardian Joshaphat spoke in a soft and unhurried voice. On account of neophytes in their midst, he reviewed the history of the Essenes, of which the order of the

Covenanters was a part. He recited portions of their foundational document. "For you know that we have separated from the multitude of the
people of the congregation and from all their uncleanness. . . ."[15] The
rule of God in the land, the Guardian explained, had long been compro-
mised by wicked men and the most dangerous Pharisees, who claimed
to guide the people.

Seth knew the Pharisees were smooth and lax interpreters of the law.
Where the Essenes ruled a one thousand-cubit limit on Sabbath travel,
the Pharisees ruled two thousand. Where the Essenes kept the faith by
preventing marriages with the Ammonites and Moabites, the Pharisees
softened the ban on marrying Ammonites and Moabites found in the
fifth book of Moses, by cleverly noting the male gender of Moabite,
thereby permitting marriage with the Moabitess.[16] For this reason,
among others, Pharisees were popular with the common folk, and the
Covenanters ridiculed them as *Dorshe-ha-Khalakot,* literally "Seekers of
Smooth Things," but it also meant "Flattery-Seekers."[17]

Guardian Joshaphat then turned to the dangers that lay before them.
He called to mind the visions of Daniel, the powers of darkness, and the
battle between the Sons of Light and the Sons of Belial, even Satan, who
is the ruler of this age. The battle in the heavens cast its shadow on the
earth, and true Israel must wage war against the doers of evil. He reminded the brethren of their original calling, and summoned them to
vigilance, for evil times lay ahead, as they must before that great and
terrible day when God would vindicate True Israel and punish the
deceivers.

The community entered behind the sabbath veil, where the soul,
immortal and imperishable, gave itself to meditation, and the body, mortal and perishable, to hibernation. They drank water sparingly, ate mea-
ger cold victuals from a table laid the day before, and suffered not their
bowels to be relieved on that day.[18] When evening to evening passed, the
brethren gathered to return in unison from behind the veil, with lus-
trous hymns and solemn rejoicing.

The next morning, after prayers, elder Ananias summoned Seth. He
went to the small council chamber and found the Guardian seated on
the plain wood benches with the chief elders. Guardian Joshaphat
spoke: "You have a reputation as a very good scribe, brother Seth."

Seth bowed his head slightly in humble admission. "The Holy One
gives his servants gifts for his glory."

"We have need of a good scribe," continued Joshaphat. "Our chief
scribe Eliezer, may his name be remembered among the blessed ones,
has gone the way of all the earth, and our other scribes have not his
knowledge or ability. They are only apprentices and prone to error."

Elder Ananias said, "The Covenanters require your service. Therefore, we are sending you to them."

Seth bowed again, more deeply. "Your servant awaits his task."

"You will leave this morning," said Ananias. "Go now and prepare."

Seth went to his chamber. What the elder meant by prepare was to gather up his appendages, ink, and quills, and wait, which he promptly did. He was standing at the gate when the Guardian came. One of the brothers brought Seth a traveling cloak and a long, smooth curved knife for protection against thieves.

They departed south along the Jordan Valley road for a destination just beyond Jericho, in the Judaean Hills above the Salt Sea. Seth could walk the distance in two days, less than sixty miles, but at the more moderate pace of Joshaphat, Seth anticipated a three-day journey. They walked down along the Jordan Valley ridge in silence, to which they were both accustomed, gazing little at the hills of Samaria to the right or the verdant river valley to the left. They might have walked from Dan to Beer-sheba with no greater disturbance than belabored breath, had not an eagle risen from a terebinth toward the river and swooped down upon some unsuspecting rodent, or more likely a hare, as best Seth could tell. Joshaphat too watched, and took that common act of nature as a text for commentary.

"Kittim, Kittim," he intoned, "who destroy the many with the sword, old men, young boys, woman and child, even in the womb."

Seth understood that he spoke of the Roman armies, for Daniel prophesied that the ships of Kittim would come, and Rome came like a bird of prey and took from Persia all the lands around the Great Sea, and defeated all who opposed them.[19] Less than two years past, Rome invaded Armenia and drove Tigranes out of Syria. The shadow of Rome encroached on Judah.

Joshaphat stood in the road, clinging to his staff. "Woe is Israel. The righteous are few and the wicked are many. God will bring this eagle against us, for we have grievously turned from the straight path." Only after the spell of the eagle dissipated into the valley breeze did Joshaphat seem aware of Seth, the road, and the journey. He turned to Seth. "We are few, and of ourselves, we are weak."

"Of whom do you speak, Guardian?" Seth ventured.

"We, the Sons of Light, brother Seth."

"The Covenanters, Guardian?"

"Here in the wilderness you may call me brother," Joshaphat smiled faintly. "The Covenanters, yes, but you too, are a Son of Light, brother Seth. You too are weak in that your contentment gives birth to apathy."

"Wherein are we apathetic, brother Joshaphat?"

"The Essenes are among the elect, but they await the call to battle only as a well-fed goat awaits a handful of barley. Though you follow the law rightly, you no longer fight for the Land of Israel as you once did. Our forefathers, the Pious Ones, were the fiercest warriors Israel ever knew because they only fought in holy wars and death brought everlasting glory. Now, only the Covenanters wage war with the Sons of Darkness. Until God raise up for us an anointed one, another Teacher of Righteousness, we rage against the wind, and no one hears our voice."

It was true, Seth conceded inwardly, that over the generations the Essenes withdrew somewhat from the power struggle of the land. They turned to quiet contemplation, to meditation on the life of holiness and simplicity. They strove to glimpse the abode of the righteous beyond the ocean, the isles of the blessed. A different order of Essene communities took wives, though only for the purpose of procreation.[20] Seth ventured, "What should we hear from your voice?"

Joshaphat raised his eyes to the sky as if seeking a sign. Seth waited at length, until he thought they might lose the thread of the conversation. "The voice, brother?"

Joshaphat kept his gaze upward, but replied, "The voice of heaven which speaks through our mouths, for we alone read the heavens." He turned to Seth. "Therein lies our strength."

"How are you alone, brother, for many Essenes have the gift of prophecy. Did not our brother Judas of Jerusalem foretell the death of Antigonus by his brother Aristobulus, and many other events?"[21]

"Brother Seth, did I say we *alone* have the gift of prophecy? From time to time, here and there, a man's life may be read in the stars, or God reveals a word to the faithful and reminds us that the span of every life is numbered. By your virtue, Essenes excel in prophecies. But we Covenanters count the span of this age, and to us alone has God revealed the darkness that lies ahead. Will the many rally when the saints of the Most High are called? Though I am old, the Kittim will come in my life and the end times will begin. I fear we are not prepared." Joshaphat faced south and they resumed their pace.

Seth pondered Joshaphat's words. It was true, from time to time events seemed to augur the catastrophe of end times, but when the years marched on as if without end, few could sustain the imminent expectations. There were fields to plough and ploughs to mend. But the Covenanters did sustain their expectations. From their desolate outposts the warlike Guardians of the pious kept vigil betwixt the northern horizon and the clouds of heaven. Perhaps the end times were truly at hand. The end, though it delay, must in the end, come.[22]

The first night they slept under the stars near the Jordan River, and Seth rose early to cut a handful of choice reeds that grew along the river bank. When the reeds dried, he would make quills of them. The second night they stayed with Essenes to the north of Jericho, and in morning they quickly passed around the city, to avoid defilement, and descended to the northern shore of the Salt Sea. In this arid lowland of the earth, the weight of the heavens bore down on them, bowing their backs and pressing their feet into the blistering sands. The long expanse of crystal-line water invited them to plunge in and be refreshed, but so great a deception would not be found anywhere else upon the earth. The brackish depths of the Salt Sea killed all life, and embalmed it for eternity, rightly earning the name Dead Sea. It was said the pillar of salt that had once been Lot's wife could still be seen along its southern shore amid the residue of Sodom and Gomorrah.[23]

The Covenanters dwelt in a complex of buildings first begun by their forefathers during the early years of the Maccabaean revolt. A handful of Hasidaeans occupied the ruins of a building that stood before the exile on a plateau above a small wadi north of the oasis, where once lay the ancient City of Salt.[24] They built up new walls of unhewn stone and dug new cisterns. During the reign of John Hyrcanus, son of Simon, more Essenes joined the Elect and expanded the building with more rooms and cisterns, an upper room and a tower. The Covenanters controlled the infrequent but furious flash floods that coursed through the wadi by a dam, trenches, and aqueducts. In the wadi below, a small spring allowed the community to plant gardens and raise livestock. Among the maze of storage rooms, courts, and secret chambers, hid six cisterns and seven baths. They channeled water to the ritual baths, and so much surface water kept the chambers cool so that within the sheltered walls a man might remain vigorous the length of the day. For five generations the Covenanters retained this outpost as one of their camps, a monument to the call of Isaiah, "Prepare in the wilderness the way of the Lord."[25]

Joshaphat spoke with the elders. They welcomed Seth, and after refreshing him with sweet dates and cool water, they led him to a small courtyard within the stone walls, where he reposed beneath a thatched canopy until the day's labor had finished. He then joined them in the baths and the evening ritual. They were indeed all elderly men, except for two apprentice scribes, none younger than thirty. If possible, they were more severe and regulated than his group of Essenes, but what truly set them apart, as brother Joshaphat said, was their understanding of the heavenly battles and their warlike visions.

On the morrow, after the communal prayers, Seth entered the upper room, where a council of ten had gathered. They set him at a proper settle with a slightly inclined desk on which to write and wasted no time in laying before him the substance of their proposed mission to the myriad communities of the Essenes across Israel. Guardian Joshaphat said, "The time of catastrophe draws near, and we must alert the faithful. This we will do by our *pesher* on the prophecy of Nahum, the explanation of his words for our times. Your task, brother Seth, is to write down accurately our *pesher,* to be read by the other groups of Covenanters and Essenes, that they might know the end times are at hand." Seth humbly bowed his head in acceptance of this holy task.

They set before him a copy of the scroll of Nahum, to serve as a guide while they quoted it from memory, and after each small passage, they would give him their commentary. They began by quoting the prophet. *An oracle concerning Nineveh. The book of the vision of Nahum the Elkoshite. The Lord is a jealous God and avenging . . .* and ended with *his way is in whirlwind and storm, and the clouds are the dust of his feet.*

"The meaning of the passage," said one elder, and he went on to explain what the words meant. The others elders offered minor changes here and there on the precise wording, but when Joshaphat nodded his approval, discussion ceased and Seth wrote down their explanations. The commentary seemed reasonable to Seth, though even if he thought them mad, he would not venture to challenge their interpretation. The wrath of God needed little comment, for it is everlasting, and will soon pour out upon the earth. His enemies are the enemies of the Covenanters. The "whirlwind and storm" refer to the "firmaments of his heaven," and the "dust of his feet" is the earth which he has created.

As they progressed, Seth saw the immediacy of the ancient words come alive. *Whither the lion goes, there is the lion's cub, with none to disturb it.* "This refers to Demetrius, king of Greece," said brother Joshaphat, "who sought, on the counsel of those seekers of smooth things, to enter Jerusalem. But God did not permit the city to be delivered into the hands of the kings of Greece, from the time of Antiochus until the coming of the rulers of the Kittim. But then she shall be trampled under their feet."

Seth wrote the explanation. The true enemies, the "Seekers of Smooth Things," were revealed at last in the prophecy of Nahum. Herein lay a true prediction, that the presence of Rome in Syria augured trouble for Jerusalem. Seth thought it a safe prediction: Rome would rule the land of Judah one way or another, and the presence of Gentiles would increase. Had not Judas Maccabaeus himself sought a treaty of friendship with Rome? The empire of Rome had long cast its shadow over the land, and now stood at the gate.[26]

The next phrase of Nahum: *The lion tears enough for his cubs, and chokes prey for its lionesses.* An evil portent, thought Seth. True, the Pharisees asked Demetrius, king of Syria, to come and make war against Alexander Jannaeus, and Demetrius defeated him in battle. Seth was two years old at the time. That battle near Shechem had been his earliest awareness of turmoil, and of the accursed Pharisees. But after the defeat of Jannaeus, the multitudes who fought against him repented and deserted the forces of Demetrius, so the Greek king departed Judah and let Jannaeus take his revenge.

*He fills its cave with prey, and its den with victims.* "Interpreted, this concerns the Lion of Wrath who executes revenge on those Seekers of Smooth Things, and hangs men alive, as was done formerly in Israel. Because of a man hanged alive on the tree, He proclaims, *Behold I am against you, says the Lord of Hosts.*" Seth wrote as the elders dictated, recalling that Jannaeus, the obvious Lion of Wrath, took his revenge against the rebels, and crucified hundreds, including many Pharisees and their supporters.

Seth kept himself bent over the writing desk, attentive to their words, though his mind wandered between times, when they discussed among themselves the precise wording for the commentary. *The prowler is not wanting, noise of whip and noise of rattling wheel, prancing horse and jolting chariot, charging horseman, flame and glittering spear, a multitude of slain and a heap of carcases. There is no end to the corpses; they stumble upon their corpses.* "Interpreted, this concerns the Seekers of Smooth Things, from the midst of whose assembly the sword of the nations shall never be wanting. Captivity, looting, and burning shall be among them, and exile from dread of the enemy. A multitude of guilty corpses shall fall in their days; there shall be no end to the sum of their slain. They shall also stumble upon their body of flesh because of their guilty counsel."

Images of carnage danced before Seth's eyes, for indeed, they spoke of the ten years since the death of King Jannaeus, and the reign of Alexandra Salome. She brought Pharisees into her court, and into power. They reversed many of the laws of the Sadducees and reaped a revenge of long standing upon all their foes. War against the Pharisees loomed when their protectress, Salome, should die.[27]

The text continued: *Because of the many harlotries of the well-favored harlot, the mistress of seduction, she who sells nations through her harlotries and families through her seductions.* One brother exclaimed, "This is Salome, whore of Ephraim." But others demurred at naming a living leader, no matter how weak and subject to the wicked Pharisees she may be. They debated for some time, until Joshaphat pronounced the interpretation. "This concerns those who lead Ephraim astray, who lead many astray through their false teaching, their lying tongue, and deceitful lips." Seth wrote down diligently all that Joshaphat declared, amazed that the ancient prophecy knew a woman would rule.[28]

A half-hour later, they came to another interpretation of the Pharisees: *Nineveh is laid waste; who shall grieve over her? Whence shall I seek comforters for you?* "Interpreted, this concerns those Seekers of Smooth Things, whose counsel shall perish and whose congregation shall be dispersed. They shall lead the assembly astray no more, and the simple shall support their counsel no more."

That settled it in the mind of Seth. The Pharisees were about to be destroyed. Although Nahum prophesied against Nineveh of old, God placed words in his mouth that came again to life at the appointed time, a second fulfillment of prophecy, a second manifestation of divine foresight. And so they proceeded, until they reached the end of the prophecy of Nahum, in which the dynasty of the debased Hasmonaeans would come to an end. At last the true meaning of the ancient prophecy lay inscribed on parchment.

Seth remained among the Covenanters through two sabbaths. Despite their severity and regulation of life, he found the Covenanters ate better than his community of Beth-shean; they served mutton or goat twice a week, and even beef and veal at times, he was told. The brethren were more solicitous of his presence than he anticipated. True, they needed a learned scribe, and his priestly status was important, for in the absence of the temple many important tasks required the presence of a priest. They asked him if he required anything? Was he comfortable at the writing desk? Did he require more rest between sessions? They were grateful for his presence. Seth responded that his stay among them was an honor he had never dreamed of obtaining. They seemed very pleased by his response. He produced four more copies of the commentary on Nahum and oversaw the apprentice scribes in their work on lesser documents.

At the close of the second sabbath, Joshaphat and the council of elders summoned Seth. "We are sending you to the Jerusalem Essenes with a letter and a scroll of our Commentary on Nahum." Seth grew rigid and imagined the color draining from his face. He dared not tell them that he was banned from the holy city. They would ask why. Eleven years of quiet solitude suddenly rose up to choke him by the throat. "Brother Seth," said Joshaphat, "when you have finished this mission, you may return to your camp. But know that we invite you to join us. Brother Ananias has given me his consent. We would surely make restitution to your camp for their loss."

"I, I am honored," Seth stammered, and drew a needed breath. "I will consider your words as I fulfill my duty."

Seth departed after prayers the next morning. Joshaphat embraced him and repeated their invitation.

The Covenanters avoided the Jericho road, preferring the isolated paths of the Judaean wilderness. A brother led Seth up through the cliffs to the plateau. "From here," the Covenanter said, "follow the wadi path that leads to the Hyrcania fortress and on to Jerusalem along the Kidron Valley." Seth shouldered his small haversack and began walking. Jerusalem lay about fifteen miles distance, but initially the path was difficult and the pace slow. And though called wilderness, it was not without its shrubs and trees, and the wildlife that dwelt among them. He found pools of water at various points along the wadi and he refreshed his face from time to time. By the fifth hour he saw the Hyrcania fortress in the distance. Soon he reached a smaller path that avoided the fortress and led over a ridge where he would meet the road between Hyrcania and Jerusalem. Seth rested in the shade of a small acacia. He had not been so alone for many years. A strange sense of freedom surrounded him. In truth, he might go this way or that. Momentarily he pondered his life. In a year or so he would be thirty, the age at which he would be given leadership responsibilities in the camp. But what if he simply chose a different path. Suppose he went to Joppa and opened a scribal booth? He might even take a wife after all. Or should he return to the Covenanters? He considered their invitation, until he recalled his mission. He rose and found his way along the mountainous path to the road to Jerusalem, that is, two paths where carts and chariots traveled.

He picked up his pace and within an hour reached a fork, one leading south toward Tekoa, the other to Jerusalem with a few small villages along the way. He found the territory vaguely familiar and had not walked long upon the Jerusalem road when a group of travelers approached, hurrying toward him. As they drew near, a man called out, "Have you heard? Have you heard?"

Seth shook his head and instinctively stepped away to avoid contact with the man. "What is it, friend?"

"Queen Salome is dead," he burst out, "Jerusalem is in turmoil." And on they hastened.

The end of days begin, thought Seth. He pressed on, and the nearer he got to Jerusalem, the more people he met hurrying away. At about the time of the evening sacrifice, Seth reached the southern gate, called the gate of Tekoa, located at the lowest point of the city near the pool of

Siloam. He made his way westward toward the Essene camp, a small cluster of houses around a courtyard situated near the upper city. Jerusalem was indeed agitated. Everyone seemed to be on their feet, compelled to race hither and yon across the city. People had begun hoarding food and storing water. Prices had risen, even doubled, he guessed, as they argued frantically over any item of food. Women shrieked in anger and fear, as children hung to their cloaks.

Seth arrived at the Essene house and knocked on the aged oak door of the front gate. They opened, and recognizing a brother, quickly drew him in and locked their door. He told them of his mission from the Covenanters and gave them the scroll. After the evening meal, they asked him to read it to them. As he read, the members lauded the *pesher,* murmuring "Amen, Amen," "Even so," "Verily, verily," "God be praised." Afterwards, they took counsel on how to spread the word and encourage the faithful. Great things were about to happen, of that they were sure. As they carried on into the night, Seth begged leave and wearily retired to their guest chamber.

Next morning word came on the rays of the sun that Aristobulus had declared war against Hyrcanus. The brothers and their armies were marching toward Jericho to meet in battle. Civil war had come again and the people, ruled by God, must choose sides. But both sides, the Essenes agreed, would succumb to the Kittim.

Seth thanked his brethren for their hospitality, and they thanked him for his mission. He left the Essene house and reentered the turmoil of Jerusalem. Already fires burned in the streets. Groups of men gathered in heated argument, and fights broke out between the supporters of Aristobulus and Hyrcanus. The priests performed the morning sacrifice—only God could interrupt the daily sacrifices—but the temple gates were heavily guarded as supporters of Hyrcanus the high priest sought to protect his control of the sacrifices. Some money lenders took wagers on which brother would succeed the queen. Young boys, as directed by their fathers, waited to throw stones at the opposition. Pharisees predominated, and the Sadducees hired day-laborers to throw stones for them.

Seth descended toward the Tyropoeon Valley. Suddenly, he paused. By which gate of Jerusalem should he depart? The western gate to Joppa? The northern gate to Damascus? Or back through the Tekoa Gate to the south? As he pondered, a woman in need approached and offered her body to Seth. He could have his way with her for a few copper coins. These he had, for the Covenanters gave him a silver dinar and three bronze coins for his travels. He could go into her, relieve a long suppressed desire, and depart unobserved. Then he could simply press on toward the sea coast, and set himself up as a scribe in Joppa, or go north to Straton's Tower, or south to Alexandria in Egypt. Immediate pleasure and a new path lay before him. But if the end of days had begun, it lay in the midst of chaos. The Sons of Light would soon wage war against the Sons of Darkness. Seth straightened, and drew a deep breath. He handed the woman his coins and hurried away toward the Tekoa Gate and the path that led to the sheltered bosom of the brotherhood.

# 7

# Of Dung, Dust, and a Dog

There is a vanity which takes place on earth, that there are righteous men to whom it happens according to the deeds of the wicked, and there are wicked men to whom it happens according to the deeds of the righteous. I said that this also is vanity.

Qohelet

The earth had begun to tremble. In the first year of the hundred and eighty-seventh Olympiad, Italy and the western provinces swore allegiance to Gaius Julius Caesar Octavianus against Marcus Antonius, the second member of the disbanded Roman triumvirate. Octavian declared war only against the strong-willed Cleopatra, but it was, in truth, a contest between himself and Antony for sole control of the Roman legions; and, as many believed, the very survival of the Empire. Because Antony had helped Herod secure the throne of Judaea, Herod now assembled an army to come to the assistance of Antony, but Cleopatra prevailed upon Antony that he should send Herod to war against the Nabataeans. She reasoned that if Herod defeated the Nabataeans, she might become mistress of Arabia, or, if Herod lost, she might gain Judaea. By whatever means, she sought to destroy one of those kings by the other and expand her territory in Coele-Syria as it had long ago been the provence of her Ptolemaic ancestors.

Herod knew well enough he was but a puppet king caught between the hands of the two most powerful Romans and subject to the wiles of the most powerful woman in the world. Already Cleopatra persuaded Antony to give her the prized aromatic balsam groves of Jericho. But if a puppet, Herod was a shrewd one, and he performed his part in the birthing of the Roman Empire by subduing Malichus, king of Nabataea in the territory of Arabia. Herod waged successful battles against the Nabataeans, but Cleopatra sent her general Athenion to help Malichus, and Herod, unsuspecting of the treachery, suffered a defeat and lost a considerable force of his soldiers. So, in the seventh year of his reign, he withdrew to his fortresses and regrouped his loyal soldiers.

Slightly below the chief players in the imperial drama, the Judaean aristocracy, from lowered lids and upturned noses, watched each move of Herod and conspired to aid him or to aid his enemies, whichever went best to their advantage. Below the elite class, the townsfolk quietly set aside what coins they could, and kept full grain jars, hidden and sealed by wax. Further below, in the pyramid of society, lay the villagers, those subsistence farmers, artisans, and day laborers who went about their lives as if the storms of nature and the schemes of the mighty were wholly and equally beyond their control.

Leah groaned. The child within struggled. "Elohim!" she breathed between the pangs, "it is time." She groaned again as she lay on the straw mattress next to her husband. He had ceased snoring and must be near to awakening. The travail started early in the night, and she lay awake hour upon hour, near to rousing her husband from his sonorous sleep. The whitewashed walls of the room began to take shape as the first light of dawn mixed with the darkness. The cool spring air chilled the thin layer of perspiration on her brow and upper lip.

Momentarily, as if summoned by a guardian angel, Jose stirred. He opened his eyes to the faint light. He turned to his wife. "Your pain increases?" he whispered. Leah nodded. He said, "Will the child come today?"

"I pray it comes, it must come; for I cannot endure." The babe, her first, had passed its stay of days, those days that make up months, but not years.[1]

"A sturdy son, perhaps, already fit for labor." Jose tried to make light of the moment and lessen her anxiety. "I will alert the midwife."

Leah attempted to rise. "Do not stir," said Jose. "Let the womenfolk perform their duties. For such they are created. I will make my own way this morning."

Jose rose and went out back of the dwelling where his dog, Balsam, lay curled by the door. Balsam greeted Jose with a slight anticipation in his soft brown eyes. Of unknown ancestry, the dog was a mixed breed as best anyone in the village could tell, certainly unorthodox, they judged, if not an outright cur. Because he spent his days with his master in the tannery, the family named him Balsam as a joke—something aromatic, they laughed, to help offset the tanner's odor. Balsam's teeth had yellowed from age and diet, approaching the drab color of his short hirsute pelt, and a dark blotch appeared on his tongue, as if he sucked on a scribe's quill. Where he came from, nobody knew. He attached himself to Jose, who threw him pieces of flesh scraped from hides. Balsam kindly defecated near the tannery, and gave back to his master what he had to give.

Jose and Leah dwelt in a single room that formed part of a complex of mud and stone walls. Successive generations altered and expanded the rooms, reusing the stones. A sister with her husband and two daughters dwelt in a room above his, while to the east, lay a small courtyard, beyond which his parents lived in the largest room, and an uncle and his family kept an upper level home above them. In due course Jose might add a room to the west of his dwelling, though he would have to dig out space in the hillside. For now the single room was sufficient. Forty or so complex dwellings, set precariously upon the raw-boned terrain of the Judaean hills, made up the village. Farther up the eastern ridge lay the town of Anathoth. Beyond Anathoth to the southwest stood Jerusalem, a half day's ascent.

Jose poured water from a jar into a small pottery bowl and washed his face. He sipped again from cupped hands, rinsed his mouth, and swallowed. He took his work tunic from a peg in the wall, oblivious to its inherent stench. His own nostrils had formed their ability to smell surrounded by the tanner's trade and accustomed themselves to odors that made refined noses shrivel. Such is the human ability to adapt to humanness, that dung becomes odorless, and even the putrid stench of Gehenna must become commonplace with time.[2]

Jose brought Leah a cup of water and found her leaning her head against the wall, her legs spread out and her hands upon her belly swollen beneath her disheveled robe. Beads of perspiration glittered softly on her forehead as the light penetrated the room. Leah received the cup and sipped. She breathed heavily and handed the cup back to Jose. He set it on the floor beside the mattress.

"Be courageous, my wife. A woman who gives birth is worth twice that of a barren woman. By nightfall your value will have doubled, and I will be a wealthy man."

Leah smiled wanly. Though his hands were stained of various dyes and his flesh permeated with the odor of his trade, she loved her husband. The betrothal had not been a difficult decision for her. Yes, her father gave her the right of refusal, because Jose's father insisted the *ketubah* contain a phrase that she would not ask her husband for a divorce because of his occupation.[3] As a child of the village, Leah knew

Jose for many years. He was a strong squat man, barrel chested, his face plain and unremarkable. But between his head shod with brown hair that took on a tint of orange in the sunlight and a thick beard that Leah kept closely cropped above his apron and devoid of mites, his eyes had always drawn her to him. They bore a striking similarity to Balsam's, moist and faithful.

"I will summon Miriam as I make the rounds," he said. Leah nodded.

Jose stepped outside the front door and into the street that led into the village on the left and on his right narrowed into a path that led down a hill and passed his tanner's pit, a distance of some two hundred cubits westward. He took a clay pot and a small shovel, and walked through the village, as he did each morning, looking for the excrement of dogs or other animals. Excrement was needed for removal of the hair from the hides. The village gladly let their tanner remove it from their midst, and they left outside their doors the droppings from dove-cotes.

Jose reached the door of the village midwife. He knocked and called out, "Mother Miriam, Mother Miriam." Mother Miriam came to the door. An older woman who had ushered a goodly share of the villagers into the world, she knew the secrets of birth and the laments of death. "Is it time?" she asked.

"Today must be the day," Jose nodded. "Leah is certain, but I fear the labor will be difficult. Have you herbs to soothe the pain?"

"My herbs are few."

Jose nodded. "The pain is great and the herbs are few. She cannot endure, yet she must endure. Such is the way of the earth. As it is written: *I will greatly multiply your pain in childbearing; in pain you shall bring forth children.*"[4]

Jose walked down the path to his tannery, and Balsam the cur followed. Balsam walked with his head upright and his nose in the air, and the villagers laughingly ridiculed him as "Your Excellency." Perhaps in this jest they ridiculed the high and mighty, or even Herod, the mixed breed Jew. It is, after all, impossible to say what feelings lie behind a jest. But they did not pay other tribute to Balsam that would sustain him. Balsam ate what he could find—scraps and carrion—though from time to time he scented, chased, and caught a badger. Balsam knew to leave chickens alone, an obedience learned well through the time proven lesson of a severe beating. Now Balsam recoiled from any domestic fowl, so that even a helpless chick felt safer the nearer to Balsam than far, and they would all cling to him when the hawk circled.

Tanneries always lay outside a village, usually downwind and always downstream, for the runoff of the vats could pollute water for a thousand cubits or more, and the fetid skins give no one pleasure. As the saying goes: The world cannot exist without a perfume maker and without a tanner; happy is the man whose craft is that of a perfume maker, and woe to him whose craft is that of a tanner. Or as others said: The world cannot do without either a spice-seller or a tanner: happy is the man. . . . [5] One could coin a hundred maxims, each one with a pleasant occupation contrasted to the tanner. Only coppersmiths and fish picklers took a distant second to the craft of the tanner. But leather served men far better than perfumes or spices—from parchments to shields, from saddles to sandals. If the world were deprived of spices, the food would be bland; but deprived of leather, men would walk with sandals of straw or bark and defend themselves with shields of bare wood.

Such are the ways of justice. From the comfort of shoes, men despise the occupation of tanning; from the protection of leather shields they joke about the stench of leather-makers. What did the leper say to the tanner? "Unclean! Unclean!"—Ha-ha-ha. Who is Baalzebub, Lord of the Flies? The village tanner—Heh-heh-heh. What is the difference between a tanner's pit and a privy? Oh, perhaps ten cubits—Ho-ho-ho. Yes, the jests are as innumerable as they are countless. To be sure, the difference between privies and tanneries was not apparent to look at the door, for both were exempt from a *mezuzah* on the doorpost. And tanners were not required to go up to Jerusalem at the great feasts; nay, they were discouraged, and entire guilds of tanners were forbidden to attend *en masse.*[6] Pilgrimage festivals were of the greatest economic importance to Jerusalem, and everyone but tanners and their families agreed that the city was a more pleasant place without the offensive cloud that hung above a group of tanners and the pillar of stench that moved before them wherever they wandered.

Sons of tanners are pitied by their friends, and Jose counted it a blessing to have found a wife at all and a double blessing in Leah, who accepted him, despite the clause in the *ketubah*. True, according to the law, only the husband could write a bill of divorce, but if a woman asked to divorce a tanner, public sentiment invariably fell on her side. As a child, Jose asked his father: "Abba, why are you a tanner?" And his father answered: "Why am I a tanner? For three reasons, my son, and for four. The world needs leather, my father was a tanner, I was trained in the tanner's craft, and fourthly, you must eat." And because his father was a tanner, so Jose was a tanner. Now in the third decade of his life, he was about to become a father, by which he too could pass on the wisdom and woes of the tanner to an unsuspecting and guiltless son, should the Almighty give him a son. Perhaps even today.

Jose reached his tannery, a large stone building built by an ancestor of long ago, before the exile it was said, and repaired by every forefather since. Four thick oak pillars separated the chamber down the middle, supporting the roof beams, and on which hung the tools of his trade: the blunt-edged concave scrapers, a currier's knife and the crescent knife, awls, staves, hooks, and iron pincers. In half the room, he stored his hides and jars of tanning agents, salt, alum crystals, dyes, and baskets of bark from oak trees and sumach bushes. A low stone wall separated the work area from four round pits some five feet in diameter and equally deep, used for depilation and softening the hides. Two other rectangular pits three feet deep and lined with wood were for the tanning process. Outside of the chamber stood two oaken racks for drying hides and a large rounded stone over which hundreds of hides had been scraped and pummeled.

Jose knew the leather process thoroughly, from the butcher's hand to the cobbler's bench. First the hide was salted and dried to preserve it against initial putrefaction. The hide was cleansed, the epidermis and hair were removed on the outside, and the inner flesh was scraped away. Jose soaked the rough hides in two pits holding a solution of dung, urine, and lime to remove the epidermis and hair. The depilation brine could eventually be sold as manure, but it should to be diluted lest it kill the grape vines. When the epidermis had been softened, the tanner scraped and washed, and scraped again, washed and pummeled, until the hide had been reduced to the middle layer, the corium, or derma. Then, depending on the type of hide and the quality of leather desired, Jose would apply cold pigeon or chicken dung, or warm dog's dung to remove the remaining lime and dissolve any albuminous material, until the skin was soft and pliable. Herein lay the tanner's art, a process done by feel, which varied from hide to hide.

The second stage was the tanning proper. The hide was soaked in the baths of tannin, a solution made from the bark and leaves of the sumach bush, or from oak bark, or when available, oak-galls, the swollen nodules under oak bark where insects had laid their eggs. Jose used one vat for the mineral bath of alum and salt, an ancient process known as tawing. After soaking the hide in the mineral bath, he would lay it in a trough of flour and work the flour into the leather. He lay the stiff white leather on a mat and set children walking on it all day, and he would feed them grapes or honey as payment. Such child-walked leather was pliable and could be stretched, but had no resistance to water. It was destined for finer garments and bags for the wealthy. The hides of cattle provided thick leather that made good sandals, saddles, or armor. These hides he soaked in a large square vat with crushed sumach bark for many months, even a year. The final stage was the dye process. Jose knew how to dye the leather red from kermes or sumach berries, or black from iron sulfates, or yellow from the rinds of the pomegranate.[7]

Near the cities, tanners worked the larger firms and hired indigents to work the dung pits. Each man learned his skill and his place, be it salter, scraper, cutter, dresser of hides, or dung collector. In the country, a tanner usually worked alone or with family members, and did a finer job of it too. Ask any peasant. Jose could sell his leather for a better price, but only when the city tanneries were not producing a glut for the leather workers. The skirmishes of King Herod, as well as the impending war of the Romans meant a greater demand for thick and heavy leather armor and shields. The leather merchants came by more often, either to bring a few dried skins for tanning, or to pick up whatever prepared leather Jose had ready. But the availability of hides depended on the demand for meat, except during the great feasts when many animals were slaughtered in the temple. Of course, priests owned all those hides, and they sold them to large tanneries in the cities. And tanners profited from the misfortune of cattle owners, when plagues or drought caused the deaths of many cattle. Such is the justice of life: one man's misfortune was another man's fortune. As it is written: *Restore our fortunes, O Lord.*[8]

A tanner was expected to know the important traditions about leather. Did not Rebekah dress Jacob in the leather skins of Esau to deceive Isaac and secure the blessing of Abraham upon Israel and not Edom? Blessed is the tanner to whom Israel owed its gratitude. Was not the tabernacle of the covenant clothed in tanned ram's skins and goatskins? Blessed is the tanner who sheltered the Ark of the Covenant. Did not Elisha the Tishbite wear leather about his loins? Blessed is the tanner who clothed the prophet of God. But did not God himself clothe Adam and Eve in skins? Was not God the first tanner? Of course, God no doubt skipped the unpleasant dung process and invoked the power of his command: "Let there be fine leather garments for the man and the woman." And the animals brought forth fine leather garments, and God said: "that is good." But as part of the curse, men had to till the ground and tan the leather by the sweat of their brows and the dung of their dogs. The wages of sin is bitter indeed. Blessed be the ways of the Lord.[9]

Jose removed his tunic and put on his leather apron. "What task for the day?" he asked Balsam. "I should begin removing hides from the pits, but," he shook his finger judiciously, "I should not be knee deep in dung on a day when my wife may give me a son." And as the "should not" herein outweighed the "should," he sharpened his scraper and set himself to scraping a dried hide upon the rock. Balsam watched Jose beneath upraised and attentive eyes, but in due course he rested his head on folded paws.

Officers of Herod's makeshift army reported on their raid of two villages in the Nabataean plateau across the Salt Sea, the old lands of Ammon and Moab. They pillaged livestock, killed scores of men, and set many buildings on fire. From his palace in Jericho, Herod directed his campaign against the Nabataeans. Until he gathered sufficient forces, he must resort to the tactics of the Hasmonaeans, the mobile surprise attacks, avoiding open battle. He would fight as a brigand, raiding the defenseless villages or attacking troops as they moved through mountain passes. These tactics had brought victory to Judas Maccabaeus and King David. Before they secured the unity of Israel they had scoured the land as brigand raiders.

Herod, son and grandson of Idumaean aristocrats, by the twists of fate was a Jew and king of the Jews. Nearly a century earlier, the Hasmonaean John Hyrcanus, having conquered the walled cities of Samaria and Gaza, also subdued the land of Idumaea, the wilderness territory twenty miles south of Judaea, which Jews called the Negev. John Hyrcanus permitted the Idumaean inhabitants to remain in their land if they would observe the laws of the Jews. For men that meant circumcision, and many of the Hellenized Idumaeans accepted the condition, and thus, in the eyes of John Hyrcanus at least, the Idumaeans became Jews.[10] After the civil war between the sons of Alexandra Salome, in which Aristobulus emerged the victor and became king, Herod's father, Antipater, supported Hyrcanus and kept the conflict alive until both sons of the queen appealed to Rome for a decision. The general Pompey intervened, and in the course of affairs, desecrated the temple by entering the Holy of Holies—thus fulfilling the prophecy of the Covenanters that rulers of the Kittim would come.[11] Eventually Rome gave Antipater jurisdiction over Judaea, and he set his son Herod as governor of the Galilee. Finally Mark Antony persuaded the senate of Rome to declare Herod the king of the Jews, and thus far Herod had not disappointed his benefactors.[12]

While the officers drew up plans for another skirmish, Herod brooded over his plight. Cleopatra desired his kingdom. Antony recently required him to receive Cleopatra with all royal honors when she visited Judaea on her return to Egypt from the Euphrates. She plied her sexual allure upon Herod as a ploy to trap him in disloyalty to Antony, but Herod rebuffed her seduction, having long ago determined that no pleasure and no price would undermine his friendship with Rome, wherein all power was grounded.[13] He must prevent Cleopatra from taking his kingdom or even his life; and he must remain loyal to Rome, whether in Antony or Octavian. Even now, Antony sailed into the Ionian sea with five hundred ships, and one hundred thousand soldiers; Octavian crossed the Adriatic Sea with four hundred ships and eighty thousand soldiers. The two were circling each other like gladiators, maneuvering their ships, troops, and cavalry, preparing for the engagement that would leave only one in control of Rome. Herod's fortunes now lay with Antony and thus encumbered by the wiles of Cleopatra.

Jose's mother, Anna, and sister-in-law, Rachel, came to Leah and began to massage her belly and chatter away to distract her. Mother Miriam came in the late morning. She found Leah shivering in a pool of perspiration. The freshness of the spring morning had given way to the heat of the day. "Fetch the birth chair," said Miriam. They returned with the village birthing chair and huddled around Leah, ready for any command. Jose's mother made all the preparations but gave way to the experience of the village midwife whose presence was sought for every first-born, or any difficult birth.

In her weakness, Leah felt a shame near to disgrace. Jewish peasants took pride in their robust constitution, and the women prided themselves in their courage and the overall ease with which they gave birth. Leah determined to demonstrate courage to her last breath. She mounted the birthing chair and planted her feet firmly on the rests. As men gird up their loincloths for battle, she grasped her long damp hair and twisted it into a thick cord and looped it around her shoulder. She summoned all the strength left to her by the oblivious and unbreathing soul in the dark abyss of her womb.

Mother Miriam opened her box of herbs: cumin, caraway, mint, wormwood, and hyssop.[14] She tossed a pinch of each into her small stone mortar and ground them with a pestle. She poured the powder into a clay bowl and filled it with unmixed wine. This she gave to Leah and commanded her to drink all of it. She smeared a foul smelling ointment of bitumen and fish beneath Leah's nostrils to keep demons from entering.[15] At last the pain and the contractions signaled the moment had come. The fountain burst forth, and the women fell into formation like an elite squadron of Roman soldiers. Leah briefly recalled the words of her husband: "For this women were created." She knew the truth of it. She must suffer and shed blood and risk her life, that no soldier, no man whatsoever, should declare that women had not paid their due of pain to the pain-bearing earth. A memory flashed through her mind. She recalled the first night of marriage, and the carefully placed testing-rag that caught her first drops of blood. Jose took it proudly to the wedding guests and they praised her virginity.

Meanwhile, the women continued to chatter while they massaged Leah's thighs and buttocks, slapping her flesh to dissipate the pain. One daubed the sweat from her brow and rubbed ointment on her lips. Her mouth lay agape in agony. Tears trickled from the corners of her eyes. Miriam placed her hand in Leah's opening. She felt the tightness and the head of the child. She quietly nodded. "The child lies well, but is too large. I must cut you and begin the tearing."

Leah nodded. "If I perish, I perish" she gasped.

"You will not perish," the women comforted, "but you will bring forth in joy and rejoicing."

"Who will inform my husband?" asked Leah, looking up at the women.

"I will fetch Jose," said Rachel.

Miriam took a small bronze knife, less than a thumb's length, and cut the corners of Leah's opening. She poured water over the wounds and applied a pinch of cumin with her finger, but Leah felt nothing. Rachel placed a wool cord in Leah's mouth and she bit down on it. As the women gathered round her, she panted through her nostrils and wailed through her clenched teeth. Miriam bent over her womb and guided and pulled at the head of the child. Blood from the freshly torn flesh of Leah trickled down the head of the mute infant, its eyes closed, awaiting life. Anna pressed on Leah's belly according to the command of the midwife. At last came the final tormented cry of Leah, and it broke through, the lump of flesh vaguely resembling humanity, blueish, covered in blood and slime. The afterbirth followed. The girl child lay still in Miriam's hands, unwilling or unable to open its mouth to life. A birth had not yet occurred. She wiped clean the babe's mouth and inserted a reed into the tiny nostrils and sucked out the mucus. But the infant showed no sign of life. She took the afterbirth and began rubbing it over the head and chest of the babe, gradually increasing the vigor.[16] Leah lay still in her exhaustion awaiting the wail of life or the pronouncement of death from the midwife. Then she heard a faint and high-pitched cry.

Leah smiled and even laughed faintly while Miriam lay the wailing infant on the mat, tied and cut the naval cord, and washed away the residue of birth. She rubbed salt lightly over the delicate flesh, and then covered it with a sheen of olive oil.[17] The womenfolk washed away the blood from Leah's thighs and cleansed her wearied womb. Miriam inspected the torn flesh, and decided to stitch one ripped corner closed. When she finished, they helped Leah stand and walked her to the mattress where she would spend the fourteen days of impurity and recover her strength. The infant suddenly ceased crying as Anna swaddled it in a linen shawl, a long kept gift of Leah's dowry, and only then did she hand the infant to her mother. Leah gazed in awe at the tiny face and offered it a nipple from her bursting breast. The child began sucking greedily. The women clucked and praised Leah's courage on her first birth. True, it was a girl child, but without women where would we be?

Jose heard a woman's voice calling from up the path. "Jose, Jose, you are a father. Come to your house." The voice was that of his sister-in-law, Rachel. Jose looked out the open door and saw her running down the path.

"Now suddenly I am a father," Jose said to Balsam. He let the scraper fall to the floor. "Now I am a father," he shook his head. Jose fumbled at the thongs of his apron. Balsam raised his head and followed the movements of his master, and Balsam wondered at the nervousness of his master; wondered, that is, if we may read thoughts from the eyes of a dog. But why should we not? We read them in the eyes of others who remain mute. Yes, we may say with certainty that Balsam wondered at the hurried, yet halting, movements of his master, and set up his ears in anticipation.

Rachel arrived at the tanning pit. "You are a father," she announced again.

"Now I am a father, just so," said Jose. "But am I the father of a son or of a daughter?"

"Blessed is the increase of your house," she said.

Jose nodded grimly. "Leah has given me a girl. As it is said: The world cannot exist without males and females; happy is he whose children are males; alas for him whose children are females."[18]

"Yes, your wife has given you a girl," said Rachel, hands on her hips. "Honor now your wife for her labor, for her labor was great."

Jose hung up his leather apron. "Come then, Balsam, and let us welcome this 'increase' into the world."

Mother Miriam met Jose outside the door. "Know that your wife is very weak."

"Will she live?"

"Leah will live," said Mother Miriam, "but it was hard and without God's help she will not give birth again." Jose nodded in resignation and started toward the door, but Miriam stayed him with a hand. "And you must give her more time to heal than the fourteen days of impurity.[19] I forced open her mouth," she said, employing a common euphemism used with menfolk.[20]

Jose went in to his wife. Her face was pale and drawn, yet peaceful. Leah looked up into the eyes of her husband, searching behind the disappointment for his true thoughts.

"Your worth has doubled," he said, and smiled gently. "You have brought 'increase' into the world." He came and knelt beside her. "Let me behold my riches."

Leah pulled the infant from her breast and its little mouth continued vainly to suck. Jose held the bundle in his hands. "As is it written: *I will make for him an helper*. Blessed is the fruit of your womb." He handed the babe back to Leah, and she lay it again to her breast.

"What shall we name her, my husband?"

"After a matriarch?" he shrugged. "Sarah, Rebekah, Rachel, or Leah?"

"Or after a queen?" said Leah. "Esther, Salome, Miriam, Alexandra?"

Jose stroked his beard reflectively. "I will ponder for a few days, that no possible wisdom escape me, and then you decide." He bent over Leah and kissed her forehead. "Rest and be healed, that I may come again unto you. If you have need, you have but to command your servants, for you are now a matron among the women."

Jose carried the afterbirth wrapped in old cloth outside. Balsam's nose told him the master held something to eat and he lifted his head in anticipation. "No, Balsam. Although we may eat the afterbirth of flocks and herds, this you may not eat. This I must return as a pledge to the earth that it not take back my daughter before her time." Jose took a pickaxe up into the hill and buried the afterbirth, five handbreadths beneath the rocky soil. He pronounced a blessing: "You are dust, and to dust you shall return. May the last day of my female child be more favorable than her first." Then he returned to his labors and Balsam to his post.

The first hint of doom came from the animals—chickens, goats, and birds in the trees—a forewarning to those closest to the soil. Balsam rose and whimpered and ran in circles around the tannery floor. There was something not right with the earth. Jose looked curiously at his dog. "What troubles you, Balsam?" he said. "Have you eaten that which you ought not?" Then it came, the earthquake, the trembling throughout the Jordan Valley and the hills of Judaea. The trees swayed, the ground shook, vessels rattled, voices screamed, walls quavered. Balsam ran out the door, but Jose was struck by the falling roof beams. Leah pulled herself up and handed the infant to Rachel, who ran toward the door. The entire village shuddered and collapsed upon itself, stone upon stone, and some homes slid down the wadi ravine.

In a span of minutes the trembling ceased. Trees stopped swaying, birds returned to roost. Dust filled the air above the village and hung in the stillness. Here and there stones toppled and beams tottered precariously. Leah choked beneath the stones that had been her wall. Her mouth was dry. She heard faint crying from her nameless babe.

Jose came alert from under the beam and stones that fell on him. He pressed his hands to the ground and attempted to raise himself up, but the weight upon his back was too great. In his stupor, he grimaced, his barrel chest heaved, and he fell again to his troubled repose.

Balsam waited near the rubble of the tannery, but when he heard no movement, he turned back to the village where voices groaned and wailed from beneath the stones. A child staggered alone along a path, crying for her mother. Balsam sensed that bodies under the rubble were still alive, immovable and thirsting, but with slow bouts of breath. He whined and sniffed around the stones, and sensing the breath of the babe, he poked his nose toward the scent. Balsam clenched a bit of cloth in his teeth and pulled. With halting tugs he pulled the swaddled and salted bundle from the rubble and into the street. He licked at the dusty face and waited. A few villagers came into sight, climbing up the hillside and over the debris. They picked among the heaps of stones, looking for signs of life, of which there were few.

Darkness fell upon the land. Balsam remained beside the bundled infant throughout the night. In the morning, Balsam sensed the bodies under the rubble were dead, though the infant yet breathed. A woman came toward him. Mother Miriam picked up the babe and took her to the stream to give her water.

Along the Jordan Valley of Judaea whole villages lay in ruins. Such an earthquake had never been in Israel. Ten thousand souls were lost, some say thirty thousand, but estimates of a tragedy are notoriously inaccurate, and for this reason we coined the word innumerable.[21] The living buried the dead as quickly as their strength allowed. The family tomb overflowed long before its time. And the dead cattle could not be numbered, except that they outnumbered the people lost. They lay beneath the rubble, bruised and broken, lowing and bleating and dying of thirst. The meat rotted, but thousands of hides were saved—a boon to the tanners, who dried and salted them and made a plump profit for years to come.

Herod took stock of the damage across the land. His officers informed him that his army emerged safe from their camp in the open fields. Reassured, Herod went and encouraged them. The Nabataeans, he told them, would hope to take advantage of the devastation and attack the weakened Judaea. Rather than be afraid of the enemy, now is the occasion to strike. In the end, Herod prevailed against Malichus, king of Nabataea, and Octavian defeated Antony and with him Cleopatra. Octavian became the ruler of the Roman Empire, and Herod ran to him, swearing fealty and offering his services, even as he had been faithful to Antony. Octavian confirmed the kingship of Judaea upon Herod the Idumaean, and added to his territory and his wealth, including the balsam groves of Jericho. Friends of Herod who had wagered wisely profited, and those who had not, did not. The lesser folk reassembled their broken lives and began profiting from the *pax Augusta* of the Empire.

# 8

# A Fence around Torah

Moses received the Torah from Sinai and committed it to
Joshua, and Joshua to the elders, and the elders to the Prophets;
and the Prophets committed it to the men of the Great Assembly.
They said three things: Be deliberate in judgment, raise up
many disciples, and make a fence around Torah.

*Sayings of the Fathers*

The six-sided courtyard was an architectural triumph of haphazard
construction over four centuries. The briefest of the stone walls,
some three paces, defined an arched opening that led to a narrow alley,
two cubit's width, that wound its way to a street, which if followed to
the left would lead to a broader street that brought one to an avenue
through the Tyropoeon Valley, a ravine in the city known also as the Valley of the Cheese-mongers—for very good reason—and from there to
the temple mount.[1] If taken to the right, one soon entered a maze of
dwellings, cloistered passageways that twist and turn, and openings in
the most unexpected places such that only the dwellers themselves are
confident of coming out. The adjoining wall on the left contained a
small door that led directly to a sheltered *mikveh* and a cistern, each cav-
ity separated by a wall, and appropriately constructed for its intended
use. Of the remaining walls, two were indeed simply walls, exteriors of
other homes rising, in one case the height of two stories, while the other
two contained doors leading to the dwelling of Zoma ben Eliezer, the
olive merchant, and of Jonathan ben Uzziel, the sandal maker. The erratic nature of the polygon courtyard notwithstanding, the space served
as a school where Jonathan and Zoma instructed young minds in the
laws of God and the correct interpretation thereof.

On any afternoon of the first three days of the week, for two or three
hours, one might find in the courtyard cross-legged scholars, both high
and low, learned and unlearned, sitting on mats at the feet of Jonathan.

On other days they sat at the feet of Zoma. On some days the learned
were a majority, and the discussion flew over the heads of the rest; but
on other days the unlearned were a majority, and the learned yawned
and sighed and shifted from one aching buttock to the other. On this
particular afternoon, cross-legged scholars, both high and low, learned
and unlearned sat upon the mats in the courtyard, with the unlearned in
a slight majority. By learned, we do not mean like Moses—rather, having
a sound familiarity with Torah and tradition. Likewise, by unlearned, we
do not mean ignorant of *aleph* and *bet,* but having only a slight familiarity
with Torah, and uncertain about the traditions, the whys, and where-
fores. But the unlearned made the most of their time by cupping their
hands behind their ears, so as not to miss a single syllable, or pause, or
inflection, which we all know can invert the meaning of a phrase, or
parse it differently. Thus they sat, models of discipline and attentiveness,
yet with the occasional interruptions of youth.

The discussions would begin with a precept, and a series of "how?"
questions dealing with the fulfilment of the precept. But Jonathan
would move in reasonable rhythm to the "why?" questions, which invariably brought them to the big picture of living a sanctified and holy
life, though at the moment they were still engaged in the "how?"; that is
to say, how does one follow a particular law of Moses in a particular situation. This particular law was a puzzle sprung from an anomaly; that is
to say, it did not derive from the obvious or literal meaning of Torah;
rather, it was an inference whose origin lay deep in the well of tradition.
Pious Jews had observed the law in some manner or other as far back as
anyone could remember, but sages still disputed the how of it, and the
why was a thorough enigma. We are speaking, of course, of the prohibition against eating milk and meat together, which is derived from the
law of Moses: *You shall not boil a kid in its mother's milk.*[2] Now, many scholars argue . . . ah, but enough of this dry and distant narration: let us lean
inward ourselves and, cupping our ears, listen.

". . . And by analogy with the prohibition against diverse kinds,
wherein two diverse seeds may not be sown in the same field, or two diverse fibers may not be woven in the same cloth, we might think the emphasis of the prohibition lies in the mixing, even though the law says
'boil' in milk." Jonathan smiled slightly as he gazed at the little cupped
ears scattered about and lining the walls of the courtyard. Momentarily

he pulled on his voluminous black beard that covered his chest and often got in the way of his sandal making. "Shall we say then, if you are carrying a fine slice of mutton from the roasting pit and you accidently drop it into a bowl of milk, that you have thereby mixed the two and may not eat that fine slice of mutton or drink the bowl of milk?" Jonathan added a sense of urgency to the dilemma by licking his lips. He held up a hand to forestall the learned and waited for an answer from the unlearned. "Yes," said some. "No," said others. But another, called Hanina, whose learning lay between the learned and unlearned, said, "That depends."

"Good, good," said Jonathan, "we have left no stone unturned." He clapped his hands together. "Now, who shall speak for the ayes?"

The contingent of unlearned affirmative voices looked among themselves and their eyes fell upon one who seemed to speak with the most authority, as if to say, "You are our champion," while their un-learned opponents snickered, as if to say, "Now, master know-it-all, see how you fare." The lad shrugged and offered his reasoning. "The milk and meat are mixed, such that some of the one remains with the other, and it is better to throw away both than to transgress the law."

Jonathan nodded his approval. "Indeed, better safe than sorry, though perhaps we are too safe, and we may go to bed on empty stom-achs needlessly. So then, how do the nays speak?"

Their champion stood. "May we not save the meat by washing it with water, and the milk by passing it through a cloth to remove any shreds of meat?" His companions grinned and nodded vigorously, but looked to the master for approval.

"Good, good. You take great precaution. But have you removed even the taste of milk from the meat, or of meat from the milk, so that you have not transgressed? How do we know that taste is the same as the substance itself?"

One of the pupils abruptly and rather loudly broke wind. Hanina re-cited, "Blessed is He who has formed man in wisdom and created in him many orifices and many cavities, for we are fearfully and wonderfully made."[3] The other pupils snickered.

Jonathan, aware that young minds are more attuned to the essentials in life, gave them time to settle themselves. When he received their at-tention, he said: "Long ago we determined that if a man take upon him-self the vow of the nazirite, to abstain from wine or grapes for a set time, he is forbidden to soak grapes in hot water, for the infusion of the one into the other is sufficient for prohibition. From this it follows that taste is like substance, and if this follows from a temporary condition, such as the nazarite, who may be released from his vow and partake of wine and grapes, how much more will it apply to a permanent prohibition, such as seething meat in milk? This principle of exegesis we call *kal vehomer,* that is, from a light matter to a weighty matter."[4]

Jonathan looked to Hanina. "Now then, it depends. . . ."

"It depends if the milk is already boiling," Hanina replied. "If it is cold, nothing has been boiled, but if it is hot, seething has taken place."

"Good, good. If the meat was hot, already roasted, and it fell into hot milk, such as prepared for porridge, then infusion takes place, and we deem the meat and the milk forbidden. But if cold falls into cold, washing is deemed sufficient, and we may eat. If hot meat falls into cold milk, then some say paring away the surface of the meat is sufficient."[5] Jonathan straightened up and leaned against the wall. "Now, some argue that fowl also falls under the prohibition against meat and milk, and why is that?"

Again the lad broke wind with such alacrity and power that the other pupils immediately put their hands over their mouths and pinched their noses. But Hanina again recited the blessing: "Blessed is He who has formed man in wisdom and created in him many orifices and many cavities, for we are fearfully and wonderfully made."

Jonathan sighed and attempted to go on, but the foul odor reached even to him. "By my life!" said Jonathan, "what have you eaten, my son?"

Someone in the back row whispered, "Rotten eggs?"

Another giggled, "Old cheese and roast cow dung?"

Unembarrassed, the lad shrugged, "Turnip greens and lentils."

"Turnip greens and lentils," Jonathan said. "These, the Holy One, Blessed be He, created on the third day for food. But it may be that for you, the two were not meant to be eaten together, just as meat and milk are not to be eaten together." Jonathan cleared his throat, and returned to the study. "So, why do some argue that fowl and milk are prohibited?"

Several students raised their hands, but a clamor from the street again disturbed the conclave of scholars. All heads turned to the entrance as the sound of running feet approached. A young man burst in upon them, tunic fluttering and the thongs of one sandal slapping the earth, while his hands grasped at the air as if to pull himself along. He stopped and heaved dramatically, "The king has decreed that everyone must swear an oath of loyalty, and Simon the Pharisee has declared we will not swear the oath, and the king's officer is wroth and . . ."

"Thank you, Assi," Jonathan replied softly. "Will you join our discussion?" The master resumed, "Concerning fowl . . ."

"Master!" Assi blurted out, "Shall we not be concerned? The people are near to rioting"

"Is Herod at the gate?" asked Jonathan.

"No, master, I only heard this from others near the temple."

"Then Herod will wait, yes?"

"But is this not a grave matter?"

"My son, if you burst in disturbing scholars who discuss the law, and told me that my ox has fallen into a ditch, then I would immediately rise and go out and save it, for *that* would be a grave matter. But you have told me only that a temporal king issued a command that we may or may not obey, whereas we are concerned with the commands of the King of kings, even the Lord our God." And he returned to the discussion.

The disciple, crestfallen and confused, sat down, whispering to his neighbor: "Has master Jonathan an ox?"

"Concerning fowl," Jonathan began again, "shall it fall into the category of flesh? There are some who maintain it does not fall under the prohibition, and others who maintain that it does. What arguments may be given for each position?"

"Fowl is also flesh, for it is an acceptable sacrifice to the Lord," said one of the older scholars, who thought the obvious should not detain them.

"But what does the prohibition say?" replied Jonathan, in an effort to sustain his pedagogical thread. "The words 'in its mother's milk,' include kid, lamb, or calf, but may exclude fowl, for with fowl there is no mother's milk."

From there, Jonathan moved quickly to the question of cheese on the one hand, as a product of milk, and fish on the other, as a type of flesh, and at length he brought his gaggle of young minds to the "why?" question. "Why all this care to distance ourselves from a prohibition that plainly says only: You shall not boil a kid in its mother's milk? The law does not even say we may not eat of it—if perchance a Gentile offers you flesh boiled in milk—only that we may not boil it. But from our tradition, we refrained from eating milk and meat together. Some say tradition is our best guide as to the intention of Moses and of the Holy One. Others say these are *only* traditions, and our judgments are *only* the words of the sages among us. Therefore, in the Galilee, fowl is often eaten with milk and cheese, but in Judaea not; just as the priests wear sashes of linen embroidered by wool, but our sashes are of one fiber only. Jews in Alexandria interpret the law narrowly, and boil meat in milk not from the mother or, to be certain, a kid's meat in cow's milk, but they eat milk and meat together without compunction."[6]

Jonathan smiled faintly at the confusion and wonderment on the faces before him. He nodded to them. "Even so, even so" he said, "we do not lose sight of the purpose behind the human restrictions surrounding divine law. Will we say that you may taste swine's flesh, though you may not eat it? Or was Eve not culpable at the point of tasting the forbidden fruit, even before she swallowed it? Surely holiness requires setting a safe boundary around the law, to keep us far from sin, and for this reason our wise men before us said, 'Deliberate carefully, raise up many disciples, and make a fence around the Torah.' But, as my wife reminds me, for every prohibition the Holy One, Blessed be He, has given us a benefit. If your desire to taste of the forbidden is a temptation beyond your resistance, if you crave meat and milk, then eat roast udder, which is permitted, and be satisfied. Or if you yearn to eat swine's flesh, ask for mullet or sturgeon, which is permitted, and which the Gentiles tell us tastes like swine's flesh."[7]

The pupils nodded, eyes wide, at the provisions of the Holy One. Said Jonathan, "Now then, how far out should we extend our fence lest we break the least of the commandments? For example, shall we forbid ourselves to place cheese and meat on the same serving table?"

Just then they heard the sound of many feet approaching. Through the alleyway came a crowd of Pharisees led by Zoma, but as Jonathan was in the midst of a comment, they paused and waited silently at the gate.

"According to the teaching of master Shammai," said Jonathan, "fowl may be served on a table together with cheese, but may not be eaten together; whereas according to master Hillel, it may neither be eaten nor served up on the same table."

"Herein," Zoma said, taking the opportunity to interrupt them, "master Shammai is more lenient than master Hillel." Zoma, a follower of Shammai, spoke with a certain proud irony, in that Shammai had the reputation of being the more strict interpreter of the law, and Hillel the more lenient.[8]

Jonathan shrugged his shoulders, "Eh, lenient, strict. Master Hillel only wishes to avoid confusion and temptation."

"Have you heard?" asked Zoma.

Jonathan nodded. "A bird flew before you."

"We have called a council to deliberate the matter," said Zoma.

"That, too, is against the king's decree" replied Jonathan.

"Even so," another member of the group joined in, "Pharisees must be united on this, and our brethren will take no courage from leaders who themselves refuse to take council together."

"Yes, so we must."

"We will meet in the synagogue of Pollion after the evening sacrifice."

Jonathan sighed, "I will come." As the contingent of Pharisees departed, he also dismissed his pupils.

Jonathan entered the synagogue, presently awash with anxious dialogue. The chamber, large by Jerusalem standards, supported two substantial dwellings above and comfortably held 120 men, though it now strained to remain comfortable. Two rows of cedarwood pillars, four a side, divided the stone pavement floor lengthwise in three sections and supported the ceiling above. At the head of the room, opposite the double door entrance, an ornate mahogany cabinet containing scrolls of Torah stood upon a low platform of cypress planks and naturally drew all eyes to it. At any rate, the stone walls, covered in white-washed plaster, did nothing to detract one's gaze. The evening light, already bronze tinted, diffused itself upon them from small square windows lining the walls near the ceiling. The windows allowed for ventilation and light, but not the distractions of the city.

Pollion, the owner of the house that served as synagogue, was their most prominent Pharisee. Years before, when Herod sought admission into Jerusalem as the lawful king of the Jews on the authority of the senate of Rome, many of the leaders of Jerusalem refused to acknowledge this choice of Rome. Pollion and his colleague Samaias urged them to admit Herod, despite their wavering support of Antigonus, the last Hasmonaean ruler.[9] Herod rewarded Pollion from time to time with gifts.

The assembled men were the acknowledged leaders of the Pharisees, the well-established party of the pious who numbered over six thousand across the land.[10] To become a leader, one had to attain the age of thirty, demonstrate mastery of Torah and oral tradition, and be a forceful interpreter thereof.[11] The qualifications required conviction, not diplomacy, and among the Pharisees would be found a diverse array of tact and eloquence, so that reaching a conclusion on anything was a contest of rhetoric worthy of the gymnasium, where none of their members, to be sure, would ever be found. Men continued to arrive, but when Hillel entered the hall, a natural pause ensued, for the presence of Hillel seemed to calm the anxiety, or perhaps he gave the gathering a sense of order and a completion of their number. Hillel, an immigrant from Babylon, had gained a reputation for quiet diplomacy in the academy of the sages and in the ways of the world. Jonathan ben Uzziel became Hillel's first disciple, and now his right hand.[12]

Samaias called the council to order. "Brethren, brethren . . . come, let us assemble." The men took benches from along the walls, arranged them into uneven rows between the pillars, and sat wherever they found themselves. Hillel began to sit where he found himself, but Jonathan and several other disciples guided him toward a place of honor near the dais. "Brethren," Samaias resumed, "you are all aware of the king's decree, but let me report the precise nature of it, and then we may turn to its implications. Herod demands that we submit a sworn declaration of loyalty as his subjects and subjects of Caesar: that we will remain favorably disposed to Herod, his family, and to Caesar Augustus in deed and word and thought all the days of our lives. He requires the signatures of our principle men, by which I suppose nearly all of us are included. Certainly Herod retains his own list of our members in the city."

"Curse him, gladly I will," a voice called out, "but to swear loyalty is sacrilege." The declaration summoned an energetic, if uneven, chorus of approbation throughout the chamber.

Samaias gazed disapprovingly at the brother who blurted out the obvious. "We have gathered to discuss how to respond and then to prepare for the outcome of our response." He waited momentarily for the somber air to return. "The oath is due to the impending visit of Caesar Augustus to Judaea," Samaias continued, "for Herod is eager to demonstrate the stability of his rule and thereby extend it further. Our chief concern is that we speak with one voice, so that the consequences come to us all, for good or ill. On the one hand, we know the Essenes will refuse the oath and that Herod will not compel them, and it is a travesty that they should be esteemed as more separated unto God than ourselves. On the other hand, the people look not to the Essenes, but to us for guidance, and we do not want to be the cause of much shedding of blood. I have asked Shammai to lay down our chief concerns and propose a course of action."

Shammai, a prominent sage of equal stature to Hillel, rose from his bench and mounted the dais. "Friends, any oath to the king must be sworn by a power greater than the king, and there is none but God, so that we will be compelled to swear by the name of the Holy One, and that we ought not do. But even if we are not required to swear by the Name, we ought not call any man king who is not of David. If so, is it not more impossible to swear allegiance to Rome? Such an oath of loyalty to Herod will forbid us from opposing him in any of his public works or any other royal whims that may follow, most particularly in his expansion of the temple, which we know he is determined to do, that his name be remembered forever. I have heard that Herod intends to place a golden eagle above one of the gates, and who knows what else? He will likely want to dedicate it to Augustus as he did the temple in Sebaste. No, we cannot, we must not, give in to Herod this time. The line must be drawn and a fence erected to contain him."

Immediately others of like mind and yet more vehement tongue, quickly rose to vent themselves. Zoma cried, "I, for one, refuse to call any man sovereign, for God alone is sovereign. It is enough that we submit to the rule of Herod, if that be the will of heaven—and of that I am not yet convinced. Herod has amassed great wealth by executing aristocratic families and confiscating their possessions. Wealth and power go hand in hand, and the two rise, like the scented steam of a Roman bath, to the king's head."

"How far we have fallen, O Israel," lamented another, "that we must swear loyalty to a half-Jew and a Gentile in one breath. Surely we are being punished for the folly of Hyrcanus.[13] Well then! Let us learn the lesson once and for all. Being a Jew is a matter of conviction. You cannot wave a knife and make Jews of Idumaeans. See how their revenge falls upon us!"

From the wailing and breast beating one might have thought the thousands of Pharisees spoke for the tens of thousands of Judaea, and in some way that would be true. None but the Herodians and Boethusians and abject sycophants were eager to swear loyalty to Herod, but among the Pharisees, certain voices urged compliance and submission.[14] In due course, Samaias regained a semblance of order and asked for other views.

Jonathan looked over at Hillel, expecting him to speak some word, but Hillel inclined his head indicating that Jonathan should speak. Amid the uneasy silence, he rose, and even as he stepped onto the dais, he shrugged his shoulders. "Brethren, we are subjects of Herod, who is himself subject to Rome, therefore we owe some loyalty to Caesar. Did not Nebuchadrezzar receive an oath of loyalty from Zedekiah, which Zedekiah then broke, as it is written, *he rebelled against King Nebuchadrezzar, who had made him swear by God;* and did not Zedekiah thus die in Babylon?"[15]

"Then the better for him not to have sworn the oath," Shammai said.

Jonathan replied, "And did not the Holy One take away the rule from Zedekiah's hand? As it is written, *surely in the place where the king dwells who made him king, whose oath he despised, and whose covenant he broke, in Babylon he shall die.*"[16]

Zoma objected, "But the prophet Jeremiah declared Nebuchadrezzar to be ruler. Has any prophet declared Herod to be our king and Caesar our emperor? Did the senate of Rome speak for God?"

"Herod *is* our king, and Caesar *is* our emperor," Jonathan said more forcefully. "We have been under the rule of Rome since we invited Pompey into the land. Did not Judah the Maccabee make a treaty of friendship with the senate of Rome, and did not his heirs confirm it?[17] If Herod's rule is not the will of heaven, then let us either take up arms against him and Rome, or let us await the hand of heaven."

"Jonathan," Zoma demanded, "are you saying that we are to swear loyalty, or no?"

"I say 'on the one hand and on the other'—it depends. An oath of loyalty need only conflict with our loyalty to the Holy One when Herod requires us to disobey the laws of God. We may avoid most of his abominations and counsel him concerning the law. Certainly he is more likely to heed us if he trusts us. Is not our good standing with Herod due in large part to his friendship with Pollion and Samaias, and the wisdom of Hillel?" All eyes turned again to Samaias and Pollion, who remained placid. They beckoned the master of Jonathan to speak.

Hillel rose, but remained in place. He said, "We have no power save that of persuasion. Let us be like the sons of Aaron, loving peace and pursuing peace, loving men, and bringing them near to the Torah.[18] Our task is to lead the people, to make of us a kingdom of priests, a holy nation. If bowing to Herod and Caesar gives us leave and liberty to guide the people, then it may be a price we must pay. A temporal allegiance to temporal rulers is not worth the loss of a single life."

"Nay and never!" shouted Zoma. "We are five thousand strong, and each of us can rally ten of the people of the land. Not even Herod will confront fifty thousand of his subjects, precisely when he wishes to show the stability of his rule to Caesar. We have the upper hand here, and now is the time to set the tone for his rule. Even a king must know his place. As Shammai said, let us set a fence around him."

"The king's place," said Hillel, "is to protect the boundaries of the land, to keep the roads open, to provide for the general welfare, and to negotiate with other kings. All this Herod has done."

"That and much more. How many temples to pagan idolatry will Herod yet build?"

Jonathan intervened. "And despite these, he cut taxes by a third after the famine out of concern for the people."

"He cannot tax barren land. Will he squeeze blood from a turnip? His actions are of necessity, not charity."

Hillel raised his hand and shook his finger in warning. "We are not responsible for what Herod does, only what we do. We must distance ourselves from politics, and incline ourselves toward piety." Hillel nodded absently. "We are called to set a fence around Torah, not around the king." Then he sat down.

Shammai replied, "Nevertheless, we are called to set limits on the king, even as Moses our teacher instructed us."

"Then from the housetops condemn Herod for his many wives," said Jonathan, "as Moses warned against kingship."[19]

"Nay," someone shouted, "the more wives the more woes. Do not lessen this curse upon Herod."

The entire assembly laughed—a rare and remarkable event—and Shammai took the opportunity to sit down. Jonathan continued, "Will Herod listen to our voice more than did King Jannaeus? Surely you know Herod will not hesitate to execute whomever he wills."[20]

Zoma raised clenched fists beside his face. "Our fathers died for Torah! And we must be ready to die thus."

"Brother," replied Jonathan with grave deliberation, "the Almighty will hold you responsible for the lives you take with you to an early grave. If we refuse to reconcile ourselves with Herod, the people will be confused and many people of the land will suffer for it."

Samaias waited for both sides to speak their mind, until he saw the same words supported by the same reasoning returning again and again. He called the assembly to order. "We have already agreed that we must speak with one voice. How shall we answer the king? Let the nays speak." And speak they did, in a swelling growl. Samaias then asked for the ayes. To which there was not a sound; for it was clear that the majority had spoken, and while the minority voice would be included in the record, it was no longer relevant to the moment.

When the silence became neutral, Hillel rose. "I say again to you, we have no power but that of persuasion, which always speaks in a soft voice and with conviction. If we are committed to refuse, we must offer the king some honorable way out, and we must tell the people they are permitted to make the oath, particularly those who depend on Herod's public works for their livelihood."

Samaias nodded. "Let us send a delegation to the king from those most favorable to him, led by Pollion."

Many a voice now joined in support of Hillel. "Go thou, Hillel, and take Jonathan ben Uzziel with you, and may the Holy One go before you all. Beseech the king to accept our apology, and whatever else you think wise to say. Only return not with the yoke of the king upon our shoulders."

Thereupon, the assembly of Pharisees delegated both Hillel and Jonathan and also Shammai, who went only as the mute eyes and ears of the majority, to attend with Pollion and Samaias, and make their position known to Herod, at the king's pleasure. Pollion sent a young servant running to the officer of the king to make request for an audience. The delegation still debated the formulation of their appeal when word came that the king, out of his friendship for Pollion, would receive his council within the hour. The Pharisees sent their most prestigious members to the palace of Herod in the upper city, escorted by a few men bearing torches. People in the streets attached themselves to the momentous happening.

The throng in the avenue outside had only begun to speculate on Herod's response to the refusal of the oath, when the delegation came out from the palace gate. The audience with Herod, whatever transpired, was appropriately brief. Herod had listened to their plea, and their reasoning, and dismissed them, saying only that he would give his reply on the morrow. The crowd grumbled, but what could they do?

Jonathan walked Hillel to his house, sharing in his master's relief that the cares of this world might again be placed in the holding jar and the concerns of heaven again be taken up.

"It is written," said Hillel, *"The king's heart is a stream of water in the hand of the Lord; he turns it wherever he will."*[21]

"If only this were so with King Herod," Jonathan said.

Hillel nodded. "Were it so."

"Good night, master," said Jonathan.

"Good night, Jonathan." Hillel placed his hand upon the disciple's shoulder and whispered, "Pray for the peace of Jerusalem."

The next morning, Jonathan rose at dawn, and after rubbing the sleep from his eyes and a ritual cleansing with a handful of water from his wash-basin, he went out into the courtyard to pray. Zoma followed soon after.

Jonathan bowed slightly. "Blessings upon you this day, companion Zoma."

"Blessings upon you, companion Jonathan. This is the day that the Lord has made."

"Let us rejoice and be glad in it."

They put on their *tefillin,* and lost themselves in devotion and contemplation.[22] Rhythmically they prayed. *"Hear O Israel, the Lord is our God, the Lord is One. And you shall love the Lord your God with all your heart and soul and mind . . ."*[23]

Thereafter, Zoma departed to inspect his olives. Jonathan brought out his stool and small work table. He laid out a sheet of leather, opened his box of knives and needles, and began fashioning sandals. At the sixth hour, Jonathan put away his work, dipped himself in the *mikveh,* and received a meal at the hands of his wife. By the seventh hour, the pupils who would be scholars arrived and seated themselves on mats in the courtyard. Jonathan put on his scholar's robe and went out to greet them.

"Welcome," said Jonathan, as he sat upon his stool.

"Blessings upon you, master," they chorused. "May we sit at your feet; may we drink from your fountain."

Jonathan surveyed them to determine at what level the discussion should begin. Once again, the unlearned formed a majority. "Now then," he began, "let us consider the sabbath rest. What says the Torah? Let us recite the fourth commandment." And together the pupils recited: *Remember the sabbath day, to keep it holy. Six days you shall labor, and do all your work; but the seventh day is a sabbath to the Lord your God; in it you shall not do any work.*[24]

"This we know and this we understand," said Jonathan. "But, what is work? We know Moses forbade us to gather food on the sabbath, or perchance only manna is forbidden? Why did Moses not tell us what activities are forbidden?"

Jonathan paused, as if awaiting a response to his questions, giving them time to understand the nature of the problem. "Perhaps Moses foresaw that as the children of Israel would leave the wilderness and settle the land they would discover new labors, and in time all the earth shall learn new work. After all, the first man Adam, and his wife Eve, knew only to gather fruit, and his sons to till the earth and raise flocks. Only later, his descendant Jabal began making tents, and Tubal-cain began forging implements of bronze and iron. Who can say what labors are yet to be devised for the good of mankind? Therefore, Moses left it to us to determine the nature of forbidden work." Jonathan spread open his hands. "Who can recite the categories of work?"

Hanina rose up. Jonathan nodded to him, whereupon Hanina recited: "The main classes of work are forty save one: sowing, ploughing, reaping, binding sheaves, threshing, winnowing, cleansing crops, grinding, sifting, kneading, baking, shearing wool, washing or beating or dyeing it, spinning, weaving, making two loops, weaving two threads, separating two threads, tying a knot, loosening a knot, sewing two stitches, tearing in order to sew two stitches, hunting a gazelle, slaughtering or flaying or salting it or curing its skin, scraping it or cutting it up, writing two letters, erasing two letters, building, pulling down, putting out a fire, lighting a fire, striking with a hammer and taking out aught from one domain into another. These are the main classes of work: forty save one."[25]

"Thank you, Hanina. It would be good that we all learn the classes of work." Hanina then stated the classes, portion by portion, and the pupils repeated it until they committed it to memory.

Jonathan resumed his teaching. "We say all these activities fall under the ban of forbidden labor. Have we then, fulfilled our duty? We have only said that it is forbidden to strike with a hammer, but what instrument qualifies as a hammer? Is a large stone a hammer? We have said one may not take anything from one domain to another. But what constitutes a domain? So, the sages are given the responsibility of clarifying what may, and may not be done on the sabbath, all based upon the single commandment of the Holy One, Blessed be He. For this reason . . ."

A commotion in the street left Jonathan open-mouthed. All the students turned to the entrance way. Assi came running in, arms flying, and chest heaving. "Master, master," he panted, "the king has exempted the Pharisees from the oath!"

"Blessed be the name of the Lord," Jonathan replied.

"But the king," said Assi "has levied a fine of fifty thousand denarii upon us."

The students turned back to Jonathan awaiting his response.

"Thank you, Assi. Blessed be the name of the Lord. Will you join us?"

"But master . . ."

"Assi," said Jonathan, "have you been asked to collect the silver?"

"No, master, I only heard of the fine."

"Then the fine may wait, yes?"

Assi's shoulders slumped. "Yes, master." And he sat down with the others.

"For this reason," Jonathan resumed, "the sages say, the rules about the sabbath rest are as mountains hanging by a hair, for the teaching of Scripture thereon is scanty and the rules many.[26] This, too, is a fence around Torah."

# 9

# Sacrilege

No foreigner is to enter within the forecourt and the balustrade around the sanctuary. Whoever is caught will have himself to blame for his death which follows.

Engraved warning outside temple barrier

Just as there are degrees of purity, so there are degrees of separation. Jerusalem is the holy city, and things permitted outside of Jerusalem are not permitted within.[1] As we approach the temple we draw near to a greater holiness and greater separation from the world and all that is profane. On the temple mount, all humanity is welcome, and all may proceed into the Court of the Gentiles, that is, of all nations. Beyond the chest-high and exquisitely carved stone balustrade surrounding the temple, only Israelites, whether born or proselytes, may enter. From east to west, we pass through a gate and mount fourteen steps to a higher pavement of elevated sanctity, and proceed across the terrace to the high wall surrounding the inner courts and the temple sanctuary. Before us, yet five steps higher, stands the Nicanor Gate fashioned of Corinthian bronze, that rare alloy formed by the chance mixing of molten metals during the burning of Corinth.[2] This gate alone on the temple mount is not overlaid with beaten silver and set in gold. Israelite men enter the Nicanor Gate and pass through the Court of Women, mounting fifteen broad and shallow semicircular steps to the great inner gate which towers fifty cubits high and forty cubits wide, entirely plated with silver and gold, and proceed into the temple complex. Israelite women enter their court through two gates in the north and south walls, where they may attend to their offerings and purification, or they may ascend to a balcony on the east wall of the Court of Women and watch the priests at work.

Within the temple area men are restricted to the perimeter of the court surrounding the sanctuary known as the Court of the Israelites.

Beyond this, and elevated another cubit's height, lies the Court of the Priests, where stands the great altar and where priests go barefoot on holy ground in performance of their sacred duties. Above and beyond stands the porch of the sanctuary, where only priests chosen by lot and purified of all impurities may enter to perform their duties. There, if the lot fell to him, a priest might enter once in his life to burn incense on the golden altar of incense or trim the wicks of the golden menorah or place the twelve loaves of shew bread on the golden table. Beyond the veil, into the Holy of Holies, only the high priest may enter, and only once a year, on the Day of Atonement. But every day without fail, come rain or snow, come earthquake, famine, or war, the Whole-offering is offered up morning and evening by austere priests and dedicated Levites, that the blessings of the covenant might endure.

The tomb lay in the wooded hillside of the vale of Shechem. Within the tomb of his father, Simeon knelt beside the stone sarcophagus, raised his face, and prayed, "God of Abraham, Isaac, and Jacob, remember me this day, and remember the deeds done against me and my father's house. God of Moses, grant success and vengeance for thy true Israelites."

Simeon lifted the stone cover and set it aside. He reached in with one hand and grasped the bones of his father. He took ribs and the fingers of both hands, some vertebrae, a leg and an arm bone, and placed them in his cloth sack. The rest he left undisturbed in the stone burial container. He replaced the cover and departed the tomb with his sack, crouching through the small opening. Two companions awaited him: Jacob, a cousin; and Manasseh, from the city of Sebaste. They rolled the stone over the entrance and walked back past the ruins of the ancient city of Shechem.

Simeon, Jacob, and Manasseh were true Samaritans, sometimes called Shechemites, to distinguish them from mere residents in the district of Samaria who might be Greeks of Macedonian and Syrian descent and could worship any god, and would better be called Samarians.[3] When Herod renovated the ancient city of Samaria and renamed it Sebaste, he rebuilt a temple dedicated to Augustus, which pleased the pagan Samarians. A true Samaritan claimed descent from the tribes of Ephraim and Manasseh, the sons of Joseph, or of the other ten tribes of Israel, and therefore a true Israelite with no desire to be

called a Jew, or even a half-Jew. Mixed blood? Of course Simon's ancestors had Gentile blood. Whose did not? When Assyria conquered
Israel and dispersed the ten tribes, King Shalmaneser resettled the land
with Gentiles. But many Israelites remained, and despite the intermarriage and many temptations to idolatry over the years, they remained
faithful to the Torah of Moses.[4] Many Samaritans claimed descent
from the Jews who fled Jerusalem with the priest Manasseh during the
days of Alexander the Great. At that time, Sanballat, the governor of
Samaria, built the temple on Mount Gerizim and his son-in-law,
Manasseh, a Zadokite priest, became the first high priest of the Samaritan temple.[5]

Simeon and his companions each took his bag, filled with the
bones of an ancestor, and departed for Jerusalem, or as the Jews would
say, they *ascended* to Jerusalem. For the Jews, of course, Jerusalem was
the navel of the earth, and all paths inclined to the "holy city," so that
one ascended toward, or descended from, the center of the universe.
This geographical error came about long after Moses led the Israelites
to the promised land and the Almighty from his pillar of fire established the place of worship at Shechem.[6]

The returned exiles from Babylon never recognized the lineage or
inheritance of the descendants of Ephraim and Manasseh. Ever since
the Samaritans offered to help rebuild the temple in Jerusalem—even
though it should have been built at the foot of Mount Gerizim—and
the Jews refused their help, contention arose between them. Each side
vied for recognition by the reigning power, from Darius to Alexander,
the Ptolemies, and Seleucids.

Many of Simon's ancestors were slaughtered by the Hasmonaean
king John Hyrcanus. His father died at the hands of Galilean pilgrims
passing through Samaria. Some Galileans in turn were killed, and re-
prisals continued as occasion served. Besides the occasional battle between mobs of Samaritans and Jews, individuals continued to harass
and annoy. One time, during the reign of Herod, a couple of Samaritan
wags substituted two mice for the two doves a Jew brought up to the
temple for his sacrifice. When the pilgrim opened the bag the startled
priest jumped, screamed, and let the mice get away, which disrupted
the solemnity and sanctity of the temple service for all, to say nothing
of the defilement. The Jew was badly beaten as he protested his innocence, and Samaritans relished the joke for years.[7] Thus did each
side attack the other by words and deeds, and the blood feud renewed
itself with every generation. The feud now fell to Simeon and his
companions.

Levites are the *hoi polloi* of the Lord's portion in Israel. When Moses, of the tribe of Levi, anointed his brother Aaron, he gave the priesthood to him and his descendants, and all other Levites became caretakers of the tabernacle. When Solomon built the temple, he appointed Zadok, a descendant of Aaron, as high priest in perpetuity. All high priests ought to be descended from Zadok—as they were until the Hasmonaeans usurped the position—all other descendants of Aaron are priests, and all other descendants of tribe of Levi are lowly caretakers of the temple. According to the sacred tradition, King David himself established that priests and Levites serve in twenty-four deputations, each for one week, four times a year. He further divided the priestly deputations into "father's houses," which served for one day, whereas Levites served for the entire week.[8] But at the pilgrimage feasts, all the priests and most of the Levites came to attend upon the multitudes and partake in the rewards. Thus it came about that Levi the Levite ascended the temple mount for duty after the morning burnt offering on the fourteenth of Nisan, in the third year of Coponious, the Roman Prefect of Judaea.

Moses forbade Levites to work the land, for their inheritance was service to the Lord, and their payment came from the temple tithes. Levi's father was a gatekeeper, and his father's father a gatekeeper, and so on back to their return under Ezra; therefore, Levi's lot in life was a gatekeeper. By comparison to priests, a Levite was an inferior servant of the Lord, but among Levites, the gatekeepers were deemed superior to the singers, which pleased Levi well for he had not a pleasant voice, nor the inner sense of rhythm required to clang a cymbal of fine brass, and harps, whether the ten-stringed lyre or the twelve-stringed psalter, were far beyond the ability of his thick and stubby fingers.[9] But gatekeepers were meant to be robust and strong, and Levi's stature and strength, like his thick dark reddish hair, flaring nose, and high cheekbones, no doubt reflected breeding from a distant forefather, chosen perhaps by Solomon himself. Levi had just come of age, thirty years, and because Levites served between the ages of thirty and fifty, not a day less or a day more, he now entered his first tour of duty.[10]

Gatekeepers opened and closed the temple gates each day, but also stood guard at them and watched for forbidden items or forbidden people. No one might bring in a weapon, except a knife with the lamb during the Passover slaughter. Gentiles halted beyond the balustrade surrounding the temple complex. At every entrance, plaques written in Aramaic, Greek, and Latin, informed all pilgrims: "No foreigner is to enter within the forecourt and the balustrade around the sanctuary. Whoever is caught will have himself to blame for his death which follows." And from time to time, Levites had to drag an arrogant offender out of the holy area and split open his skull with clubs.[11] Herod never intervened, and Rome likewise respected this divine justice. Only two Romans had entered and walked out. Crassus, the legate of Syria, desiring funds for a campaign against Parthia, plundered the temple on his way to war. His army was defeated and he himself slain. Before him, Pompey entered the very Holy of Holies. He went on to Egypt, where he perished at the hand of Julius Caesar.[12] What do we learn from this? The cost of sacrilege is dear.

Levi entered the temple precinct through the Triple Gate at the base of the southern wall, reserved for priests and Levites, and emerged onto the great esplanade of the temple.[13] Pilgrims mingled freely within the vast Court of the Gentiles and gazed up in awe at the pillars of the Royal Portico, the magnificent triumph of Herod's reconstruction of the temple. The roof of the Royal Portico was sustained by four rows of pillars, polished white marble toped by Corinthian capitals, one hundred and sixty-two in all. The pillars stretched for the astounding length of a full *stade* along the southern wall—that is, six hundred feet, since Herod's Greek architects used the Greek foot for measurement, and not the archaic cubit. And the height! The center columns were one hundred feet tall. One grew wobbly gazing up at them. Levi, however, was not a pilgrim on a once-in-a-life pilgrimage to the holy city, and he had seen it all before with his father; therefore, he proceeded toward the gathering point of the Levite guards. He heard his name called out. Levi turned and saw Phinehas, a friend and fellow temple attendant, seated in the shade of the Royal Portico. Phinehas was a priest, a small, sinewy man, a decade older, and like all priests, he was an expert butcher.

"Shalom, Levi," Phinehas greeted. "Are you well rested?"

"Can you not tell from my eyes?"

"Because of that I asked."

"It will be a long night," sighed Levi, as he sat down beside Phinehas. "I slept poorly."

"Anticipation?"

"Yes, I suppose. My father performed year by year without fail."

"You will acquit yourself nobly in your father's place," Phinehas encouraged him. "Thus you will honor him and live long upon the land."[14]

"May it be so," Levi nodded. "Have you heard how many Passover sacrifices we should expect this year?"

"Thousands upon thousands," Phinehas shrugged. "More than last year, I am told, perhaps twenty thousand, perhaps thirty thousand, perhaps more."

"Then the evening Whole-offering can not be far away," said Levi.

"Yes, and the high priest himself will perform it."

"Of course. And how well does Ananus perform his duties?"[15]

"You have not seen him perform?"

"No," Levi replied. "Should I?"

Phinehas wagged his head in a so-so manner. "He is suited to the pomp, though he delegates more responsibilities than he ought. He performs well enough, certainly better than his predecessor."

"I suppose I have not yet reconciled myself to a high priest appointed by the Roman legate of Syria. What were we thinking when we asked Caesar to make us a province of Syria?"

"We thought we could no longer endure the son of Herod."

"Ah, yes, so we thought."

"Your family is well and in good health?" asked Phinehas.

"Thank you, they are. My wife is again in the way of women."

"May God be praised."

They heard the call to the evening Whole-offering. The two men rose.

"My hour has come," said Levi, "perhaps I shall catch a glimpse of the sacrifice and even his holiness the high priest."

"Indeed, judge for yourself. And find me again tonight that we may share the meal."

The law of Moses states: *One lamb you shall offer in the morning, and the other lamb you shall offer between the evenings.* But the Lord also told Moses concerning the Passover sacrifice that *you shall slay the lambs between the evenings.* These instructions were no doubt clear at the time and in the wilderness, when every man could slay his own Passover sacrifice anywhere in the camp at the same moment. But when Moses later restricted the Passover sacrifice to the *place which the Lord will choose* he squeezed a great deal of blood-letting into a small space and narrow stretch of time. It may be that he did not reckon on the great numbers of lambs to be slaughtered at one altar after the daily burnt offering, in the evening at the setting of the sun. Of course, it is not possible to catch the Omniscient One in an error. The Lord said "between the evenings," a nebulous measurement providing ample room to maneuver around any difficulties raised by Moses. Therefore, the interpreters of Scripture expound "between the evenings." Some say it is the time when the sun is on the decline and before it disappears beyond the horizon, that is, from the eighth hour to sunset. Others say from the first moment of decline to utter darkness.[16] So the priests calculate the size of the Passover throng and adjust their schedule accordingly.

On this day of preparation for the Passover, after the morning Whole-offering, pilgrims brought individual sacrifices and offerings, and the priests ministered to them until the shadow of the sun reached a predetermined mark along the temple court. The priests who served in the morning sacrifice returned to perform the duties again, but a fresh group of priests who had never performed the incense offering also entered the court and gathered in the Chamber of Hewn Stone—a chamber in the Court of Priests where priests deliberated and decided.

Swiftly and silently the priests went to their posts. Levites brought new wood from the wood chamber, pushing their way through the crowd in the Court of Israelites, and handed the faggots to priests, who lay them on the glowing embers. Immediately the wood burst into flame. Priests brought the lamb, lightly bound in cord, and handed it to the priest who slaughtered. He lay the lamb on its left side upon a marble table, head to the south, face to the west. The priest slit the lamb's jugular vein, being careful not to cut the windpipe, lest the lamb choke on its own blood. Another priest caught the blood in a gold basin and sprinkled it on the altar at the northeastern and southwestern corners. The priest who slaughtered then hung the lamb by its hind leg upon a ring embedded in a slaughtering pillar to the north of the altar. He flayed it, cut it into pieces, taking care to cut only at the joints so that no bone was broken, and gave each part to the appropriate priest. They washed the parts and the inwards in the swilling chamber, then in solemn procession brought the parts and placed them on the lower half of the ramp, where they salted the meat to remove any blood.[17]

The priests then retired to the Chamber of Hewn Stone to recite the Benediction, the Ten Commandments, the Shema, and other portions of Scripture.[18] When they completed their hymns, they cast lots to determine their respective duties, except that during the great festival, the high priest Ananus was minded to offer the incense in the afternoon, that the pilgrims might see their high priest in the performance of the sacred duties. His presence required additional priests to minister beside him, thus increasing the pomp and the circumstance and the solemnity.

Thereupon, Ananus made his entrance into the Court of Priests. The high priest was distinguished by a blue wool robe which he wore over his linen undergarments, and from which hung golden bells that tinkled as he walked. An embroidered sash bound the robe at his chest, and over his chest lay the ephod, a vest fastened by sardonyxes at the shoulders, on which were inscribed the names of the twelve tribes of Israel. Upon the ephod lay the breastplate studded with precious stones.

Atop his elaborately woven turban sat a three-tiered gold crown. At the sight of the high priest in his resplendent glory, a thick murmur of laud and approval rose from the court of the Israelites and flowed down from the balcony of the Court of the Women, which overflowed with worshipers like the famed hanging gardens of Babylon.

The priest in charge of the incense burning took a golden ladle filled with incense, and another priest went up to the altar and scooped a shovel of embers which he emptied into a golden firepan. They came to the space between the porch and the altar, and a priest threw down the magrefa, a musical instrument in the form of a large shovel, with pipes and holes that made a hundred different sounds when it clattered along the marble floor. The cacophony could be heard across the temple mount, and some say even to Jericho.[19]

The priests entered into the porch. One cleared away the ashes from the altar of incense with a silver firepan, prostrated himself, and came out. Another priest came to the golden menorah, took the flame from the one lamp that had been left burning in the morning, and lighted the other six wicks of the seven-branch candelabra. He prostrated himself and came out. A third priest piled up the embers on the altar of incense, smoothed them, prostrated himself, and came out. A fourth priest took the dish heaped full of incense from the ladle pan and handed it to the high priest who took it up to the altar of incense. The officer of the priests proclaimed, "My lord high priest, offer the incense!" When the other priests had backed away off the porch, Ananus poured the incense on the altar, from back to front so he would not be scorched by the flames that sparked and flared up. Three priests came up to Ananus as he entered further into the sanctuary to prostrate himself. One priest held him by his right hand, one by the left, and the third stood behind him, grasping the two sardonyx stones at his shoulders. Thus they attended as he bowed down and worshiped. And they came out, and from the steps of the porch, Ananus pronounced the blessing of the priests over the people.

Ananus, with the captain of the priests at his right hand, then ascended the ramp of the altar. A priest below handed up the lamb's head and a hind leg, which Ananus laid his hands upon and cast them upon the altar. Another priest gave to the first priest one of the fore-legs, which he handed up to the high priest, and in this way all the parts of the Whole-offering were blessed and thrown on the altar. Ananus descended the ramp and they gave him the wine for a drink offering. He proceeded around the altar, slowly and solemnly, beginning at the southeast corner, then to the northeast, northwest, and southwest. At each corner he stooped and poured out wine. When he poured, the Prefect of the Priests waved his towel, and at his signal a Levite clashed a great bronze cymbal and the Levite choir broke forth in song. When the Levites reached a pause in the singing, two priests blew on silver trumpets, a long blast, a quavering blast, and another long blast. And at every sound of the trumpets, the people throughout the temple complex prostrated themselves. At the completion of the wine libation, the evening ceremony of the daily Whole-offering ended, but the great event of the day yet lay before them.

Simeon and Jacob surveyed the vast Court of the Gentiles from the shade of the colonnades of the northwest corner below the Antonia fortress. Roman soldiers stood guard atop the portico roofs surrounding the temple mount, and Levite guards lingered near every gate to the temple complex. Pilgrims littered the entire esplanade, though the sanctuary of the temple remained the center of activity while the evening offering went on.

"This truly is magnificent," Jacob brooded, "greater than the temple to Augustus in Sebaste."

"The greater the magnificence," Simeon breathed, baring his teeth, "the greater the defilement."

"So it is, and so it should be. Had Herod rebuilt our temple, instead of one to Augustus, there might be peace. Had Archelaus let us build a temple, there might be peace."

Simeon laughed. "The last peace with Jerusalem was to rid ourselves of the son of Herod."

"The enemy of my enemy is my friend," replied Jacob with bitter irony, recalling the joint delegation three years earlier that appealed to Caesar to depose Archelaus, son of Herod, and bring Samaria and Judaea under the jurisdiction of Syria and therefore of Rome. Herod himself had been good to the district of Samaria. He made the city of Samaria his refuge from the strictures of Jewish law and a defense against any uprising by the Jews. He married a Samarian woman, Malthace, who became the mother of Archelaus and Antipas, the tetrarch of the Galilee. But even with his Samarian blood Archelaus had been unwilling to rebuild the temple on Mount Gerizim.[20]

They left the colonnades and walked to the east entrance of the temple. Simeon whispered, "From here we may defile even the renowned gate of Corinthian bronze."

They walked up the steps through an opening in the balustrade, where many people strained to see over the crowd that filled the Court of the Women. As worshipers of the one true God—they were not, after all, idolaters—the Jews did not prevent them from entering the temple, though few Samaritans sought to do so for worship.

"Are we not circumcised?" Jacob grumbled. "Are we not devoted to the laws of Moses? Are we not like the Sadducees in rejecting the oral traditions of the Pharisees?"

"Shh," Simeon cautioned him. He stared up the height of the open gate. One of the Levite guards scrutinized them, and they moved along the courtyard.

Levite guards herded the throng of worshipers out of the temple complex so that a far greater throng might enter. Most of the men and women who had watched the Whole-offering hurried down the steps of the Hulda Gate in the south wall which passed beneath the Royal Portico to their temporary homes in Jerusalem to prepare for the Passover ceremony, and the men who brought their lambs for the slaughter pressed forward up the other Hulda Gate, or they came over the archway to the Western Gate.

Levi stood guard at the Western Gate. Thousands of worshipers streamed onto the temple mount. Each pilgrim carried a lamb or flocked around one carrying a lamb. They held their knives prominently displayed near the face of the lamb. One by one, Levi and his fellow guards checked the size of the knives and let them pass. Often young boys scampered through, crouching beneath the waves of elbows and sacrifices.

"Whoa, easy there. Slowly, slowly," guards kept shouting.

"Shalom, shalom," the wide-eyed pilgrims greeted the austere Levites.

The Levites nodded authoritatively, never returning a smile. Order and dignity were the watchwords. The Passover slaughter was serious business.

Every imaginable form of humanity passed before their eyes, in all sizes, colors, and shapes, as if the whole earth sent delegates to Jerusalem. Aramaic and Greek were the common languages, but in dialects Levi found strange to the ear, and a smattering of Latin here and there. The rest he lumped into his vast repository of unknown tongues.

"How many Babylonians do you count?" a guard called to Levi. To pass the time while guarding, the Levites guessed at the origins of pilgrims from Babylon, Alexandria, Greece, and Rome.

"Fewer by half than Alexandrians," replied Levi.

"The merchants will bless this festival," said he, for everyone knew that the wealthy Alexandrians brought the greatest second tithe and spent more in Jerusalem than other pilgrims of the Diaspora.

Levi watched a large man carrying a lamb under one arm, a kid under the other, and a knife clenched in his teeth lumbering up the steps of the archway. He stopped the man and made certain no other weapons were hidden beneath the sacrificial animals. On and on they came.

As the sea of pilgrims tossed and turned upon the Court of Gentiles, an army of priests that waited beneath the colonnades converged upon the temple complex like a procession of the Praetorian Guard in its precision. Each priest had closely trimmed his beard and bound up the sleeves of his tunic at his wrists to allow for the strenuous and rapid work that awaited. A new choir of Levites took up its position on the flanks of the steps leading up to the inner gate and prepared to sing the Hallel psalms. The efficiency displayed was a marvel that could only be described as orchestrated in heaven, for only such divine efficiency would allow the thousands of lambs to be slaughtered, flayed, their blood sprinkled, and their dedicated portions burned upon the altar. Even so, thus it happened.[21]

In solemn procession, two lines of men flowed through the Court of Women and into the Court of the Israelites. Each man brought his lamb to the perimeter of the Court of Priests, so that upwards of a hundred men could participate in one sitting. There, he leaned over the low wall and when the basin reached him, slit the throat of the lamb. The priest caught a spurt of blood in a gold or silver basin, which passed from priest to priest, and was tossed against the base of the Altar. The priest held the lamb and let the rest of its blood flow into a gutter, then immediately took and flayed it, giving the fat and kidney to another priest who sprinkled incense upon it and took it up the ramp and cast it into the inferno of the altar. Dark smoke billowed up, forming a cloud of burnt flesh over the temple. The priest who flayed the lamb, bound it back in its fleece and returned it to the pilgrim, who by now had stepped back along the wall of the Court of Israelites, and who continued the slow procession out into the Court of Women and on to the Court of Gentiles. Fresh priests relieved the slaughtering priests after every few lambs so the pace never slackened. Periodically, priests with buckets of water sluiced the pavement of the inner court to wash away the blood, which flowed into gutters and through drains down to the Kidron Valley.

Twilight fell, and the last of the sacrificers hastened off the temple mount, through the Hulda Gates or over the archway that spanned the broad avenue between the temple mount and the hillside of the city, and to their families and friends who prepared the Passover meal and awaited only the roasting of the lamb. The gates of the temple complex closed. Soon the outer court lay barren and peaceful. The Levite guards, along with many priests, would receive food and a token portion—an olive's bulk, or perhaps an egg's bulk—of roast lamb.[22] Levi again found Phinehas and joined a small group of priests and Levites. Phinehas had bathed himself, but the odor of flesh lingered around him. The men were weary, priest more so than Levite, but the latter had the whole night yet to work, whereas the priests might find quiet corners in the upper courts and sleep. While they now rested, speaking in hushed tones, the initial darkness of the evening yielded to the light of the full moon.

The temple workers formed groups and received their meal. They sang their hymns and took turns reciting portions of the Exodus story, and argued points of uncertain history, oral traditions, and the legends of Moses. Why, for example, did the sacred tradition omit the life of Moses as a general in the army of Egypt, and his ten-year campaign against Ethiopia in defense of the Egyptians, and his marriage to the Ethiopian princess Tharbis? Why does Scripture reduce all this glory to a single phrase, as it is written: *Moses had married a Cushite woman?*[23] And such theological quandaries as occupy priests and Levites in their leisure. For example, when God said to Moses, *I will make you as a god to Pharaoh,* as what god did Moses appear? Was this the origin of the pagan god Hermes, as some Jews from Alexandria attested?[24] Soon they diverged into the complexities of dealing with a Roman governor, whether such a governor was better or worse than a bad "Jewish" king. Shadows grew sharper as the web of light bathed the entire temple mount in spectral hues, and any moving thing took on a ghostly appearance like the shades of Sheol. For the superstitious and weak of heart, it could be terrifying. The white stone columns of the porticoes rose up like pillars of ice from a blanket of snow. When the gates should be reopened after midnight, pilgrims would enter, and gasp, and reverently mount the Royal Portico just to behold the city in the hoary light, and stretch their gaze over the Kidron Valley as far as the eye could reach. Such a sight was possible only from the temple mount and only during a clear night at full moon.

Near the first watch, when the Passover meals across the city had ended, the temple officer came round and ordered the gates opened. Among the thousands of pilgrims, many came for the first time in their lives. Many would never come again. Many had no room to lay down for the night. Many had not yet seen the Daily-offering and wished to be on hand when it began. Levi joined his squadron of gate openers. Ten men placed their outstretched hands against each door of the gate and at the hushed command of their leader, they strained and pushed, and slowly the towering doors swung open, rolling upon their brass cylinders.[25]

Already a few pilgrims awaited in the streets below, and throughout the rest of the night they came. Although the moonlight illumined the temple grounds such that one could read by it, the guards lit torches at the gates. Levi kept watch by patrolling the perimeter of the court for two hours until another Levite replaced him. He returned to rest with Phinehas, who slept.

Levi noticed three pilgrims wandering about under the portico of the eastern wall. They appeared to squat down for a moment, fumble amid their robes, then rise and wander off to another spot, repeating this behavior. Levi nudged Phinehas awake. "What do you make of them?" he pointed.

Phinehas gazed across the court. "Perhaps they are drunk," he replied, "perhaps ill."

"If the one or if the other, they should be ushered out of here. Between the two of us, I shall have to remove any vomit." They watched a little longer, but the men began walking away toward the balustrade. "Let us see if they have vomited," Levi said, and he walked toward the eastern wall. They came under the shadow of the portico, and Levi saw a few objects laying near a pillar. He drew closer and suddenly a tremor of alarm ran down his spine.

"Sacrilege! Sacrilege!" Levi shouted and pushed Phinehas away. "Human bones. Corpse impurity!"[26]

But even as he shouted, the men under suspicion began running toward the temple.

Simeon threw an arm bone as far as he could beyond the balustrade and it slid along the pavement toward the Beautiful Gate. The sound of dull clattering echoed across the temple mount. He shouted, "Mount Gerizim is the sacred mountain of the Lord." He threw another bone. "This temple is an abomination!"

Scores of Levite guards emerged from all sides. The people gathered themselves under the Royal Portico, aware that if they got involved, they too would fall under the clubs of the guards. Levites ran toward the commotion, priests ran away, but Levi was atop the miscreants first.

Simeon turned toward Levi and threw bones at him. Levi jumped aside, dodging as best he could, and decided on which man he would tackle. The men scattered in different directions, but they had no chance of escape. Levi ran after his man and quickly fell upon him, sending him to the pavement.

"Dry bones, dry bones," Simeon spat in his face, "can these bones live?"

"Dog! Samaritan dog!" Levi shouted back, for he knew the Samaritan accent, as well as the Samaritan rancor.

"Swine!" Simeon shot back. "The words of Moses are profaned by the Jews."

They struggled on the pavement, locked arm in arm and calling each other by the names of various animals and body parts. But they struggled only out of a deep frustration and anger that had accumulated over the centuries. Simeon had achieved his goal, and Levi only had to keep hold of him until more guards reached them. The greatest danger lay in a riot among the pilgrims, in which they would tear the Samaritans limb from limb, and perhaps trample a few Jews in the chaos.

But soon enough the Levites subdued the men. Roman soldiers rushed out of the Antonia and took up positions along the portico roofs. Levi dragged the man to his knees. He gasped, "For this foolishness, you will pay with your life!"

"Many a man has died for less," replied Simeon, heaving deeply.

"Why do you keep alive the old grudge against us?" Levi grunted, as he pulled the man to his feet and led him away. "*Lama? Lama?*"

"Why do you refuse to acknowledge our status as Israelites?"

"Why do you deny us the prophecy of Ezekiel? Has not the valley of dry bones come to life? Do you think your defilement by these dry bones will destroy us?"[27] Levi pushed the Samaritan ahead as they walked around the temple toward the Antonia fortress.

"Why do you not let us rebuild our temple at Mount Gerizim?" Simeon retorted.

"Why do you ask me questions to which every child can give answer? Did not Moses say that we are to perform sacrifices and festivals 'in the place which the Lord your God shall choose'?"

"And how do you know Moses meant Jerusalem?"

"David chose Jerusalem for his city."

"Ah, so David chose, not God."

"God chose through David."

"But did not Moses say: *And when the Lord your God brings you into the land which you are entering to take possession of it, you shall set the blessing on Mount Gerizim?*[28] This much you must admit."

"If Moses said it, I admit it!" Levi replied. "But that does not mean the temple should be on Mount Gerizim."

"And Moses also said, on Mount Gerizim, *there you shall build an altar to the Lord your God of unhewn stones; and you shall offer burnt offerings on it to the Lord your God.*"[29]

"Moses said that concerning Mount Ebal."

"You Jews corrupted the words of Moses.[30] But even so, Ebal is in Shechem."

"We protected the words of Moses from Samaritan corruption, and that altar was not forever, or in the place which the Lord your God shall choose."

"But even in your traditions," continued Simeon, "you admit that Joshua established a covenant with the people and made statutes and ordinances for them at Shechem."

"He obeyed Moses, that I admit. But all of that occurred before God chose his place on Mount Zion."

"The sacred vessels of the tabernacle are hidden on Mount Gerizim, and one day they will be revealed."[31]

"When you discover the sacred vessels of the tabernacle, we will flock to Gerizim. But for now, Jerusalem is the place that God has chosen."

"So say the Jews," Simeon laughed bitterly.

"So say the Jews," Levi granted him, shaking his head.

As they reached the northwestern corner of the temple mount, the oft rehearsed dispute between Samaritans and Jews came to an abrupt end—an end without a resolution. As with many disputes of grave consequence, the resolution would come only with the Messiah. And he, according to the Samaritans, a prophet like Moses, the anointed Son of Joseph, would come on Mount Gerizim, but according to the Jews, he, king and conqueror, the anointed Son of David, would come on Mount Zion.[32]

Levi handed his captured Samaritan into the custody of the temple guards who were armed with swords. The others were also handed over. The temple guards bound the Samaritans and took them to a cell in the Antonia fortress. Simeon, Jacob, and Manasseh walked defiantly to await their fate, which lay in the hands of the governor Coponius and Roman justice. They would become martyrs of Shechem, and their names revered in Samaritan lore. They would inspire the next generation. Glory be to the God of Abraham, Isaac, Jacob, Joseph, Ephraim and Manasseh, and Moses.

Levi returned to the terrace of the temple courts and began collecting the bones. He was already defiled and it was a good deed to save others from defilement. His Passover week had ended. Other Levites came with torches, and they brought him a sack. Levi nearly filled the sack with the bones of three different skeletons, while the Levites paced the terrace looking for any small fragments. By now, the Prefect of the Priests had summoned all the officers. The Levites emptied the Court of the Gentiles until daylight when Levites would search and sweep the entire court. The morning Whole-offering would not be delayed, but it would occur without the Passover crowds, and discontent would spread among the pilgrims and hostility across the land. Coponius would station troops at strategic locations to avoid mob violence. All the Levites who touched the Samaritans must remain in isolation for seven days and be sprinkled by water mixed with the ashes of the red heifer on the third and seventh days.

Even so, the Prefect of the Priests commended Levi for his awareness and quick actions. He spared the temple a greater impurity and the pilgrim festival a greater loss. As the moon's light paled against the first light of dawn, Levi wearily departed the temple for his house of isolation outside Jerusalem.

# 10

# The Wedding

Meanwhile, the customs of this accursed race have gained such influence that they are now received throughout all the world. The vanquished have given laws to their victors.

Seneca the Younger

Jews began to settle in Rome around the time of the revolt of the Maccabees, though only a few wealthy aristocrats were approved by the xenophobic republicans of the day.[1] In the decades that followed, more Jews squeezed themselves in, so that when Pompey brought back thousands of Judaean Jews as slaves, the Jews of Rome had produced a community able to purchase many of their Aramaic speaking brethren and free them—thus increasing the numbers substantially and adding to the strength of the *populares*. The Jews threw their collective weight behind the rise of Julius Caesar, and he in turn granted them the right to observe their customs.[2] The charter allowed Jews to assemble for cultic purposes and to send money to their temple in Jerusalem. It also exempted them from compulsory military service on the grounds of sabbath and dietary restrictions. Caesar Augustus confirmed the privileges and by the time of Tiberius Caesar, the Jews in Rome numbered upwards of fifty thousand.[3] This infestation caused considerable alarm among the old guard of Italy.

Now, there is no good time for a public embarrassment, but some times are worse than others, and what occurred next, all Jews agreed, was particularly ill-timed. A fugitive from Judaea concocted a scheme with three other scoundrels among the Jews in Rome to defraud a Roman matron of high society, Fulvia, who inclined toward the beliefs and practices of the Jews. Pretending to be scholars, they induced Fulvia to learn the laws and customs of the Jews from them, and when they gained her trust, they persuaded her to send costly gifts to the temple in Jerusalem, which they promptly embezzled. The indignant woman told her husband, the senator Saturnius, and when Tiberius learned of it, he put the matter before the Senate. Suddenly, the long festering "Jewish problem" erupted, and the ash of animus settled, widespread, across the imperial city: "banish all Jews from Rome." A practical reprisal and first step toward the desired goal was to conscript thousands of Jewish prose-lytes of military age, all freedmen, and send them on a suicidal campaign to Sardinia where brigands had reduced the island to anarchy. Men who refused the conscription out of regard for sabbath laws would be banished with their families.

Marcus Licinius tightened his jaw and breathed slowly through flared nostrils. No one doubted his courage, though one might question his wisdom from time to time, as one lingered upon the austerity of his face, which in the afternoon sunlight gave the appearance of an unfin-ished statue. One might suppose a Greek sculptor had begun the bust of a gladiator from a block of marble, but had given up on it before he rounded off the severity of the edges. His angular flat forehead, like a sloping mountain cliff, overshadowed his intense blue eyes, and contin-ued its decline along the bridge of his nose, deviating not a single degree in its declension, nor veering rightward or leftward. His mouth, defined by perfectly formed lips set firmly beneath the overhang of his nose, be-trayed the only hint of sensuality, a hint that disappeared again like spring water flowing over the square jaw and cleft chin. The chiseled face was crowned by a tightly waving crop of dark and dense hair. In short, the gods had bequeathed Marcus certain aesthetic advantages for a military career: the mien of stability and sobriety, given neither to laugh-ter nor retreat. Of course, no fortress wall is immune to an earthquake and no heart shielded to Cupid's darts. Knees that withstood the screaming hordes of Cherusci barbarians might quickly buckle under a woman's glance, as indeed, they had. Thus do the gods keep mighty men in submission and amuse themselves to boot.

Marcus traced his ancestry to the stock of Sabini, a people from the northeast of Rome, renowned for their bravery and simple devotion to the gods but conquered nonetheless, and long ago entwined in the race of Latins. At age eighteen, he joined the army, served in southern Italy and in Syria under Varus, and after the minor revolt in Galilee he was stationed briefly in Caesarea under the Prefect Coponius, the eques-trian governor of Judaea. While in Judaea, he once had occasion to visit

Jerusalem for their festival of Passover, and though he had known Jews before, it was there, perhaps, that his attraction to the god of the Jews began in earnest. He returned to Italy with Coponius, where he was promoted to the rank of centurion. Under the command of Germanicus, he helped quell the mutinous troops in Germany following the death of Augustus, where he served two years in campaigns against German tribes and the great opponent of Rome, Arminius. Thereafter, he transferred to the Urban Cohorts of Rome and with three years left until his retirement, he sought no further glory in war but turned his gaze to the simple life of farm and family that awaited a veteran. That vision of a simple life now led Marcus to the Jewish section of the Transtiberine quarter of the city of Rome with its crowded foreign population of strange tongues—though everyone spoke Greek with passable proficiency—and strange odors—though as a soldier, he had grown accustomed to a variety of odors.[4] After all, Rome was no longer the capital of a republic but of an empire, and must adapt to its imperial population.

He stood upon the ancient stone Aemilius Bridge over the Tiber, satchel in hand, awaiting Vitalis, a Jew and companion of three years, who would guide him to the house of Domitius Abbas, the glass-maker. Marcus began his association with the Jews of Rome by observing the sabbath, which many Romans did, whether as a fad of superstition or out of conviction.[5] Then he abstained from pork, for which he took a fair amount of ridicule from his comrades, and soon found himself lingering outside of synagogues. The Synagogue of the Augustesians, the oldest congregation of Jews in Rome, welcomed Marcus to their sabbath services in their large meeting hall.[6] Vitalis took him in arm, introducing him to everyone of significance, and insignificant members who asked to meet the Roman soldier. In due course, the most beautiful Domitia Felicitas, dark haired daughter of Domitius Abbas the glass-maker, passed before his eyes, and the rest is cast in bronze. Never had the god of the Jews presented a more enticing invitation to worship him. At any rate, Marcus now believed in Providence, the Jewish Fate, and the recent embezzlement of the Roman matron spurred him to bring his marriage to a swift settlement, for the signs within the Senate augured an ill wind for the Jews of Rome.

Already the bridge crawled with the working throngs, coming and going beneath the afternoon sun as they hurried on their way seeking taverns, homes, or late purchases at the shops. Men and women glanced cautiously at Marcus in his scarlet military cloak fastened below his chin by a polished bronze clasp. Vitalis appeared amid the throng and made his way to Marcus. Though younger than Marcus by a few years, and shorter by a hand, Vitalis, a cosmopolitan Jew, educated himself in Latin and the ways of the Latins, clothed and shaved himself like a Latin, and appeared as comfortable among Romans as he was among his own community. Vitalis agreed to serve as arbiter for the marriage, for when Marcus made known his intentions to take a Jewess to wife, his own father had refused to make the arrangement. Vitalis met with Domitius several times, showing proof of Marcus's honorable intentions and wealth, which though not great, was sufficient, for his inheritance of silver had already been given him, and Marcus had set aside a good portion of his wages with a reputable creditor who returned to him five percent annual interest.[7] Marcus knew that the inheritance his father's farmland was now in doubt, but the once strict order of lineage in Roman society was giving way to the loyalty of bloodline, and Marcus hoped that when he produced a male heir of his own, with an ancient Sabine name, his father would soften and embrace his posterity. Vitalis and Domitius quickly came to an arrangement on the dowry. There remained only the nuisance of an official betrothal contract, so important to Jews, and the delicate matters of the wedding ritual, the guest list, and invocation of blessings.

"Hail, noble Marcus," Vitalis greeted, hopping light footed toward him. "The crush, the crush, one must dance the tread of the grape vat to cross this bridge at this hour; yet like a grape in the vat do I endure elbows and heels."[8]

"Vitalis, only a fool or a pauper would step onto this bridge in sandals rather than boots," replied Marcus, and he embraced forearms with his companion. "The bridge was not built for such traffic, but for a promenade over the once pristine river and onto the ridge of the Janiculum. Come, let me forge a path for you."

"And let me carry your betrothal gifts," said Vitalis. He snatched the satchel from Marcus and lightly stepped in behind him.

They broke from the tumult of the bridge and turned along the avenue that flanked the Tiber. As the crowds thinned, Vitalis drew alongside Marcus. "What word of the conscription?"

Marcus frowned. "The Senate has heard the arguments, and the consuls are drawing up the requirements. Within the week the enlistment will begin. I have heard they will target mostly proselyte Jews, and a few Egyptian worshipers of Isis or other mysteries."

"I fear for the men who will be forced to choose for the first time in their lives whether to join the army or flee. Even I am not immune to conscription."

"True," replied Marcus. "They will call up a great many, take payments from those who can afford it, and send only those who cannot, but particularly proselytes. We shall simply have to wait and see what comes of it."

Vitalis took note of the way Marcus used *they* and *we*. "This is not a propitious time to wed yourself to the Jews, my friend."

"The time is most propitious," said Marcus, "I intend to remove the beautiful woman from harm's way."

"Beautiful woman? Has she no name?" he chided.

Marcus reddened. "To myself I call her Venus, so statuesque is she— a child really, yet mature."

"Ah yes, that perfect moment at which a girl is transformed into a woman, neither one nor the other, yet fleetingly both in perfection." Vitalis jabbed Marcus in the side. "And you cannot speak her name for fear of losing all the strength of your loins?"

"You are near the truth, Vitalis. But if you breathe a word of any weakness, be forewarned, I've sufficient strength to strangle you."

"Tsk, that would be a strictly unkosher slaughter."

"No matter. Strangled or not, I've given up swine's flesh."

"I am relieved to hear it," Vitalis laughed.

Making haste down the avenue along the river, they turned into a street that led through a maze of smaller streets. The sun disappeared behind the tall tenement houses, built of wood and plaster upon foundations of brick or stone. City law limited the height of a multi-family dwelling to seventy feet, but left its design largely unregulated, and many were stacked haphazardly one against the other around communal courtyards with ovens and latrines, and often separated by an alley of no more than four feet between them.[9] Marcus heard water splashing into the street behind them and glanced back to see a woman shaking a basin from a window in the upper levels, and a woman in the street called up a greeting, stopped, and began to gossip.

At the dwelling of Domitius Abbas, they ascended the steps through a dark passageway to the second floor. A third generation Roman citizen, Domitius resided in the more Romanized section of the Jewish populace, where the Jews had integrated into Roman life, accepted Greek and Roman art as a gift of the Muses, not idolatry, and more often than not took Latin names, particularly for their daughters. Accordingly, Domitius named his daughter Domitia Felicitas. Domitius dwelt in a small apartment on the second level of a moderately towering tenant house, a complex of dwellings four levels high, just above his glasswork shop and among other shops on the ground level. His son Petronius, and his daughter-in-law, Regina, shared the home.

Marcus knocked at the door. "Courage," Vitalis breathed, "I hear footsteps." Marcus cast him a sideways glance of scorn. Both men straightened as the door opened.

"Welcome, master Marcus Licinius," Petronius bowed to the distinguished visitor. "And you, too, Vitalis. Enter, please."

The two entered a small atrium and passed into the central room of plastered walls, newly whitewashed. A wool carpet, the color of faded sienna surrounded by a border of yellow in which were woven dark green palm branches, covered half the floor. Two low couches with a low table between them lined a corner of the room. Domitius sat on one couch and by his side another man, whom Marcus recognized as Julianus the gerusiarch, the head of the council of elders for their congregation.

Domitius rose from his place. "Greetings, my future son-in-law, peace be to you," said Domitius, and he embraced him with a touch of Semitic airs, kissing his cheek. "Pray, be seated here," he motioned to the open couch. Julianus also greeted Marcus and gave his warm congratulations. Vitalis sat next to Marcus on the inside corner, and Petronius drew up a chair. Marcus fleetingly glanced about the home of his future *familia*. On the street side-wall stood a small brick hearth beneath one side of the solitary window of double winged wood shutters, which opened wide to the light and sounds of the city. Nearby, a table, three stools, and a chair filled the rest of the room. A copper seven-branched candelabrum sat on a shelf embedded in the wall opposite and beside it a shinny conch shell. Other than the menorah, nothing particularly un-Roman leapt out at Marcus shouting "Jew." Marcus noticed a curtained archway that led to the other small rooms, in which his betrothed surely lay hidden. Summoning his military protocol, Marcus turned back to the company and engaged in the ritual preliminaries of conversation and fought an urge to let his eyes wander toward the bedroom.

Indeed, behind the curtain stood Domitia Felicitas, bare feet at curtain's edge, ear gently rubbing the cloth. At fifteen she was fully capable of bearing children, and might have married earlier, but the death of her mother six years before made her father cling to her, as he kept saying, until the Lord blessed him with a new wife. Then the centurion Marcus came to their synagogue and cast his gaze upon her. She detected it beneath lowered eyelids and suddenly returned a gaze of her own. Her heart fluttered and she went quickly on her way behind her father. Now she awaited the marriage with burning desire, but fears tormented her daily that some twist of cruel fate—some incantation uttered by a jealous woman—might prevent the wedding. Of course, she should not eavesdrop, but if she remained in the bedroom, the sounds from the street overpowered the voices. And she must be ready to make her appearance and offer them cakes she had baked and wine she had prepared.

"With regard to the contract," Domitius addressed Vitalis, in keeping with the formal negotiations, "I believe we may use a standard formula. Will the groom object to a wedding in our synagogue?"

Marcus shook his head, and Vitalis responded, "The groom favors a wedding in the Synagogue of the Augustesians. He offers his apology that his own family will not attend, though a few friends and military personnel will be present."

"And the ceremony, will the groom wish to include certain procedures of Roman tradition? I assure you, we have an ecumenical ceremony that we use often with God-Fearers."

"Only the exchange of rings, which the groom will provide." Vitalis looked to Marcus, and suddenly added, "Ah yes, also the groom will make his own vow, in addition to any others. And of course, there may be the usual drinking songs during the festivities."

Petronius chuckled, "Eat, drink, and be merry, but sing not out of tune."

Vitalis laughed. "Master Marcus makes no promises on that point."

"Concerning offspring," said Julianus, "will the father of the children permit his sons to be circumcised on the eighth day, according to our law?" Again Vitalis looked to Marcus.

"Yes," said Marcus. "I fear the god of the Jews, and I intend that my sons and daughters be in all ways both Roman and Jew. We shall put that in the contract. Though it has no legal force in a common-law marriage, I want it known to my betrothed that she and her children shall remain among her people."

Domitius clasped his hands to his chest and with head bowed spread out his open palms in grateful submission to the will of Marcus.

"Blessings of our fathers upon you," said Julianus. "In our eyes, you are a Jew, for your kinship is far deeper than bloodline and parentage. It is sufficient that you renounce allegiance to all other gods."[10]

"I renounce them all," Marcus replied. "May the Lord your god forgive me if I continue to engage in military rituals to the gods, which I do of necessity but not of the heart."

Julianus said, "Our God is father to all mankind, and God knows we suffer sufficiently for our belief in him alone, that we need not offer more opportunities to those who ridicule us."

In the silence that followed, Marcus suddenly sat upright, and clasped his hands to his knees. "If we have removed all questions between us, I propose that the wedding be performed as soon as possible," said Marcus, "before the politics of Rome hinder us."

"Yes, that is best," replied Domitius. "The times are uncertain."

"How soon?" asked Petronius, who would take on the responsibilities of the festival.

"Tomorrow I will seek leave and permission to marry. Perhaps the
day after?"

"Impossible!" cried Petronius.

Vitalis laughed. "He jests, Petronius. Do you not jest with him,
Marcus? You meant the day after the day after, yes?"

Marcus grinned. "Within a fortnight?"

"That is possible," Petronius sighed. "With the help of God, even ten
days is possible."

"Let it be so," said Marcus. "Ten days."

Behind the curtain Domitia brushed away a tear from her cheek and
pressed her hands against her bosom, that she might bless the womb that
would harbor the sons and daughters of so noble a man. Then she crept
back into her bedroom to await her summons, which came soon
enough. When the contract had been signed, Petronius went to the window overlooking the inner courtyard and called to his wife, Regina, who
had prepared food in the apartment above them. He entered behind the
curtain to escort Domitia into the company where she might serve her
cakes and in other ways demonstrate her modesty, charm, and considerable talents. She came barefoot in her plain woolen frock, hair cascading
over her shoulders in a most alluring decore. Marcus sprang to his feet,
and stammered somewhat awkwardly, "Greetings, child."

"Shalom, master Marcus," Domitia replied softly. "Welcome to my
father's house."

Finding Marcus utterly speechless, Vitalis played his part of inter-
cessor. "You see, master Marcus, how this lovely woman *cum* matron
will grace your home, keep your hearth, and open the door to greet your
guests? Now, sit back and watch in awe and wonder at how she will
serve them and secure your reputation of hospitality."

Domitia smiled, bowed her head slightly, and went to a cupboard for
the glass goblets. Soon, Regina arrived along with other guests who carried baskets of food, and the air of festivity flowed in through the doorway behind them. For an hour they feasted and toasted the bride and
groom and called down blessings from on high. As twilight descended,
Marcus called for his satchel of gifts for the bride. Ceremoniously he
presented a long sleeved linen robe, perfume, an ivory hairpin, and a
woven wool girdle with a silver clasp. The guests praised each gift as
they passed it around, and then Domitia went to her bedroom to don the
robe and the girdle and anoint herself with the perfume. When she returned with her radiance thus enhanced, Marcus produced the ring,
made of etched iron in the ancient Sabine tradition, a bond that cannot

be broken. Domitia slipped it on her left hand finger next to the small-est, for it is believed a nerve reaches from there to the heart.[11]

The next morning Marcus appeared in full military dress at the hour of his appointment in the headquarters of his cohort. He waited while the guard announced his presence to the commanding officer. Though completely at ease among the military decorum, Marcus became sud-denly aware of the distance his soul had traveled from its Latin origins during the night.

Marcus entered the office of Tribune Severus Arsinius. The guard closed the door behind him.

"At ease, centurion," said Severus, who shuffled a small stack of pa-pers and replaced them in a gilded leather portfolio. He looked up and smiled wryly. "Your request for a common-law marriage is not unusual," Severus began, "but your desire to marry a Jewess is. Are you quite set on this course of folly?"

"Yes sir," Marcus replied stiffly. "Marriage is not an obligation one takes up lightly."

"You have been a sympathizer of the Jews for some time now, have you not? I believe God-Fearer is the term used, a *metuentes* of the invisible god of the sky."

"Yes sir."

"And do you believe a flayed *membrum virile* fires up a greater plea-sure, as they say?"

"I am not submitting to circumcision."

"No? It is a wonder they will accept you with a foreskin."

"It depends on the community, sir. Many Jews of Rome are far more concerned with proper worship of their god than the customs of their heritage."

"By the gods, man! Worship the clouds if you must, or the head of an ass for all that, but why do you desire to be wed to the Jews?[12] Are there no women in your father's village who will give you a more noble lineage?"

"This is the woman, sir."

Severus threw up his hands. "Ach," he laughed sarcastically, "if it is not their seventh day of laziness, their bootlicking and sentimentality, it will be their women." He paced the floor behind his desk. "What do you find so attractive about the Jews? Besides their women. I know soldiers who succumbed to the Isis mysteries, in some vague hope of immortality. I understand the appeal many soldiers find in the cult of Mithras, or the Bacchanalian rites.[13] And women will fall for every foolishness, but what does a Roman officer with a distinguished record find in the barbaric superstition of the Jews? Speak openly, Marcus."

"Peace."

"Peace?" Severus replied in amazement. "What peace have the Jews brought? Every time they congregate before Caesar it is to ask Rome to bring *them* peace. Eight thousand Jews of Rome lobbied Augustus Caesar to remove their prince from the throne and rule Judaea ourselves.[14] Peace?"

"I believe they worship the one true god, which the philosophers have long declared, and as they pray to this god for the peace of Rome, so shall I."[15]

Severus shrugged. "Can you not delay this until you retire from the army?"

"No sir. For another woman I might delay, but not for this woman, sir."

"So be it. Your timing is very poor, and your future in the public arena will have washed into the Tiber, along with the foul smelling garbage of the Jews. You understand?"

"Yes sir."

"Very well. Have your request drawn up." He laughed sarcastically, "And may the god of the Jews smile upon you."

Marcus returned to his quarters, wrote up his request, and submitted it through the normal channels. He sent word to Vitalis that he should begin the preparations and that they should make haste. Within the week, the orders for the conscription were posted in the markets of the city, requiring Jews and Egyptian worshipers of the Isis to register for the army. A few young men fled Rome, but most, though they appealed to the edict of exception granted by Julius Caesar, remained and registered out of concern for the future welfare of their families. The Urban Cohorts were charged with enforcing the conscription, and Marcus received a detailed list of Jews to bring in for medical observation and confinement. Then certain senators began calling for a general expulsion of Jews from the city, and a dark cloud of dismay settled on the entire Transtiberine quarter of Rome.

In the house of Domitius, the bride remained secluded. Petronius reserved the synagogue and enlisted the help of the community. Regina

was in charge of the bridal preparations and arranged for every need of
Domitia. A friend, Prima, and other women of the synagogue prepared
the gown, a white gown made of expensive Indian linen embroidered
with purple that was loaned from bride to bride in their congregation
and altered accordingly. But they gave the bride her own veil of deep saffron, as was the custom among the Latins. Domitia scrubbed her face
daily and cleaned her teeth with a thin piece of wood and a rough cloth.
She massaged her body with ointment, and her breasts swelled in
anticipation.

Three days before the wedding, Domitia began to preen her body
with the same care and reverence by which she lighted sabbath lamps.
Alone in her room, she bent near to the bronze mirror and plucked her
eyebrows with a small pincers. It was well known that most Roman men
loathed stray hairs on the body of women. Nearly all Roman men
shaved their faces and many their bodies, and they even plucked out the
hairs of their armpits. One could hear their screams in the street-side
booths of the barbers. She had often removed all the uncomely hair of
her legs by coating them with a barley paste and scraping it off when
dried. But that left her skin splotchy and rough. Petronius brought her a
vial of expensive oil of myrrh, made from unripe olives. She rubbed herself with the oil and the hairs fell out and her skin became like silk. With
a bronze razor she carefully shaved and trimmed her private parts as she
had watched her mother do and had been thus instructed.[16]

On the day of the wedding, Prima, came early in the morning with
iron curlers, which Regina heated in the hearth. Domitia sat on a stool
and let herself be pampered and sculpted. They curled Domitia's long
auburn hair and wove yellow ribbons into it as a wreath, intricately piled
it upon her head as a crown and affixed it with hairpins, of which the
most prominent was the ivory pin given by Marcus. Regina knelt before
her. "Close your eyes," she ordered. "Dream of this night and the good
fortune that comes to you."

"Have I not dreamed thus every night since the betrothal?" replied
Domitia, her eyes closed and a slight smile on her lips. They lightly
whitened her face and neck with chalk powder and applied vermillion to
accent her cheeks. With a fine charcoal stick, Regina defined and darkened her eyes. At last, they completed their artistry.

"Now arise, bride of Marcus the centurion," said Regina, "and let us
inspect you for any blemish, however small, that hinders your radiance."
Domitia stood still as the two women scrutinized her like a gem cutter
evaluating a rare diamond, from the helmet of ringlets on her head to the
trimmed and filed nails on her toes.

"Perfection," Regina announced. "Not the least fault to deter him whom you long to receive." Domitia began to blush.

"Exquisite," said Prima, holding the mirror before her. "He will hunger and thirst to touch and kiss, and his longing for you will not be quenched. Like the bulls of . . ."

"Enough! Please, I beg of you," said Domitia, blushing a deep crimson. "I am a virgin still, and my ears tingle at your words."

Regina laughed, "It will not be only your ears that tingle this night. Sing to him the Song of Songs and gaze upon him incessantly and prepare your bed of spices that he may enter in."[17]

They gathered up the wedding clothes and bundled Domitia off to the bridal chamber of the synagogue. Prima went to round up the young virgins who would serve as the escort maids and to make other preparations.

The Synagogue of the Augustesians provided an open and aristocratic venue for the wedding of any Jewish bride. A sheltered porch on the south side of the building, supported by four pillars, gave entrance to a small walled garden, with a pool and shade trees, wherein birds made their nests. If the skies favored them, weddings were conducted in the garden, even as Adam and Eve were first united. And on this day, the cloudless heavens attended upon the company that gathered. As the hour approached, Domitia perfumed her body and donned a linen shift and tied it under her breasts. Over this, Regina helped her into the white gown of soft Indian linen, which they fastened below her bosom with the girdle given by the groom.

Ancient tradition decrees that brides prepare the wedding, while grooms merely arrive and are told what to do, all of which augurs well for future domestic peace. Marcus arrived surrounded by a handful of soldiers, friends who fought with him in the past, appreciated beauty, and were willing to set aside any prejudice against the Jews for the sake of their comrade-in-arms. They wore their military apparel, while Marcus came dressed in a plain white wool tunic, looking more like a muscular Sabine shepherd than a centurion, though he comported himself like a soldier. One escort carried a cloak which he guarded for Marcus until after the ceremony, when he would take the bride to his home. Vitalis greeted them and led them to a table on the porch, a place of honor, yet suitably segregated, where they might begin the merriment. The guests of the Jewish community congregated at other tables, though many passed by the groom and his men to pay their respects and good wishes. Not a word of the conscription escaped anyone's lips—indeed, despite their anxiety, the wedding itself seemed to assure them that Jews could live among the Romans. Two musicians played lyres in the garden off to one side, while a handful of young girls carried trays of finger foods, and young men brought around pitchers of wine and water which they mixed in the goblets, according to the proportions prescribed by the guest, from a third wine to a third water.

When the guests had all arrived, and the afternoon sun had given way to a diffused and gentle light among the shadows of the porch and trees, Julianus stood with a cup of wine and pronounced a blessing on the assembly. "Amen, amen," they responded. Immediately, four young men of the synagogue brought out the canopy, a large square of heavily woven cloth embroidered with signs of the zodiac, which symbolized the new home into which the bride now entered. They held it above their heads and waited. Vitalis led Marcus to the canopy and stood him beneath it, facing west. Soon, a procession of the young girls with lighted lamps came out and formed two rows leading from porch to the canopy. The door of the bridal chamber opened, and the bride came forth, robed in white and veiled in saffron, as if led by an unseen hand. Domitia descended one step and walked between the rows of lamp-lit virgins. The people sang a wedding hymn of thanksgiving, and the girls escorted the bride around the canopy three times, depicting the protection she would offer to her lord and husband in his dwelling. Then she entered and stood beside Marcus, to his right, as custom dictates according to Scripture: *A queen shall stand at your right hand.*[18]

Julianus again rose and faced the couple and Jerusalem. He raised a cup of wine and recited the blessing: "Blessed art Thou, O Lord, our God, King of the universe, Creator of the fruit of the vine." As prompted, when Julianus finished the blessing, Marcus said, "Amen."

Thereupon, Vitalis came forth with a gold ring, and gave it to Marcus. Marcus took the right hand of Domitia and placed the ring on her forefinger. Still holding her hand, Marcus repeated after Julianus, "Behold, you are consecrated to me with this ring according to the laws of Moses and Israel."[19] Marcus then added his own vow. "By the loyalty of my ancestors," he proclaimed firmly, "and by the courage of a Roman soldier, and by the cardinal virtues, and by all that is sacred upon the earth, I vow to defend you against all evil and want, as long as I have breath."

Accordingly, Julianus declared them husband and wife. He said to Marcus, "Is this one not betrothed to you from eternity? And she shall be your wife from now on and forever and ever." Domitia lifted her veil, and Julianus turned them around toward each other face to face. With his left hand he guided the chin of Domitia, and with his right, the chin of Marcus and brought them mouth to mouth and joined them by their lips, and they kissed each other.[20]

While they lingered and breathed into each other's breath so their spirits became one spirit that their flesh might become one flesh, Petronius stood up and read the marriage contract, which detailed the obligations of the groom in the presence of all the witnesses, and proclaimed the date in the fifth year of Tiberius Caesar.

Julianus then concluded the ceremony by raising his cup of wine and pronouncing the ancient blessings, divinely translated into Greek, which hearkened back to the creation of Adam and Eve, and by them covered the whole human race.

"Blessed art Thou, O Lord our God, King of the Universe, who has created all things to his glory and the Creator of man, and who has created man in his image. In the image of the likeness of his form, and has prepared unto him out of himself a building forever.

"Blessed art thou, O Lord, Creator of man. May Zion greatly rejoice and exult when her children will be gathered in her midst in joy.

"Blessed art Thou, O Lord, who makes Zion joyful through her children, who makes the loved companions greatly to rejoice, even as of old in the Garden of Eden.

"Blessed art Thou, O Lord, who makes bridegroom and bride to rejoice.

"Blessed art Thou, O Lord our King, God of the universe, who has created joy and gladness, bridegroom and bride, rejoicing, song, mirth, and delight, love, and brotherhood, and peace, and friendship.

"Blessed art Thou, O Lord, who makes the bridegroom to rejoice with the bride."[21]

Julianus then gave the cup to Marcus. He sipped the wine, and gave it to Domitia who drank. Thereafter, the four stalwart youths removed the canopy cloth. Vitalis escorted them to the seat of honor in the garden, and the feasting began. As night fell, more lamps were lit and torches placed in their brass holders on the porch and in the garden. Everyone came by to congratulate Marcus and Domitia.

Between times, Domitia sought to speak with her husband. But what, she wondered, does a young woman of fifteen say to a Roman officer? Sir, what is your opinion of the troubles brewing in Armenia? Sir, do you favor the double-edged broadsword or the lance in close combat—no that were silly, of course he favors the broadsword. While Domitia considered what to say, she held his hand beneath the table, and caressed his fingers, one by one. She did not seem to notice that her husband's ability to communicate with the guests had grown distant and halting. Suddenly Domitia said, "You are ever so strong, my Marcus, my stag."

"Ah . . ."

Domitia bent in and kissed his ear and whispered. "Come, my beloved, let us get up early to the vineyards; let us see if the vine has budded, whether the grape blossoms are open, and the pomegranates are in bloom. There I will give you my love. Make haste, my beloved, and be like a gazelle or a young stag on the mountains of spices."[22]

"Ahh . . ."

She placed her hand on his thigh.

"Ahhhh . . ." Marcus nearly screamed, eyes wide.

Domitius, seated at a nearby table, leaned forward, "Are you quite all right, my son?"

Marcus straightened up, "Yes, my father, I was only . . . ah . . . delighting in the wine."

"Good," replied Domitius. "I am pleased you approve. The wine is Cypriot, a favorite of mine—both delightful and powerful."

"Indeed," Marcus smiled. He grabbed Domitia's hand from further exploration. "Tame yourself, Cyprus."

"Save yourself, Italy," Domitia giggled.

The wine flowed and the soldiers began to sing their Latin songs of sexual bravado. As custom bade, they uttered well chosen obscenities, which only a few in the congregation understood, and Domitia not at all.

"What are they saying," whispered Domitia.

"They are simply distracting evil spirits by declaring your ugliness." Marcus smiled at his companions. "But in truth, they are a troop of jealous soldiers." Marcus whispered in her ear, "And they have never had greater cause for jealousy."

Domitia murmured, "They haven't the faintest idea." She grasped his hand again and felt it utterly pliable and obedient.

In due course Marcus and Domitia joined the table of her father. Marcus sat with them briefly, and then he joined his besotted companions, who continued their coarse and vulgar jests with the best of intentions.

As the evening wore on, the festivities began to wane and various guests begged leave to return to their homes. Regina took Domitia to the chamber where she changed out of her gown, and prepared for the walk to her new home. Marcus remained among the soldiers, good-naturedly submitting to their abuse and ribbing them in turn, while he awaited his prized bride and lover.

A young man came out of the synagogue, and after glancing briefly at Marcus, hurried to Vitalis and whispered in his ear. Vitalis sprang up and came to Marcus. "Have you summoned a greater escort party?" he asked. Marcus shook his head in bewilderment. "Soldiers await you at the entrance." Marcus grew somber. He asked his friends, "Did you invite others?"

"Have the whores arrived?" one laughed.

"No, a military presence," said Marcus, and his companions sat up alarmed.

Marcus rose and went with Vitalis. At the gate stood three officers of the Urban Cohorts, torches in hand.

"Marcus Licinius," said one, "you are ordered to present yourself at headquarters immediately."

"By whose orders?"

"Tribune Severus Arsinius," he said, handing him the document.

"But I have a leave of absence," replied Marcus.

"Your leave is cancelled, Jew! You are transferred to the Jewish conscripts. You depart for Sardinia in the morning. Be thankful that you have not been stripped of your rank."

Marcus clenched his jaw. The officers waited, smiles of disdain gradually spreading across their faces. "Wait here," he said, "I must inform my guests and get my cloak."

"Do not tarry. The tribune awaits us within the hour."

Marcus hurried back to the porch with Vitalis at his side. He rasped, "I charge you, Vitalis, protect Domitia and keep her safe until I send for her. Swear that to me."

"I swear it, Marcus, by all that is holy."

They went to Julianus and Domitius and told them of the development.

"The time of travail has begun," Domitius groaned. "Go quickly to your wife and consummate the marriage. Let the bridal chamber be your bedroom."

"No," Marcus gritted. "I will not draw her blood, but my own."

"What do you mean?" asked Vitalis.

"Am I a Jew?"

"Not fully, but . . ."

"To Rome I am a Jew," replied Marcus. "And if so, then I shall be fully to all. Let me be circumcised."

"My son," Domitius replied, "do not take this obligation on yourself now. Do you not see how we are ridiculed and chastised for our faithfulness?"

"I see, and I am not yet worthy," said Marcus. "Let my devotion to the Lord your god be manifest." He turned to Julianus. "Can you do this?"

"Yes," he said, "but listen to your father-in-law. The Almighty knows your heart, and we have accepted you. For everything there is a season."

"The season is now. Make haste."

Julianus rose and called the men to assemble in the main hall. One who had the most experience at circumcision retrieved the ceremonial knife, while another asked Regina for ointment of any sort. She brought a small jar of cream in the belongings of Domitia. There was a formal procedure for circumcision, but under duress, the ritual could be shortened. With a minimum of ceremony, in the presence of Vitalis, Domitius, and a few male guests as witnesses, Julianus briefly questioned him again on his desire to become a Jew. Marcus declared his free and full desire, and they formed a circle around him. Marcus disrobed. Uttering an invocation to the Most High, the man carefully but swiftly sliced away the mark of the Gentile, and stanched the blood with a small cloth. As ointment was applied and the wound bound up, the men chanted in unison, "You are our brother, son of the covenant, you are our brother." Marcus wrapped his loin cloth carefully, and dressed. He asked for the cloth that had stopped the flow of blood, and returned to the porch. The anxious guests poured out their admiration and promised to remember him daily in their prayers.

Marcus took the bloodied cloth and went to Domitia, who remained in the chamber. She waited bravely but sprang to him in tears as he entered the room. He held her to his chest, and caressed her head. "Domitia Felicitas," he said, "look into my face and listen now to my words." Domitia stepped back at arm's length, sobs in her breast and tears rolling down her cheeks. Marcus pressed the cloth into her hand. "Take this pledge and guard it to your bosom. I shall return for the sign of your blood pledge to me."

Domitia looked down at the bloody cloth in her hand. She removed her iron betrothal ring and pulled the cloth through it, and held it to her heart. "Go forth and conquer. I shall await your return as faithful as the angels."

Marcus kissed her brow. Domitia again began to cry and would not let him go, but Petronius and Regina came and took her away into the waiting and tender arms of her people.

Marcus placed his military cloak around his shoulders and fell in behind the officers for the march back to the encampment of the Urban Cohorts. He clenched his teeth and breathed through flared nostrils. He was a Sabine and soldier of Rome. He had suffered greater wounds in battle.

# 11

## "I See"

A man once gave a great banquet, and invited many; and at the time for the banquet he sent his servant to say to those who had been invited, "Come; for all is now ready." But they all alike began to make excuses. . . . So the servant came and reported this to his master. Then the householder in anger said to his servant, "Go out quickly to the streets and lanes of the city, and bring in the poor and maimed and blind and lame."

Jeshua of Nazareth

Wisdom tells us that a life of sloth leads to poverty, a life of debauchery leads to sickness, too much wealth leads to anxiety, too much wine leads to a hangover. As the sage has said, "You reap what you sow." That much seems clear. But innocent people also suffer unjustly, as we know by sight and intuition. Therefore, the question has been posed: Is there an ultimate justice; is there a final symmetry to the cosmos? The Pythagoreans answered in the affirmative: Justice is a square number and in the end, all wrongs will be squared.[1] That is how the Greek mind sees it, but Pythagoras did not say who will square all wrongs. Better then to avoid injustice while we can.

Sophia again offers us her advice. Thales of Miletus, first among the reputed Seven Sages of Greece, advocated reciprocity in this life. When asked, "How shall we lead the best and most righteous life?" he replied, "By refraining from doing what we blame in others."[2] It is likely, as most Jews believe, that Thales got this wisdom from Moses, who lived six or seven centuries earlier and wrote according to the dictates of YHWH, "You shall not take vengeance or bear any grudge against the sons of your own people, but you shall love your neighbor as yourself: I am the Lord."[3] But if Thales got his wisdom elsewhere, we know that Hillel the Elder received it from Moses, as every schoolboy can attest. The story is told how a Gentile seeking to convert to Judaism came to Hillel and said,

"'Make me a proselyte, on condition that you teach me the whole Torah while I stand on one foot." Hillel said to him, "What is hateful to you, do not to your neighbor: That is the whole Torah; the rest is the commentary; go and study."[4] The dictum is repeated, usually in the negative, since it is easier to know what your neighbor dislikes, than to determine what actions fulfill the command to love, but the sage from the Galilee, Jeshua of Nazareth, a disciple of Hillel in spirit if not in fact, is reputed to have rephrased it as a positive command, and included the prophets as well: "Whatever you wish that men would do to you, do so to them, for that is the Law and the Prophets."[5]

For so widespread a proverb, more's the pity so few heed it; but since so few heed it, we are driven back to the question of ultimate justice; as it is written: *Vengeance is mine, I will repay.*[6] It may be that the universal wisdom "do unto others as you would have them do unto you" is God's invitation for man's best attempt at ultimate justice, before the Almighty himself steps in and "squares all wrongs." But all agree that ultimate justice will require more time, hence the notion of an afterlife, the peg on which a great deal of mortal hope hangs.

Now, while the desire to live forever likely goes back to Adam who, despite his 930 years, gave back the breath of life reluctantly, the dogma of an afterlife developed late among the Jews and late dogmata are always suspect. Perhaps, for many souls the desire is something too good to be true and, therefore, consigned to the heights of wishful thinking. Others say it is unprovable and unworthy of the self-sufficient man. Even the sage who called himself Qohelet seemed incapable, in all his wisdom, of coming to a decision on the matter. On a moral symmetry to the universe, he simply asks, "Can the crooked be made straight? Can what is lacking be numbered?" On eternal life, he merely wonders, "Who knows whether the spirit of man goes upward and the spirit of the beast goes down to the earth?" Yet he declares, "The dust returns to the earth as it was, and the spirit returns to God who gave it."[7] If a single soul may be of two minds, how much more a whole people? But rather than worry about a late formulated belief in the eternal scheme of things, we should instead go back to the desire. If the desire for eternal life, which in itself is good, springs from the heart of man, ought it not also spring from the heart of man's Creator?

Jokim was not one to complain. Born blind, he could not say that he had lost his sight, for a man cannot lose what he does not

have. Indeed, sight, which admittedly helped get others from hither
to yon without stumbling in a rut of the road, was not a sense for
which he pined, except when someone sent him down the wrong
path. But even that misfortune he took in stride, for the Lord had
already laid down justice: *Cursed be he who misleads a blind man on the
road,* and Israel ratified it with "Amen."[8] Blindness made his life sweet.
He knew Bilhah was less than beautiful, far less even; perhaps so far
as to be outright ugly if one used plain and unsympathetic words,
such that both she and her father despaired of securing a match, and
rather than settle for solitude and bareness, she took a blind man to her
bosom. Did Jokim have a complaint in the world? Not even one, with
respect to his wife. What had a large and bent nose, or warts, or whatever else he had failed to discover of her reputed lack of beauty, to do
with companionship, lovemaking, and procreation? Perhaps her dispo-
sition was not the sweetest in the Galilee, but they lived well enough,
day by day.

At the cock's first herald, Bilhah rose each morning from her place
beside Jokim on their straw mattress. She prepared a basin of water for
her husband who followed close behind her. Jokim stepped out into the
courtyard, relieved himself in the latrine pot, and washed the mucus
from his eyes. He was quite accustomed to the odor of his eyes, but others found both the odor and the spectacle of his mucous laden eyes offensive, and a poor man cannot afford to give offense. When he had
cleansed himself, he recited the Shema.

> *Hear, O Israel: The Lord our God, the Lord is one. And thou shalt love the Lord
> thy God with all thine heart, and with all thy soul, and with all thy might. And
> these words, which I command thee this day, shall be in thine heart. And thou shalt
> teach them diligently unto thy children, and shalt talk of them when thou sittest in
> thine house, and when thou walkest by the way, and when thou liest down, and
> when thou risest up. And thou shalt bind them for a sign upon thine hand, and they
> shall be as frontlets between thine eyes. And thou shalt write them upon the posts of
> thy house, and on thy gates.*[9]

This oath of loyalty, recited in the archaic Hebrew tongue, was among
the many passages of Torah that Jokim memorized. The ancient Hebrew
Scriptures, when read in the synagogues, were often translated into Aramaic for the sake of understanding, but Jokim took pride in memorizing
the sacred words as Moses himself spoke them. And he delighted in the
"frontlets between thine eyes" because it made equal the sighted with
the blind. He also remembered what was taught to him by Pharisee
sages who came from time to time to teach in the town of Nain, at the
edge of the Lower Galilee.

Jokim sat on his stool in the corner of the room and Bilhah gave him a cup of sour milk to drink. As the faint dawn began to separate light from darkness in their small dwelling, Bilhah looked her husband over. "You are ready for the day, my husband."

"So it seems to me," replied Jokim.

"Here, then," said Bilhah, and she pressed into his hand a small cloth pouch with a piece of coarse barley bread and a boiled egg. Bread she gave him always, with some additional item from her larder; figs, olives, eggs, or, when he brought home three days' labor in a row, perhaps a small piece of smoked fish. She tucked a clean cloth under his sash with which to wipe his eyes. Then she handed Jokim his staff and sent him off. "Go earn our daily bread, my husband."

"I depart in health," said he, "and pray God to return in health and wealth."

Jokim left the town of Nain and set his face toward the estate of Dositheus in the plains at the foot of Mount Meggido. He found the walk pleasant and invigorating. He listened to the morning and laughed with the liquid sounds of the brook he passed over on his way. His world of sounds and touch he knew well enough, but the sounds of the world ever amazed and amused him and gave no end to his imaginations. Every sound induced a picture in his illustrious mind. Images unfolded relentlessly as he walked along the paths of the earth, spawned by the birds, raindrops, rustling leaves, or the belabored tread of travelers and beasts of burden he met along the way.

Jokim reached the estate of Dositheus soon after the warmth of the sun broke above the eastern hills and touched his face. He found his spot near the threshing floor of Dositheus. He sat down and awaited the overseer, or on some days Rufus, the master's son, or on rare days the master himself, who would tell him if they had work for him and whether he should begin immediately or wait awhile. When Jokim heard not the voice of the overseer, but the voice of master Dositheus himself, he knew it would be a rare day.

"Jokim," said the master.

"Shalom to you, master," replied Jokim. Men of lowly estate were punctilious about lowering their gaze in the presence of any man of high estate. But Jokim, being sightless and therefore without a gaze to cast low, generally kept his ears uplifted and fully attentive to what sounds might come his way, and because he was below the lowly, he got away with a rather arrogant demeanor in the presence of his superiors. Jokim remained entirely oblivious to their facial disdain and therefore treated each superior with grace and openness, of the sort found only among the most well-bred matrons who never give or take offense.

"Today you will work the new corn mill," said Dositheus.

"Yes, master."

"This is the finest grindstone to be had, and you may count yourself fortunate to be allowed to work it."

"I see," replied Jokim, spreading his lips in a broad smile that bared his crooked teeth. "Indeed, master, I am a fortunate man."

"Come," said Dositheus.

Here, Jokim gave a supplicant's bow and followed the voice of his master across the threshing floor yard and through the gate of the wall that surrounded the mill and his granary. Jokim rarely asked for a physical description of anyone, preferring to picture the appearance of a person according to the limits of a blind man's imagination. A man's height, for example, he gauged by judging the audible distance of the voice and the angle of its origin, in a sort of intuitive geometric triangulation, allotting for a normal distance from the mouth to the top of the head, using his own head and facial features as a standard. Accordingly, he imagined Dositheus to be quite tall, and from the sound of his tread and belabored breathing, to be saddled with fat fore and aft. Jokim gave his master a beardless aristocratic chin beneath a satisfied face, soft and fleshy as the hands Jokim had kissed. He imagined his master's hair was silvery gray, and, because the master was a Sadducee, cut short in the Roman fashion that he might glide unhindered in the affluent circles, oiled and glistening, which in Jokim's dark world glistened dramatically. The curious thing is that Jokim was not far from the facts, and we need imagine nothing further ourselves, except that Dositheus was not quite as tall as Jokim pictured. But then, the aristocracy rarely are.

"Over here, under the storage roof," said Dositheus, "three paces."

Jokim advanced into the shade of the roof three paces and stopped.

"Feel the mill," said Dositheus, "so that I may explain how it works." Jokim ran his hands over the new mill. The new grindstone, set upon the circular stone base, was freshly hewn and rough to the touch. "What you feel is the stone grinding cap. Feel into the open throat on top. The bottom side is identical, and fits over the cone shaped stone fastened to the base."

"I see," said Jokim with great interest. "We have a stone cylinder with cone shaped orifices at each end, and all of it sets upon a cone shaped base."

"Exactly. You will fill the open top with grain, and turn the stone by pushing against the lever attached to it. You should push to your left."

"I see," said Jokim, as he walked around and found the wood lever. He positioned himself against it and gave a slight push. Yes, he felt the stone move.

"The grain falls down around the central stone, and beneath the crush of the revolving cap stone it will become course flour."

"I see," said Jokim. His normally placid face contorted with slightly exaggerated appreciation. "I see."

Annoyed, Dositheus asked, "Why do you always say 'I see'?"

Jokim shrugged and pulled at his beard. "It pleases me, master, to express my understanding in that way, in the hope that it pleases the Holy One, who gave me understanding but not sight. Have not the sages said, if you incline your heart to understanding, if you cry out for insight, if you seek it like silver, and search for it like hidden treasure, then you will understand the fear of the Lord, and find the knowledge of God?"[10]

"Hmm, I suppose they have," said Dositheus, further annoyed at the keen memory of a blind man. "You like to listen to sages, do you not?"

"Yes, master," replied Jokim. "The words of a sage provide grist for the mill, and give me much food for thought."

"A very apt turn of phrase," Dositheus smiled patronizingly, the tone of which Jokim utterly failed to appreciate.

"As I see it, master," Jokim continued, enticed by this rare conversation with his master, "the sages are guides for the blind and keep us from falling into the pit. Not only do they tell us how to live this life as we ought, but they lead us on the path to eternal life."

Dositheus shook his head. "Jokim, my poor fellow. Eternal life is truly the falsest dream ever dreamt. Torah says nothing. There is not a shred of evidence for it."

"I hope," said Jokim, "and therefore I believe that when this body returns to dust, God may raise up my soul and animate a new body with whole eyes and join me to it."

"Such unfounded hope is sheer folly, Jokim, though I do not begrudge you this folly if it makes you happy. But you may as well hope and therefore believe that food will appear in your dish thrice daily."

"I have uttered folly, master," Jokim nodded. "My lack of wisdom surpasses that of a lost sheep. Even so, unfounded hope is better, like day from night, than no hope at all. That, forgive me, is how a blind man sees it."

"Well," Dositheus replied, "the day is soon spent, so off to your labor."

Jokim took a gourd and scooped grain from a bushel basket and poured it into the open top of the mill. He listened to the grain trickle around the top of the cone shaped central stone. Then he pressed his hands against the lever, leaned into it and pushed, walking in a slow circle. Pigeons cooed incessantly from a nearby coop, adding a pleasant background of music to the steady grind of the wheel. Pigeons he imagined were little angels. Of course, he knew a pigeon by feel, but he imagined they were angels in the form of pigeons, praising the Most High and occasionally commenting on this Jokim fellow, a fine and steady miller. Jokim felt the press grow light. He rested momentarily and ran his finger through the course flour at the base. Good, he thought, the crushed grain would easily become fine flour in the grinding bowl of another servant and end up as fine-flour bread. Jokim filled up the throat again from the bushel basket, and wiped his eyes, before he resumed his tread.

Was Jokim pleased to be pushing the lever of a coarse stone mill round and round, hour upon hour, day after day? Yes, he was! The overseer paid Jokim less than a healthy laborer received: five, sometimes seven copper aspers, ten or twelve of which equaled the fair day's wage of a silver denarius. But for a blind man to have respectable work that gave status to his wife was no small blessing. Jokim never begrudged his master or thought an evil thought against him, or in any way summoned the Evil Eye.[11] Dositheus was wealthy and therefore favored the views of the Sadducees and aligned himself with their position. Accordingly, the five books of Moses were the bedrock and final authority on all matters pertaining to God and his people: strict interpretation of the law, no binding oral traditions of the Pharisees or false calendars of the Essenes or false places of worship of the Samaritans. Above all, Sadducees had no patience for fables about resurrection of the body and eternal life.[12] Jokim secretly admitted that from what little he knew of the sacred writings there was little support for his hope in the hereafter.

Toward midday, about the sixth hour, Jokim heard the sound of many voices out in the road. Some cause for excitement, he thought, but not for alarm. He paused and listened. One man was telling another of a preacher passing by, one whose reputation had begun to spread across the Galilee. The man was a Galilean, of Nazareth, just up the road toward Sepphoris, and such an inauspicious origin for a wise man was a considerable source of pride to Galileans—a one-upmanship over Judaeans and Jerusalemites who imagined all wisdom found its way from their sages to the rest of the world. The people were telling the steward, and soon Jokim heard the patronizing voice of Dositheus, who sent his steward to invite the wise man to come and preach to his laborers and afterward partake of refreshments. After all, to patronize a preacher was a good deed and might well bring its reward, to say nothing of admonishing the day laborers to be pious and humble. Jokim resumed his measured gait, and the ground corn trickled down into the trough. A rare and fortunate day indeed, thought Jokim.

The preacher arrived at the house of Dositheus with a few disciples, and the steward led him over to the courtyard of the threshing floor. Soon enough Jokim heard the workers gathering in the outer courtyard, settling themselves on the threshing floor, and servants of the household and a few passers-by joined them. Jokim waited patiently for a call to join the assembly, but it appeared that he had been forgotten. When he heard the preacher begin to speak, Jokim left the shade of the grindstone and squatted down against the wall near the gate. He had been forgotten but not forbidden to pause and listen.

The preacher spoke in a clear and melodious cadence, like a rippling brook, enunciating distinctly so that every word was easily understood by someone squatting behind the courtyard wall. He began in good humor and spoke of his recent travels around the Galilee with his disciples, recounting some of their misfortunes, and the crowd laughed and nodded sympathetically. Then the preacher posed a question. "To what shall we liken the kingdom of heaven?" There followed silence, except for the occasional shuffling of arms and legs. Again, the preacher asked, "To what shall we liken the kingdom of heaven?" *Nu,* thought Jokim, someone should answer. Clearly the preacher wished his audience to participate in the exchange of wisdom. Finally a voice offered, "To a treasure?"

"Yes," said the preacher, "the kingdom of heaven may be likened to a treasure. One day a man was digging in a field, and he found a strongbox filled with gold coins and precious jewels. Immediately he covered the box back up and arranged the stones so that no one would know he had been digging there, and he went quickly away. What did he do?" The preacher paused and Jokim could feel the perplexity on the faces of the assembly, for he felt it upon his own brow. At length the preacher continued, "He went and sold all that he had and bought the field, and he began to lend money at interest. So it is that whoever gives up all that he has in this life will have treasure in heaven."[13]

"I see," Jokim whispered to himself. Yes, treasure in heaven was worth far more than all he had on earth. Even a blind man could see that.

"Preacher," said Dositheus, breaking the contemplation of Jokim. "Preacher, can you mean what I hear? Let us leave aside the ethical dilemma of buying field for less than its known value, but surely you are not annulling the law of Moses that forbids usury."

Jokim held his breath in alarm, for he had not considered the ethical dilemma.

The preacher said, "Give to him who begs from you, and do not refuse him who would borrow from you. But to the Gentiles you may lend at interest and thereby give more to your brethren and to your laborers."[14]

Jokim sighed, and nodded to himself knowingly. This preacher breathed the spirit of the law of Moses.

"To what else shall we liken the kingdom of heaven," the preacher asked.

This time, a voice answered quickly, "To a bountiful harvest?"

"Even so," said the preacher, "the kingdom of heaven is like a bountiful harvest. Now a farmer went out to sow his seed. As he sowed, tossing it back and forth, here and there, some seed fell along the path and was trodden under foot, and the birds flew down and devoured it. And some fell on rocky soil, and it quickly sprang up, but the sun scorched the tender plants and they withered away. Other seed fell among thorns, and the thorns grew up and choked it, and it yielded no grain. But other seed, most of it, fell into good soil, and it brought forth grain, thirtyfold, sixtyfold, and even a hundredfold. He who has ears to hear, let him hear."[15]

Jokim nodded in deep reflection, but suddenly he heard the voice of his master, Dositheus. "A hundredfold? Is that possible?"

"With God all things are possible," replied the preacher. "Is it not written of Isaac our father, that he sowed the land and reaped a hundredfold, and grew very wealthy and the Philistines envied him?"[16]

Dositheus replied, "Ah, indeed, those were the days of bounty and blessing. May they once more fall upon us."

The preacher continued, "Again, a man sowed his field with good seed, but while he slept, an enemy of his came and sowed weeds among the wheat. So when the young shoots of grain came up, the weeds appeared also. His laborers came and told the owner of the field that the two crops grew together. 'Shall we dig up the weeds?' they asked him. 'No,' he replied, 'let them all grow, lest you dig up the wheat also. When all is ready for harvest, we will gather the weeds into bundles for burning, and then gather the wheat into my barn.'"[17]

Jokim smiled to himself, as the word pictures played across the stage of his mind. Here was a preacher who understood life. How extraordinary!

"Again, the fields of a rich man brought forth a great harvest, and he thought to himself, What shall I do, for I have nowhere to store my crops? And he said, 'I will do this: I will pull down my storage sheds and build bigger barns, and there I will store my goods. And I will say to my soul: Soul, you have ample goods laid up for many years. Take your ease. Eat, drink, and be merry.' But our father in heaven said to him: 'Fool! This very night your soul is required of you; and the things you have prepared, whose will they be?' So is the man who lays up treasure for himself; he is not rich in the eyes of our father in heaven. He who has ears to hear, let him hear."[18]

The preacher paused, and Jokim felt the heaviness of the air that suddenly hung, like a rain laden cloud, over the gathered workers. It was one thing to admonish workers, give comfort to the lowly, and to promise everyone a happy ending, but to preach to the master of the house in his own courtyard . . . well, that was unexpected. Mind, it wasn't that Pharisees never prodded the opinions of the Sadducees, or poked fun at their interpretations of Torah, but a man's wealth, like his private parts, was generally left alone. And if not an offense against humanity, preaching against wealth to the wealthy was at least a breach of social custom. Jokim sensed that the workers were afraid to smile approval.

The preacher, however, did not seem to notice the heaviness of the air, or else he wished rain to fall upon them. "To what else may the kingdom of heaven be compared?" he asked again.

Dositheus spoke up, as if he had not heard any offense thus far. "Let us liken the kingdom of heaven to a feast." Good, thought Jokim. Here is something they might all enjoy.

"A feast," agreed the preacher. "A feast is a good likeness, though I fear that if we linger too long upon it, we shall all grow hungry. Now, there was a very rich man who gave a great banquet. He invited all the nobles and every important merchant and landowner in the city. On the day of the feast he sent his servant to bring the guests to the magnificent table. He said to his servant, 'Tell them all what we have prepared— fatted calves, sheep, chickens, legumes, and savory sauces, breads of fine white flour, fruit of every tree and bush, honey from the desert, pastries and nuts, and wine without end.' And the servant went out, praising the delicacies of the feast to the limits of his vocabulary. But the invited guests insulted the master, and made excuses, and they went off to their labors, one to his business, another to his farms. So the servant returned and reported his failure to the master. The master set his hands on his hips; he tucked his thumbs in his sash, rocked back and forth, and frowned a great frown. He said, 'Very well, go out quickly into the streets and alleys of the city, and invite the poor and maimed, the lame and blind.' The servant went out and found as many as he could and led them to the banquet. They came in, each one marveling at his good fortune; the maimed led the blind, and the blind carried the lame, and the master set them down to his feast. But still the house was not full, so he sent out the servant into the highways and hedgerows to call more guests and told him to beat the bushes and find anyone who might be sheltered under them and bring them in, so that none of the food would be wasted. And more hungry people came, and they ate and ate until their sides hurt."[19]

The preacher stopped. Jokim pondered such a strange, even remarkable tale. His stomach had begun to growl softly. The blind carrying the lame into a great banquet. Yes, he would gladly carry a cripple into such a feast, if only someone would lead him to it.

The preacher continued. "You see, to be in the kingdom of heaven is to do the will of our father in heaven. And what is the will of our father in heaven but to love your neighbor as yourself, to give to those in need. Let the needy be members of your household. Therefore, when you give a banquet, however humble, invite those who cannot repay you, and our father in heaven will repay you. Invite the poor, the maimed, the lame and the blind, and you will be blessed now because they cannot repay you, but you will be repaid at the resurrection of the righteous."[20]

"Ah yes," someone said solicitously. Jokim recognized the harsh voice of Rufus, the son of Dositheus, whom he imagined was shorter than his father, always intent on measuring up, and was born with a worried brow, a permanent scowl, and a fat lower lip. Again, Jokim imagined with uncanny accuracy. Jokim also rightly supposed Rufus had become visibly uncomfortable and took this opportunity to change the flow of the preacher's words. "Yes, yes," said Rufus, "sooner or later we come to the next world, and I speak figuratively, of course. But what did King Solomon tell us on this matter, except that the body returns to the earth, and the spirit to God who gave it. When we die, we go the way of all the earth; therefore, let your garments be white, and let not oil be lacking on your head; eat, drink, and be merry. Heaven rewards piety *in this life.*"[21]

"Have you not read the prophet Isaiah?" said the preacher. "*Thy dead shall live, their bodies shall rise. O dwellers in the dust, awake and sing for joy! For thy dew is a dew of light, and on the land of shades thou wilt let it fall.*"[22]

Ah, thought Jokim, that is wonderful. So pure and full of promise. Why had he never heard this passage before? Shout it from the mountain tops! The face of the preacher suddenly burst into the imagination of Jokim. A sage to be sure, with a sage's high and smooth forehead, and a sage's beard, sufficient in length for caressing when deep in thought. But more than a sage, a prophet perhaps, or the son of a prophet who walked with the authority of the prophets, and whose eyes gazed steadily and without fear, seeing all humanity, high and low, as a single throng in need of help.

"Of course I am familiar with the poetry of Isaiah," said Rufus. "But surely that is metaphor. The prophet speaks of the restoration of Israel after our exile in Babylon, and he goes on to speak of the days to come when Jacob shall take root and Israel shall blossom. Perhaps there is some continued existence in the land of shades, but to what end I am sure we do not know. Scripture says nothing about a resurrection of the body. How can the flesh possibly be restored from the maggots that devour it? And even if witchcraft may disturb the shades, as the necromancer of Endor did with the prophet Samuel, God has forbidden it; and in any case the prophet did not wish to be disturbed from his sleep. That is the sum of the law and the prophets on life after death."[23]

"Did not the patriarch Job declare: *For I know that my Redeemer lives, and at last he will stand upon the earth; and after my skin has been thus destroyed, then from my flesh I shall see God, whom I shall see on my side, and my eyes shall behold, and not another.*"[24]

"No proof text may be taken from the book of Job," replied Rufus. "We do not even know that he was an Israelite."[25]

"Have you not read Daniel?" replied the preacher. "*Many of those who sleep in the dust of the earth shall awake, some to everlasting life, and some to shame and everlasting contempt. And those who are wise shall shine like the brightness of the firmament, and those who turn many to righteousness, like the stars for ever and ever.*"[26]

"The words of Daniel are not binding in matters not taught in Torah.[27] Where in the books of Moses do we learn that God will raise up anyone? I know of no such teaching."

"Even so," replied the preacher, "Moses wrote in the passage about the bush that God said to him, *I am the God of your father, the God of Abraham, the God of Isaac, and the God of Jacob.*[28] What do we learn from this? God is not God of the dead, but of the living."

"I see," Jokim whispered to himself, and pulled on his beard with delight. "Everywhere the promise abounds for those that have ears to hear."

"Such an answer," cried Rufus, "how very like the Pharisees, they who twist grammar like twine and bind up words to say something new."

The preacher turned back to his audience. "There was a rich man clothed in fine linen who feasted sumptuously every day. And at his gate lay a poor man, full of sores that the dogs came and licked. He asked only to be fed with what crumbs fell from the rich man's table. Now the poor man died and was carried by the angels to paradise. The rich man also died and was buried; and in the land of shades, amid the burning refuse, he lifted up his eyes and saw Abraham far off and the poor man by his side. And he called out, 'Father Abraham, have mercy upon me, and send him to dip the end of his finger in water and cool my tongue; for I am in anguish in this flame.' But Abraham said, 'Son, remember that you in your lifetime received your good things, and he in like manner evil things; but now he is comforted here, and you are in anguish. And besides all this, between us and you a great chasm has been fixed, in order that those who would pass from here to you may not be able, and none may cross from there to us.' And the rich man said, 'Then I beg you, send him to my house so that he may warn them, lest they also come into this place of torment.' But Abraham said, 'They have Moses and the prophets; let them hear if they have ears to hear.'"[29]

In the silence that followed, Jokim imagined Dositheus sitting in his wicker chair under the pergola, with a deep furrow in his forehead such that his eyebrows came together, and his lips frowned uncomfortably. But Rufus sighed heavily, "Ah, when Torah fails, we always have folktales to frighten us."[30]

"Be at peace with your own soul," said the preacher. "Those who say there is no resurrection of the dead have no share in the world to come."[31]

"Good heavens!" cried Dositheus, struggling to rise from his chair. "The hour of rest has passed, and the day is half spent. Well, we thank you for your words, Jeshua of Nazareth. No doubt we have all profited, and we shall carry them with us back to our labor, which, after all, is how we put bread on the tables of the poor. May God grant you safe wandering whither you go today."

Thereupon, the crowd hastened to their feet and fled to their appointed tasks, the promised food already forgotten. Jokim, too, rose and returned to the grindstone. He staggered beneath the weight of the preacher's words. Much grist for the mill. The preacher came like a herald from the king, from the inner chambers of heaven. Like a prophet of old, he delivered good tidings to the poor and evil tidings to the rich. Jokim kept his pace around the millstone, pressing against the wood lever. He listened to the crush of the grain and the falling of the coarse flour into the trough at the base. He listened to the cooing of the angelic pigeons, who praised the preacher without end. He that has ears to hear, let him hear.

At the tenth hour Jokim lined up before the overseer to receive his wages, today five copper coins. He fingered the irregular bits of metal with imprints of palm branches. A modest day's wages even for a blind man, but Jokim thanked the overseer, and tucked away the coins in his sash. He took his staff, oriented himself to the road and walked back to Nain, rather more oblivious to the evening sounds than he had been to the morning. Even the babbling brook went unnoticed. Jokim walked by intuition, while he contemplated the words of the preacher, and repeated over and over all that he had heard, engraving it on tablets of stone hidden away in his darkness.

Jokim found himself at the door of their mud brick house, worn as it was from years of wind and rain. Jokim entered and Bilhah rose to meet him.

"You found work this day," she said hopefully.

"Ah," said Jokim, "a day's labor, yes, but far more than a day's wages did I receive."

"How so, my husband?" Bilhah replied. "What treasure have you found?"

"Treasure, my wife? Yes, how you prophesy and prepare the way. But first, take my wages," he said, handing the coins to her. "Now, let me sit and rest my feet, and I will tell you of the treasure, as you say, for indeed, it is." Jokim sat on his low stool in the corner of the room and rested his back against the wall. Bilhah sat on the mat nearby, awaiting the good news.

"Today," Jokim began, still in a state of wonderment, "I listened to Jeshua of Nazareth." Jokim sighed and repeated the name, "Jeshua of Nazareth." He clapped his hands together. "He speaks of the kingdom of heaven almost as if we were there, and yet it awaits in the world to come." Jokim spread out his hands. "The best of both worlds. He invites all to enter, and yet, it seems, the most deserving do not desire it." Jokim pulled methodically at his beard. "Heh-heh-heh. He said to Rufus, son and heir of master Dositheus, 'Be at peace with your own soul; those who say there is no resurrection of the dead, have no share in the world to come.' Heh-heh-heh."

Bilhah waited patiently for her husband to come to the good news and the "more than a day's wages" part.

"He is a fair and lovely man," said Jokim. "Not tall, not short, about my height, I think, with a face of kindness the likes of which you have never seen." Bilhah, well versed in her husband's imaginations, listened to his rapid flow of words and fantastic descriptions of the preacher. Indeed, the description had blossomed since he first imagined the preacher. "His eyes, above all, glow like coals of fire and penetrate into the deepest recesses of the darkened soul. Even from behind the stone wall I felt his gaze prick at me. I am certain that he knew I was there, crouched and listening, for he said 'He that has ears to hear, let him hear,' and that must have been for Jokim the blind. His words, too, cut to the quick, like a two-edged sword. He bows to no one and listens to all. My wife, if he is not a prophet, he is an angel."

Bilhah now realized there was no pot of gold at the end of this tale. "He sounds like a perfect Jokim," she replied.

"What is this you say, my wife? How wise and wonderful your words. If everyone imagined the preacher as a perfect example of himself and altered his life to match his imagination, surely the kingdom of heaven would fall on us like the deluge."

"God help us," said Bilhah. "A landscape awash with preachers?"

Jokim straightened up. "Wife, listen now to your husband and lord. We must go out and find someone poor, or two and three, the more the better, and invite them to a banquet."

"But, my husband, *we* are poor."

"Yes, but we are not alone. We poor folk are many. We should not be hard to find."

"How shall I prepare a banquet, when your measly supper comes to-gether only by scrimping and saving and arguing in the marketplace."

"Let it be a humble banquet, my wife, only we must have some meat, a leg of lamb or a turtledove for each."

"The head of a chicken, you mean," said Bilhah, not knowing whether to take her husband seriously or not. "There is no one poorer than us."

"And good bread, not barley bread, but wheat bread, dripping with savory sauces. Such as you prepared once or twice."

"Why not honey cakes, Jokim, why not dates stuffed with walnuts?"

"Wonderful," he replied, "yes, all of that is excellent for a banquet."

Bilhah threw up her hands. Her husband was again walking on the clouds of his blind imagination.

"So long as they cannot repay us, that is the key," continued Jokim, shaking his finger in the air. "And we must have wine."

"Enough to color water the faintest purple? The coins you have brought will not suffice, my husband."

"Perhaps we can sell some of our belongings, in exchange for the banquet. What have I that you may sell or barter?"

"We have nothing," Bilhah whined in exasperation.

"My stool perhaps? Sell whatever we have, dishes, my cloak."

"Your cloak—no one will buy. My dishes? How shall we lay this banquet without dishes?"

"It is very important that we do this. Tomorrow you must prepare a meal and invite guests who cannot repay us. Surely we can find some who are unable to work—the lame and maimed, even other blind folk— anyone who cannot repay us. Perhaps I will meet some on the way. I will beat the bushes."

"You'll find no one poorer than yourself," she shouted. "Rather invite your master and employer, the mighty Dositheus, and invite him to bring a jar of wine and a leg of lamb that we may all feast at his largess, which he has and we do not!"

Jokim laughed. "Now that is a good one, my wife. That would be the kingdom of heaven indeed. No, we must not ask God for the impossible. Master Dositheus supping at my table? Heh-heh-heh," he laughed and wiped the tears and mucous from his eyes.

"We have no table," Bilhah reminded him. "Have we not always eaten on the mat under your stool?" She rose up, shaking her head. "Come my husband, wash yourself that you may eat your measly supper from your lowly stool."

The next morning Jokim awoke full of expectation and rose before Bilhah. He washed his face and paced the floor, energetically reciting the Shema. When he finished, Jokim pressed his hands to his breast. "Today the kingdom of heaven is at hand," he said loudly.

Bilhah rose from her bed. "Today we will display our poverty," she grumbled, "and make a mockery of all banquets past and all banquets yet to come."

"Not so, my wife. I believe God will provide the banquet and the guests. As the sages say, God will not command you to fly without giving you wings."

Jokim received his cup of sour milk and his day's provision. "Prepare the banquet, my dear wife and see if God does not bring us into the kingdom of heaven."

Bilhah watched him walk down the street to the city gate. When he had gone, she sighed and pondered her dilemma. Her husband so desired a banquet, as if the kingdom of heaven really did depend on it. She could not disappoint him, he who labored at any task to give her a home and a livelihood. She anguished for an hour, then went to her chest and withdrew the small bag of copper coins she had cached away for hard times. Bilhah put her shawl over her head and went out to squander their savings on a single extravagant meal, with a leg of lamb.

Jokim arrived at the estate of Dositheus. The overseer acknowledged his presence and summoned him back to the grindstone. Jokim set his staff against the wall, oriented himself to the baskets of grain and the millstone, and settled himself in to the circular tread, and the cooing of the pigeons, and his inner world of thought.

"Jokim!" A voice—nay the voice of his master—summoned.

"Yes, master."

"Thank heaven you are here." Dositheus entered the grindstone court. "See here, take your staff and come with me." Jokim took up his staff and followed Dositheus away from the grindstone, toward the private courtyard of his estate. Jokim listened to the belabored breath of his master, saddled with fat fore and aft. "Come, sit you down . . . here, sit in my chair."

"In your chair, master?"

"Yes. Sit here and listen to me, for I have not slept well this night on your account."

"I am sorry to hear that, master." He felt the arm of the wicker chair and carefully sat himself into it. The cushion, very soft, must be filled with goose down, he thought.

"Well you should be," said Dositheus, "though I lay blame equally to the preacher of Nazareth."

"The preacher?" said Jokim.

"Yes, the preacher. In the night I dreamt a dream. Now hearken to my dream and tell me what you think."

"I listen, master."

"I dreamt that I died and awakened among the shades in Sheol.[32] It was like unto a pit of refuse, and the smoke burned my nostrils and scorched my throat. I thirsted. That is not a pleasant situation, I assure you."

"Not pleasant at all," Jokim gravely replied.

"I looked about," Dositheus continued, "and I saw that you sat in a garden, not far-away, beyond a chasm, with Abraham, Isaac, and Jacob. Do not ask me how I knew the patriarchs, but . . . well, who else could they have been? And I recognized you. Indeed, you wore the very tunic now on your back."

"I see," said Jokim. "The very same tunic, with these patches?" He fingered a patch on his sleeve.

"Yes, I think it had patches, certainly it appeared threadbare. But never mind that. I recognized you and I called out to you by name. 'Jokim, Jokim,' I called. And you looked up. 'Hail, Dositheus,' you called back. And I said, 'Come hither and bring me to your garden.' And you said, 'The cost of passage is a denarius. Have you the price?' 'I have nothing,' I said. 'My purse was left behind.' And you said, 'I have but eleven copper coins, twelve of which make a denarius.' I said, 'Can you not ask the patriarchs for a copper?' But they shook their heads. And then you rose and walked away, and the patriarchs turned their backs to me. Now tell me, Jokim, because it was you in my dream and not another, what do you think of this? Speak the truth, for this is no fawning matter, you understand."

"Your dream, master, is wonderful," said Jokim. "By that, I mean, terrible. Perhaps remarkable is what I mean. To think that but for lack of a single copper you might have entered the kingdom of heaven. That is wonderful, and terrible, and remarkable indeed."

"Well? Terrible and remarkable, is that all you can say?"

"Surely I would have come to help you had I been able."

"But you could not, and I could not cross over."

"And I am disappointed that I did not have a new tunic."

"By the temple gates, Jokim!" Dositheus shouted in exasperation, "what does it mean for me?"

Jokim pondered the dream, rocking back and forth in the down-filled wicker chair while he stroked his beard. "Ah," he said, suddenly. "Could it be?" he asked himself, scratching his cheek thoughtfully. "It must be, for on this night only do heaven and earth agree, dream and interpretation."

"Yes?" said Dositheus.

"Last night," Jokim began, "last night I decided to do as the preacher said and invite poor people to a banquet. My woman, Bilhah, she says to me, 'You'll find no one poorer than yourself.'" Jokim looked up with mucous laden eyes into the face of Dositheus, and smiled. "Master," he said, "I invite you to my banquet."

Dositheus frowned. "I see."

# 12

# The Embassy

Being puffed up by their delusion, they sought to overthrow the government of the universe by unholy words; and they set themselves up as rulers and kings, attributing the undestroyable sovereignty of God to creation which passes away and perishes and never continues in one stay. Therefore these ridiculous men give themselves tragic airs and using boastful absurdities are accustomed to speak thus: we are the leaders; we are potentates; on us all things depend.

Philo of Alexandria

We Jews lifted up YHWH from being our god to the exclusion of all other gods, and made him the Most High God of the universe. That is not an ontological statement, rather an expression of human understanding. It is one thing to say the Senate voted Augustus into the Olympian mansions, thereby officially recognizing him a god, and quite another to say the Senate recognized that Augustus had always been a member of the pantheon, recently come down to earth for the purpose of helping to stabilize Rome. Mankind believes all sorts of strange things, none of which impinge on the true nature of the cosmos or the nature of the Deity. Tiberius refused divine honors, and the Senate declined to deify Caligula and Nero, they who so wanted to be gods, but curiously, the Senate did vote an apotheosis for Claudius, much to the amusement and disgust of Seneca, as may be appreciated from his bitter satire, *Apocolocyntosis,* or "The High Drama of Claudius the Gourd."[1]

So much for Roman dilemmas. The Greek-speaking Jews, having lifted YHWH to his rightful position of Most High, yet retaining the Hebrew tradition as Father and King who cares for his people, searched about for a concept to describe the rule of this benevolent Most High God of the Universe, that we might fulfill our mission as a light to the nations.[2] We found a suitable concept in Greek, which in fact had no

Hebrew counterpart, namely, *pronoia,* or in Latin, *providere;* that is, fore-thought that provides. Jews of the Diaspora quickly appropriated this concept, so dear to the Stoics, of a kindly providence which sees the goal and ordains for the best everything that takes place in history. The Jewish appropriation transformed *pronoia* from an impersonal and cosmic-centered force, to a personal God-centered force, Providence. God rules the Jews, indeed, the cosmos, like a benevolent father over his household, punishing the unruly when necessary, but caring for them all. Philo of Alexandria took this concept to great heights in his many volumes on the nature of God and the goal of humanity. He devoted an entire treatise to Providence.[3] The goal and end of history is the establishment of the rule of God. Woe to him who interferes.

The hands of Petronius, Legate of Syria, trembled as he finished reading the imperial letter. Gaius Caligula, Caesar of Rome, commanded him to commission a statue of Zeus, colossal in size, gilded with gold, and with the facial features of Gaius himself. All well and good, insofar as the worship of the emperor was well and good for the empire. The figure of Caesar had become the symbol of unity for the far-flung empire, and though Augustus had forbidden worship of him in Italy, where he was the first among equals, in the provinces he had permitted temples in his honor and let them worship him as they desired. But what made Petronius's hands tremble? The emperor had commanded him to erect the statue in the temple of the Jews in Jerusalem. Gaius insisted that the Jews so acknowledge and worship him as a god.

Publius Petronius, of senatorial family, was elected consul *suffectus* with Junius Silanus in the fifth year of Tiberius. Together, the consuls enacted the *Lex Iunia Petronia,* which stipulated that in trials concerning manumission from slavery, if the jury was equally divided, the judgment should be for liberty. In other words, Petronius must be placed among those rare Roman administrators who inclined toward the plight of the oppressed. Nevertheless, he became proconsul of Asia and later the legate of Syria. Petronius now pondered the strange and impossible command. He informed his staff officer of the letter's content, concluding, "Whoever advises the emperor on foreign affairs ought to be impaled."

"Sir," replied his staff officer, "I believe he turns to his chamberlain, Helicon, and the actor Apelles, for counsel on eastern affairs, though I dare say the gods have whispered this advice in his ears."

"If so, what have I done to the gods that they place such a dilemma in my path?"

"Perhaps there are reasons far beyond our understanding, and we must simply play our part in the divine caprice."

Petronius nodded somberly. "Send for the sculptors and commission the statue."

The officer saluted and turned to leave.

"Tell them," said Petronius, "to proceed slowly, with utmost care. The statue must be immaculate, and they must sacrifice no detail, regardless of the time required. You understand?"

"Yes, sir. A pace just shy of procrastination?"

"Precisely." Only later did Petronius learn the cause of Caesar's command. A minority of Greek residents in the coastal town of Jamnia decided to erect an altar to the new god, Gaius Caesar, long known as Caligula, "booties," on account of the little boots he wore as a child while accompanying his father Germanicus on military expeditions. The town of Jamnia belonged to the imperial property, and the Greeks hoped to demonstrate keen piety toward their god and benefactor, who would soon journey to the eastern empire, bestowing gifts along the way. So, they built a solid altar of clay brick in the town square and offered sacrifices and poured out libations to Gaius. But the Jewish majority of the town took offense at this sacrilege within the borders of the holy land, and they tore down the altar.[4] The incident might have remained a local dispute, and settled among neighbors, who, after all, must live together, but certain sycophants, always on the prowl for new ways to ingratiate themselves to ultimate power and get back at the Jews, took the matter to the emperor. The imperial response was to set up a colossal statue of Gaius *cum* Zeus in the Jerusalem temple. The task had fallen to Petronius.

Agathon awaited in the shade of a cypress. Philo sat on a stone bench, staring into the shrouded window of his vast mind. Behind him, a large stone vase set on a pedestal rose up like a pillar between the green shrubbery. Across the garden another delegation waited, the Alexandrian Greek opponents of the Jews.

Gaius Caesar had arranged an inspection of two imperial villas in the gardens of the Esquiline Hills, just outside the old wall of Rome, and it was there that he chose to receive the delegates from Alexandria. The matter at hand was the political rights of the Jews, rights granted by the Ptolemies from the foundation of the city of Alexandria and confirmed by Julius Caesar when the rule of Egypt passed to Rome. The Egyptians had never accepted Roman rule, but they directed their dissatisfaction not at the Macedonians or Romans, but at the Jews, for in Egypt the Jews were one element that everyone could dislike. The undercurrent of Egyptian anarchy and mob rule had always lain beneath the surface, but good Roman rule contained it, and the Jews made their contribution to the preeminence of Alexandrian society under Augustus and Tiberius.

Then came the reign of terror under the Roman governor Aulus Avillius Flaccus, who took up his administration of Egypt during the last five years of Tiberius Caesar.[5] Flaccus ruled well enough during the five years while Tiberius Caesar was alive, though he favored the Greeks at the expense of the Jews. He fell afoul of Roman politics after the death of Tiberius; for he had supported Gemellus, a rival of Caligula to succeed Tiberius, and upon the succession of Caligula and the subsequent death of Gemellus, he naturally feared for his own welfare. He therefore sought the support of certain Alexandrians, principally Lampo and Isidorus, who promised to intercede with Caligula on condition that Flaccus sanction their plot to take away the political protection of the Jews in the city.

These instigators of mischief drew from the deep well of animosity against the Jews among the native Egyptians, but they received an unexpected call to action when Agrippa, newly appointed as king of the Jews in Rome, stopped in Alexandria on his way east. The king came surrounded by a bodyguard festooned in armor overlaid with gold and silver, and the pomp with which the Jews received this "foreign ruler" not only put Flaccus into the shadows but gave the Egyptians reason to complain that the Jews of the city were more loyal to Agrippa than to Rome, and therefore the Jews should all go back to Judaea. Some enterprising youths grabbed an imbecile named Carabas who went around the city naked, thrust him onto a stage in the gymnasium, and clothed him in a carpet, with a shaft of papyrus for a scepter. They stood round their king with rods on their shoulders as a bodyguard and proceeded to mock the presence of Agrippa by hailing this poor soul as "Marin," that is, "lord" in Aramaic.

Flaccus did nothing to prevent this insult to a foreign ruler, who had received Praetorian honors from the Roman Senate, so the crowd grew bolder and a riot ensued. The Egyptians ransacked the synagogues and set up images of the emperor. Within a few days Flaccus denounced the Jews as foreigners and aliens who, therefore, did not enjoy the status of Alexandrian citizenship. This illegal act emboldened the Egyptians still further, and they evicted Jews from the three districts of the city where Jews were in the minority and plundered their homes. Some of the rioters set fire to the homes and burnt alive the families hiding in fear. Other Jews were dragged through the streets of the city until dead and partially dismembered. Meanwhile, the Jews who escaped fled to the Delta quarter until it was choking with bodies.[6]

If all this mob rule were not enough, Flaccus arrested thirty-eight senators of the Jewish council and publically paraded them in shackles through the market. But even here, the greatest disgrace came when they were arrayed in the theater and flogged, and several old men, among them Agathon's father, expired as a consequence of the flogging. The mob seized women in the marketplace and theater, brought swine's flesh, and ordered the women to place it in their mouths. Those who did were let go, but those who refused where handed over to gangs who abused and violated them.

The illegality of the riot was so blatant that many esteemed Greek citizens called for justice. Within a year Flaccus was arrested and exiled, though whether for his complicity in the riots or as an imagined threat to the emperor, they could not say.[7] But the Jews of Alexandria realized that they must renew their protection of law, and their rightful place as legal denizens of the city. Therefore, they requested permission from the new prefect, Vitrasius Pollio, to send a delegation to appeal their case before Caesar. The prefect granted permission and the embassy was formed. Though reluctant, Philo agreed to lead the delegation, and chose Agathon, both for his rhetorical skills and as compensation for the death of his father.

On arriving in Rome, Agathon and the delegates learned that their judge would be their accuser. They had been given the right to appeal to Caesar, but Caligula had decided he was a god, and he listened only to those who addressed him as such. And having leapt to the realm of divinity, Caligula began to act like a god and dress in the costumes of the demigods. He had statues of the gods decapitated and revivified with his own bust on their necks. So wild and delirious Caligula had become, he determined that he must rise above the demigods and become a full god. But not just any full god—no that would not do—he had to be Gaius the New Zeus Manifest, and his statue had to stand in the temple of the Jews, who alone among the peoples of the empire did not acknowledge him as a god. This, then, was the Caesar and god with delusions of grandeur before whom the Jews would make their appeal.

The approach of a servant of Caesar shook Agathon from his thoughts. Philo rose from the stone bench, but the royal servant went only to the Greeks. Agathon knew three members of the Greek delegation—

Apion, Lampo, and Isidorus. These three loathed Jews with such a loathing as no diplomatic rhetoric could plaster over. The servant ushered the Greeks into the villa. Philo sat back down. His usual stately demeanor was tinged by anxiety. Now, in his seventh decade, Philo had become the elder statesman of the Alexandrian Jews.

Born of an illustrious Jewish family, thus into the luxury of leisure, Philo entered the gymnasium in his youth and came out the most learned Jew in the land or, as they said by means of humble understatement, he was certainly no novice in philosophy.[8] Soon the master took on pupils, among whom a most energetic student was Agathon. The teachings of Philo allowed Agathon to rub shoulders with the Greeks and advance in the politics of Alexandria. But never in his most ambitious moments or delirious daydreams had he pictured himself in the gardens of Caesar awaiting the summons of Caesar. Even so, that is where he now stood, along with Philo and three other delegates. Philo found himself in Rome out of a sense of duty to his people, and for no other reason. A lifelong scholar, he preferred the library to the courts, and he stepped to the fore only when pushed from behind. Yet here he sat, a learned and revered old Jew about to be humiliated in front of Caesar for the sake of his people. *Oy li! Oy lanu! Oy!*[9]

Petronius and his legions wintered in the coastal city of Ptolemais, formerly called Akko. Jewish leaders came to him and he explained his plight, begging them to find a way to permit the obvious sacrilege of a statue on the temple mount. But the Jews begged him not to proceed with the impossible command. Petronius gathered up his retinue and traveled to the city of Tiberias, where he sought a full evaluation of this predicament from all the Jewish leaders. The Jews came by the thousands.

The legate suggested placing the statue in some sheltered corner of the Royal Stoa. After all, the Court of the Nations was open to all, and had not Herod placed a golden eagle in the temple?[10]

"No, no," the elders of Jerusalem replied. "Even coins with the imprint of Caesar are not permitted within the temple area.[11] A statue of Zeus is an abomination."

"If I were Caesar," said Petronius, clearly agitated, "and had issued this command of my own caprice, then your words would be justified, but I am under oath to obey Caesar, and I come to you looking for some conciliation, some diplomatic way out for both of us."

The Jews merely shook their heads, acknowledging the dire straits for all concerned; they had no conceivable path of conciliation to offer him. They recalled the insurrection of Judas Maccabaeus under Antiochus Ephiphanes and even the five thousand Jews who confronted Pontius Pilate over the smaller offense of iconic military standards within the walls of Jerusalem as precedents of what would surely follow.[12] War to the death, pure and simple. Was Petronius ready to take this much blood upon his hands?

"Will you go to war against Caesar?" Petronius asked.

The Jews replied, "We will not fight, but we will perish, for we will sooner die than violate this law of our God and erect an image of Zeus in Jerusalem." And the leaders knelt and bared their necks, as lambs for the slaughter.

Now, Petronius too, shook his head. In one simple command, Caesar had condemned a tenth of the empire to death, for the six million Jews comprised a tenth of the population of the empire. It was decimation on the most grand and impossible scale. He saw his own life pass before his eyes. He dismissed the Jews and promised to do what he could. After consulting with a few royal relatives of Agrippa, he determined to write a letter to Caesar, explaining the situation and seeking his counsel.

Agathon, son of a well respected member of the Jewish council, with a finely crafted aristocratic face and its typical features, including a tendency to lower his eyelids and raise his nose, became a childhood friend of Tiberius Alexander, son of the wealthy Alexander, Minister of the Nile customs. Together they entered the gymnasium to pursue the same education as all aspiring Greeks, and together they came of age. The coming of age for Agathon had been a keen awareness of the faint line between the theoretical sovereignty of God and the political realities of daily life. Agathon acknowledged his debt to Tiberius Alexander for the reality of politics, and to his mentor Philo, for the sovereignty of God. The two pillars towered in his hall of contemplation, and he paced reflectively between them, day after day.

The coming of age, Agathon recalled, occurred during those fraternal symposia in the taverns of Alexandria, where intellectuals gathered, poets, artists, writers, all aspiring to make a mark on life—and a living of it too, if possible—where philosophy in all its forms, politics, art, or

religion, could be threshed and winnowed, crushed and fermented
to obtain the pure essence of knowledge and truth. One afternoon,
Agathon and Tiberius Alexander (he insisted even his friends address
him by the double name), and a third companion, perhaps it was Philip,
retreated to a tavern in the shadows of the colossal granite library, a
favorite among the elite of the city. No doubt Agathon's recollection had
become a synthesis of numerous such occasions—and so it should be,
for no one wants to recall everything, when a condensation of the many
recollections into an epitome is far more economical—but as he recalled, Philo had lectured on the universal rule of the universal God,
known as *Theos Hypsistos,* the God Most High.[13]

"Does Philo mean to say," asked Philip (if indeed, it was Philip, and
not another), "that whenever Greeks or Egyptians speak of the most
high god, they refer to the God of Moses?" He reached for his goblet,
drank long, and wiped his mouth with the back of his forearm. As the
youngest among them, slender, smooth of chin and curly haired, and the
one still clinging to the more literal interpretations of tradition, Philip
recognized no shame in playing the rôle of poser of the questions, which
all brilliant observations require for a starting point.

"Certainly not!" said Agathon. "Egyptians? Really, Philip! What have
Egyptians to do with high-minded thoughts?"

"Mea culpa. The Greeks then."

"First we must agree that logic allows for but one most high god, no?"

"One at a time, I grant you that," said Philip, "but if there is only one
god, he cannot be the 'most high,' for that is a comparative term."

"Well, our tradition is replete with comparative assumptions which
serve us well in a polytheistic world. Long ago even our forefathers believed other gods existed, and therefore we are left with the tradition of
their beliefs, and for sake of clarity these gods also exist, even if only in
the imaginations of men."

"I was going to say," continued Philip, "different peoples will call
different gods the most high god, depending on what help their souls
require."

Tiberius Alexander shrugged his muscular shoulders, upon which
sat the column of his neck supporting a handsome face, clean shaven and
self assured. "Philip, why should we care about their souls? As long as
they call on the same god as the Jews, they will not be slandering us,
their fellow supplicants." Tiberius Alexander, it is fair to say, was not a
philosopher; that is, he was not a "lover of wisdom" per se. Rather, he
enjoyed many mistresses, among them Sophia, and sought them out to
his advantage. A thoroughgoing rationalist, he appreciated the down-to-
earthness of Rome and nurtured himself in her soil.

"Ever the political strategist," laughed Agathon. "But surely it is the duty of the wise to enlighten the ignorant, for a wiser public makes for a more stable society."

"It is the duty of the shrewd to devise ways of controlling the ignorant," replied Tiberius Alexander. "You are not so naïve as to think Philo will make Jews of everyone."

"Whether Gentiles wish to become Jews or not is beside the point, so long as they suppose that we Jews worship their most high god in our own way."

Philip pursed his lips momentarily. "Has not this stratagem been exercised for over two centuries? Aristeas, for example, in his letter to Philocrates, declared that Zeus and Jove are the same as the Unnamed Deity worshiped by the Jews?"[14]

"Even so," Agathon confirmed. "And the translation of our sacred Scriptures into the universal language of Greek, permits all the world to accept the rule of the most high God."

"Well," said Philip, "I would not call this mission a great success."

"It will never succeed," said Tiberius Alexander, "until Jews are true Alexandrians, indistinguishable from Greeks and Romans."

"In the baths, too?" Philip quipped.

"Why do you imagine Philo allegorizes our customs," said Agathon, "if not to demonstrate the universal truths of moderation and piety that they symbolize? I myself have explained to Greek friends that the prohibition against eating swine is meant to convey discipline in the practice of moderation. We eschew gluttony, that is, eating like a pig. And many of my Greek friends understand and have praised me for it. Similarly, circumcision is a symbol of the excision of the pleasures which delude the mind."[15]

"Just the same," Philip said, "Philo insists privately that Jews ought not throw off the symbol by which we proclaim to all the world this principal of virtue. For one thing, you ostracize yourself from the community of Jews who never get beyond the literal understanding. For another . . ." he broke off, realizing that he should not have said 'for one thing' because he did not have a second point to make.

"Moderation is the golden mean," Agathon replied somewhat impatiently. "We have to wage war on two fronts: on the one hand, against the Gentiles who ridicule our customs as archaic and provincial, and *on the other,* against the backward literalists who add custom upon archaic custom to enhance our holiness. Philo's translation of Torah into allegory opens our laws to the universal truths that intelligent Gentiles can appreciate.

Tiberius Alexander shook his head. "Both of you place far too much confidence in truth. But as you delight in it, I will give you a morsel to nibble upon. Most Greeks see through this ploy, and Philo's proclamations and books only rankle their ire. They do not wish to share power with Jews, nor even a meal, for that matter. Not until you chew and swallow swine's flesh and ask for more will they be satisfied that you are no different and certainly no better than they."

"We do not have to convince the Egyptians of anything," said Philip.

"By the gods, you do," replied Tiberius Alexander. "You must show your superiority unassailable."

"Or worth emulating," Agathon suggested.

"On the contrary, you must demonstrate to Rome that Jews are better subjects than Egyptians and as good as Greeks, and better administrators than either. To achieve this, you may begin by admonishing our Jewish brethren to give up the arcane customs that make us a laughing-stock, the fodder for comedians."

Agathon shrugged. "Our comedians are as good as theirs."

"As long as men are laughing," said Philip, "they are not likely to be throwing stones."

"There you are either naïve or foolish," said Tiberius Alexander. "They laugh to disarm you even as they prepare to dance on your grave."

"Suppose," said Philip, "Caesar required you to offer incense to him as a god?"

"I would offer the very best incense."

"And transgress against all our heritage in one act?"

"What do I care what Caesar thinks of himself?" Tiberius Alexander threw up his hands. "When Alexander the Great required the Greeks to acknowledge him as a god, what did the Spartans answer? 'If Alexander wishes to be a god, he is a god.'[16] Was the conqueror thereby a god? I tell you, only fools do not suffer the folly of power."

"I for one," Philip proclaimed, "will die before I blur the distinction between us and them on the worship of God."

Tiberius Alexander replied, "And I will plant a tree in your memory."

Another imperial servant came out of the villa and hastened toward them. With a slight sneer on his lips, he said, "Caesar will receive you now." Agathon took his place beside and slightly behind Philo. The other members of the delegation found their places, and they followed the servant through the garden shrubs, up the marble steps of the south-ern porch, and into atrium of the villa. Agathon wished that Tiberius Alexander might have joined the delegation, but that was not possible now that Tiberius Alexander served as a soldier of the Roman army. To advance in the ranks, he dispensed with all the dietary restrictions, and gave gifts liberally from his father's wealth which was the envy of all Egypt. His loyalty to Rome was exemplary. He asked nothing of his men that he himself would not do. Tiberius Alexander became a centu-rion within two years. He accepted any assignment and swiftly rose among the career officers, serving under several generals in the eastern provinces.

Tiberius Alexander, when he learned that Agathon was to participate in the delegation, sent a brief message: "Caesar is mad, and even Rome will not tolerate him for long. Therefore, do as the Romans: humor him." Agathon shared the message with Philo and prepared himself to go as far as necessary in placating the emperor with divine adjectives. But Philo cautioned him, for they had come as representatives of the entire Jewish community. "Humoring folly," said Philo, "ofttimes encourages it." And if their audience did not go well, not only were the Jews of Alex-andria in dire straits, but all the Jews within the empire. The Jews of Judaea would never allow a statue of Caligula in the temple, and Jew haters across the empire would take the emperor's example to force Jews into idolatry. At stake, Philo whispered, was the very survival of the Jewish way of life. The phrase he used was "the catholic polity of the Jews," that bound them together across the empire.[17]

Augustus had built the residence farther from the bustle of the city which had been constantly in a state of repair and reconstruction. His well-known boast, "I found Rome of clay, I leave it to you of marble," was not altogether untrue.[18] But Augustus had been something of a stoic, certainly frugal, and Caligula could not enjoy existing villas until he refurbished them to his more extravagant tastes. Agathon saw the emperor at the far side of the room, surrounded by his architects, with the Greek delegates off to one side, enraptured by every suggestion he made. The emperor was very tall, pale, and wan-colored, his body shapeless beneath royal robes, out of which rose his exceedingly slender neck. Caligula's eyes sunk in his head. His temples, too, were sunken, of the classic hollow sort, flanking a broad forehead with deep furrows. The hair of his head grew thin, and his crown was all bald; but his arms and hands were hairy.[19] The Jews approached to within a respectful dis-tance and stopped. Caligula continued his survey, sizing up a wall, sug-gesting a minor change. Then looking at the nodding heads of his audience, he changed his mind and watched them nod more vigorously.

Finally he turned to the Jewish delegates. He scowled and said: "Are you then, the god-haters who do not believe me to be a god; I who am already confessed to be a god by every other nation but am refused that appellation by you." Then he stretched out his shaggy hands toward heaven and bellowed, "I am God, Eyaoo! Eyaaaooo!"[20] And thinking that he had uttered the unspeakable Divine Name, as indeed he had attempted, the Greek delegates burst into raucous laughter; they gesticulated mock adoration and they danced about, invoking the names of all the gods in blessing the emperor's wit, for it becomes one god to jibe another.

Agathon began to smile, for the scene was so comical in its puerility that he found himself indulging them as one smiles at the silliness of children's defecation jokes, but he saw that Philo's face had grown white, and so he too grew solemn. He reasoned that perhaps Philo knew better what sort of response would please the emperor. As Caligula intended to offend by his sacrilege, offended they should be and should not disappoint him with anything less than abject mortification.

When the jocularity began to subside, Agathon said: "Lord Gaius, as we know, the philosophers have long noted the fine distinction between the human and divine. Certainly your grandfather, the most noble Augustus, was in all respects divine in his rule, imitating God, god-like, we may say, and is held in the greatest esteem by the million Jews in Alexandria and, indeed, by every Jewish subject of Caesar in the empire. And you also, Caesar, are loved by all Jews who look to you for protection against their foes. As the saying goes: 'What is a god? The exercise of power. What is a king? God-like.'"[21]

Caligula pursed his lips and raised his eyebrows, apparently pleased with so adroit a response. That impression, at least, worried the Greeks, and Isidorus immediately blurted out, "Master, with yet greater vehemence you will hate these men whom you see before you and their fellow countrymen, once you are acquainted with their disaffection and disloyalty toward yourself; for when all other men were offering up sacrifices of thanksgiving for your safety, these men alone refused to offer any sacrifice at all." He sniffed, "And when I say, 'these men,' I refer to all Jews."

Immediately the Jewish delegates voiced their outrage at such an accusation. Said Agathon, "Lord Gaius, we are slandered; for we did indeed sacrifice! We offered up entire hecatombs, the blood of which we poured in a libation upon the altar; nor did we carry the flesh to our homes to feast and banquet upon, as it is the custom of some people to do, but we committed the victims entire to the sacred flame as a burnt offering."

Philo added somberly, "And this we have done three times already at our temple in Jerusalem, and not once only; on the first occasion when you succeeded to the empire, and the second time when you recovered from that terrible disease with which all the habitable world was afflicted at the same time, and the third time we sacrificed in hope of your victory over the Germans."

The emperor appeared to be touched by their proclamation of loyalty and gratitude. But after a moment of such affectation he replied, "Grant, that all this is true and that you did sacrifice; nevertheless you sacrificed to another god, even if it was *for* me. What good is that to me? For you have not sacrificed *to* me."[22]

The Jews stood mute. What could they do? Every law in the books of Moses was negotiable or might be broken in order to save a life, except the one law that gave meaning to the very essence of being a Jew: *Thou shalt have no other gods before me.* That law stood stiffly beyond the twist of allegory. Caesar might as well kill them all. But Caligula left them in their speechless consternation and resumed his survey of the villa chambers, and all the Greeks followed boisterously in his train. "Tsk, tsk," he clucked, pointing to a small chamber, "have this wall torn down, and enlarge the two chambers as one, with pedestals in each corner and far more elaborate decor." On he went from room to room redesigning the villa.

As they had not been dismissed, though all hope seemed to have vanished, Philo led his delegation behind the Greeks. They continued to weather the taunts and barbs of the Greeks, making no response, until suddenly Caligula stopped, came to Philo, and asked, "And why do you refuse to eat swine's flesh?" The question was scarcely out of his mouth when he began to drool and chuckle uncontrollably. The Greeks laughed and held their sides, as if enjoying a comedy of Sophocles, and they clapped in spontaneous applause at the wit of the leading rôle.

Agathon stepped forward to make answer in humorous form, for indeed, the entire affair was becoming a farce, but Philo held him back with a hand and responded. "My Lord, different nations have different laws, and there are some things which are forbidden both to us and to our adversaries."

One of the Greeks, Apion, then said, "There are also many people who do not eat lamb's flesh which is the most tender of all meat."

Caligula laughed, "Quite right too, for it is not nice."

The foolery resumed, but Agathon was not yet ready to concede rhetorical advantage to the Greeks or Caesar. It was evident that the stature of Philo held no sway in these halls, and despite his learning and eloquence, in the arena of comedy, Philo was destitute. Therefore, against the elder's constraint, Agathon said, "Our abstention from pork is a symbol of temperance, and against gluttony; that is, eating like a pig or an Egyptian. All our customs, Caesar, are symbols of piety, and our opponents here have quite forgotten, it seems, that many of their esteemed philosophers, from Pythagoras to Plato, have borrowed from the customs of the Jews. Even the priests of the Egyptians are circumcised and abstain from swine."[23]

"So I have heard," replied Caligula as he began walking off. Then he abruptly turned around. The Greeks parted between him and the Jews.

"Very well," said Caligula, wagging his head like a mother over her child's spilt porridge. "It is our desire to hear what claims of justice you make about your citizenship in Alexandria."

Philo bowed his head, as if they had only just come before the emperor and had been received with the respect due a delegation from the provinces. "My Emperor," he began, "your Jewish subjects in Alexandria have long sworn allegiance to Caesar and have lived in peace under the benefactions of Caesar. As your lordship knows, Julius Caesar established our charter in Alexandria, and your grandfather Augustus Caesar renewed it."

Caligula began to show ennui, or more likely an aggravation at being reminded of the nobility of his ancestors.

Apion took the opportunity to interfere. "If the Jews be citizens of Alexandria, why do they not worship the same gods with the Alexandrians?"

Philo's shoulders sank wearily, for he thought they had dispensed with the theology.

Immediately Agathon responded. "And should we join in the riots you Egyptians have over your differing gods? Jews are forbidden by our ancient laws to worship any god other than he with whom our fathers entered into a covenant of the most sacred nature. Out of respect for our ancestors, we are not at liberty to break with this covenant. Our God is a jealous god."

"But, how can this be?" asked Apion. "The ass is not known for its jealousy."

"That Jews worship the head of an ass is an old wive's tale which passes for truth among those who deal in old wive's tales as truths.[24] But even if Jews did worship the ass, wherein do Egyptians reproach us? The ass is a more noble animal than the cat, he-goat, ibis, crocodiles, and other strange animals such as one rarely sees that are worshiped by Egyptians. Yet, Jews are commanded not to revile the gods of other nations, on account of the very name God ascribed to them, so I shall say no more."[25]

"All the world knows," said Apion, "that Jews were once themselves Egyptians, but because they were lame and blind and diseased by a plague of tumors on their groins, they were expelled from Egypt."[26]

"All the world knows what Apion wishes it to believe of his fabrications. But the records show that the Jews were given their quarter of the city by its founder King Alexander, and ruled alongside the Macedonians. I, like my fathers before me, even to the tenth generation, was born in the city of Alexandria, whereas Apion, who imagines himself among the elite of the city, a veritable descendant of the Macedonians, was born in Oasis, in the very heart of Egypt. The forgeries of fools are not to be confuted by words but by facts."

"Do you take me, then, for a fool?"

"That I cannot say, my dear Apion. You ask of me the impossible, for if I say no, then I shall have to explain you to myself. Pray, ask something within my power of reason."

Caligula laughed, and Apion struggled to stifle his anger, whereupon, Philo continued with utmost economy, "The Alexandrian Jews consider Egypt to be their fatherland, even as the Jews in Europe and Asia and on the islands esteem the lands in which they are born and reared to be their homelands."

"But what claims are you making now?" asked Caligula, hands still on his hips.

"Caesar, the first injustice committed by our accusers against their Jewish fellow-citizens was the desecration of our synagogues, thereby depriving us of the means by which we reverence our master, for in our synagogues we pay homage by our prayers for you."

Caligula tossed his head and began to survey the room in which they stood. Philo pressed on. "When our meeting houses were thus destroyed, they attempted to deprive us of our citizenship, denouncing us as foreigners and aliens, without right to plead our case before the law of the empire. Thereafter, they incited the base Egyptian mobs to drive us out of our homes in the five quarters and take refuge all in a single section of the city, and then ransacked the properties, thus depriving us of our livelihood, by which we support the empire. And many families were put to the sword or burned to death by those who show no mercy to women and children or respect for old age."

"What was that again?" Caligula called from where he had gone in his preoccupation of the survey. "What were you saying?"

Philo began again, word for word, and moved on to the fourth injustice. "Not only were many of our senators deprived of their property, but thirty-eight were arrested and publically paraded in shackles through the market. But even here, the greatest disgrace came when they were arrayed in the theater and flogged, and not with the wood blades as their rank requires, even if they were guilty of some offense, which they were not, but they were scourged as are the debased Egyptians, and many expired as a consequence of the flogging." Philo might have saved himself the trouble, for Caligula had rushed off to the next room of the villa, and by the time the Jewish delegates caught up with him, he was measuring the windows with his arms outstretched.

"See here," Caligula said to his master architect, "have these windows restored with that transparent slate."

The architect replied, "Caesar, *lapis specularis* cannot be cut to a height greater than five feet and still maintain the thinness required for transparency. We shall have to fashion panes for so large an opening."[27]

"You shall make it transparent and one piece," the emperor commanded. "Things not possible are quite the norm in the mansions of the gods." Then he walked leisurely toward the Jews. "You were saying?"

Unperturbed, Philo picked up the thread of his argument. "These brutalities occurred, Lord Caesar, at the very time when we might have performed the notable celebrations in honor of the birthdays of the Augustan house. . . ." And off flew Caligula to yet another room, where he ordered original paintings to be installed.

By now it had become apparent that—and we may suppose even to Caligula—the laws of Rome had been breeched, and the case of the Jews against their accusers, chiefly Isidorus and Apion, was justified. Therefore, the emperor, determined to spare himself any further embarrassment, gave his verdict. In words dripping with benevolent pity, he said to the Greeks, "These men do not appear to be wicked so much as unfortunate and foolish in not believing that I have been endowed with the nature of a god." And so saying, he dismissed the Jews, and bade them be gone.

Philo, Agathon, and the entire delegation bowed to the absent emperor, who had already turned his back upon them and returned to his survey. The Jewish delegation departed the villa with as much dignity as they could summon in their minds upon this blatant humiliation. Said Agathon, "We have been to the throne room, but the throne is empty."

Said another, "Disaster has been diverted, but the battle is not yet won."

"We shall simply have to outlive him," replied Agathon.

Philo nodded sadly. "Such a cruel irony that the fate of all Jews should rest precariously on us five envoys. Now, we must await judgment from Providence."

And so they made arrangements to return to Alexandria.

Petronius proceeded haltingly, insisting that the statue be perfectly gilded and without a blemish whatsoever. But in due course the artisans completed the statue in all its perfection. War and slaughter could no longer be delayed. Petronius decided that he would forfeit his own life, for if he slaughtered the Jews, would not the god of the Jews require their blood of his hands, as had occurred with Flaccus? He was not a superstitious man, but he believed there was such a thing as ultimate justice, and if not, at least the ultimate good of the empire. Petronius wrote a second letter asking the emperor to rescind the decree. The Jews showered him with praise and promised to pray for his welfare.

Meanwhile, King Agrippa, a favorite of Gaius, had come to Rome and appealed to the emperor not to erect the statue, for if he did, Agrippa, his loyal servant, would have no kingdom to oversee, and no tribute to give. Perhaps because he loved to shower his friends with great gifts, or perhaps a moment of sanity came upon him, Gaius agreed to the request of Agrippa and dispatched a letter to Petronius saying that, if the statue were already in place, leave it, but if not, he should abandon the project and return to Antioch.

Shortly after Gaius had sent his directive to Petronius, he received the letter of Petronius asking him to reverse his order concerning the statue. Gaius flew into a rage, and sent another missive instructing Petronius to commit suicide for having challenged his orders. But the messengers were delayed by the winter weather, and on the twenty-fourth of January, at long last, Gaius Julius Caesar Germanicus was assassinated. Word of the death of the emperor reached Petronius early in March. The missive of Caesar commanding him commit suicide arrived in April.[28]

Petronius smiled wryly at the twists of fortune and the pace of messengers. The Jews in Judaea, and indeed across the empire, offered up prayers of gratitude to the Most High. Again, God had delivered his people. Again the haughty were brought low and the humble uplifted, proof to all the earth of divine Providence.

# 13

## Persuasion

Being then God's offspring, we ought not to think that the Deity is like gold, or silver, or stone, a representation by the art and imagination of man. The times of ignorance God overlooked, but now he commands all men everywhere to repent, because he has fixed a day on which he will judge the world in righteousness by a man whom he has appointed, and of this he has given assurance to all men by raising him from the dead.

Paul of Tarsus

From the exile on we were instructed to be obedient carriers of tradition, but when once we picked up the sword of Greek logic, when we had felt the grip and run our thumb along its blade, many of us silently swore never to lay it down. It is by reason, *logos,* that the war of ideas is waged. Polemic, after all, comes from the Greek *polemos,* war. Hellenism had conquered us, but just as our ancestors set aside their bronze weapons and took up the superior iron weapons of the Philistines, so we took up the argumentation of the Greek mind and made it our own.

We began by arguing that, since Moses lived five hundred years before Homer and the more so before Thales or Pythagorus, Socrates or Plato, Judaism is the source of all knowledge; thus Greek wisdom must come from Moses. Demetrius of Alexandria, Eupolemus, and Artapanus recounted the fame of Moses and Solomon for all Greeks to read, and Aristobulus assures us of the impact of Moses upon the Greek philosophers.[1] Others, such as Qohelet and Ben Sira, gave Greek currency to Jewish wisdom, and Aristeas praised the kingship of Ptolemy because the king praised the wisdom of Jewish sages and the rule of God.[2] Philo deftly wielded his *logos* and *logia* and made converts of many Gentiles and not a few Jews to his way of thinking, among them Josephus, who harbors ambitions for yet another treatise or two on the wisdom of the Jews. Other Jews, such as Paul of Tarsus, have done well, though were less rewarded by fame, but the argument of one god over all the universe, the sheer beauty of divine linear thought, has become the *cause célèbre* of the Jews, even as we skirmish endlessly amongst ourselves on how to retain that which is distinctively Jewish on God's most singular earth. By persuasion toward Divine Reason, this Logos, we Jews will wield the sword and God will conquer.

Demetrius plunged himself up to his neck in the small *frigidarium* pool, rose, flexed his muscles, and plunged again. After several repetitions, he stepped out like a god from the sea, walked naked and dripping through a small archway and across the marble floor to the *tepidarium*. His athletic body was entirely clean shaven, save for a small patch of pubic hair, the symbolic separation between men and boys, and he kept the hair of his head cut short and curled in the style favored by the classic sculptors. With a sigh of contentment, "Ahh . . . ," he slid into the tepid water of a large rectangular tiled bath. Two nude women, professional courtesans in the employ of Probus, lounged, slightly submerged, on the pool steps nearby. They smiled at him. He gazed momentarily at their hair and breasts—one of dark complexion beautifully sculpted, the other reddish blond with inviting pink breasts—and spreading his arms up like wings behind him at the pool's edge, he smiled in return, closed his eyes, and slid further into the water to ponder the choice of which beauty he might enjoy first. Such were the dilemmas presented by Probus, a wealthy Roman who fled Rome to escape Caligula and chose Athens for his retirement. For years Probus had provided the Emperor Tiberius with a variety of lecherous pleasures, until Tiberius grew weak with disease, and his adopted son, Caligula, unable to wait on the disease, suffocated him. Probus joined the emigration from Italy, lest, for the reaping of his estate, Caligula accuse him of some crime against Rome. Probus might have returned to Italy after Caligula's assassination, but he enjoyed his life in Athens.

Probus gave extravagant dinners three or four times a year, and it was the goal of every class-conscious sophist in Athens to attend one such orgiastic adventure in his lifetime. For Demetrius, it was now his third invitation since he had come to the notice of the rich Roman. Demetrius sought out different patrons for his different goals. Probus, for example, took delight in surrounding himself with clever men or men who sounded clever and were able to confound his guests with their rhetoric.

The reputation of sophistry was far too undervalued in the academy. His apartment came from Probus. But to be taken seriously in the stoas, one needed mentors. Dionysius the Areopagite, though a Platonist with Stoic sympathies, had taken him under his wing, and provided him with the occasional forum from which he gathered his own pupils willing to pay a tutor. Dionysius carried on the tradition of the ancient Athenian elite, to support the university both in grants for the libraries and stipends for teachers and pupils alike.

Demetrius had already come far from his humble roots in Crete. As a gifted youth, he became a lover of philosophy and migrated to the center of all philosophy, Athens. He soon learned that "lover of philosophy" was redundant, since philosophy was to be a lover of wisdom, and to be a lover of a lover of wisdom was redundancy or pederasty, or in his case, both. He found that wisdom had long since been assessed, sifted, evaluated, and catalogued, from Socrates and Plato to Aristotle then Epicurus and Zeno.[3] A few significant philosophers came before them, a few after, but none so enduring. Nothing remained but to repeat their positions in different words, or pick and choose portions of each to one's own liking and ridicule what remained. Men might continue to gather knowledge, but wisdom can only be refashioned into hybrid monsters.

Admiring the wit of Diogenes the dog, the Cynic, Demetrius became cynical, but he had not the stamina for the poverty of a true Cynic.[4] He leaned toward the *tetrapharmakos* of Epicurus, his fourfold cure: there is nothing to fear from the gods; there is nothing to feel in death; good is readily attained; evil may be readily endured.[5] In short, do not deny the existence of the gods, do not trouble yourself over them, they care not, neither should you; rather, seek the good for yourself—seek pleasure, which is the absence of sorrow, pain, and fear. If there were anything to be added to the meaning of life, it was simply an expansion of the concept of pleasure. Demetrius thought Epicurus's absence of sorrow and pain too restrictive, emanating from the climes of a sober and archaic era; rather, pleasure ought to be the amassing of enjoyment, and to this there was no theoretical limit. Such a verdict gave one an impossible goal, and an impossible goal was a perfect goal. Spin your cobwebs of rhetoric, he concluded, and enjoy all that the web entraps.

Demetrius felt movement and the disturbing of the waters. He opened his eyes, half expecting to see the immaculate bosoms of one or both of the women drooping above his eyelids. But he was disappointed, as life often disappoints, to see only the buttocks of his friend Lucian descend into the pool. Lucian was shorter than Demetrius by a hand, and far more subdued.

"Disturb not yourself," said Lucian. "I divine that you linger at the precipice of pleasure, and I would not prevent you from plunging in."

"Lucian, you ass," Demetrius laughed, "why did you not tell me you were a guest of our benefactor Probus."

"Last we spoke, I was not," said Lucian, as he settled in beside Demetrius. "It seems that one of the guests became indisposed, and I moved up a rung on the ladder. Though I am neither accustomed to, nor comfortable in, such opulence, I cannot let pass a free bath and food."

"I've mentioned your name on more than one occasion."

"There. The gods in their benevolence again reward importunity."

"The gods care not, Lucian. The sooner you learn the truth of it, the faster you'll climb the ladder."

Lucian closed his eyes and together they lay still for some minutes. Demetrius watched the gathering crowd of bathers, all invited to the evening feast and festivity. As the male guests arrived, the hired women too, multiplied in their scant wraps or unwrapped, much as the appetizers at any fine banquet, such as dainty pastries, oysters, and long-legged grasshoppers.

"Speaking of the gods," said Lucian, "I chanced upon an orator in the market place today, a Jew from Tarsus in Cicilia."

"Dark, bearded, and intense?" Demetrius queried.

"Even so."

"Caustic?"

"Yes, a tendency toward."

"Hmm, as they invariably are."

"But no more caustic than any Cynic worth his rags."

"Is he competition for our own crowds, then?"

"For you, Demetrius? Not a bit of it. His Greek, though rhetorically effective, is stylistically unimaginative."

"Permit me to hazard a guess," said Demetrius. "He expounded on the god of the Jews, the lord of the cosmos, to whit, all Greeks ought to bow down and in due course denude our privy members and abstain from pork. So far so good?"

Lucian opened his eyes and turned toward Demetrius. "Except that he said nothing of circumcision or other quaint customs of the Jews."

"Of course not. First, feast and flowers, then famine and scourge."

"Perhaps. He did not strike me as your typical provincial Jew; rather, he argued something new out of Judaea, as he appeared to be preaching the virtues of some foreign gods."

"Speaking in the market, introducing new gods? Surely he mimics Socrates. Which gods?"

"One called Jesus, another, Anastasia."

"Foreign indeed."

"But when a few of the council members chanced upon him—Paul, he is called—they insisted that he come up to the Areopagus and expound on his views."

"Did they, indeed?" asked Demetrius. He shifted himself upward, somewhat.

"And as I had no pressing engagement, I followed them."

"Very well, Lucian, you have aroused my curiosity. Summarize his position, if you can."

"He began as follows," said Lucian, and he cleared his throat rhetorically. "Men of Athens, I perceive that you are cautiously pious. . . ."[6]

"Ingratiating, but clever. Did he then wipe the irony drooling from his lips?"

"He seemed impressed, actually, with the many temples, particularly the Parthenon."

"A well-heeled tourist. But for some reason, most Jews are unable to distinguish between art and idols, between aesthetics and worship."

"He referred specifically to the old altars with defaced inscriptions, and unnamed foreign gods, and announced he would enlighten us on the great unknown creator god."[7]

"The god of the Jews, though imageless and nameless, is scarcely unknown, as can be verified when passing by beggars on the street, or any of their numerous synagogues."

"Well, his position does not seem oppressively Jewish. He took his starting point not from the sacred writings of the Jews but the poets."

Demetrius yawned and reclined back into the water until it lapped at his chin. "A babbler, then. Whom did he quote?"

"I recognized only Aratus, when he quoted a few lines of *Phaenomena:*[8]

> Never O men, let us leave him unmentioned,
> all ways are full of Zeus and all meeting-places of men;
> the sea and the harbors are full of him.
> In every direction we all have to do with Zeus;
> for we are also his offspring."

"Then his unknown god is Zeus? Really, Lucian, are you not slightly abashed? Equating the Jewish god with Zeus is hardly novel."[9]

"His point, Demetrius, was that all enlightened men from ages past know they have a creator and come in some ill-defined way from the creator god. Only we Greeks have since then got things confused and corrupted."

"A favorite tactic of the Jews, my friend. They are certain our ancestors, even Plato, borrowed from their philosophers, one called Moses

foremost. Did he not mention Moses? You would not believe their au-
dacity." Demetrius suddenly grinned and raised his head. "Macro!" he
shouted to a man approaching the pool, "deadly weapons must be left
outside the gate, sheath and all." A number of men laughed, both at the
jest of Demetrius, and the fact that the man's name was not Macro, but
Menelaos. Certain women stared wide-eyed at the sight of the leather
sheath, retained by a thong around his waist, covering the man's privy
member.

"By the gods," said Lucian, "does he carry his wallet in that sheath
as well?"

Demetrius lowered his voice, "It is he and only he, I assure you. I
used to think he wore his loin sheath out of discomfiture, but one day
while playing ball in the courtyard, his covering fell off. The poor man is
circumcised!"

"A Jew?!" asked Lucian.

"A medical necessity I am told."[10] Demetrius sank beneath the water
and emerged, wiping the droplets from his face. "Anyway, you were citing the poets this orator quoted."

"I did not recognize the other lines, something about 'in you we live
and move and are'."

Demetrius frowned. "An excerpt of Epimenides, perhaps. 'They
fashioned a tomb for thee, O holy and high one—the Cretans, always
liars, evil beasts, idle bellies! But thou art not dead; thou livest and
abidest forever; for in thee we live and move and have our being.'[11] It is
all very well, I suppose, to quote a Cretan who castigates Cretans. But
again, this refers to Zeus, even Zeus Cnossos—hardly suitable to you
Stoics. And, my dear Lucian, I yet await the novelty."

"Well, having argued that all men should recognize their creator, but
also that we are his offspring, it follows that images of any sort cannot do
justice to the creator, since they point only to that which is created. Indeed, a living god can only be represented by a living being, the highest
of which is mankind."

"Then we are all gods."

"That point was made. Paul replied that he scarcely thought himself
a god, nor did he suppose any of us were, but that we may all live our
lives in a god-like manner, thereby worshiping through our lives the creator of life."

Demetrius frowned in contemplation. "I see your attraction. The
man trumpets a Stoic position somewhat. But again, wherein is the
novelty?"

"Just here, Demetrius. Although in times past, this god has overlooked our ignorance of his requirements, now he commands all men

everywhere to repent, because he has fixed a day on which he will judge the world in righteousness by a man whom he has appointed."

"Judgment? And by what man?"

Lucian pursed his lips and whispered: "By a Jew called Jesus, crucified some twenty years ago, whom, he claims, this god raised up from the dead."

Demetrius looked into Lucian's eyes and wrinkled his brow in disbelief. "You really are joking now, aren't you? Pray, admit it, Lucian."

"You asked," replied Lucian, stifling his laughter. "I do not recall all he said, but I am quite sure of the essentials. He thought it obvious that repentance is the natural response to the recognition of, and belief in, this god—the reward of which will be a bodily resurrection from the dead to eternal life."

"Resurrection? *Anastasia, anastasis.* Hah! Very good! Clever indeed, not a goddess at all, rather an impossibility. And with that they laughed him off Mars' Hill?"[12]

"Actually," said Lucian, "your Epicurean colleagues did ridicule, whereas many of the Stoics wish to hear more of it. Among them myself, and, if you can believe it, Dionysius."

"By Zeus! I am shocked and dismayed. Still, if so noble a patron as Dionysius showed interest, then I must feign interest too. But another time, dear Lucian. Tonight I shall be concerned not with resurrection, but erection and re-erection." He winked. "So will you."

The invited guests bathed in the private bath complex of Probus which though small, was complete and lavish. The *frigidarium* contained three plunge pools; as many as eight could enter the steaming *caldarium,* and the *tepidarium* would admit twice that, so the guests, all men of some repute, numbering twenty, plus the professional courtesans, reveled in luxury without uncomfortable crowding. A handful of slaves, male and female, stood by with towels, perfumes, and ointments. Demetrius and Lucian took turns on a marble massage table, as a Libyan slave rubbed them with oil and scraped it away with a bronze strigil.

At the appointed hour, when the sun's shadow had grown ten or eleven feet long, a bell sounded, alerting them to the feast at hand. They converged on a rectangular courtyard, sheltered round the perimeter by walls and a burnt clay tiled roof, but with a large open space in the center. The central floor beneath the open roof was lower by a half-step. Presently the space contained two large brasiers, over which cooks prepared a variety of seafood. Around the walls lay a host of ornately carved couches, light and slender, in the classical style, yet able to hold two individuals in a variety of positions. Near each couch stood low portable tables, large round bronze trays, each set on a tripod. Cups were already set, along with plates of finger foods and pastries, including roast grasshoppers, a delicacy long cherished in Greece. At the center of each table lay a wreath filled with aromatic herbs.

Demetrius and Lucian, rubbed and scented and clothed in their best tunics, walked round the hall to the end opposite the head couch of Probus, for although trained in noble airs, being neither Athenian nor Roman, they knew better than to presume, and took the position of least among the guests, as the others made their way to the couches, and the ladies in waiting took their places on small stools, or they reclined on the couches. Demetrius encouraged the two women who first smiled at him, Damaris and Daphne, each now seductively dressed in a loose and flowing robe, to join them. The names of the women were, of course, professional names, stage props in the art of their performance. Demetrius guessed that "Daphne," the reddish blond with fair skin and full pink breasts, was born of Germanic descent. Damaris, on the other hand, the dark one, had a Syrian air about her, with some Egyptian blood perhaps. Both young women were trained as high-bred courtesans, but each sought an opportunity for marriage and escape from this elite form of prostitution. As Demetrius took Daphne to his couch, Damaris stayed near Lucian, and all seemed pleased with the arrangement.

Probus soon entered to the applause of all, and reclined his bloated frame. A wig covered his bald head, which nicely accented a pocked nose and a small crooked mouth—all in all the picture of decrepit aristocracy and immoderate living, though wealth made him appear as a philosopher king to his retinue. He welcomed them, recounted briefly his family history replete with anecdotes of famous orgies in Italy, then introduced the entertainment, musicians, and jugglers, and bade them enjoy the feast: first the *deipnon,* the banquet proper, with foods of every sort; thereafter the *symposion,* comprised of wine and words, in all their myriad combinations, and of course, women, in all their delectable delights. "Gentlemen, pace yourselves," Probus warned, "lest in the end you fail and disappoint the ladies."

With that, the music began, harp, drum, and flute, including an accomplished musician on the *syrinx,* the pan-pipes. Soon the servants brought in trays piled high with food. They came, wave upon wave, and deposited the overspilling dishes onto the tables of each guest. The feast began with greens and pulses, asparagus, cheeses, raw oysters, olives, and fine wheat loaves. The cups were filled, but lightly, one part wine to three parts water, for at this stage, liquids were meant only to help the digestion. After the first course had been sampled, servants brought in fresh bread and distributed a dazzling array of seafood hot from the brassier: sole, red mullet, sea urchin, cuttlefish, perch, tunny, and eel, all heavily garnished with sesame seeds, mashed raisins, fennel, anise, mustard, cumin, capers, marjoram, hartwort, rue, leek, vinegar, fig-leaves, olive oil, almonds, onions, shallots, salt, and eggs. The fish were arranged on large circular platters with a central reservoir of savory sauce. Lucian, eyes wide, made a point of identifying each succulent seafood and garnish.

"Hush," Demetrius whispered, "lest they think you've never dined before."

For an hour they feasted, the women more daintily than the men. A few household dogs lay strategically around the hall awaiting morsels of meat and bread that fell from the tables. In the end, the dogs were as sated as the guests, for according to Greek custom, one wiped one's fingers with bread and tossed it to the dogs.

Darkness descended and the lamps were lit; one double wicked terracotta lamp to each table, and numerous lamps with eight wicks hung from the walls to illuminate the entire hall. The third course entered: ham in sweet mustard, roast duck, and peacock, surrounded by an assortment of dried fruit. They picked at the peacock and feigned appetite. Finally the feast drew to a close. The platters of uneaten food were cleared away, and small dishes of nuts and pastries replaced them. The slaves brought in water to wash the hands of the guests, along with drinking bowls. The wine steward led five slaves into the hall, each carrying an amphora of different wines. In a loud and authoritative voice, the steward described the wines: Rhodian, Cyprian, a Falarian, and several local varieties, all with their vintage years. One was twenty-seven years old. When the selections had been made and the cups filled, the host declared: "Let the *symposion* begin." Guests rose to the challenge: riddles were posed, songs were sung, and some men allowed themselves to be dragged from their couches to dance. Wine flowed.

Lucian moaned, "The days of the abstemious *symposion* have gone the way of Socrates."

"Moderation in all things, including moderation," Demetrius chided. "How shall we know the moderate if we do not indulge from time to time in excess by way of contrast?"

"As always, you have a way out, or in, depending on your destination."

"Besides, we could not possibly afford to indulge ourselves at our own expense, therefore, we must indulge at other's expense at every opportunity. How does the saying go . . . one bowl for health, two for love and pleasure . . . ?"

"Three for sleep," said Lucian, "and then the sensible man goes home."

"Yes, yes, but how many for carousing?"

"Six."

"Six it is," he laughed and quaffed a long swallow.[13] He offered Daphne the rest, delighting in the red droplets that ran from the corners of her mouth down her neck to her breasts.

With their appetites sated, and wits abated, the attention of the guests departed their stomachs and descended to places somewhat lower in the anatomy. Demetrius had begun kissing and caressing Daphne, and she let her robe slip down to her waist, offering him her bounty and more. Damaris awaited some overture from Lucian, but he seemed content to feast his eyes on the exquisite beauty beneath her robe, which she had dutifully opened to her waist. Lucian offered his wine bowl to her and, by way of contrast to his companion, began quoting philosophers on the virtues of simplicity and moderation. Damaris gave the appearance of treasuring Lucian's every word as wisdom. Her pay was the same, whether she spent the evening beside a Stoic or beneath an Epicurean, and because she had some education, she appreciated that Lucian conversed with her as an intelligent being and not simply a brothel girl.

"That's the value of moderation, you see," said Lucian, "that it allows desire a longer reign, and I have always found the desiring every bit as enjoyable as the having." He smiled, "What say you?"

Damaris arched her brows. "True," she replied, "a meal is more enjoyable while you still have appetite."

"So with wine," said Lucian, casting a disparaging glance at Demetrius, "moderation is the key."

"So with sex," replied Damaris, mimicking his glance.

"Ah, yes, well," Lucian stumbled, "I presume you speak of pace."

Damaris laughed and blushed somewhat, in her amber hue. "I speak wantonly, without wisdom or forethought, only to please you. Take nothing I say seriously."

Lucian smiled, "But you do please me, and I should rather like to take you seriously. Philos, after all, is a union of the mind, whereas Eros is a union of a different sort. What wisdom of the poets can you share?"

"A line from *Ajax*," Damaris said. "A woman should be seen, not heard."

"You've read Sophocles?" asked Lucian in surprise.

"No," she smiled, and shrugged slightly. "A man once told me that was the wisest thing Sophocles ever wrote."

"It is merely a well-worn phrase Sophocles quoted."[14]

As the evening wore on, the naturally uninhibited guests around the hall began the gymnastics of coupling in every conceivable combination, on the couches or on the floor. Probus sat watching, his reward for all the expense.

For this, Lucian found himself entirely unprepared. He said to Demetrius, "When may one depart without offending our host?"

"Depart? Just as the sweet meats are served?"

"I think it an opportune moment to escape. Orgasm is one thing, an orgiastic circus quite another, and it is impossible for me to perform amid all this commotion."

Daphne then sided with Lucian. "If we remain, I shall be fair game for anyone," she murmured, writhing seductively, "and I would devote myself to you alone, for as long as you can endure it."

"Ah, well that is a different argument altogether," Demetrius replied.

Damaris smiled and said, "If you explain Lucian's predicament to Probus, I am sure he will grant us to you for the night."

Lucian admonished him, "And we had best go quickly, while you can still walk."

They watched Demetrius push himself up from the couch and go to the master of the feast. Probus, without taking his eyes off the spectacle smiled, nodded, and waved Demetrius away. So the four departed the villa and each couple took a separate path, for Lucian dwelt farther down the hill than Demetrius.

"I will call on you tomorrow," said Lucian. "I should like you to hear the Jew yourself."

"Yes, yes—not too early though," Demetrius saluted farewell. "We'll untangle this resurrection affair. Now go do your duty, stout fellow."

Demetrius took Daphne by the hand and led her down the streets to his room in a long row of small stone-built apartments. Behind the pinewood door, he succumbed to Daphne's charms—as a starving man succumbs to a loaf of bread—and threw himself into his twisted Epicureanism with abandon, the description of which may be left unspoken; for although the definition of debauchery changes from generation to generation, the details remain the same, and are too well known to arouse the curiosity of a cultured audience. Suffice to say that if one stood outside the window, one would hear a good deal of wine-sodden gibberish: "Dearest treasure, I am burning to yield myself to voluptuous sport, lying on your bosom, to let my hands play with your thighs. Aphrodite, why do you fire me with such delight in her? Oh! Eros, I beseech thee, have mercy. Oh! my adored one, I adjure you, open for me your gate of desire. Oh! my jewel, my idol, you child of Aphrodite,

the confidante of the Muses, the sister of the Graces, you living picture of erotica, oh! open for me. . . ."[15] Surely even Demetrius would
have thought it embarrassing babble had he been competent to stand
outside the window and listen. His only defense would be that it is poetic and semi-learned, not the mere panting and grunting of a peasant or
he-goat.

Thus the night passed, methodically and at its usual pace, while the
passions of humanity ebbed and flowed throughout Athens.

"Demetrius, Demetrius, wake up!" Demetrius awoke on the floor,
on his face. But had not Aristotle, among his many catalogues, determined the science of drink: with wine you fell on your face, with beer
you fell on your back.[16] His nymph Daphne lay on the bed, unclothed
and yet inviting, but spent he was and very thirsty. He heard his name
again: "Demetrius, Demetrius, wake up!" Demetrius staggered naked to
the door and opened it. There stood Lucian and behind him, Damaris.
Demetrius beckoned them in, then he staggered to a wash basin, poured
water from a pitcher, plunged his face in the basin and drank deeply. For
decorum's sake, he splashed what remained on his face.

"I thought," said Lucian, "that you might like to listen to Paul of Tarsus with your own ears. It is the seventh hour." He added slowly, "If you
can hear me, signal with your hand." Demetrius waved away Lucian's
impertinence and drank again straight from the pitcher. "Good," cajoled
Lucian, "now if your legs and remaining senses hold, perhaps we can arrive at the agora in time to hear him."

Daphne awoke, and seeing the faces, she moaned and pulled the
linen sheet over her face. Damaris laughed and went over to help
Daphne hide herself.

At length Demetrius regained his clarity and natural wit. "Where is
my tunic?" he asked. Lucian searched about and handed it to him. He
put it on. "To the agora, then, but let us take the scenic route, while the
exercise and fresh air revive me."

"Damaris comes with us," said Lucian. "She is quite interested in
this new philosophy."

Demetrius shook his head. "You discussed it half the night, I'll be
bound."

Lucian smiled. "Very nearly, among other things. There is, after all, a
certain attraction to living forever."

"The Elysian Fields, Lucian? The Isles of the Blest, or the merging of your divine spark back into the Divine Fire?"[17]

"The Jewish version of Elysian Fields, I think. I have discussed it with Jews before, something to do with the end of the world, rather than the ends of the earth. Only they said nothing about flocks of Gentiles entering at will."

Damaris said, "Daphne will also come, only give her time to prepare herself."

"And why not?" Demetrius responded. "The more the merrier. We shall form a chorus for the main players."

"Have you a comb?" asked Damaris.

Demetrius found an ivory comb in a box beside the basin. "Here then," he said. "Make yourselves presentable to a Jewish philosopher. Lucian and I will await you outside."

Shortly thereafter, the four descended the south side of the Areopagus Hill, and walked toward the center of Athens, pausing at a public latrine near the Middle Stoa. Their search was short-lived, for as they crossed the avenue of Panathenaia and entered the Stoa of Attalos, a small crowd signaled an orator, and on approaching they found the Jew. Dionysius the Areopagite stood beside Paul, while others listened to their dialogue. The Jew was not so dark and intense as Demetrius had pictured him. He appeared remarkably placid and genial.

"I quite agree," Dionysius was saying, "that the gods, or God, can be known from creation, but you say God is not only the Cosmic Mind, but a Father who would treat us like his sons and daughters."

The Jew replied, "This God, Lord of Heaven, who created the heavens and stretched them out, spread forth the earth and what comes from it. He, who gives breath and life to those who walk in it, has called you in righteousness, even as he called me, for we are indeed his offspring and therefore brothers."

"And this righteousness," said Dionysius, "is it other than the goal of philosophical inquiry, that is, to live the good life?"

Demetrius mumbled to Lucian, "What sort of *inquiry* is this? He does not query, he gently leads by the hand and invites unbridled speech."

"Perhaps he is already persuaded," replied Lucian.

"By Zeus, I wonder."

The Jew said, "Is not the good life that which conforms to the natural world?"

"It is," Dionysius nodded.

"But since God is the creator of the world, we may suppose he knows best how mankind ought to live in his world."

"That too, follows."

Demetrius grew agitated and cleared his throat. Dionysius glanced up. "Ah, welcome, Demetrius and Lucian," he said. "Would you care to question our visiting philosopher?"

Demetrius bowed his head. "I would, indeed, most excellent Dionysius."

"By all means, Demetrius," replied Dionysius. "There are some points I myself am uncertain of."

Demetrius said to Paul, "You are a Jew, are you not?"

"I am a Jew," said Paul, "circumcised on the eighth day, of the people of Israel, of the tribe of Benjamin, a Hebrew born of Hebrews; as to the law a Pharisee."[18]

"Very impressive, I am sure. This god you proclaim, is he not the god of the Jews?"

"He is—that and more. He is the god of creation, the Lord of Heaven, whom the Jews have long worshiped, but to say he is the god of the Jews is not to say he is the god of the Jews alone, but of all the earth, including the Jews."

"Is your message then not that of the Jews?

"It is—that and more; for as a Jew, I am sent to the Gentiles to fulfill the command of God to bring the light to the nations, to open the eyes that are blind, to bring out the prisoners from the dungeon—all those who sit in darkness—and therefore, I am under obligation both to Greeks and to barbarians.[19]

Demetrius tried to keep to the thread of his query, while granting the Jew talent with his extended sentences. "Are not the customs of the Jews divinely given and must be observed as part of the worship of your god?"

"The customs of the Jews are divinely given, but since they are Jewish customs, they are given only to the Jews, for we are chosen and separated from creation, that out of our stock the Christ may come, by whom the world is judged and redeemed."

"Yes, we will come to that presently," said Demetrius, "but do your fellow Jews agree with you on this?"

"Many of my fellow Jews do not accept that God has raised up Jesus as the judge."

"If your fellow Jews do not accept this, how do you expect learned Greeks to accept it?"

"My expectations," replied Paul, "are dampened by the abundance of ignorance. Nevertheless, many Greeks have accepted this good news. In Thessalonika and also in Beroea learned Greeks turned from idols, to serve a living and true God, and they wait for his Son from heaven, whom he raised from the dead, even Jesus who delivers us from the wrath to come."[20]

"And may these converts continue to dine on pork?"

"They do, whenever they can afford it."

A voice from the crowd proclaimed: "I will believe in your god if you will eat pork."

Without seeking the speaker, Paul said to all: "If it is well cooked and properly garnished, *and* you pay, I will eat and thank you for it."

"Indeed?" said another man, who stepped into view. He was a member of the synagogue in Athens. "What kind of a Jew are you that eats swine?"

Paul looked him in the eye. "A swine-eating Jew, brother, for the sake of the gospel."

"For this reason alone it is right that you be thrown out of the synagogues."

Demetrius waved away the objector. "Surely being cast out of a synagogue is an honor. But this is too small a thing, for I know of other Jews who eat pork. Rather, come with me this night to a feast, garnished by wine, women, and song. Show me that you know how to live, and to-morrow even I might become a devotee of your god."

"That I will not do," said Paul, "not even for the sake of your soul."

Someone from the crowd shook a finger at Demetrius and tittered, "Tomorrow may be too late, Demetrius; many a man has succumbed to the rigors of the night."

"Ha! But I am in superb condition, a true athlete, a gladiator of the lance: grapple and thrust, thrust and grapple. Indeed, I have just come from a night-long contest," he said, and pulling Daphne to his side, he pinched her. Daphne giggled and amorously pushed her body against Demetrius. Some of the gathering burst into laughter and light applause, while one voice, no doubt a Stoic, or perhaps a Jew, shouted, "Epicurean dilettante!" Demetrius stretched his arm toward the Acropolis. "You are in Athens, sir, the soul of Greece. We Greeks have long shown the world how to worship the gods through beauty in all its forms and to enjoy all that the gods have given, or at least what they have not taken away. Seeking pleasure gives meaning to life, and therefore a banquet of wine, women, and song must be very near the ultimate meaning of life."

"The meaning of life," said Paul, "is to secure life eternally. For nei-ther does the soul perish into extinction at death, according to Epicurus, nor does it merge back into the Cosmic Mind, according to Zeno; rather, the soul seeks its source in the creator. All agree that self-love is the starting point, and love of God is the end point, the *telos* of our exis-tence. He has showed you, Demetrius, what is the good life, as it is writ-ten in our Scriptures: *What does the Lord require of you but to do justice, and to love kindness, and to walk humbly with your God?*[21] Therein lies happiness."

Damaris noticed Lucian nodding to the words of Paul. She whispered to him, "It sounds wonderful, if only it were true."

Lucian turned to her. "If his god is true, why should it not also be true?"

Damaris smiled. "As Dionysius asked, a father who would treat us like his sons and daughters?"

"Yes, then you would be like my sister." Lucian took her hand, and Damaris felt warm and wanted—in love with Lucian, Paul, and Jesus all at once.

"Ah," said Demetrius, "so the Scriptures of the Jews are authoritative after all. I return to my point. If I were to accept your god, you will at least require circumcision of me."

"God has given you and all gentiles a substitute."

"And what is that?" Demetrius tilted his head. "Decapitation?" The audience laughed, and even Paul had to smile. Demetrius added, "Figuratively speaking, of course, or will a simple head shaving do?"

"Baptism," said Paul.

"A dunking? A bath? So simple as that?"

"Simple, yes, but not at all easy. Baptism signifies the transformation of your old nature into your new nature in Christ Jesus. You enter the bath a sinner and come out a son of God. Baptism is the symbol of your faith."[22]

"A son of God, a new nature?" cried Demetrius. "What can all this mean?"

"When you are in Christ," said Paul, "you will see yourself and the world differently, from God's perspective. You are transformed, so that the natural becomes unnatural, and the supernatural becomes the natural. Though you still do what you desire, your desires have changed." Paul turned to the crowd and adopted a condescending air. "Where now you are occasionally tempted by virtue and painful acts of altruism," he said melodramatically, "then you will be tempted by vice and deeds of degradation."

The crowd laughed, but Demetrius paused and gazed upward, attempting to apprehend the complex notion of human transformation. Lucian took the opportunity.

"If I may," he said by way of introduction. "Tell us how in a cosmic scheme that a crucified man, even if raised from the dead, as you say, unites us with the cosmic creator?"

Paul replied, "Listen carefully, if you wish to understand. Stoics seek true conformity to the world while Epicureans seek freedom from pain, fear, and death. God offers you both." Paul closed his eyes as if pondering his soul's creed. "Identify yourselves," he said, "with the mind of

Jesus, who, though he was in the form of God, did not count equality with God a thing to be grasped, but emptied himself, taking the form of a servant, being born in the likeness of men. And being found in human form he humbled himself and became obedient unto death, even death on a cross. Therefore God has highly exalted him and bestowed on him the name which is above every name, that at the name of Jesus every knee should bow, in heaven and on earth and under the earth, and every tongue confess that Jesus Christ is Lord, to the glory of God the Father. That is the good news I have received, and this I deliver unto you."[23]

Lucian nodded reflectively, but Demetrius had found his voice. "That is a great deal of blind faith to hang on the crucifixion of a condemned criminal. Can you offer us nothing more? You are not, after all, in the backwaters of Thessalonika but in Athens."

Paul looked intently into his face. "Demetrius, my friend, this Jesus troubled himself to appear to me, even while I was intent on honoring God by destroying his followers. Jesus appeared to me in the heavens. Why? I have asked myself why, over and over ever since, and here is my answer. I sought the truth. Though I thought I had grasped it, I had not, and God in his mercy led me to it. I am a Jew, of Jewish inheritance and education. You are a Greek, of Greek inheritance and education. But in Christ, there is neither Jew nor Greek. What can be known about God has always been plain, his power and deity are clearly seen. God does care, my friend. Though you once knew him, God has given you up to your base desires. Now, you have every pleasure, Demetrius, everything but hope."[24]

Demetrius stood mute and still, momentarily unnerved by an echo from his long ago childhood, the yearning for truth that sent him on his quest and to Athens. Then he said, "That is true. I have no hope, for there is nothing in which to hope save grasping the most out of this life, a task at which I am better than most."

The Jew smiled. "Not so, my friend. You are lost in the infernal maze of seeking pleasure without direction." Paul placed his hand on the shoulder of Demetrius. "Follow me, Demetrius. To be in Christ is to be reunited with God. I offer you dignity in this life and hope in the afterlife."

Demetrius again paused, and the entire audience paused with him. The moment of decision had arrived. Daphne suddenly grew fearful of losing Demetrius. She opened her robe and drew a seductive breath, and her breasts rose dutifully in response. "If you follow him," she said, "you will never taste of these again." Demetrius gazed at her, bemused perhaps, by the irony of his predicament.[25] He turned to Paul. But the dark, intense Jew had averted his gaze, turned his back, and left Demetrius to make up his own mind.

# 14

## The Power of the Name

And this became known to all residents of Ephesus, both Jews
and Greeks; and fear fell upon them all; and the name of the
Lord Jesus was extolled. Many also of those who were now believers came, confessing and divulging their practices. And a
number of those who practiced magic arts brought their books
together and burned them in the sight of all.

Luke the Physician

From hoary antiquity, before mankind learned to work with iron or
subdued the horse for war, we succumbed to the power of words and
their symbols engraved on stone. Whence the power? No one knew, and
few cared. In those days, before philosophers and historians, we were
less concerned with origins than with efficacy. In due course, words, like
those who uttered them, were seen as good or evil. Good helped, evil
harmed. Finally, we discovered the names of the powers themselves; and
of all words, the name of a power became the most powerful. Practitioners of the dark arts, by means of secrets to which all invisible powers
are subject, discovered that a name contained its power and the control
of the name gave control over these powers. Therefore, when demons
surrender their names, they surrender their power. But truth is, we
know not what powers and personalities lie hidden from view or prance
behind our backs, and we invent names for them as we go along, and
make puns of their names, which in itself has certain magical power by
way of a disarming, if nervous, laughter.

The names of the gods are of a different order, for they are too well
known to be of great use in magic, except in curses and invocations,
in which Persephone and Hermes are favored. But the mysterious Ineffable Name of the god of the Jews has become a most popular name in
magical formulae throughout the Mediterranean world, a clear contra-
vention, we note, of the third commandment: *You shall not take the name of*

*YHWH your God in vain.*[1] Because the Name is ineffable, the six million Jews honor it by their silence, and the tetragram YHWH, while revered by all, is pronounced by Gentiles with penetrating uncertainty, and written variously as *Iao, Iae, Iaoue,* along with his titles of adoration, Adonai, Eloai, Elion, Sabaoth.[2]

The power inherent in a name led lowly mankind to believe that a name given at birth destines the soul to the vicissitudes of life which we define by the vulgar terms of fortune and misfortune. Many a man has taken a new name in the hopes that he might enhance his destiny, but the Fates have decreed that only a name given at birth truly affects destiny, as if it were a sacred or accursed talisman that might illuminate the soul's passage through life or destroy it in flames. It is a different matter for Jews, however, when God himself bestows a new name, as he did for Abram, and even Jacob, renamed by his divine antagonist, for it is within the authority of YHWH to change human destinies.[3] We cannot say whether it was fate or coincidence that Asteria, which means starry or heavenly, betook herself into magic, or that Thalassa, which is the sea, symbol of unfathomable mystery, became Asteria's protectress and mentor, but we should incline toward the belief that they followed the destiny of their names.

Thalassa, a small old woman, smaller still by the bent of her aged back, was an herbalist, a maker of medicine, and therefore a healer. Some thought she was a witch, but if so, she kept her fatal potions and incantations hidden. She dwelt alone in a windowless hut, its walls of wood thinly smeared with mud under a roof of goat skins and grass. Straw mats hung on two inner walls and covered the dirt floor. It was easily recognized as the simplest of dwellings among the trees of the wood, which a humble woman might call home. The low-ceiled hut contained no furniture except two wood chests. In one she kept bowls, pots, and cooking ware, in the other the utensils of her trade; for she sold her medicines, herbs, and spices to physicians and others in the markets of Gordium and the surrounding villages.

The old woman often searched the hills before sunrise for mushrooms and rare herbs that must be picked before dawn while the dew weighed heavy, and on one starlit twilight she chanced upon the faintly wailing child. The nameless infant was no doubt an untimely and unsought conception, perhaps of a poor elderly couple, or an unwed girl, or a father with too few sons and too many daughters. We do not know, and therefore it must remain a mystery. But the infant, being of the female sex, found herself on a rock to die of exposure in the hills of northern Galatia, and surely she would have perished in the night had not the Fates taken pity. Such a discovery under the waning light of the stars compelled the old woman to save the child, which she named Asteria, perhaps because the child survived the night under the heavens or perhaps because she wished to set a destiny. Thalassa took Asteria to her dwelling and weaned her on the teats of a goat, and she mashed boiled greens and pulses in her own mouth and kissed them into Asteria's hungry mouth.

By these means Asteria grew from infant to little girl. Nature contributed to her destiny by giving her a hag's body; or at least by comparison to the perfect beauty of Aphrodite, somewhat deformed: longish arms and legs attached to a slightly curved spine, and when she came of age, smallish breasts. Her only jewel was her thick woolen hair, black as pitch and uncut since birth, a mantle that enhanced her aura of mystery. In an earlier era, Asteria might have made a home in one of the oracular shrines.

Asteria's earliest memory saw the old woman seated on her mat, hunched over a brass bowl in her lap, crushing and mixing herbs. Thalassa's white hair was always pulled tight into a knot at the back, and the folds of wrinkled skin at her throat hung like a cock's comb and swayed as she worked. From her large dark eyes, Asteria watched Thalassa day by day and followed her into the hills in search of herbs, roots, and mushrooms. Thalassa walked slowly, staff in hand, and Asteria, robed with an old shawl, learned to walk with the same careful and deliberate tread, lest a rare herb be crushed and lost. Thalassa seldom spoke except to teach Asteria the names and the lore of herbs and simples.

"This herb, reseda," she would say, showing her the gray green plant, "cures inflamation, but requires spittle and an invocation. These herbs stave off consumption, but should be wrapped in a cloth and tied around the neck by red string. This herb must be mixed with milk curdled by fig juice to heal a wound. These, taken with wine, bring soothing sleep to a troubled soul." Often she would remind Asteria, "Some herbs have the power to give life and others to take life; but they do so only if cut with a bronze knife, as in the days before the gods gave men iron." Thalassa knew many of the cures written down by Hippocrates without ever knowing the man existed, for Hippocrates merely catalogued what old women had long known. The universal treasure of the female sex was the knowledge to sustain life.

Soon Asteria recognized the herbs, and she learned to speak by reciting their names. With her youthful eyes, she found them in the more hidden places, and she picked them delicately at Thalassa's direction or when necessary cut them with the bronze knife. Asteria learned their properties, their effects, and the times when herbs must be picked for their greatest power. When Asteria knew the names and nature of the herbs, she learned the compounds that make cures for numerous diseases, as well as protection against the spirits. And because knowledge increases a thirst for knowledge, and power a quest for power, the more Thalassa taught, the more Asteria longed to know. By age ten Asteria had grown as tall as Thalassa, and they were like sisters of time, youthful and swarthy, aged and white.

One morning as they walked the wooded hills in search of plants, they came to a round gray rock, like a half-buried Phoenix egg, rising out of the earth to the height of a man. They stopped and gazed at it. "Asteria, my sister," Thalassa said, "climb up and sit upon the rock." Asteria nimbly climbed up and sat, crossing her legs. "From this rock you were given to me," said Thalassa. "From here I took you and raised you. I have given you life, but my own will soon be taken from me. Soon you must decide a path for yourself. Whether to seek a husband and dwell in a village or to live another life. This choice is yours."

Asteria tilted her head slightly to the left as she was inclined to do and gazed down into the eyes of Thalassa. "I wish to be like you."

Thalassa nodded and offered Asteria one of her faint and rare smiles. "You will be like me, yet far more, for you have learned much in your ten years of life. But knowledge is endless. I have given you knowledge of herbs and invocations, but like the soul of man and the spirits of the woodlands, knowledge leads to good and to evil. Beware of knowledge, and beware of the Evil Eye, within and without."

"Have you not given me this amulet against the Evil Eye," Asteria replied, fingering the ceramic disk fastened to the knotted red cord around her neck. On the red disk was painted in black a solitary staring eye.[4]

"That protects only from without," Thalassa said, "not from within."

"How shall I protect myself from within?"

"Do not envy those with power," replied Thalassa, "and do not reach too high or too deep."

"What is too high?" Asteria asked.

"The clouds are too high, my dear."

Asteria stood and gazing upward, stretched her long arms high above her head. She laughed, "The clouds are much too high." Gazing down at Thalassa, she asked, "And what is too deep?"

"The spirits of the dead are too deep. Do not delve in necromancy or tempt the demons of the netherworld." Asteria jumped off the rock. "See here, my sister," said Thalassa, pointing to the base of the rock, "if you were to dig beneath this rock, to see on what it rests, would it not fall on you and crush you?"

"I will not dig beneath the rock," she replied.

"You will not avoid spirits and demons, for anyone who heals must confront the powers of sickness, madness, and death. Spirits and demons are enticed and cajoled by herbs, but they are bound by incantations. Seek only to help and to heal." Asteria gazed innocently into the wizened old eyes of Thalassa. "Come now. We have herbs to glean and dry branches to gather for the fire."

In Asteria's twelfth year of life, Thalassa died. The old woman had lived a full life and found comfort in her daughter-sister of the stars, so at the appointed hour, known only to her, she lay down on her mat and stopped breathing. Asteria suspected she drank a potion. As her mother-sister had commanded her, Asteria took Thalassa's cloak for her own and the wool haversack in which she placed the herbs, bronze utensils, vials, mortar, and pestle. Then she set fire to the hut and recited a dirge while the flames consumed the wood. When she finished her task, she departed.

Without family or inclination toward betrothal or social pleasures, Asteria wandered through Galatia, collecting and selling herbs and gleaning knowledge and secrets from others. She associated easily with old women and witches, who were attracted to her hag-like beauty and the earnest hunger of her dark eyes. Asteria learned the mixtures of aphrodisiac potions, for which men and women always searched, as well as the prayers to Venus and Aphrodite. From aphrodisiacs, she learned spells that prolong ecstacy and the number of kisses required to disarm the Evil Eye of those who out of jealousy wished bad luck on their lovers. Folks told her repeatedly that the great center of magic was the city of Ephesus, and she set her sight toward the west.

After two years she found herself near Iconium, where Perseus cut off the head of the Gorgon Medusa.[5] Both men and women trusted Asteria in her uncomeliness, and she made a decent living in the traffic of passion and unrequited lust. Yet she herself did not go entirely unloved. There is, it seems, always one soul more unloved, or less lovable, than oneself. Such a one to Asteria was a simpleton called Balas; not a lunatic, but a brute of a man by nature who drooled over her as she passed by one day. He worked a small field, breaking the ground with regular and powerful strokes of a long handled mattock. As she passed by, he stopped and watched her. Then he called out, nay, let us say bellowed, "From where do you come?"

"The hills," she said, waving her hand in a far-away fashion.

"Where are you going?" he asked.

"I wander here and there," she replied, "but my destined end is the city of Ephesus."

"Where is Ephesus?"

"Near the sea."

"Why do you go there?"

"To learn the arts of magic."

Balas shook his head nervously to and fro as he lowered it. "It is not safe to do magic. It is not safe to travel alone."

Asteria smiled. "I have a charm against the Evil Eye to protect me." She pulled the red ceramic disk from under her robe.

Balas stared momentarily at the amulet, and then at her. "Take me with you."

"But you have a field to plant."

"It is not my field."

"What are you planting?"

"Seeds."

"Seeds," she nodded. "What kind of seeds?"

He looked into a bag. "Little seeds." He took a handful of seeds to her. "My master gave me the seeds and told me to plant them."

"Coriander," she said. "Such powerful strokes for little seeds."

"I am strong," he said. "Strong as an ox."

"What are you called, strong one?"

"Balas," said he.

"My name is Asteria."

"Take me with you," he begged.

"You may come with me, if you like."

Immediately he lifted his long-handled mattock to his shoulder and followed. The owner of the field, the seed, and the mattock never learned what became of the dim-witted peasant he had hired to plant his coriander.

Asteria appeared most beautiful to Balas, a nymph shrouded in a black lamb's wool cloak; and she, with her natural limitations of gender and strength, found him a good companion both for protection and the lifting of heavy bundles. Balas inhabited a powerful frame, thick-limbed, thick-lipped, thick with hair—a beast of burden with a soul. Asteria playfully called him "my ox." Thus, he followed her from village to village and ate from her hand. She trained him to look for herbs and creeping things in the hills and roadside. Despite his lumbering size, Balas had quick enough hands and caught toads and even lizards with ease.

The two journeyed ineluctably westward to Ephesus, the city with the revered title "First and Greatest Metropolis of Asia," and the dwelling of Artemis, whose temple was numbered far and wide among the seven wonders of the world. Near the city, Asteria met a shepherd willing to part with an old tent for a few pieces of silver. Balas lifted the bundled goatskin tent over his broad shoulders and carried it three miles to a site in the hills overlooking the great city. There Asteria chose to dwell, and there they dwelt. Asteria began dealing in her herbs, aphrodisiacs, and secret incantations. Balas crouched by the tent, ready to rise at her command, a threatening behemoth against the slightest frown of a customer.

Magical practices and paraphernalia were popular in Ephesus, but there were rules to its acceptable use. These rules were and are timeless and universal. We encourage any action or incantation that aids the medicinal value of herbs. You may add any disgustingness to the brew, fox tooth, toad liver, a lizard's heart or penis, and place it on the head or under your armpits, turn around three times and spit at your feet or into a colored glass cup—all these are acceptable forms of magic. Other forms of magic are frowned upon: necromancy, altering the outcome of a game of chance, or causing someone to fall in love through potions and charms. Beyond that, magic becomes dark, shadowy, and illegal: specifically, causing someone's death, inducing serious monetary loss, altering justice in a trial, intimidating a magistrate, or in any way threatening the safety of the throne. In the face of such dangers, Augustus ordered the burning of two thousand scrolls of magical formulae in Rome, including numerous Sibylline oracles.[6] Other burnings occurred as the times required throughout the empire.

The Jews of Ephesus also had their share of practitioners in the arts of magic, as we have always had from antiquity. This we know from the prohibitions in Torah against certain forms of magic, which, like the prohibition against adultery, need not have been given if no one practiced.[7] Jewish monotheism assumes the evil spirits are on a long tether, permitted for this age to plague and corrupt humanity, but Torah does not permit Jews to invoke the spirits of demons or ancestors, or in any way manipulate the dark powers for their own advantage.

Jewish tradition traces our knowledge of magic back to Solomon. God granted him great wisdom, such as a single man has never known.

He could talk about the plants, from the cedar of Lebanon to the hyssop growing on the wall. He knew the constellations of the stars, the tempers of wild beasts, the powers of spirits, the varieties of plants, and the virtues of roots. Solomon talked with the trees, and ruled over the devils, the spirits of the night. He composed incantations to alleviate distempers, and bequeathed us the method of exorcisms, by which we drive away demons, so that they never return, and these cures are still used unto this day.[8] Because this magic comes from God, it is good and may be used, but because it is magic, it must be used with care. Amulets against evil and formulae or charms to aid cures are allowed. For example, many carry a hargol locust egg to prevent earaches, a tooth from a dead fox helps one sleep, a tooth from a live fox helps one who sleeps too much, and the nail from the gallows of a convicted felon is a prophylactic against numerous types of disease; the liver and gall of a fish smoking on charcoal keeps demons at bay.[9] And all humanity believes in lucky days, astral configurations, charms, and incantations against a nebulous, seamless, and dangerous web of power.

One day, among Asteria's clientele came a middle-aged man by the name of Sceva, a magician in his own right, a self-proclaimed exorcist. He lacked a particular knowledge, however, for a certain task, that of helping a "friend" bring a woman into amorous relations. The unusual nature of the union, he said, was that the woman is quite elderly, certainly past child-bearing, and likely past much interest in coitus, though his friend was eager to tempt her. Asteria gave Sceva two potions. One contained the penis of a lizard caught while copulating, which would render a woman of any age amorous and longing for the one she gazed at provided the man recited under his breath the proper incantations while she drank. The second potion was for his friend to drink before the first act of copulation, which would render him potent beyond his or her greatest longings. Sceva paid the fee and promised a good deal more should the potions prove successful.

Thereupon, Sceva wooed and married the wealthy old woman. But certain other suitors who lost out on gaining the woman's wealth, accused him of having charmed her by means of a magical potion from the liver and heart and gall of an unusual fish. Sceva defended himself in court by noting that if he was looking for unusual fish, it was an interest in natural history, not magic; if he had been dealing in magic, he would have used not a fish but herbs, as everyone knows; if he had distilled some liquid from the fish, that would have been science not magic. In any event, he had done none of these things, for he was a legitimate exorcist and soothsayer, with no interest in cheating at love or games of chance, or in using unnatural charms where natural charm is called for.[10]

The court dismissed the charges and Sceva resumed his luxurious life and his soothsaying, much to the pleasure of his wife who had married him for that very reason, or so she thought, charmed as she was. Sceva made good on his promise to Asteria and paid her handsomely both for his success and her silence.

Asteria moved out of her tent and into a modest but comfortable stone apartment within the crowded city. One wall of the two-room dwelling presented a beautifully painted scene of woodlands, a stream and trees, deer, hare, and Pan with his pipes. Balas was overwhelmed by his good fortune: a room of his own, with a bed, a stool, and a chamber pot, and occasionally meat in his bowl.

Now within Ephesus, a considerable number of itinerant exorcists plied their trade, for in great centers of magic, there naturally resided a greater concentration of demons. As Sceva established himself in the city, he garnered seven men who practiced exorcism and taught them greater skills in their chosen trade. Sceva portrayed himself as both Jewish and a chief priest, because as a former high priest, he was believed to know the powers of the Ineffable Name. He claimed to know the most ancient incantations composed by King Solomon and had in his possession the rare *baaras* root, so named because it was found only in a certain place of the same name near the Lake Asphaltitis, also known as the Dead Sea. The plant's color is like a flame, and toward evening it shoots out rays like lightening. It is difficult to pluck up, for it recedes from the hand unless a woman's urine or menstrual blood is poured over it, and even then it will kill one who touches it. Once it has killed, however, it may be used by anyone. So, those who found this root would dig up the earth around it and tie a cord to its shoot, which they then attached to a dog. When they departed, the dog tried to follow, and it easily wrenched out the root, but the dog died instantly. Thereafter, the root, rendered harmless through the vicarious death of the dog, could still be used for exorcisms.[11]

Sceva's entourage called themselves the "Seven Sons of Sceva." While one, Eutyches, may well have sprung from his loins, if facial likeness may be trusted, the others were not sons but disciples. "Seven sons" carries a certain mystical authority in its own right, and the "Seven Sons of Sceva" rolls off the tongue like a solemn invocation. Were they to add "scam" to the rolling phrase, truth would be served, but business harmed. Even the name of the one "son," Eutyches, which means "good luck," is suspect and begins to strain the tie between a name given at birth and destiny. Moreover, that Sceva was a chief priest associated with the Jerusalem temple is out of the question, not even as a distant relative. Indeed, some within the Jewish community questioned his Jewish lineage, for if he were, it would have been fortuitous indeed that his parents named him Sceva, which is not a Jewish name, but a Greek rendering of the Latin *scaeva,* meaning "left-handed" literally, and metaphorically, "favorable omen." Whoever he was, whatever his origins—and no people is without its rascals—he affixed a bronze plaque to the wall of his soothsaying lair which read "Seven Sons of Sceva, a Jewish Chief Priest," and the helpless and gullible flocked to his door.

Asteria, now a woman of sixteen years in the full luster of her feminine power and scent and mysterious airs, attracted suitors. Balas, too, who slavishly did her every bidding, deep down desired her flesh as any bull would. That Asteria cherished the power of the virgin above all pleasures of the flesh, only made her *mysterium* the more powerfully attractive. When Balas understood her desires, he made himself as a eunuch in charge of a harem of one, the bodyguard of an immortal queen. Balas kept suitors at bay, but among the most persistent was none other than Eutyches, who, contrary to the male tendency, craved the woman's knowledge more than her body and felt certain it was a match made in heaven. He vowed he would not give her up, and regularly sent Sceva with overtures of marriage.

About this time a certain Jew, Paul of Tarsus, arrived in Ephesus. Among the bustling pantheon of the city and amid the many advocates of every god and goddess, the indefatigable messenger of the Gospel of Jesus the Christ entered the city gate. He came with companions, Aquila and Prisca, a well-to-do couple who settled in the city and established their business of tent-making. Paul, being an expert tent-maker, worked in their employ and slept in their home.[12]

Soon enough the message of Jesus reached every quarter of the city. Some Jews embraced the news, as Paul explained it, but other Jews rejected it out of hand as anathema. There were whisperings in the back corners of taverns and synagogues that Jesus of Nazareth had practiced magic in the performance of his miracles, that is, he called upon the powers of darkness rather than the powers of light emanating from God. Some said he learned magic as a child from the Egyptians. Others believed that Jesus not only knew the correct pronunciation of the Ineffable Name, but also the combinations of divine titles used at creation, by which words brought the world into being. That is how he produced bread from air and fed thousands.[13] The biographers of Jesus are aware of the charge of sorcery, or at least of being in league with the devil, and recount an accusation that he cast out demons by the power of Be-elzebul, or Ba'al Zevuv, "Lord of the Flies," as Jews have long punned the name Be-elzebul.[14] For a Greek, these Jewish squabbles were confusing indeed, but they revived an interest in the power of the name of the Jewish god. And whether the accusation of sorcery against Jesus was true or not, those who sought the powers of darkness followed the whisperings in search of the keys to this kingdom. Paul himself had the power to heal, but he was more than a physician; he was a bona fide thaumaturge, and people snatched away bits of cloth with which he wiped the sweat from his brow and used them to heal the sick or cast out demons. While Paul preached his Gospel, a good many other things were going on in the name of Jesus.[15]

Are we surprised that Asteria, too, became enamored of the quest for the power of the name? Not at all. Power thirsts for power, and having mastered so much, she could only reach for more. She sought out Sceva and persuaded him to write down the names of his god. Asteria then copied the letters of each name individually on small square tiles of laurel wood, which she arranged in different combinations, silently pronouncing the sounds. Balas sat by and watched her lips move, and he inwardly shuddered.

On the eve of a full moon, Asteria left the city for hills to the south. Close behind, Balas carried a cloth sack containing her magical paraphernalia. They climbed up on a flat rock jutting out from a ridge in the hillside. Here and there, ragged clouds glided overhead. The full moon illumined the rock as if it were black glass or obsidian and made luminous the dark sea. The light from torches around the harbor danced in the distance. She waited for the moon to reach its zenith, when her beams form the ladder between heaven and earth. Asteria untied the cloth bundle and took out a small water skin, two vials, a bowl, a bone from a dog's foreleg, and a pouch holding the wood squares inscribed with the letters of the divine names. When the moon entered the upper third of the heavens, Asteria gave one of the vials to Balas. "Open it," she said, "and with your forefinger, daub the ointment on my ears, my lips, my eyelids, my nostrils, and my inner wrists." Balas removed the stopper and poured a drop of the sweet-smelling oil on his finger. He applied one drop to each part of her body as she had instructed, and some beneath his own nose as well. The sweetness brought on pangs of hunger. Asteria hunched down on the rock, and Balas, too, squatted not far from her.

Asteria placed the tiles, each containing one letter of a divine name, along the flat rim of the bronze bowl. She took the dog's bone and tapped the side of the bowl until a letter fell in. She took it out of the bowl and lay in on the rock. She tapped again until another tile slipped into the bowl and placed that letter next to the first. She lay them in groups of three, four, and five. Each time she pronounced the name it spelled as best she could.

Asteria stood and raised her longish arms to the night, spread her palms to the moon and called out: "Iao, Adonai, Eloi, Elion, Sabaoth, by the power of your name and all derivative names, I beg your secrets and knowledge to dwell in my soul and breathe through my mouth and nostrils and see through my eyes. Give me a ray of your divine knowledge. Indwell and empower, I adjure you, I adjure you, I adjure you." Thus she called out to the dim stars and the ethers for a long time, repeating the names in different order. But feeling nothing, no infusion of power, she dropped her hands and bowed her head. She knelt down, returned the letters to the rim of the bronze bowl, and repeated the knocking and arranging process. Again she called on the power of IAO, over and over, but again the night remained silent.

When the moon passed its zenith, now in the decline of the upper third, she knelt and tossed all the letters into the bowl and swirled them around. Then with her left hand she took one out and lay it before her, B. She reached into the letters without looking and took another, E, and a third, L, then I, A, L. An owl swooped overhead, its moon shadow raced across the rock. She felt a dread and stared at the combination of letters: BELIAL.[16] She stopped, stood, and disrobed. "Open the other vial," she commanded Balas. "Daube the backs of my hands, the tops of my feet, my breasts, and my forehead with the ointment." He pulled out the stopper and shrank from the stench, but summoning his obedience, he did as he was told. Balas stepped away and in attempting to replace the stopper in the vial, he fumbled it and spilt the foul liquid down the front of his tunic and dropped the vial at his feet, where it broke and the remaining liquid trickled off the rock. He grimaced, hunched back down, and pointed his nostrils into the night air.

Asteria, her hag-like body naked in the moonlight, threw back her raven hair and raised her arms again to the moon. "Iao," she called out, "who shines by night, who is ruler of the secret mysteries: I bind you to myself, I adjure you, I adjure you, I adjure you." She began speaking sounds in eery monotones, but meaningless to Balas. "Oai, iole, noile, mihole, thoabas, ianoda." She repeated her pleas and her adjurations. A wind stirred, but nothing else in the heavens suggested an answer to her longings. Yet she remained still, arms outstretched.

Then she heard Balas grunt repeatedly, and she looked over at him. He squatted, mesmerized in the light of the moon. His bovine eyes had changed, now fearful or cunning, filled with apprehension and malice, resembling a wild beast, staring out from a crevice in the hillside that led to the netherworld. He shielded his eyes from the moon, turned, and glared at Asteria. Suddenly, he raised himself up. "Bitch!" he bellowed, "female fungus, slut of Hades, pus-bag, you who have overreached the putrid bounds of your putrid flesh, you do not know me, but do I not know you? Asteria, Airetsa, whore of Leviathan, the earth has deep gutters for the poisonous blood of your wet and cankered womb. There, in the waterless depths my companions await with outstretched tongues." Then he sprang upon Asteria and brought her down on the rock and savaged her at great length. She did not scream, but silently writhed as her virgin blood flowed, while heavens turned and the moon fell further in its arc.

Growling, he stood and urinated over her wretchedness. When the oafish body of Balas had vented itself, the will too, changed, and the demon, or evil spirit, withdrew into its hiding place in the cavernous chest of Balas, who, as quickly as he had begun, returned to his docile state.[17] He knelt beside her and by the declining moonbeams he watched over her, lest the Harpies come to snatch her away.[18] Asteria lay upon the rock under rotating heavens. She had unleashed powers far beyond her control. The name of the god of the Jews was a fathomless terror when summoned under compulsion, and the netherworld awaited just such an opportunity to fill the vacuum of the God who turns his back. Her simple-minded companion was no longer hers, but a brute she could neither trust nor control. She must find a way to return her beloved friend to herself, and release him from his bondage.

Dawn dispelled the night and extinguished its heavenly lamps, though the moon lingered in the western dawn. Asteria returned to the city with Balas walking behind her. Balas went to his room, dropped the sack containing the divination bowl and wood tiles in the corner, and collapsed on his mat and slept though the day. Asteria washed her body and applied an ointment to her wounds. She rested until the early afternoon then made her way to the place of the Seven Sons of Sceva. Eutyches opened the door to her.

"Eutyches" she said helplessly, "Balas is possessed by a demon, and I fear for my life."

He grinned. "What will you pay for me to exorcize him?"

"What do you require?"

"You," he replied. "You must agree to become my wife."

"As you demand, so I will do."

The Seven Sons of Sceva marched to the house of Asteria. She opened the door, and they solemnly filed in. She knocked on the door of Balas. No answer, no sound. She opened the door. Balas squatted on his chamber pot, his soiled and stinking tunic pulled up around his waist. He stared at his male member. The Seven Sons of Sceva solemnly entered the room tinkling little brass bells, and formed a semicircle around Balas. Eutyches held a root under the nose of Balas. In unison, they chanted: "We conjure you by the Name! Be off! Be off! Depart! Depart!" Balas did not move, but he gazed up at them. They huddled together, conferred, and nodded. Eutyches held the root and again they chanted: "We conjure you by Asmodeus: Be off! Be off! Depart! Depart! We conjure you by Mastema: Be off! Be off! Depart! Depart! We conjure you by Azazel: Be off! Be off! Depart! Depart!"[19] Still, Balas simply gazed at them like a cornered bull trying to make sense of the gibberish of men. They stepped aside and conferred longer. Several of the men shook their heads, but finally they formed their half circle, and while they tinkled their brass bells, Eutyches alone intoned: "I adjure you by the Jesus whom Paul preaches: Be off! Be off! Depart! Depart!"

Balas opened his mouth. His eyes grew cunning and dangerous, even rabid. In a rasping voice clearly from the netherworld, he said, "Jesus I know, and Paul I recognize; but who are you?"

They looked at him, mouths agape. Eutyches stammered, "We are the S-s-seven S-sons of Sc-c-ceva."

Balas laughed deeply from the pit of his bowels, or rather the unfamiliar spirit within laughed, for we must grant the spirit possession of the lungs and larynx of Balas. "Decloaked charlatans and sons of jugglers!" he hissed. Like a crouching leopard, he sprang upon the men, clawing at them and heaving them across the chamber. Asteria heard the terrible growls and the crashing of bodies against the wall. The chamber pot clattered amid muffled groans and cries for help. The door flew open and Eutyches ran out holding his torn loin cloth in his hand, and the others followed as best they could. They fled the house, terror in their eyes and altogether naked.

Asteria fled behind them. She ran through the streets to the western quarter of the city asking for the house of Aquila and Prisca. If the demon knew this Jesus and recognized the messenger Paul, perhaps he would come and help her. When she found the house, she knocked at their door and waited breathlessly. A young woman opened the door. "May we help you?" she asked.

"A friend is possessed by a demon," Asteria cried. "Is Paul the exorcist here?"

"Paul is not here. He has gone away with the master of the house on business."

"But the demon knows Paul of Tarsus," she said, "and this Jesus he preaches."

The young woman's face paled. "Wait here," she said, and hurried away.

Soon, a tall elderly woman in a long blue tunic, fastened by a white wool sash, came to the entrance. She had a kindly face, and her dark hair was streaked with silver, and bound up behind her. "My name is Prisca," she said, and invited Asteria into the atrium of the immaculate home of white stone, with walls plastered a light rose color. "What is your name?" the matron asked.

"Asteria," she replied and bowed respectfully.

Prisca motioned to a couch covered by an ornate wool tapestry. "Sit here," she beckoned, "and tell me what occurred."

Asteria sat beside the gentle woman and recounted the failed exorcism of the Seven Sons of Sceva, and how the demon knew of Paul and Jesus.

"How long has Balas been possessed?" asked Prisca.

"Only from last night," said Asteria.

"How did it come about?"

Asteria shrugged her shoulders.

"Asteria," Prisca persisted, "there is at work in this world an evil will, from which evil spirits come and clothe themselves with flesh and blood to kindle evil desires. You must tell me precisely what occurred that brought Balas into the power of the Evil One."

Asteria's head fell in shame. She explained what she had done and how she sought the power of the Name of the god of the Jews. "I reached too high," she said, and began to sob.

Prisca let her weep for some moments. "No one can reach so high, my daughter," she replied somberly. "That is why God has reached down to us."

Asteria looked up. "Reached down to us?" she managed between uneven breaths.

"Yes. The power of the name is yours for the asking, but you must do so on your knees."

"How ought I ask?" Asteria asked, wiping the tears from her cheeks with her hair.

"Ask God for the forgiveness of your sins. Believe in the name of Jesus and confess him as your Lord."

Asteria nodded. "This I will do," she sighed peacefully, "but what of my friend, Balas?"

"We will go now to see him."

When Prisca and Asteria arrived, Balas sat forlornly in the doorway of the house. Pedestrians walked to the other side of the street out of fear of the grotesque figure. At the sight of Asteria he grew agitated, swaying back and forth, but as Prisca drew near, Balas jumped up and ran into his room. Prisca, with Asteria just behind, went in after him. Balas squatted in the corner of his room. He emptied the cloth shawl of its contents, erratically placed the brass bowl beside him, and tossed in the laurel wood tiles, mixing them as if washing his hands. Then he scattered the tiles across the floor. Next, he picked up the vial of sweet scented oil and rubbed the oil on his face.

Asteria said, "Balas, we have come to help you."

Balas looked up, his eyes darting back and forth. "Flee, flee!" he said, as he crawled away from them along the wall, whimpering like a frightened dog.

"What is your name?" Prisca asked.

"Balas," he whispered.

"No," replied Prisca, "I speak to you, the evil spirit who dwells in Balas—you who has left the wastelands and come to roam upon the earth and steal souls from the Most High. I command you in the name of Jesus to reveal your name."

Balas grimaced, closed his eyes, and repeatedly banged his head on the floor. "I am Salab. Leave me alone, Salab says, lest I drag you down to the abyss."

Prisca stepped forward and stretched out her hand toward him. "Salab, son of darkness, I charge you by the authority in the name of Jesus, the name above all names: Be gone!" Balas stood up and ripped off his soiled tunic. Naked, he appeared ready to savage Prisca and tear her limb from limb.

Asteria shouted, "Balas, no!"

Trembling, Prisca stepped back slightly, but she did not retreat. She stood her ground, eye to eye. Balas bellowed in anguish and clawed at his chest and collapsed in a great thud at her feet, prostrate on his knees. The ox was felled. In the corner of the room, the bronze divination bowl suddenly shook, and, as if by an unseen finger, flipped over, spinning round and round on its rim, until it came to rest and the chamber grew quiet.

Prisca sighed and her shoulders slumped. "Thank you, God," she whispered, and she staggered backwards to lean against the wall.

Asteria cautiously approached the fallen Balas. She ran her fingers through his bushy hair and called, "Balas, my brother, my ox. Rise up. You are free."

# 15

## Destinies

But now, what did most elevate the Jews in undertaking this war, was an ambiguous oracle that was also found in their sacred writings, how, "about that time, one from their country should become governor of the habitable earth." The Jews took this prediction to belong to themselves in particular and many of the wise men were thereby deceived in their determination. Now, this oracle certainly denoted the government of Vespasian, who was appointed emperor in Judaea. However, it is not possible for men to avoid fate, although they see it beforehand. But these men interpreted some of these signals according to their own pleasure; and some of them they utterly despised, until their madness was demonstrated, both by the taking of their city, and their own destruction.

Flavius Josephus

The Jewish revolt against Rome is said to have begun the moment we stopped offering the daily sacrifice on behalf of Caesar. The daily sacrifice of two lambs and a bull "for Caesar and the Roman people" as a Roman "tribute to the Most High God" preserved the ultimate, if uneasy, rule of God over the Jews through the fiction of Roman obeisance to God.[1] If so, the war could be blamed on Eleazar ben Ananias, son of the high priest, who, in the summer of the twelfth year of Nero, persuaded the priests to reject all sacrifices of Gentiles, including that of Caesar. But his authority only came from sufficient wrath by the Jews, in sufficient numbers, with sufficient faith in their cause.

Over the past decade, indeed, even as far back as the prefecture of Pontius Pilate, Roman administration had deteriorated, and the numbers of "malcontents" grew accordingly. In the most peaceful of times there had always been a small number of Jews sworn to rid their land of Rome, and probably take down the Jewish aristocracy and all rich landowners into the bargain—a revolution in the fullest sense of a dirt-poor peasant's vocabulary. But against all claims to the contrary, the majority of Jews understood that in an age of empires, every land and ethnic people must lie within the hegemony of one empire or the other, and an educated ruling class was essential for any government. The Jews of Babylon, with their ruling aristocracy, lived under Persian rule; the Jews of Judaea and Alexandria and all parts west, with their ruling aristocracy, lived under Roman rule. Rome kept the peace and provided security for Jews throughout its empire for one hundred and twenty years. But the quality of the Roman empire depended on the quality of its emperor. The deterioration of Roman rule began at the top, and the poison of Nero found its way down the chain to Gessius Florus, governor of Judaea. We need not rehearse the many atrocities Florus committed, for Josephus has left no stone unturned in his *Jewish War*. Florus, by his own acumen, multiplied the malcontents and haters of Rome more than any charismatic and divinely appointed Messiah ever could have done.

Therefore, the true rebels, the fanatic followers of Phinehas, grandson of Aaron, whether Sicarii or Zealot, gained strength. They were zealous indeed. The Sicarii were renowned, and so named for their deftness with the *sica,* a curved double-edged dagger that entered beneath the ribs and rose swiftly to the heart, and for using it to slay fellow Jews who conspired with Rome. The Zealots, in former times a ragtag group of zealous activists, were now a faction deserving of cognomen and capitalization, a force to be reckoned with, and their sons were good at slinging stones.

Zeal for God, in itself good and praiseworthy, can quickly go astray. Among the many shameful executions, such as of the high priest Ananias himself, a most dishonorable and portentous incident occurred on the seventeenth of Elul.[2] The Roman garrison in the Antonia fortress of Jerusalem sued for a surrender. The Zealots granted the soldiers security to depart Jerusalem, leaving their weapons behind, and sent a delegation to seal the capitulation by an exchange of oaths. While the soldiers marched through the city still armed, they were left alone, but when they reached the gate and lay down their weapons, the Zealots surrounded them. The Roman soldiers neither resisted nor appealed for mercy, but cried out "the oaths, the oaths!" And they were thus butchered, save for their general who entreated them, promising to be circumcised and become a Jew. Him they let live. But in this the Zealots betrayed their true colors, and the sages and most of the Pharisees turned against them.[3]

Cestius Gallus, legate of Syria, marched on Jerusalem and reached Judaea during the month of Tishri, while the city celebrated the Feast of

Booths. On the thirtieth day of the month, Gallus took the north suburb of Bezetha and burned it. But his first assault on the temple mount failed, and inexplicably—that is, by any military evaluation—Gallus retreated. In a gorge near Beth-horon, Zealots fell on his army and routed it—to the loss of over five thousand soldiers, though Gallus and a much reduced force managed to escape.[4] We may say that the failure of Gallus was the true cause of the war, because this victory convinced many Jews that God fought for their cause and the time of Messiah had come. If this were not proof enough, other omens lent their weight. A comet appeared in the sky, like a sword hanging over the city, and continued for a year. A pilgrim brought a cow to sacrifice and it gave birth to a lamb in the temple court. The great bronze gate of the temple that required twenty men to open it, one night opened of its own accord.[5] Yes, God's anointed would come, but who would it be: The despotic Zealot, Eleazar ben Simon, who received supreme command of the Jewish army, or another? It was a day of hotheads and therefore heated arguments.

Jews who sought peace were obliged to remain silent, as the country succumbed to the euphoria of victory and prepared for war. Rather than leave matters in the hands of fanatics, a number of the Jerusalem aristocracy took up the cause of the war; among them were Simeon son of Gamaliel, a leader among the Pharisees, and Josephus son of Matthias, an energetic member of the priestly aristocracy. And war came. The following spring, Titus Flavius Vespasianus, with three legions, twenty-three auxiliary cohorts, six regiments of cavalry, and other auxiliaries provided by client kings—a total of sixty thousand men—marched against the land of the Jews. The Galilee fell with scarcely a struggle. After a brief siege of Jotapata, in which the commander of the Galilee, Josephus, was captured, Vespasian captured the fortified town of Gamala, and by the end of that year, all of northern Israel had fallen to Roman control.[6] The steady breath of blame blew upon the smoldering embers of defeat and sparked a civil war in Jerusalem by which the Zealots gained complete control. They unleashed the Furies and began their tyrannical reign of terror. They executed many of the prominent leaders of Jerusalem, including chief priests. At this point, the community of Christians, under divine guidance they said, fled from Jerusalem to Pella in Peraea.[7] The temple had been overrun by men thinking themselves chosen by God and therefore above his laws. A civil war between the Zealot factions of Simon son of Giora and John of Gischala raged day by day, and the closed gates of the city and the guards posted at them, prevented anyone from leaving Jerusalem.

Vespasian wintered in Caesarea, and in the spring he secured the western Peraea, southern Idumaea, and most of Judaea. While he prepared for the siege of Jerusalem, word came of Nero's death.[8] Suddenly, the future of the empire was uncertain and Vespasian suspended the war effort to await events in Rome. When news came in December of Galba's coronation, Vespasian sent his son, Titus, to pay homage to the new emperor. Meanwhile, the legions of the Rhine, Gaul, Britain, and Spain declared their general, Vitellius, emperor, and within a fortnight on the Ides of January another general, Otho, organized a conspiracy among the Praetorians to assassinate Galba and declare Otho emperor. Soon the legions of Egypt, Africa, the Danube, and the Euphrates supported Otho. Titus, having got no farther than Corinth, learned of Galba's assassination and returned to Caesarea. Seeing the throne up for the taking, Vespasian immediately consolidated the support of key leaders in the provinces of Syria and Egypt. In the month of June, by the Roman calendar, on the fifth day of Sivan by the Jewish reckoning, Vespasian resumed the subjugation of Judaea.[9] He took the mountainous country north of Jerusalem, the towns of Gophna, Acrabette, Bethel, and Ephraim, and garrisoned them. The city of Jerusalem had been under siege for two years. But now, with the war about to be taken to the walls of the city, many pleaded for surrender. The sages said to the Zealots, "Let us go out and make peace with the Romans." The Zealots would not let them, and retorted, "Let us go out and fight them." The sages said, "You will not succeed."[10]

Johanan ben Zakkai, elder sage and Pharisee, walked the streets of Jerusalem. A slender figure of medium height, Johanan, well into his ninth decade of life, retained his upright stature, and though his shoulders were rounded and his skin sagged like aged tallow upon his upright frame, the light from his brilliant mind still shone through his eyes. Longevity among the Jews is not as rare as among other peoples—one need only consult the ages recorded in Sacred Writ—but there is some dispute whether it is virtue or garlic that serves as a preservative. Certainly, the blessing of many years must be considered a reward for virtue by all believers in the promises of God; although there are so many exceptions that a great deal of faith is required, and for lack of firm evidence the matter cannot be deemed conclusive. But Johanan ben Zakkai had lived long enough that the honorary 120 years could be applied to him, as to Moses, without embarrassment. His glossy silver beard was trimmed to a half-hand-breadth. His once ample head of hair, cut short in good Roman fashion and now thinned by age, also gave him the appearance of youth despite the fine wrinkles of wisdom across his waxen brow. As a Pharisee, he was an innovator among the traditionalists—one not immune to slight alterations with the times. Had he not been a venerable sage of Israel, he might have passed unnoticed among the philosophers in Alexandria, Athens, or Rome.

The city suffered, and Ben Zakkai suffered for it. The infighting of the Zealot factions left the people starving. Each group, in order to prevent the other from gaining access to the grain supplies, carried away what they could and then burnt the storehouses. The poorest, with their empty jars, suffered soonest. But even the wealthy learned that no amount of gold could buy what was not there. After two days respite from the civil strife, Johanan ventured out along the burnt and barren passageways; two of his young disciples, Eliezer and Judah, walked with him; that is, a respectful step behind. Eliezer ben Hyrcanus, the handsome son of an aristocratic landowner, gave up his vast inheritance to devote himself to the study of Torah under Johanan. But Eliezer's father could not withhold the inheritance of an exceptional memory, which Johanan likened to a plastered cistern that never lost a drop.[11] Joshua ben Hananiah, a Levite cantor, was a large and robust man, impetuous, even brash, but for all that, he had the ability to think quickly on his feet.[12] Both were devoted to Johanan, attending to him as if to the Holy One, Blessed be He, that they might not miss an utterance that sprang forth from their master. To them Johanan ben Zakkai was living scripture. From time to time, fiery-eyed Zealots of the Simon faction passed by, offering a slight bow of respect, tempered by innate suspicion for anyone who did not openly declare for their side. Eliezer and Joshua quickly advanced close to Johanan, that they might shield him from abuse. As they walked through the lower city, a poor man recognized Johanan and approached them.

"Master," he said, "have you heard that Martha, the daughter of the wealthy Sadducee, Boethius, who was one of the richest women in Jerusalem, died yesterday."

"How did she die?" asked Ben Zakkai.

"From hunger or shame," he replied. "They said that she sent her servant out saying, 'Go and bring me some fine flour.' By the time he went it was sold out. He came and told her, 'There is no fine flour, but there is white flour.' She then said to him, 'Go and bring me some.' By the time he went he found the white flour sold out. He came and told her, 'There is no white flour but there is dark flour.' She said to him, 'Go and bring.' By the time he went it was sold out. He returned and said to her, 'There is no dark flour, but there is barley flour.' She said, 'Go.' By the time he went this was also sold out. She had taken off her shoes, but she said, 'I will go out and see if I can find anything to eat.' In the street, some dung stuck to her foot, and she fainted and soon she died."

Johanan applied to her the verse: "*The tender and delicate woman among you which would not adventure to set the sole of her foot upon the ground for delicateness and tenderness.*"[13]

"If so," said Joshua, "the curse of God foretold by Moses our master has come upon us."

"I fear it is so," said Johanan.

"And the siege will end in our destruction," said Eliezer.

"I fear it is so, of the city, the temple, and the nation."

The man asked, "Master, what then may we do to secure the mercy of heaven?"

Johanan shook his head and replied, "If we had food to eat, we could fast."

They walked on and passed by an open door from which a stench emerged. A short distance within lay a dead child, emaciated, perhaps two years old, but now scarcely larger than a newborn. The mother sat forlorn in a dark corner, herself waiting to die. Ben Zakkai stopped and prayed over the child: a girl child, it appeared, so crumpled, her birdlike shoulder raised against her inclined head, her small blue lips slightly opened, awaiting anew the breath of life.

They walked on and reached a small marketplace where the people, gaunt and sallow-eyed, boiled straw in water and drank the broth. He said to his disciples, "Can men who seethe straw and drink its water withstand the armies of Vespasian?"

Joshua and Eliezer huddled nervously around him. "Master, pray speak not thus in the streets," said Eliezer, "lest a Zealot hear and report, and they accuse you of treason."

Suddenly a cry went forth from the temple mount, and others echoed it across the city. "He comes! He comes!" The people cowered in alarm, as the Zealots rushed up to the city walls. Johanan said to Joshua, "Go up and see." The disciple ran to a stairway along the wall above the Kidron Valley. He pushed his way through the Zealots and onlookers. Across the valley, a contingent of Roman cavalry appeared along the ridge of the Mount of Olives, their banners fluttering in the afternoon breeze. Joshua studied the army on the hill, while those around him bravely shouted vulgarities, curses, and cries of defiance. Having gazed, he ran back to his master.

"What did you see?" asked Johanan.

"Master, it must be the general himself come to assess the siege of Jerusalem."

Johanan stared absently into the face of his disciple, and Joshua did not stir lest he disturb the vision while it played itself out across his brow. At length Johanan murmured, "This is of the Lord."

"May it be so, my master, but how?" asked Eliezer.

"My disciples, already I have waited too long. Reason cannot prevail. The Holy One has departed, and I too must depart."

"May it be so, my master, but how?" Eliezer repeated. "No one may go out or come in, except the Zealots permit it."

"I will speak with my kinsman, Ben Battiah," said Johanan.

Joshua said, "I will go and find him."

"After the first watch," said Johanan. "Now, let us go to our chamber for prayers."

They left the market and returned to the compound in the upper city where many of the sages and their disciples dwelt. The small complex of buildings and a courtyard with a mosaic tiled pool had been the academy of Hillel while he lived. There, amid the distant sounds of tumult, they swayed and recited the evening Shema. Before they finished, they heard the throngs descending from the walls. The Romans had departed the Mount of Olives. After the first watch, Joshua went further into the upper city and inquired of the Zealot guards for Ben Battiah. The guards, dirty and illiterate peasants from small villages, enamored of their power and authority and still reeling from the bravado of the encounter with Vespasian, sneered at Joshua. "What does a Pharisee jackal want with the lion Ben Battiah?"

Joshua looked them straight in the eyes and said, "The lion's great uncle and revered sage, Ben Zakkai, sends for him." So they went and reported to Ben Battiah, and he came down to Joshua. Ben Battiah was the grandson of Johanan's sister, a man now in his early forties who had never been close to his great uncle. He briefly joined the Pharisees in his youth, but when he found they lacked a vision for the ancient glory of Israel, he took the dagger in hand and renounced them as allies of Rome and therefore traitors. Nevertheless, he respected the sages as leaders among the common people, and took some pride that Johanan ben Zakkai was a leader among the leaders.

Joshua led him aside and said, "Your uncle requests you come visit him privately."

"I will come this night after the second watch. He must be alone."

Late in the darkness, Ben Battiah came to the dwelling of the sages. They directed him to the small windowless stone chamber of Johanan. Ben Battiah entered, and by the light of two small lamps, found Ben

Zakkai seated on a carpet with Joshua and Eliezer. "We must be alone," he said to his uncle.

Said Johanan, "I am an old man, and these are my right hand and my left hand." Ben Battiah hesitated. Johanan said, "They will keep their oaths of silence."

He closed the door. "What do you need?" he asked.

"Sit, son of my sister," Johanan commanded, motioning to a cushion on the floor. "Sit and let us consider the fate of our people." Ben Battiah pulled the cushion back and sat cross-legged against the wall opposite his uncle. The lamps cast an erratic light upon the stone walls of the chamber. He waited quietly for Ben Zakkai to begin.

At length Johanan did begin. "Will you not give to Rome the tokens of submission, an arrow and a bow?"

"Never! As we sallied forth and defeated Cestius Gallus, so we will sally forth and defeat Vespasian."

"How long will you carry on in this way and kill all the people with starvation?"

"Every soul in Israel must be prepared to die for our freedom," replied Ben Battiah.

"Do you think liberation from the rule of Rome will bring freedom? Autonomy is not freedom. And the way your Zealots tyrannize the city, I can only tremble at the thought that they should rule all of the land."

"Never in our history," Ben Battiah growled, "has the people followed the zeal of Phinehas."[14]

"And never shall we," replied Johanan. "The zeal of Phinehas was for the Lord, against the sin of Israel. He slew one man that the wrath of God against Israel be averted. But you slay without reason, without justice."

Ben Battiah paused. He knew that in a contest of Scripture with Johanan, he was like an unarmed man before a lion, but unwilling to admit defeat without a struggle, he ventured, "Never, has the people sought the sovereignty of God with one heart and soul and might, as it is written: *Shema Israel* . . ."

"Yet our God is sovereign, whether we seek it or no. As it is written: *I saw the Lord sitting upon a throne, high and lifted up; and his train filled the temple.*"[15]

Ben Battiah replied, "Shall we not fight to rid the land of uncleanness that the Jews may be the people of God as in the days of old? Has not the prophet Daniel foreseen this day? I, too, know some Scripture, my uncle, as it is written: *And in the days of those kings the God of heaven will set up a kingdom which shall never be destroyed, nor shall its sovereignty be left to another people. It shall break in pieces all these kingdoms and bring them to an end, and it shall stand for ever.*"[16]

Johanan nodded wearily. "The stone cut from a mountain by no human hand, which broke in pieces the iron, the bronze, the clay, the silver, and the gold."

"Has not this day arrived that God will fight for us?"

"If so, tarry; if not, plant your garden and reap its produce. Messiah is a hope to be awaited, not a strategy to be enforced."

"Most revered uncle, when do we know that God has ordained a man and a time?"

"When he comes on the clouds of heaven, as it is written: *And behold, with the clouds of heaven there came one like a son of man.*"[17]

Ben Battiah shook his head. "That I cannot accept. We have waited all our lives. On the contrary, we must prepare and show ourselves worthy of his command, that he may come. The army of the Lord must assemble."

"The army of the Lord?" asked Johanan. "You presume too much."

"Then let us die with honor and leave proof that we preferred death to slavery."[18]

"It is true that death brings liberty to the soul imprisoned in misery, but the jaws of Gehenna open wide for the reckless souls that profane the sanctuary." Ben Battiah bit his lip, his eyes searching back and forth from one disciple to the other. "Son of my sister," whispered Johanan, "God has turned his back on Jerusalem. Do not let your zeal blind you to this dark truth. The Holy One, blessed be He, will not condemn you for opening a window of opportunity even while you guard the gate to his vestibule. Heed, while there is yet time."

Ben Battiah sighed and murmured, "What can I do?"

"Devise some plan for me to escape."

"To what end? Will you preserve your old age and leave your disciples to die?"

"Though Jerusalem be lost, perhaps I shall be able to save a little."

"What can you do?"

"I will try to speak with Vespasian."

"The Zealots will never surrender. If I say a word about surrender to them, they will kill even me."

"I speak not of surrender or of Jerusalem. I seek to prepare the way for our renewal of the covenant promise."

Ben Battiah frowned. "The only way out of Jerusalem is on a bier," he said. "The dead are taken out, but some escaped that way, and the guards now stab all corpses at the gates."

"Therefore, everyone must believe that I am truly dead?"

"Yes. All the sages must believe you are dead, so their laments ring true. Then, because you are my uncle, I will accompany the bier out of the city."

Johanan stretched out his hand toward Ben Battiah. "Go then in tears, my son, for by morning your kinsman will be a corpse."

Ben Battiah returned to his camp, weeping. His companions asked him what had occurred and he told them that his uncle, the great sage Johanan ben Zakkai, was near to death and had called on him for comfort.

Johanan conferred with his disciples. "How shall you confirm my death?" he asked.

"We will attend to you, and then mourn you," they replied.

Johanan lay down on his cot and Eliezer and Joshua spread the word that their aged master was dying. They smeared oil on his face and hands, sprinkled ash upon it, and they solemnly took up their watch: Eliezer at his head and Joshua at his feet. The sages prayed, not for his health but for a merciful passage into the presence of the Holy One; for one does not, without seeming overbearing, ask God to grant a man in his nineties another decade of life. They came to pay their last respects. In the early hours of the morning, Johanan whispered to his disciples: "Go and see if the child who died is still in the chamber. If so, bring her corpse and lay it between my thighs, that I may stink of death."

Immediately, Joshua went and found the dead child and secretly brought the corpse to their room where they lay it between the legs of Johanan. At dawn the disciples came out and announced that the master had given up his spirit. Women wailed and sages mourned, "Alas, the pious man! Alas, the humble man! The disciple of Hillel has departed us!" The Zealots sent spies as mourners, and the pallor of his face and the stench of the body convinced them, so they let Ben Battiah take his uncle to place him among the dead outside the city walls.

Toward evening Ben Battiah came and told them to lay their master on the bier. The sages stood by repeating prayers. Eliezer carried him by the head, Joshua by the feet, and Ben Battiah walked in front. Many people bowed their heads as the little procession passed by. But at the gate, the guards came with a lance to run through the corpse. "Do not do so," said Ben Battiah, "for he is a great sage of Israel. Do you want people to say that when our teacher died his body was stabbed!"

"Then push him over the rocks and let the body fall," replied the gate commander.

"Do you want it said that we pushed the body of a revered sage over the rocks!" Ben Battiah exclaimed, and shook his head in disbelief.

Joshua raised his voice and proclaimed, "Lord of the Universe, I adjure you, do not depart from Israel on account of these impious men."

The commander of the guards laughed nervously, but the others looked ashamed and let them pass. They carried him down the road to a cemetery and set him among the graves. Johanan opened his eyes and drew a deep breath. He looked at his companions and glanced about the stone monuments. "Well done, son of my sister," he said with a faint smile.

"Wait now until we have returned to the city," said Ben Battiah. "Later, grave diggers will come to bury you. Ask them the way to the camp of Vespasian. He cannot be far off." He turned to the disciples. "We must return, for we have done our duty. Even now we cannot raise suspicions, or they will send out a band to kill him."

"May God go before you," said Eliezer.

"May God go behind you," said Joshua.

Johanan replied, "My sons, if God goes with me, I will come again for you."

They lifted him off the bier, with the dead child still between his legs, and returned to the city. Johanan lay still and quiet for several hours. Other bodies were brought out and placed near him. Then he heard the grave diggers come. He listened to them dig, lift a body, and cover it. They buried one man and another and another. They came to him. "My sons," he said. The grave diggers jumped and swore by their ancestors and a whole host of demons—"do not bury me, for I am not dead." They stood still, shaking, as Johanan raised himself slightly to one side and leaned upon his elbow. "By the grace of the Holy One, I am still alive."

"I know you," one of the men exclaimed.

"Whence do you know me?" asked Johanan.

"You signed the *ketubah* for my sister, eighteen or twenty years ago."

"Did I?" said Johanan. "And is she and her family well?"

"Well enough in times of sorrow, master. Her husband is dead, and her second son is with the Sicarii on Masada. But her eldest remains with her and her daughters."

"And what are you called?"

"Shammuah," said the man.

"Shammuah," said Johanan, "Listen carefully. The Holy One, Blessed be He, has sent me on a mission in which you also have your part."

"What is our mission, master?"

"I must speak with the Roman commander."

"That would be general Vespasian," Shammuah said authoritatively.

"Thank you," said Johanan. "Can you tell me where he may be found?"

"We can," he replied. "Only let us finish with the graves."

"Bury the child between my legs," he said, pulling at his robe.

They removed the corpse. "Yes, we will lay it to rest, and then we will shield you as you rise and walk before us into the shadows."

Johanan waited and did as they instructed. When they finished their task, he rose and they led him into the lower hills of Judaea, where they dwelt in tents.

"Stay with us this night," said the man, "and we will take you to the general tomorrow. He is encamped along the road to Gophna, perhaps six miles north."[19]

"That is but two hours journey. I will go even now, by the light of the stars."

The man shrugged. "Then I will go with you." And the grave diggers all agreed that if they were destined to be part of the mission, for good or ill, they must follow it.

Shammuah fetched a small donkey that grazed nearby, and they set Johanan upon it. One man walked before him, two behind, and Shammuah walked with him, telling him of all that had been happening in the land. "The troops are grumbling," he laughed. "They begrudge those soldiers in Rome, who live in luxury and cannot bear even the rumor of a war, yet choose the new emperor, while they, who toil day and night and grow gray under their helmets, cannot declare their own beloved general to be the new emperor."

"Do they," replied Johanan. "Who is the new emperor?"

"The general . . . I mean, the emperor Vitellius is emperor."

"Has Vespasian declared himself in support of Vitellius?" asked Johanan.

"No," Shammuah shook his head. "I also hear rumors that the troops will not permit it, for they know he is the better man, and has a strong son as a successor."[20]

"May it be so," said Johanan. "May it be so." Johanan fell into silent contemplation as Shammuah continued to expound on the condition of the land.

They reached the Roman camp. Large torches set in tripods lit the perimeter. Even in the darkness the standards of the general were visible in the midst of the camp. Johanan waited at a distance while Shammuah approached the guards.

"Another deserter?" the guards asked.

Shammuah replied, "I bring an elder and sage who escaped out of the city. He wishes to speak with the general."

"Does he bring an offer of surrender?"

"He does not speak for the Zealots, he told me, but for the rest of the Jews."

"Wait here," the guard said. Soon he returned. "The zodiac smiles upon you," he said. "The general will see him."

They led Johanan to the tent of the general. Inside, several officers stood near their leader, looking over a map on a table. They were still dressed in their red tunics, boots, and broadswords. The officers stood aside. Johanan bowed and proclaimed, *"Vive domine Imperator!"*

Vespasian's eyes narrowed. "Your life is forfeit on two counts," he said. "One, because you give me a royal greeting but I am not emperor, and to allow such a proclamation is treasonous. And again, if I were your king, why did you not come to me before now?"

Johanan replied: "As for your statement that you are not emperor, you soon will be, and therefore I merely anticipate what is."

Vespasian grunted, "Are you then a prophet of the Jews?"

"Neither a prophet nor the son of a prophet, O king, but it is written in our sacred oracles: *And Lebanon shall fall by a mighty one.*[21] 'Mighty one' is an epithet applied not to a commoner, but only to a king; and 'Lebanon' refers to the temple sanctuary."

"And as to the second count?"

"The Zealots would not let me."

"Yet you are here."

"As a dead man I was carried out of the city. Does not the stench go before me?"

"I suppose it does, but am I able distinguish the scent of a live Jew from a dead one?" The officers laughed. "What is your name?" asked Vespasian.

"Johanan ben Zakkai, Your Excellency."

Vespasian frowned a deep military frown of contemplation. "I will call for you again," he said; then he ordered that the Jew be given food, water to wash, and a fresh robe.

In due course, according to the dictates of military protocol, Johanan was led into the tent of Vespasian. This time, the general, dressed in a white tunic, sat alone in his ornately carved, yet portable, cathedra. His arms lay on the armrests, his hands hung down beyond. His head, with its slightly balding pate, tilted to the right as he gazed momentarily on the aged Jew, then he motioned to a stool nearby. Johanan walked over and sat upon it.

Vespasian cast a reproving air at Johanan. "Because of your many years I will listen to you. But I ask you to be forthright, and do not insult me with far-fetched excuses, such as the Zealots let no one out."

"I escaped by pretending to be dead, for only the dead are allowed out of the city."

"For three years Rome has sought a reconciliation; what do we require but an arrow and a bow as tokens of submission and the resumption of the daily sacrifice. But the Zealots have not been in control for three years. If you and your wise men were innocent of revolt, you would have attempted to remove the Zealots when you had numbers on your side. At least you should have departed Jerusalem and come before me then. But you did not." Johanan remained silent under the accusation, head bowed, eloquently admitting his guilt. "You see," Vespasian continued, "Rome requires a native class capable of ruling, or it must rule as if you were slaves. Under King Herod, Augustus left the land alone. Unfortunately, Agrippa is no Herod."

"You speak the truth, and you speak it wisely," said Johanan. "You will make a great emperor."

"Ah yes, the oracle. I have a Jewish general in my captivity now, one Josephus, who was in charge of the armies of the Galilee, but when he stood before me in chains, he said 'I come to you as a messenger of God, that you are master not of me only but of land and sea and the whole human race.'[22] There is a phrase for that, is there not? *Vaticinium ex eventu*, prophecy after the fact. Very convenient. Of course, I accept the support of any capable Jew, but you have indeed unknowingly preceded events by a day or two, and I wish to know if you speak truthfully. Do you believe that your ancient prophet speaks of me?"

"Yes."[23]

"Tell it to me again."

"If it please Your Excellency," said Johanan, "I will quote it more fully, though I must translate into Greek as I go." Vespasian nodded. Johanan closed his eyes and began methodically:

> He shall shake his hand against the mount of the daughter of Zion,
>     the hill of Jerusalem.
> Behold, the Lord, the Lord of hosts, shall lop the bough with terror:
>     and the high ones of stature shall be hewn down,
>     and the haughty shall be humbled.
> And he shall cut down the thickets of the forest with iron,
>     and Lebanon shall fall by a mighty one.[24]

Vespasian shook his head. "Though I hear the words, I do not understand the meaning."

"Our prophet, Isaiah by name, foresaw your coming to Judaea, and the towns of the district quake and quaver before you. Our God has given you the victory."

"And 'Lebanon' is the temple sanctuary?"

"Yes. Another of our prophets has prophesied: *Open your doors, O Lebanon, that the fire devour your cedars.* This, too, is for our time."[25]

"But the destruction of your temple is not a military goal. We prefer surrender and a resumption of normal life for the Jews."[26]

"The temple will be destroyed, for the very prophecy which foretells your rise to the throne also declares the destruction of the sanctuary. The two are one and the same. The Zealots themselves will burn it for they wish to force the hand of God, or take everything down upon their heads."

"And you say that I am the 'mighty one' of the oracle?"

"Yes, Your Excellency."

"Your prophets spoke oracles about Gentiles?"

"Often. The same prophet, Isaiah, who lived eight hundred years ago, prophesied that Cyrus, king of Persia, was the Lord's anointed one who would send the Jews back to the land of Israel.[27] Now, for our many transgressions, God will again destroy the city and the sanctuary, and you will become emperor before it is destroyed."

Vespasian laughed lightly and shook his head. "Do you know why I am here in Judaea?"

Johanan hesitated. "You enforce the rule of Rome."

"Yes, but why me? Why not someone of the ruling class, of ancient family and senatorial rank? Well, I do not expect you to know, so I will tell you. While I accompanied Nero on his artistic tour of Greece I slept during one of his interminable performances. Naturally, I fell into disfavor, and he sent me 'from his presence' to Syria, where I happened to be when Cestius Gallus bungled his administration." Vespasian paused and smiled at the turn of events. "But my father, of equestrian not senatorial rank, was a minor tax official, and I might have been a clerk in some office in Italy. He even fought on the wrong side, for Pompey, in the civil war. Now I am legate over a powerful army—the most powerful army of Rome."[28]

Johanan said, "The God of Heaven works in just such ways, from small to great, yet with a firm hand and clear vision."

"Perhaps you are right," Vespasian mused, and fell to pondering his rise and impending predicament. "And you?" he asked suddenly. "Are you descended from a hoary line of illustrious wise men?"

"My father was a small merchant, and I, too, have spent many years in the leather trade. We descend from a long line of commoners, of the clan of Zakkai, which returned from our exile in Babylon."[29]

Vespasian laughed lightly. "So, here we are, sons of commoners you and I. How shall we make the most of our destinies? As you are my guest, and you will remain so for a time, I shall confide in you. In two days, on the first of July, Tiberius Alexander, Prefect of Egypt—himself a Jew, did you know?—will declare Egypt in support of me for emperor. Two days

later, my officers will declare my legions for me. I will hesitate, but they
will ignore my reticence, and threaten to kill me if I do not accept. The armies of Syria will follow in orderly fashion. Of course, that means we
have another civil war on our hands, but Vitellius is a drunkard and he has
not the backing even in Rome to remain emperor. I will leave this war in
the hands of my son Titus and go to Alexandria where I will withhold the
corn supply and the empire will fall into my hands." Vespasian threw out
his hands with upturned palms of innocent submission. "So, you see, my
course of action is set." Then he leaned forward and pointed his finger at
Johanan. "But I do believe in Destiny." He nodded to show he meant
what he said, and Johanan nodded his appreciation of that fact. "It is much
better to follow Destiny than fight against it, is it not?"

The question had the firm characteristics of a rhetorical question, so
that Johanan demurred even to state the obvious "yes." But Vespasian,
seeing his reticence, said, "Speak your mind, sage of Israel."

Johanan bowed his head. "Your Excellency is wise and worthy of the
throne. Not only has Providence, which, when looking inward we are
inclined to call Destiny, given you victory over Jerusalem, but Providence has given you insight to provide on his behalf for the Jews who remain your subjects, both in Judaea and throughout the empire. Indeed,
were Your Excellency to inquire, 'Why hath Providence given me victory over the Jews?' surely there is a breadth to your destiny that awaits
seers of the whole. One man's destiny plays upon the destinies of many,
and the many upon the one, so that the whole is better ascribed as Providence. Just as it is within the nature of the highest to govern the greatest
expanse, so the God of Heaven governs the whole earth, and likewise,
under the divine shadow, the emperor governs the whole empire. As the
emperor's destiny touches the lesser destinies of all, and all touch him,
so Providence touches all and all touch Providence. In this way, God is
made all in all."

Vespasian massaged his cheeks and replied, "You are not unlike your
compatriot Josephus in your familiarity with Providence. But can you
make your point in more practical terms, something a mere soldier
might understand?"

"Your Excellency must appoint new leaders of the Jews, both seers
and overseers of your flock of Israel, men who are able to command and
obey, Jews on whom you can depend to act as administrators, and whom
the people respect."

"Why will they be better than the priests and the aristocracy?"

"They must come from among the people, gifted for their wisdom,
not their wealth; strict and authoritative interpreters of the customs of
the Jews."

"Are you such a man?"

"I am."

"What do you require?"

"Give me a city where I can establish a court for deciding the customs of the Jews, and let me fill the court with wise men."

"What city?"

"A city that is the personal possession of the emperor. Give me Jamnia."

Vespasian frowned. "That is imperial property, and *if* I were emperor, I could give you Jamnia . . . at least, I could authorize you to set up a court of Jewish customs."

"And give me the family of Gamaliel to act as leader of the Jews."

Vespasian wrinkled his brow. "The name Gamaliel is familiar to me. Is not Gamaliel, or a son of Gamaliel, a leader of the revolt?"

"Simeon son of Gamaliel," said Johanan, "was a leader, before the Zealots overthrew the elders of Jerusalem but his son, Gamaliel, has never been a party to the war."

"Why this family?"

Johanan now paused briefly. He inclined his head and said, "The oracle that proclaims your ascendency to the throne, continues."

"And?"

"It says: *And there shall come forth a rod out of the stem of Jesse, and a Branch shall grow out of his roots: And the spirit of the Lord shall rest upon him, the spirit of wisdom and understanding, the spirit of counsel and might, the spirit of knowledge and of the fear of the Lord.*[30] The dynasty of Gamaliel finds its roots in the lineage of our great king, David, whose father was called Jesse. Now that the tree is cut down, out of its stump a shoot shall come forth to rule the Jews by the ancestral laws. Only in this way can you rule the Jews, not only in Judaea, but throughout the empire."

"I have learned enough about the Jews to know that anyone from the royal line of David is dangerous and suspect."

"Gamaliel's lineage is through the maternal side, and therefore it is legitimate to the oracle but not for the throne.[31] Gamaliel son of Simeon understands that Rome must keep the peace. We would replace the corruption of the old priestly aristocracy with the virtue of sages."

Vespasian frowned contemplatively, but soon his frown became a subtle smile. "Shall I then show my faith in your oracle, and grant you what only a Caesar may grant?"

Johanan waited expectantly.

"Very well, Johanan son of Zakkai, I grant your requests, and may your god bless me for it that I may fulfill your oracle. You must remain in my custody for now—shall we say, as part of my Jewish council—but in due course I will have a letter drawn up that gives you claim to some of the imperial property in Jamnia where you can implement your vision as your prophecy unfolds. You shall be under my protection, and under my authority. Your will shall be my will; your decrees my decrees. When Jerusalem falls, you may request the life of Gamaliel and any other wise men you deem useful, so long as they have not participated in the revolt." Vespasian reclined in his chair. "Does that satisfy you?"

Johanan remained silent for as long as he thought it courteous. He said, "Would Your Excellency consider breaking off the siege of Jerusalem?"

Vespasian nodded and laughed lightly. "I would have thought the less of you had you not asked, but that is not possible, unless the city surrenders. If you can persuade the Zealots . . . but then, circumstances would be different, would they not? And prophetic oracles as well."

Johanan sighed, and his aged shoulders slumped beneath the weight of the future of Israel that lay upon them.

Vespasian clapped his hands. A steward stepped into the tent. "And now," the general said brightly, "as lowly commoners, let us drink to our destinies." The steward produced crystal goblets and poured the blood red liquid and served them.

Johanan drank deeply of the imperial and unkosher wine.

# Epilogue

We are called Israel. Tradition says the patriarch Jacob received this name because "he struggled with God," which is, in our ancient Hebrew tongue, *ISRA EL*. After wrestling much of the night with Jacob, the messenger of the Lord, being forced to utter a blessing so that Jacob would let him return to the ethereal heights, said: *Thy name shall no longer be called Jacob, but Israel, for thou hast striven with God and with men and hast prevailed.*[1] While Jacob no doubt thought he had been blessed, and the tradition continues to call it as such, any descendant of Israel will tell you the name has not been easy to live with. By our name we are labeled: contentious, quarrelsome, bellicose, pushy, stubborn, and a favorite slander is stiff-necked. Now, it is true that when we grumbled during our desert wanderings, the Almighty let out a tirade against us, in which the twice-yoked epithet "stiff-necked" was used three or four times, but we were young then and prone to complaining, and not without some justification. Moreover, that God called us stiff-necked does not give license to all the world.

In Alexandria, some Jew, perhaps it was Philo, divined a different etymology, one reckoned as far more suitable to our calling, and therefore closer to the truth, namely, "he who sees God"—in the Hebrew *ISH ROEH EL*.[2] Accordingly, Jews are seers, prophets of the Most High, who proclaim, both in word and deed, the universal rule of God. The mission, given first to Abraham, is to raise our arm, and with outstretched finger, point to the Creator of the universe, the Most High and only true God. In this task, we may not compromise, nor allow any human to usurp God's sovereignty.

Surely both etymologies are valid. They bespeak the growth and maturity of a people. We have listened now to voices over a span of six centuries. From Ezekiel's encounter with Hattil to the flight of Johanan ben Zakkai is 637 years. In the voices we hear the labored transformation of a people who declare the creed "YHWH alone for the Jews," to a people who declare the creed "YHWH the Most High alone for all the earth."

As King David wrote: *The earth is the Lord's and the fulness thereof, the world and those who dwell therein.*[3] Yet, even when we achieved a complete devotion to YHWH alone, there remained the dilemma between the universal rule of the Creator God, and the singularity of a "chosen people" with all the privileges and restrictions applied thereto. All this we have seen and heard, but let us briefly consider it again from the vantage of reflection upon a silent and empty stage.

Eliakim and Marah are not alone among the pruned branches of the genealogical tree. Their story repeated itself countless times, with countless "dead sons." For a Jew to cease to be a Jew is non-existence, and therefore death. No longer did we quote the proverb: *The fathers have eaten sour grapes, and the children's teeth are set on edge.* In the Exile, personal responsibility replaced corporate responsibility; nevertheless, we may say that for Eliakim, God slew the father for the sins of the son. Eliakim and Marah lost their hope of the promised return, but return we did and they have their place in the great progress. We may only hope that other young men in Tel-aviv learned somewhat from the death of Hattil, so that the weeping voices were not in vain.

Nor was Uriah alone in his dilemma. The rebuilding of the land after the exile was no less momentous a task than had been the first entrance into Canaan. The analogies are legion, and Ezra is rightly called the second Moses. Troubled times call for troubling measures. The fear that mixed marriages would lead the Jews back into their old ways of idolatry was genuine. Uriah made his decision, of that we may be sure, and one's love for God is never more invoked than when one must decide between God and the love of one's life. Ezra's goal probably did not require such drastic measures. Intermarriage between faiths has always been both blessing and bane. It becomes a battle of the more fervent faith, and so it should be, for in the absence of certainty, faith walks on.

Faith. There are those souls who believe and instinctively reach higher, who divine a presence beyond and above the canopy of heaven, a source to the awe inspired by the statues of gods and goddesses enshrined in their sacred space. Such a soul was Rami. She yearned for the God of Heaven, even as Egypt yearned for the waters of the Nile. We may believe that Rami's spirit carried her, and not she her spirit, so that a mixed marriage, even to a burnt-faced Cushite, will have made new converts of the villagers. And with the birth of her children, a yet greater House of Israel is born, as indeed, the Israelites who dwelt in Ethiopia appear to have done. During the latter years of the second temple, and certainly during the brief glory of Herod's temple, many offspring of Israel came up from Ethiopia to the great feasts for their once-in-a-lifetime pilgrimage. Whether or not the Jewish lineage in Ethiopia began in the days of Solomon, the community now thrives and shines the light of Yah far to the south.[4]

The Jewish colony at Elephantiné did not long survive. A few years after Natan and Rami fled Elephantiné, upon the death of the king, the second called Darius, the Egyptians threw off Persian rule. In due course Elephantiné came again under Egyptian control, and the community disappeared sometime thereafter. If they succeeded in rebuilding the temple, it will have been a far inferior building, more in line with synagogues than temples.

By the time that Alexander set out to conquer the first of an "infinite number of worlds," Jews worshiped YHWH alone, the creator of all possible worlds. The question then was whether YHWH indeed controlled history as the prophets claimed. What other answer could we give but "Yes"? Over the centuries little Israel, backwater of the empires, has succumbed to the political upheavals of the earth, but only in keeping with the visions of Daniel. There is, after all, a design to the ways of the Lord. Through weakness, we conquer. Transforming apparent defeat into victory is just the sort of tactic one would expect from an omnipotent God. How else does God amuse himself? Whether or not Tobiah grasped the divine playfulness, he seems to have understood that God moves in mysterious ways—and when dealing with Gentiles, God always sides with the stronger. Theokeles faithfully played his part in the divine design, and perhaps in the end, God will reward him for the blessings on Israel that he helped to bring about.

Then came another battle for the soul of the Jew, that is, the identity of the Jewish people. Jewish monotheism, spawned and incubated in harsh deserts and armed with a Mosaic constitution for an agrarian society, met the lush and verdant hillsides of urban Hellenism and the *polis*. Diaspora Jews, now so at home in Greek culture, will readily sympathize with our philhellene ancestors, such as Rhodocus and Glaphyra. They were among the pioneers who met with a glorious culture of art, science, and sport, and toyed with allegory, all in an attempt to reform Judaism and keep the words of Moses relevant for the progress of humanity. On the other hand, when all signs of Jewishness have been removed, we cannot endure on scent and memories alone. Whether we sympathize with the reform party or the orthodox traditionalists, we know that an adaptation of religious principles to cultural changes is necessary, and we saw that the orthodox themselves found a way. How could God expect otherwise? Did he not give us dominion over the earth, and instruct on how to exercise that dominion? Be fruitful and multiply; plant, reap, and build. Is not progress in culture part of that command? In the end, all Jews became Hellenized Jews, even the Hasidaeans, according to the will of God. And Hannah, she may be numbered among the myriads of souls, mostly women, who bowed to the vicissitudes of humanity while trusting in the benevolence of the Almighty.

With the rule of the Hasmonaeans we came into our own—an independent Israel once again. We replaced the worship of different gods with the worship of YHWH in different ways. When we look back, it appears like the democratization of Judaism, yet because it was the rule of God under review, and not a mere theory of kingship, on which the Greeks produced countless treatises, it was rather more serious. It was not just politics at stake, it was divine politics—something worth dying for. On the surface though, it looked like normal politics, and for a century, generations of the main parties—Sadducees, Pharisees, and Essenes—struggled to enforce their visions of the rule of God upon the land, and all this under a Hasmonaean ruler from an increasingly ineffective dynasty. The civil war between the sons of Salome produced a chaos that invited the order of Rome. Rome chose Herod, and Herod put an end to the power struggles, if not the ire, of the Essenes, Pharisees, and Sadducees.

Despite the internecine strife and the progressive Hellenization of Jewish life, collectively we began to observe the customs in a normative way. All agreed Torah was divinely inspired, imparted by Moses, and ought to be obeyed. But the interpreters were legion. Literal or symbolic? Strict or lenient? Oral Torah or written Torah alone? Priestly ritual purity for the few or for all? Solar or lunar calendar? May we reasonably hope that this sort of diversity, even in the form of heated bickering, is more pleasant to the eyes and ears of heaven than idolatry?

Josephus, in his effort to translate a very exclusionist sect of Jews to a Greek audience, describes the Essenes as neo-Pythagoreans. Philo, in his book on the *Contemplative Life* admiringly compares Essenes to a similar sect of celibate healers in Egypt called the Therapeutae. It appears that a portion of any people will set themselves apart for a simpler and purer life than society offers. Perhaps it is that lingering urge to return to Eden and to a time before we began obeying the command to be fruitful and multiply: a sure formula for chaos. Seth chose solitude and simplicity. But he too perished, chaste and celibate, in the great earthquake. The monastery of the Covenanters collapsed and few survived, so that the end of their days came like a thief in the night, and the great battle between the Sons of Darkness and the Sons of Light yet awaits to be fought. A group of like-minded Essenes returned to rebuild the community, but it was again obliterated in the great war. Today the once thriving monastery is a pile of rubble that lends its charm to the abandoned landscape of the Dead Sea.

The Pharisees receive a mixed review from Josephus, and that is accurate enough. One may say good and bad things about any group, for there is bound to be some unevenness among its members. Josephus admits, however, that Pharisees were the most accurate interpreters of the law, and they carried the greatest authority among the common folk. In other words, they sat in the seat of Moses.[5] However one chooses to score them, we acknowledge their ability to survive. Jonathan ben Uzziel outlived his master Hillel by two decades, well into the administration of Pontius Pilate, and raised up many disciples of Hillel. After the destruction of the temple, scores of second generation Hillelites gathered around the last disciple of Hillel, Johanan ben Zakkai, and erected their fence around Torah. But we shall refer to that at its proper place.

By comparison with the Essenes and Pharisees, the Sadducees had a good deal of power based on wealth, but very little influence. They were rich in gold and property, but impoverished of insight and imagination. Their insistence on the written Torah alone, when set against the oral Torah of the Pharisees, provides a classic distinction between the dead letter of the law and its living spirit. Yes, the Pharisees knew that the laws must change with the times, but above all, they knew that hope was the life of the spirit, and eternal life the hope of the ages. What had the Sadducees to offer? There, you see? Even Jokim the blind could see as much. And the preacher from the Galilee further opened his eyes to the invisible. As for Jeshua of Nazareth himself, I defer to Jokim's astute imagination without comment.

Some may sympathize briefly with Dositheus. There is, after all, nothing so disconcerting and open to doubt as a sustained hope in a blessed hereafter. It requires a great deal of faith, and to the rational mind there is something deeply suspicious about "blind faith." Still, a belief in eternal life gives meaning to this life as no other philosophy can. The vast majority of Jews do believe, and insofar as Jews, including proselytes, make up roughly a tenth of the Roman Empire, we may say those who believe are the Lord's portion. If a tenth of the people of the earth returns to dwell with God, that is humanity's tithe to the Lord. The rest, as the Epicureans maintain, live in pleasure or in pain, perhaps grateful in some clouded and undefined way for their brief existence yet asking for and expecting nothing else. They live like animals, spawned from animals, and if they believe that at death they cease to exist, they are justified in their belief, for so it will be. Death is an eternal sleep, and eternal life is, as it must be, the gift of a being greater than ourselves. That is all I have to say on the question. Except that in this life, the skeptics have the stronger argument.

At random we introduced Leah and Jose to speak for the multitudes of nameless and powerless peasants, and to attest to an element of meaninglessness in life that lingers about us day by day. They lived and they died, and we will follow in their footsteps, nameless heaps upon nameless heaps, marching over them to the present heights of the pyramid-like dung hill of humanity. Shalom, Most High, we who are about to die, salute you! Eternal life is essential to any notion of holiness.

We come to the third and final battle: the unity of the Jews under the universal rule of YHWH. And we admit at the outset that the Christians have both clarified and complicated the original mission of Abraham, and therefore of the Jews. As it is written: *I will multiply your descendants as the stars of heaven, and will give to your descendants all these lands; and by your descendants all the nations of the earth shall bless themselves: because Abraham obeyed my voice and kept my charge, my commandments, my statutes, and my laws.*[6] As David also said: *All the ends of the earth shall remember and turn to the LORD; and all the families of the nations shall worship before him.*[7]

The mission statement is concise. As it is written: *Turn to me and be saved, all the ends of the earth! For I am God, and there is no other.*[8] And again: *The LORD has bared his holy arm before the eyes of all the nations; and all the ends of the earth shall see the salvation of our God.*[9] And again: *It is too light a thing that you should be my servant to raise up the tribes of Jacob and to restore the preserved of Israel; I will give you as a light to the nations, that my salvation may reach to the end of the earth.*[10]

But who could foresee the implications? We note that the nations of the earth will bless themselves *because* Abraham obeyed the commandments, statutes, and laws of God. To begin with, then, is the mission to make Jews of all the earth, from India in the east, Ethiopia in the south, to Spain or Britannia in the west? Or will mere God-Fearers suffice? That is, must all who worship YHWH also obey the laws and customs of the Jews? There is no question that many of the myriad Jews today are converts or offspring of converts. Jewish women are prolific, but not that prolific. When Marcus, himself a proselyte, was sent to Sardinia, he commanded an army of Jewish proselytes, by definition born Gentiles. His offspring, of which Domitia gave him six, were all Jews, the four males all circumcised on the eighth day.

Nevertheless, Jews have exercised themselves for a long time over the question of what YHWH requires of the Gentiles. Philo alone, through his allegory of Torah, is responsible for innumerable God-Fearers, those who revere YHWH as the Most High and only god, but are unable or unwilling to cast their lot with the Jewish people in all manners and customs. Josephus too, has taken up the mission to proclaim the universal rule of the God of the Universe. But there are limits to the victory we may expect. All the earth will not become God-Fearers, much less Jews. Cyrus the Great was called the Lord's Anointed because he did the Lord's will and sent the Jews back to Judah, to rebuild the Lord's temple, but Cyrus never worshiped the Lord.[11] Caesar Augustus is praised as the perfect ruler of the Jews throughout the empire because he permitted Jews to live their lives according to their customs, but his daily sacrifices in the temple were a diplomatic gesture, and no Jew supposes that Augustus secretly worshiped YHWH. Much of the Jewish mission among the Gentiles involves self-defense. For every Petronius there is a Flaccus; for every Augustus there is a Caligula. As seers of God—according to the *ISH ROEH EL* etymology—we no longer find ourselves struggling with God, but we continue to struggle with men who would be God.

Even the Christians have begun to learn the truth of this, as a fair number were expelled from Rome under Claudius—among them Aquila and Prisca—and many were tortured and burned to death under Nero, and even now under Domitian, who is unworthy to be called the son of Vespasian. But as Jews and Christians are sent away from one city, they spread the tidings of God's salvation in another city, and by their willingness to die, they proclaim a truth worth dying for. Martyrdom for the sanctification of the Name will always be part of the mission.

The Christians, led by Paul of Tarsus, have developed a powerful God-Fearer formula for grafting Gentiles into the original tree.[12] Paul annulled the cultic commandments with respect to Gentiles, thus removing the balustrade between the Court of the Gentiles and the temple precinct. With this barrier gone, the ground is leveled and the mission becomes strictly a clash of philosophies. Demetrius of Athens is but one of many Greeks who clashed sword-philosophies with Christians. Whether or not he followed Paul, Dionysius the Areopagite, Damaris, and Lucian became Christians. If Paul and the Christians can garner another tithe of pagan souls for God, they have the blessing of Leontius the scribe. As Josephus says, the tribe of Christians, so named from Jeshua (Jesus in Greek) the sage and wonder worker, are not extinct at this day.[13]

Asteria and Balas, who entered the house assembly of Prisca and Aquila in Ephesus, also joined in their battle, not against flesh and blood, but against the world rulers of this present darkness, against the spiritual hosts of wickedness in the heavenly places.[14] For the mission of monotheism is and has always been the subjection of all creation to the rule of God, and the subjection of mankind in worship is quite the opposite of the manipulation of the powers by magic. But the human race does crave power.

Crave power well we may, but we are, in the end, powerless. On the ninth of Av, in the second year of emperor Vespasian, the temple in Jerusalem was destroyed. In the absence of a temple to YHWH anywhere in the world, the Samaritan-Judaean rivalry seems rather insignificant now, like children fighting over a pottery sherd. Samaritans called the destruction of Herod's temple an act of God, and not a few Christians have echoed the sentiment. It may be. That is how the prophets Jeremiah and Ezekiel described the destruction of Solomon's temple, but this time it cannot have been for idolatry. Something else is afoot. Until the temple is rebuilt and the sacrifices resumed, our arguments with the Samaritans will remain theoretical, and the descendants of Levi and Phinehas will have to take their inheritance from the land, as indeed, all priests and Levites have begun to do.

Master Josephus has not given up hope that the temple in Jerusalem may yet be rebuilt, but he hopes in vain. Johanan ben Zakkai's interpretation of the oracle has thus far proven true. Although Ben Zakkai did not long survive the end of Jerusalem, he survived long enough to establish his academy at Jamnia, and he issued a handful of decrees by which he set in motion the transformation of Jewish worship from temple to synagogue. Recently, Gamaliel the Patriarch received authority from the Roman governor of Syria to determine the Jewish calendar for all Jews in the empire, thereby regulating the holy days.[15] This concludes the shift of power from the class of priests to the new class of sages, who now ordain themselves as Rabbis. They will guide the people and answer to Rome. We must wait to see if the Jewish people accept them—even the Jews of Babylon and Ethiopia and Spain and to the ends of the earth.

We have come then to the present. See here, a Sibyl long ago declared of the Jews, "Every land and sea is filled with thee." Josephus wrote in his second book of the Jewish War, "There is not a community in the entire world which does not have a portion of our people." Philo of Alexandria also says that the Jews are so numerous no one country can contain them all, and they are to be found throughout the whole inhabited world, serving as priests of the Most High God.[16]

Very well then, upon these authorities let it be so. Let the Jews confirm that they are a People of the Book; for a book can go with a people in ways a temple cannot. Let the earth be the temple of the God of Heaven, as Rami foresaw, and let each supplicant be a sanctuary unto himself. Let the synagogues be filled, let wise men replace the priests, let prayers replace sacrifice; let the Jews become wanderers once again. The age of temples has passed or will pass; the age of books, scribes, and librarians begins and will never end. Let us press on with our mission to the ends of the earth.

# Notes

## Notes to Chapter 1

Primary sources are the biblical books of Jeremiah, Ezekiel, and 2 Kings 22–25. Also consulted for background are the following works: C. F. Whitley, *The Exilic Age* (Westport, Conn.: Greenwood Press, 1975 [1957]); Peter R. Ackroyd, *Exile and Restoration* (Louisville: Westminster, 1968); Susan Ackerman, *Under Every Green Tree: Popular Religion in Sixth-Century Judah* (Atlanta: Scholars Press, 1992). Karen Rhea Nemet-Nejat, *Daily Life in Ancient Mesopotamia* (Peabody, Mass.: Hendrickson Publishers, 2002). Story is set in the year 568 B.C.E. The quote is from Ezekiel 20:39.

1. Biblical tradition uses the variation Nebuchadnezzar (e.g., 2 Kings 24:1; 2 Chron. 36:6, 13; Ezra 1:7; Jeremiah 27:6) for Nebuchadrezzar (e.g., Jeremiah 21:2,7; 24:1; 25:1; Ezekiel 26:7; 29:18); the Akkadian is *Nabu-kudurri-usur* so the preferred form is Nebuchadrezzar, as the prophet Ezekiel uses exclusively.

2. Psalm 137:1.

3. Tel-aviv (Tel-abib) noted in Ezekiel 3:15; Tel-melah, Tel-harsha, Keruv (Cherub), Addan, and Immer are mentioned in Ezra 2:59 = Nehemiah 7:61; Kassifia (Casiphia) is mentioned in Ezra 8:17, without specific reference as a settlement, though apparently it held a treasury, and is included by scholars among the settlements in Babylonia. See Y. Aharoni and M. Avi–Yonah, *The Macmillan Bible Atlas* (rev. ed, 1977), map 163.

4. Zedekiah, who had been placed on the throne by Nebuchadrezzar, twice attempted to join a coalition against Babylon in alliance with Egypt, first in 594/3 with Psammetichus II, and again in 589/88 with Hophra, son of Psammetichus II. According to Josephus, Tyre also joined the coalition (*Against Apion* 1.21). The prophet Jeremiah recounts his counsel to Zedekiah in chapters 27–28. When the Babylonian army caught Zedekiah trying to escape Jerusalem, "they slew the sons of Zedekiah before his eyes, and put out the eyes of Zedekiah, and bound him in fetters, and took him to Babylon" (2 Kings 25:7).

5. "The fifth month on the seventh day of the month" (2 Kings 25:8), is the seventh of the month of Av, probably in July, in the nineteenth year of King Nebuchadrezzar, probably of 586 B.C.E. See H. Tadmor, "The Chronology of the First Temple Period: A Presentation and Evaluation of the Sources,"

(Appendix 2) in J. Alberto Soggin, *An Introduction to the History of Israel and Judah* (Valley Forge, Penn.: Trinity Press International,1993).

6. According to biblical tradition, the name Judah referred to tribal territory associated with Judah, the fourth son of Jacob (Genesis 29:35), essentially from Bethlehem to Hebron. King David's reign was identified with the territory of Judah, which included the tribal area of Benjamin where Jerusalem lay, but is called, ideally, the kingdom of Israel (1 Samuel 13:13; 15:28; 24:20). After the split of the kingdom of Solomon around 940 B.C.E. (1 Kings 12), the territories of the northern ten tribes, from Jericho to Dan, were called Israel (cf. "kingdom of the house of Israel" Hosea 1:4); in contrast to the southern kingdom of Judah (2 Chronicles 11:17), and the official histories are called the Chronicles of the Kings of Israel/Judah (e.g., 1 Kings 14:19, 29; 2 Chronicles 36:8). Prophetic writers occasionally refer to the people of Judah as an individual, harkening back to the eponymous ancestor (Hosea 5:13; Ezekiel 37:16), and poetically as feminine, emphasizing the people (Lamentations 1:3).

7. Zadok, whose genealogical lineage is uncertain, was a priest during the reign of David. He supported Solomon for the throne, and was then anointed (according to 1 Chronicles 29:22) as the high priest of the first temple. Ezekiel declared that when the temple would be rebuilt, only descendants of Zadok should attend to the altar of the Lord (Ezekiel 44:9–31). The post-exilic practice allowed any descendant of Aaron to serve as a priest in the temple, but the Zadokites controlled the high priesthood, until the Seleucid era, ca. 200 B.C.E.

8. In the absence of a temple, there arose a need for meeting places to worship, and these became the origins of the synagogue. The existence of such places are perhaps hinted at by the "sanctuary" in Ezekiel 11:16 and the "meeting house" in Jeremiah 39:8, and were no doubt supported by both prophets, as Jeremiah urges them to pray for the welfare of the land of their exile (Jeremiah 29:7).

9. The law against eating blood was ancient, and according to tradition, instituted with Noah (Genesis 9:4), and made explicit in Mosaic code (Leviticus 7:26–27; Deuteronomy 12:23–24), because it held the mystery of life (Leviticus 17:11).

10. 2 Kings 23:29; 2 Chronicles 35:20–25. The death of King Josiah occurred in 609 B.C.E.

11. Astarte, also called Ashtoreth, was a consort of Baal, the Canaanite god of the storm and fertility. Israelite devotion to Astarte is condemned throughout the biblical history, and may be "the queen of heaven" mentioned in Jeremiah 7:18, 44:17–18. Ishtar, the goddess of ancient Mesopotamia was the personification of the planet Venus, and therefore similar to Aphrodite and Venus in Greek and Roman mythology. Astarte was the west Semitic counterpart to Ishtar. Baking molds in the shape of a female figure have been found at Mari, and may represent the means by which women of Judah baked cakes to a fertility goddess. Such molds have recently been found on Cyprus.

12. Adapted from inscription, cited in Ackerman, *Under Every Green Tree,* 31.

13. Daniel and his three companions, Hananiah, Mishael, and Azariah, who rose to prominence in Babylon, are unattested historically outside the second-century B.C.E. book of Daniel (1:6), which is historically useless for the exilic era. Ezekiel refers to a Daniel (14:14, 20; 28:3) but includes him in a triad of famous pious non-Israelites, Noah, Daniel, and Job, and therefore cannot refer to a contemporary Judahite by that name. Ezekiel probably has in mind a legendary sage Dan'el found in the Ugaritic tablets of Ras Shamra, in James B. Pritchard, ed., *Ancient Near Eastern Texts Relating to the Old Testament* (3d ed. Princeton: Princeton University Press, 1969) 149–55. On the other hand, the tradition found in Daniel 1–6 is probably older than the composition of the book, mostly written in Aramaic, and it does not reflect or require a second-century historical setting; in any case, we know that some exiles rose in wealth and prestige in Babylon, and a late tradition with names is preferred over no tradition at all.

14. Jeremiah 31:29; Ezekiel 18:2. The implication is that the children suffer for the sins of their parents.

15. Jeremiah 29:7.

16. Lamentations chapter 2, especially verses 6–7.

17. Jeremiah 17:21, 27.

18. Upon the assassination of Gedaliah, governor of Judah, shortly after the destruction of Jerusalem in 586 B.C.E., a group of Judahites fled to Egypt and took Jeremiah with them (Jeremiah 43:2–7). They sided with Egypt against Babylon, and apparently felt that Jeremiah and his god had done nothing to help them against Babylon. In 570, the general Amasis led a revolt against Pharaoh Hophra. The deposed Hophra fled to the east, and supported Nebuchadrezzar's effort to subjugate Egypt. The Judahites of Egypt would be treated as enemies of Nebuchadrezzar, and very likely Egyptian and Babyloninan Judahites would be fighting each other. For a survey of the history of the Jews in Egypt until the destruction of the temple, see Joseph Mélèze-Modrzejewski, *The Jews of Egypt from Rameses II to Emperor Hadrian* (trans. Robert Cornman; Philadelphia: Jewish Publication Society, 1995) chapter 1.

19. The prophetic book of Ezekiel provides brief biographical information about the prophet. His name, *Yehezkiel,* means "God strengthens." He was of the priestly caste (1:3), therefore educated, married (24:18), and probably dwelt in Tel-aviv (3:15). It is most likely that he came to Babylon among the initial eight thousand exiles, before the destruction of Jerusalem (2 Kings 24:16). He began to have visions in the fifth year of the exile of king Jehoiachin, 593 B.C.E. (1:2), perhaps at the age of thirty (1:1). The latest dated oracle was in 571 B.C.E. (29:17). At some point the elders began visiting him for a word from the Lord (8:1), and we may assume he became an elder statesman of the Jewish community in exile, in that his oracles were preserved.

20. Ezekiel 24:1 = 15 January 588 B.C.E.

21. Ezekiel 24:15–24. Ezekiel is forbidden to mourn so that people will wonder at the lack of compassion and grief.

22. During the reign of Josiah (2 Kings 22), while workmen repaired the temple, a book was found, described as "the book of the law," which probably was the book of Deuteronomy, or a previous version of the book.

23. The later chapters of Ezekiel are filled with promises of the restoration of Judah, and the rebuilding of the temple, the most famous being the vision of the valley of dry bones (37:1–14).

24. Ezekiel 29:19–20.

25. Jeremiah 44:11–28; cf. 7:18. Jeremiah cites them: "We will surely perform our vows that we have made, to burn incense to the queen of heaven and to pour out libations to her" (v. 25). The Queen of Heaven in Jeremiah probably refers to both Astarte and Ishtar, and possibly the Canaanite goddess Anat, in other words a composite of the fertility goddesses.

26. Ezekiel 18:1–4.

27. Exodus 20:5.

28. Ezekiel 18:4, 20.

29. The concept of the god-king was prevalent in the ancient Near East, and especially in Egypt. While understandings of the true nature of the king's divinity differed, whether divine descent or a special relationship with the god, the rule of the god through the king was well established. The cry "Marduk is king" was common, and identical to the biblical cry "YHWH is king" (Exodus 15:18; Isaiah 52:7; cf 1 Samuel 8:7); and the human king was in some sense divine (e.g., Psalm 45:6; and the father-son relationship expressed in Psalm 2:7). The myth of *enuma elish* was the foundation for the kingship of Marduk, in which Marduk is victorious over Tiamat, primordial sea of chaos. With a central role in the state religion, the king of Babylon would perform an annual new year enthronement ritual to renew the kingship of Marduk.

30. "Whether they hear or refuse to hear . . ." (Ezekiel 2:5, 7; 3:11).

31. W. G. Lambert, *Babylonian Wisdom Literature* (Oxford: Oxford University Press, 1960) 281–82.

32. The prophet's dramatic performances symbolized the siege and destruction of Jerusalem: shave off hair and beard and destroy separate piles differently (5:1–4); lying on his side for 390 days (4:4–8); dig a whole in his wall (12:3–6); cook his food over cattle dung (4:9–16), which was a concession to Ezekiel, since God commanded him to prepare his food burning human dung, but Ezekiel protested.

33. The law of the stubborn and rebellious son (Deuteronomy 21:18–21) carries a strong affiliation with the theme of personal responsibility in Ezekiel 18.

34. Adapted from Ezekiel 20:33–39.

35. For this and other euphemisms for death, see J. A. Scurlock in *Civilizations of the Ancient Near East* (4 vols.; Jack M. Sasson, ed.; New York: Charles Scribner's Sons, 1995 [Unabridged 2 vol. ed. Peabody, Mass.: Hendrickson Publishers, 2000]) 3:1893.

36. Sheol is the Hebrew term for the grave, or the abode of the dead. Without cognates in other Semitic languages, and with little description in biblical tradition, the nature of Sheol and its comparison with other descriptions of the

netherworld remains difficult. Eventually it became associated with the Greek Hades (so translated in the Septuagint) and took on the imagery of Hades.

## Notes to Chapter 2

Primary sources are the books of Ezra and Nehemiah, which are traditionally one book in the Hebrew Bible, and have a very obscure textual and redactional history. The date of Ezra's return, during which the following events occurred, is debated and uncertain. The problem revolves around the relationship of Ezra and Nehemiah, both dominating figures, and whether the Artaxerxes mentioned in our sources was the first or second of that name; hence either 458 B.C.E. or 398 B.C.E., although a textual emendation has been suggested that would place it in 428 B.C.E. Secondary literature: Frederick J. Murphy, "The Restoration," chapter 2 in *Early Judaism: the Exile to the Time of Jesus* (Peabody, Mass.: Hendrickson, 2002). Story occurs around 458 B.C.E. Quote is from Ezra 9:11–12.

1. 538 B.C.E.; Ezra 1:1–2; 2 Chronicles 36:22–23. The anonymous prophet known as Second Isaiah, describes Cyrus as an anointed one of the Lord, when he prophesies: "Thus says the Lord to his anointed, to Cyrus . . ." (Isaiah 45:1).

2. Ezra 2, and Nehemiah 7, contain a long list of clans who joined in the return to Judah. Those associated with Bethlehem numbered around 123 (Ezra 2:21).

3. The Persian court commissioned Sheshbazzar to restored the sacred vessels to the cultic worship in Jerusalem and began the restoration of the temple foundations (Ezra 1:7–11; 5:13–16). There is great uncertainty over the relationship of Sheshbazzar to Zerubbabel; the former may have come in 538 B.C.E., and the latter in 520 B.C.E., or possibly they are the same person, but they are both credited with laying the foundations of the temple (Ezra 5:16; Zechariah 4:9; Haggai 1:1–11).

4. Zechariah 4:10.

5. Ezra 3:12–13. The foundations of the temple proved to be a disappointment to those who could remember the former house of God built by Solomon, although the younger generations shouted for joy. But the lack of stature of the proposed temple reflected on the glory of God, and the disappointment is also addressed by the prophet Haggai (2:3).

6. According to rabbinic tradition, two pubic hairs for a male or female were considered the mark of puberty and legal majority under the law; for example, "If a boy has grown two pubic hairs he is subject to all the commands prescribed in the Law; and he is fitted to become a stubborn and rebellious son (Deuteronomy 21:18–21) from the time that he has grown two pubic hairs until he has grown an encircling beard—the lower and not the upper one is meant for the Sages spoke in modest language" (Mishnah *Niddah* 6:11). Although the rabbinic source is late ( 200 C.E.), it probably reflects a very ancient

understanding of the legal definition of physical maturity when a person was capable of procreation, therefore of marriage and the responsibilities of society.

7. Moabites worshiped the god Kemosh (Chemosh), probably a survivor of the ancient Semitic pantheon, and Moabites were referred to as the "People of Kemosh" (Jeremiah 48:46; Numbers 21:29). Ancient (pre-biblical) sacred sites were marked by stone pillars, known as *matsevot,* but apart from the general gods and goddesses of fertility, we know very little about the cultic worship of Kemosh during the Persian period, although one Aramaic inscription suggests the cult survived into the late fourth and early third century B.C.E. (A. Lemaire, "Epigraphy, Transjordanian," *Anchor Bible Dictionary* 2:563). Kemosh is mentioned a number of times in the Mesha Stele, an inscription in praise of Mesha, the ninth-century B.C.E. king of Moab, who maintained a sanctuary to Kemosh in the city of Dibon, but the city does not appear to have been occupied during the Persian era.

8. The phrase Beyond the River refers to land west of the Euphrates River. The Persian empire was organized into provinces, and each province was governed by a Satrap, hence the provinces were known as Satrapies.

9. Ezra 7:25–26. The phrase "law of your god and the law of the king" can be (and therefore is) interpreted in two ways: either as two bodies of law, one Jewish (Torah) and the other Persian, or one law twice sanctioned (by god and by king), that is, "the law of your god which is also the law of the king." In either case, Ezra is granted the authority to implement and enforce Jewish law, which means the interpretation of whatever laws fall under the "law of your god." The phrase "all such as know the laws of your god; and those who do not know them, you shall teach," probably means Jews and non-Jews, such that Ezra is empowered to enforce laws on the entire population. It seems clear that the law Ezra enforced is very similar to our present Pentateuch, although there are differences in the details, and some laws are not found in the Pentateuch, which may suggest our extant text of Deuteronomy is a later redaction of the laws known to Ezra. Nor can we exclude the possibility that the phrasing of the letter has been reworked by a later redactor, perhaps the author(s) of 1 and 2 Chronicles, since the "law of your god and the law of the king" is strikingly similar to the "matters of the Lord . . . and . . . matters of the king" in the reconstructed judicial reform of Jehoshaphat (2 Chronicles 19:8–11). See Joseph Blenkinsopp, "Was the Pentateuch the Constitution of the Jewish Ethnos?" along with other articles in volume James W. Watts, ed., *Persia and Torah: The Theory of Imperial Authorization of the Pentateuch* (Atlanta: Society of Biblical Literature, 2001).

10. The following incident is taken principally from Nehemiah 8. Within the complicated textual tradition of Ezra-Nehemiah, the eighth chapter of Nehemiah is widely accepted as part of the Ezra tradition, the bulk of which is found at the end of the Greek 1 Esdras 9:37–55.

11. The festival in the seventh month is described in Leviticus 23:33–43 as an eight-day solemn assembly, and also in Deuteronomy 16:13–15, where it is called the Feast of Booths, and is a seven-day solemn assembly, and equates to

the Feast of Ingathering in Exodus 23:16. The command to build booths and live in them is found only in Leviticus, which gives the historical justification of God's provision of shelter during the wilderness period. The historical origins of the autumnal celebration are obscure but likely go back a long way as part of the agricultural calendar, with rituals and prayers for a good planting and harvest, and may well be the most ancient of the annual celebrations, perhaps the "yearly feast of the Lord at Shiloh" (Judges 21:19). Very likely the many pilgrims who came to Jerusalem for the celebration dwelt in tents or booths, for lack of room within the city.

12. The identity of *etz shemen* (lit. "oil tree" or "oil wood") in Nehemiah 8:15 is uncertain, and is not listed in the passage from Leviticus, upon which is it supposedly based (Leviticus 23:40). The phrase is grouped with various trees for construction (cedar, acacia, myrtle, cypress, and pine) in Isaiah 41:19, and elsewhere only for the cherubim and doors to Solomon's temple (2 Kings 6:23, 31–33). Revised Standard Version translates *etz shemen* as wild olive, but it is clearly distinct from the olive (*zeit*), is unsuitable for construction, and is unlikely to be the same as the "wild olive" (*agrielaios*) used by Paul in his metaphor of Romans 11:17, 24. See George A. Buttrick, ed., *Interpreter's Dictionary of the Bible* (4 vols.; Nashville: Abingdon, 1962) 2.293–94 for its probable identification with *Pinus halepensis,* the Aleppo pine. Rabbinic tradition identifies *etz shemen* as one of four kinds of cedar (i.e., some "resinous" wood), Babylonian Talmud *Rosh Hashanah* 23a.

13. The day of confession is described in Nehemiah 9.

14. Ezra 9:1–2. The term holy race, literally, "holy seed," is perhaps first used here, but draws upon concepts such as "a people holy to your God . . . chosen out of all the peoples that are on the face of the earth" (Deuteronomy 7:6), and the promise that the seed of Abraham would become a great nation, as the instrument of blessing to the whole earth (Genesis 12:1–2). While the goal is primarily separation from idolaters, the emphasis is clearly on the racial distinction of the seed of Abraham.

15. Asenath (Aseneth), the daughter of Potiphera priest of On (Genesis 41:45, 50; 46:20); later tradition attempts to explain how a revered patriarch could marry the daughter of an Egyptian priest; on which see *Joseph and Aseneth* (*Old Testament Pseudepigrapha* 2:177–247); and J. Aptowitzer, "Asenath, the Wife of Joseph," *Hebrew Union College Annual* 1 (1924): 239–306. The Tamar story is found in Genesis 38. On the wives of Moses, see Exodus 2:16–21 (a Midianite) and Numbers 12:1 (a Cushite), which perhaps gave rise to the legend described by Josephus that Moses married the Ethiopian princes Tharbis as a condition for the surrender of the city of Saba (*Jewish Antiquities* 2.243–253).

16. The book of Ruth recounts the story of David's ancestress, and was probably written in response to the views of exclusion found in the books of Ezra and Nehemiah.

17. On Solomon's wives, and the severe judgement of tradition, see 1 Kings 3:1; 11:1–10; Nehemiah 13:26.

18. Nehemiah 13:24. The two incidences of dealing with mixed marriages are probably separate, and demonstrate the continued difficulties in voluntary compliance.

19. Ezra 10:7–8.

20. Ezra 9:10–12; this injunction is not found in our current texts of Deuteronomy or Joshua or any of the Prophets; but may be traced to Deuteronomy 7:1–3; and other passages such as Deuteronomy 23:3–7. While Deuteronomy does ban marriages with certain groups in proximity to Israel, the Torah of Moses never bans marriages to non-Israelites *per se*.

21. Ezra 10:15.

22. Genesis 19:31–37. The historicity of this etymology is highly questionable, but it served a purpose in the traditions of Israel.

23. Deuteronomy 23:3–4; see also Nehemiah 13:1.

# Notes to Chapter 3

Our knowledge of the Jewish colony at Yeb or Elephantiné, pronounced elephan-TEE-nay, (Greek, Ἐλεφαντίνης), is based largely on the cache of Aramaic papyri and ostraca found there at the turn of the last century. To this we may add a few epigraphic and literary references concerning Elephantiné (e.g., Herodotus, *History* 2.28–30; Josephus, *Jewish War* 4.611) and the biblical record of political ties between Judah and Egypt from the eighth to the fifth centuries B.C.E. The papyri have been translated and analyzed by Arthur Ernest Cowley, *Aramaic Papyri of the Fifth Century B.C., Edited, with Translation and Notes* (Oxford: The Clarendon Press, 1923), whose numbering of the documents is the standard reference, and more recently by Bezalel Porten, *The Elephantine Papyri in English: Three Millennia of Cross-cultural Continuity and Change* (Leiden / New York: E. J. Brill, 1996). On the Jews and their life in Elephantiné, see Bezalel Porten, *Archives of Elephantine: The Life of an Ancient Jewish Military Colony* (Berkeley / Los Angeles: University of California Press, 1968); and the chapter of Joseph Mélèze Modrzejewski "The Stronghold of Elephantine" in *The Jews of Egypt from Rameses II to Emperor Hadrian* (trans. Robert Cornman; Philadelphia: Jewish Publication Society, 1995). Story occurs in 407 B.C.E. Quote is papyrus Cowley, *Aramaic Papyri* 32 = Porten, *Elephantine Papyri* B21.

1. The origin and pronunciation of the tetragram YHWH remain uncertain. The vocalization of "Yahweh" is the most plausible scholarly guess, based on grammatical considerations, and other epigraphy. The shortened form, YH, occurs in poetic passages of the Bible (e.g., Isaiah 12:2; Psalm 68:5), and is used in personal names, whereas the full name YHWH is never combined in names. Throughout the Elephantiné papyri, the consonants YHW occur, with the probable pronunciation of Yahû, whereas the full tetragram is not found at all in the surviving papyri.

2. Two goddess, Ishumbethel and Anathbethel, are mentioned in Cowley, *Aramaic Papyri* 22, lines 123–125; and Anat-Yahu in 44.

3. A home mentioned in a loan contract is described as a "brick-house" (Cowley, *Aramaic Papyri* 10:9); for further description, see Porten, *Archives,* 101.

4. A detailed account of the attack is given in the petition of Jedaniah to rebuild the temple (Cowley, *Aramaic Papyri* 30 and 31).

5. Herodotus, who visited Elephantiné after the Persian conquest, around the year 449 B.C.E., recounts how men would harness boats, as they harness an ox, to tow up river (*History* 2.29). Among the papyri we find the occupation title "boatman of rough waters," or "boatman of the cataract" (Cowley *Aramaic Papyri* 6 and 8).

6. One papyrus, with a date corresponding to 412/411 B.C.E., is an order to repair a boat, and lists the authorized materials (Cowley, *Aramaic Papyri* 26).

7. Several papyri give evidence for Jewish oaths to Sati and intermarriage, though we do not know to what extent Egyptian marriage partners accepted Jewish worship, or Jews worshiped Egyptian gods; an oath to Sati (Cowley, *Aramaic Papyri* 14); to swear by Anath-Yahu (Cowley, *Aramaic Papyri* 44 ); Egyptian woman married to Jewish man (Cowley, *Aramaic Papyri* 34 ). See Porten, *Archives,* 151–58.

8. The title God of Heaven, rare in the pre-exilic tradition, appears nine times in the Aramaic papyri of Elephantiné, as well as numerous times in the post-exilic books of the Hebrew Bible (Ezra, Nehemiah, Daniel, Jonah 1:9). This was part of the gradual shift in the Jewish view of God as the particular God of Israel, to a universalistic God of Heaven. The rationale that God is too great to dwell on earth may be traced much earlier, for example, Solomon's prayer in 1 Kings 8:27, "But will God indeed dwell on the earth? Behold, heaven and the highest heaven cannot contain thee; how much less this house which I have built!"

9. Scholars assume that Egyptian followers of Khnum, a god represented by the ram, or as a human with a ram's head, were bound to take offense by the sacrifice of rams, and possibly of lambs at Passover, within the vicinity of the temple of Khnum. Although there is no specific evidence in the papyri, this conflict would be the most logical reason for destroying the temple of Yahu.

10. The petition to rebuild the temple refers to the demise of Vidranga, as well as all those who participated in the destruction of the temple of Yahu (Cowley, *Aramaic Papyri* 30 and 31).

11. We have no direct evidence that Jews had already migrated to Ethiopia, though Esther 8:9 implies the spread of Jews from India to Ethiopia; and other earlier biblical passages appear to assume a far-flung diaspora; e.g., Isaiah 11:11–12; 19:19; Zephaniah 3:10. Modern Falashas are accepted as Jews by Israel, and they claim a heritage back to Solomon and the Queen of Sheba. For a thorough evaluation of the Falasha traditions, see David Kessler, *The Falashas: A Short History of the Ethiopian Jews* (3d ed., Portland, Ore.: Frank Cass, 1996); E. Ullendorff, *Ethiopia and the Bible* (rev. ed.; London: Oxford University Press, 1988).

12. The source for this tradition is *Letter of Aristeas* 13, found in volume 2 of James H. Charlesworth, ed., *The Old Testament Pseudepigrapha* (New York:

Doubleday, 1983). It is uncertain which Psammtik (Psammetichus in Greek), I (664–610 B.C.E.) or II (595–589 B.C.E.), is meant, since both fought against Ethiopia and Jewish mercenaries along with Greeks and others were active during both reigns. Porten, *Archives* 8–16, favors Psammetichus I, to whom Manasseh, king of Judah, had cause to send auxiliaries as part of an alliance.

13. Herodotus, *History* 2.30 and 159, describes the deserters as Egyptians of the warrior caste, and gives the probably inflated number of 240,000 soldiers. If soldiers from Judah were already fighting for Pharaoh Psammetichus, it is possible that they too settled in Ethiopia, continuing the dispersion of Jews.

14. Meroë, described as an island city and a kingdom, lay between the Blue Nile and White Nile, about 120 miles downriver from modern Khartoum. Josephus identifies it with the biblical Seba (Saba), which he says Cambyses renamed Meroë (*Jewish Antiquities* 2.249). As one of the known "distant lands" it qualified as an example of the "ends of the earth."

15. Herodotus (*History* 3.17–20) describes the Ethiopians as the tallest and most handsome of peoples. The reputation of height was known to Isaiah, who calls the Sabeans of Ethiopia tall of stature (45:14).

16. The petition to rebuild the temple (Cowley, *Aramaic Papyri* 30 and 31) describes the wearing of sackcloth, along with abstention from sexual relations, anointing with oil, and drinking wine, as part of their communal mourning.

17. Based on the recorded dimensions of surrounding houses, the temple court is reckoned, according to Porten (*Archives,* 110), to be sixty by twenty cubits, about ninety by thirty feet, and reminiscent of Solomon's temple in dimensions, but with a smaller temple shrine, called an altar house (Cowley *Aramaic Papyri* 32).

18. Although it is probable that decisions were made by the adult males, and for general community affairs only men would be present, for such a momentous announcement, the entire community would have come, including the women and children, as we saw for the convocations called by Ezra (Ezra 10:1; cf. Nehemiah 8:2–3; 12:43).

19. Forbidding holocaust sacrifices is implied by the absence of permission granted for sacrifices (Cowley, *Aramaic Papyri* 32) in response to the initial request, in which the Jews of Elephantiné promise to offer up sacrifices and prayers for Jerusalem. This would be consistent with the centralization of cultic authority begun by Ezra, although a rival temple was built in Egypt at Leontopolis (near the Delta, probably the modern Tell ha-Yehudiyeh) two centuries later (*Jewish Antiquities* 13.62–73), and according to Josephus (*Jewish War* 7.436), it stood until the destruction of the second temple, that is, from about 170 B.C.E.–74 C.E. Josephus further says that the temple in Egypt was prophesied by Isaiah (19:19): "On that day there will be an altar to the LORD in the center of the land of Egypt, and a pillar to the LORD at its border." It is just conceivable, though impossible to know, that this oracle, or one like it, also encouraged Jews to build their altar house at Elephantiné, on the border of Egypt. See Porten, *Archives,* 116–20.

20. Deuteronomy 12:5–6. Scholars have noted that the texts of Elephantiné contain no mention of Moses or the Torah, although the restricted nature of the evidence may explain the absence of many topics otherwise known. The fact that the community did perform animal sacrifice may mean they were ignorant of the book of Deuteronomy and the prohibition against sacrifices anywhere but Jerusalem, or they felt it applied only to the land of Judah. Since we know they were in communication with Jerusalem, and emissaries from Judah had come before, the latter interpretation seems more reasonable.

21. The opinion that Khnum worked against the Jews since the arrival of Hananiah is expressed by a Jew, Mauziah (Cowley, *Aramaic Papyri* 38), and witnesses the belief that the Egyptian god was real and active. On the question of Passover regulations, see Deuteronomy 16:9, and the "Passover papyrus" (Cowley, *Aramaic Papyri* 21), dated fifth year of Darius, 419–18 B.C.E., at least twelve years earlier; on which see discussion of Porten, *Archives,* 128–33; 279–82.

22. One argument made by the Jews of Elephantiné in their request to rebuild the temple was that the Persian conqueror, Cambyses, found the temple (in 525 B.C.E.) well established and sanctioned its continue function there (Cowley, *Aramaic papyri* 30 and 31). If the Jewish colony had been there since Psammetichus I (664–610 B.C.E.), the temple would likely have stood for over two centuries.

23. Based on Zephaniah 3:10. The prophet Zephaniah was active during the reign of Josiah (640–609 B.C.E.). According to the lineage, he was the son of Cushi, or "a Cushite" meaning an "Ethiopian" (1:1), and if the latter is meant, he may have had some Ethiopian ancestry. His extensive genealogy of four generations may have been an attempt to establish his lineage in the face of doubts about his ancestry.

24. One document, dated after 407 B.C.E. (Cowley, *Aramaic Papyri* 33), lists five wealthy Jews, citizens of Syene and hereditary land owners, who will pay a promised sum of silver and produce, if permission is granted to rebuild the temple. The document also notes the condition that sheep, ox, and goat sacrifices will not be made. We have no certain evidence that the temple ever was rebuilt, and the latest dated papyrus is 399 B.C.E.

25. The legend of the source of the Nile is recounted by Herodotus (*History* 2.28).

## Notes to Chapter 4

Primary sources are Josephus's account of Alexander's campaign in *Jewish Antiquities* 11.304–339, and other ancient sources on Alexander, principally Arrian, *History of Alexander,* all of which are thoroughly analyzed by Robin Lane Fox, in *Alexander the Great* (London: Allen Lane, 1973 [American edition, The Dial Press, 1974]); and Peter Green, *Alexander to Actium: the Historical Evolution of* the Hellenistic Age (Berkeley: University of California Press, 1990). Suffice to say that the Jewish legends of Alexander are every bit as legendary as any others. Besides Josephus, there are parallel accounts in rabbinic literature, principally Babylonian Talmud *Yoma* 69a; on which see Appendix C in the Loeb Classical Library edition of *Jewish Antiquities,* vol. VI; on the legend in general, see Shaye J. D. Cohen, "Alexander the Great and Jaddus the High Priest According to Josephus," *Association for Jewish Studies,* vols. 7–8 (1982–83): 41–68. Story is set in 332 B.C.E. Quote is from *Jewish Antiquities* 11.317–319; translation by William Whiston in *The Works of Josephus Complete and Unabridged* (Peabody, Mass.: Hendrickson Publishers, 1987).

1. Three men named Tobiah occur in the post-exilic biblical record: Zechariah 6:9–15 (Revised Standard Version reads Tobijah), Ezra 2:60, and Nehemiah 2:19. The name is also found in other sources, such as the Lachish Letters, 3 where a Tobiah is "the arm of the king" suggesting a position of some prestige in the service of Persian government, and a cache of banking documents dated to the end of the fifth century B.C.E. tells of a branch of Tobiads settled near the Babylonian city of Nippur. If the various Tobiahs are related, they did indeed form a wealthy clan. For a detailed study, and a possible genealogy of the Tobiads, see Benjamin Mazar, "The Tobiads," in *Israel Exploration Journal* 7 (1957) 137–45, 229–38; also Jonathan A. Goldstein, "The Tales of the Tobiads," in Jacob Neusner, ed., *Christianity, Judaism, and Other Greco-Roman Cults* (4 vols.; Leiden: E. J. Brill, 1975) 3:85–123. Josephus gives the Tobiads an important role in Jewish history following Alexander the Great (*Jewish Antiquities* 12.157–236).

2. In Ezra 2:59–60 (= Nehemiah 7:61–63), the "sons of Tobiah" are considered of doubtful Israelite lineage, perhaps due to intermarriages.

3. Ezra 2:59–63. The Urim and Thummim were probably two tiles or stones, which were kept in the breastplate of the high priest and used for divining questions put to God (see, for example, 1 Samuel 14:40–44 and 28:6). The post-exilic reference to Urim and Thummim is rather cryptic, and we have no evidence that these ancient "lots" were ever used in the Second Temple era. According to early rabbinic tradition, the Urim and Thummim ceased with the end of the former prophets, that is, before Solomon's temple was destroyed (Mishnah *Sotah* 9:12), and from the commentary it appears to have become an idiom for "never." Since the Urim and Thummim were never revived, the phrase in Ezra 2:63 was interpreted to be idiom for never, or the remote future, similar to "Until the dead revive and the Messiah, son of David, comes!" (Babylonian Talmud *Sotah* 48b; see also *Qiddushin* 69b). Nevertheless, it apparently remained part of the ideal system of knowing the will of heaven. The Temple Scroll (11QT = 11Q19), of the Dead Sea Scrolls collection, which is a law code for a new eschatological Israel, says the king shall not go to war without the high priest consulting the Urim and Thummim (11Q19, Col 58).

4. According to Mazar (The Tobiads, 336), it was perhaps during the reform of Josiah (622 B.C.E.), that the name Tob-El changed to Tob-Yah(u).

5. In the opinions of both Josephus (*Against Apion* 1.224–225) and Philo (*Flaccus* 29; *Special Laws* 3.1–5), the strife between the Jews and Egyptians in Egypt was due to the overwhelming envy of the Egyptians for the status and success of the Jewish community. Josephus also speaks of a widespread envy against Jews in the Hellenistic world (*Against Apion* 1.72).

6. Arses, the youngest son of Artaxerxes (Ochus) III, reigned 338–336 B.C.E., after his father was assassinated by the court Eunuch (Grand Vizier) Bogoas, in a palace coup.

7. Darius III, known as Codomannus, was the son of a brother and sister marriage, and a distant collateral relation to the Achaemenid dynasty. He was apparently the most suitable replacement to the throne, when the Grand Vizier Bogoas wished to regain control of the palace and assassinated Arses. When Darius Codomannus secured the throne, he executed Bogoas, and ended the court intrigue. This Darius is noted as the "fourth king" in Daniel 11:2.

8. According to Herodotus (*History,* 2.44), who visited Tyre around 450 B.C.E., the temple to Melkart was built when the city was founded, twenty-three hundred years before, that is around 2700 B.C.E.; and archaeological evidence supports this date. The island city of Tyre came into historical prominence under king Hiram I (969–936 B.C.E.), who worked with Solomon to establish trade routes and build up both kingdoms (1 Kings 9:26). Tyre continued the alliance with Israel by the marriage of princess Jezebel of Tyre and Ahab of Israel (1 Kings 16:31), and Tyrian colonists founded Carthage, helping Tyre to become a leading maritime city of antiquity. Kings of Tyre paid temporary tribute to the dominant kingdoms of Assyria (*Jewish Antiquities* 9.285–287), and to Babylon, on which see H. J. Katzenstein, *The History of Tyre* (Jerusalem: Schocken Institute, 1973), 326–33.

9. Ezekiel 29:18. For the early prophecy against Tyre, see 26 and 27, especially 26:7–8. According to Ezekiel, because Nebuchadrezzar failed to destroy Tyre and get the booty, God would give him Egypt as payment for his long suffering soldiers (29:18–20). See also Josephus, *Jewish Antiquities* 10.228; *Against Apion,* 1.156.

10. Arrian, *History* 2.21.

11. Because of the successive assassinations in the Achaemenid court, Persian loyalties were divided, and Alexander used the court struggles as justification to defeat this inbred usurper, who "unjustly and illegally seized the throne"(Arrian, *History* 2.14; Diodorus, *Library* 17.5.3–6).

12. According to Arrian (*History* 2.18), the deepest part of the channel was three fathoms (= eighteen feet), and Diodorus (*Library* 17.40) tells us the mole was about two hundred feet wide.

13. Arrian, *History* 2.18–19.

14. Plutarch, *Life of Alexander* 6.

15. Arrian, *History* 2.26; Plutarch, *Life of Alexander* 29.7–9.

16. According to Isaiah 44:28 and 45:1, Cyrus is called the Lord's anointed (Messiah) for the task of restoring the Jews to their land. Josephus (*Jewish Antiquities* 11.336–337) says that when Alexander finally came to Jerusalem to

receive the tokens of submission, the elders brought out the book of Daniel and showed him how it was prophesied that a conqueror would take the throne of Persia (Daniel 8:21; cf. 11:2–3). Besides the anachronism of having these chapters of the book of Daniel available at this time, (chapters 7–12 were probably written around 165 B.C.E.), the prophecy would have made the decision to submit fairly straightforward, assuming it was understood to refer to Alexander before his victory over Tyre.

17. The diminutive stature of Alexander became part of his legend, though no precise height is given in the ancient sources. We are told that when Alexander sat on the throne of Darius, he required a table, rather than a footstool for his feet. Arrian (*History* 2.13) recounts an incident reflecting the stature of Alexander. When the Persian royal harem found itself at the mercy of Alexander after Darius fled Damascus for Babylon, the queen mother came to Alexander, who was alone in his tent with only his companion Hephaestion. As both men were dressed in simple tunics, she prostrated herself before Hephaestion, who was taller than Alexander, and an attendant had to nudge her in the proper direction. Alexander graciously smoothed over the mistake. See Fox, *Alexander,* 41–42; Green, *Alexander,* 307.

18. According to Josephus, Alexander invited any Jews of military age to join his forces, while still following their Jewish customs (primarily dietary and sabbath laws), and that "many were ready to accompany him in his wars" (*Jewish Antiquities* 11.339). It is equally probable that many Jews moved to Egypt, and joined in the founding of Alexandria and the development of the later Ptolemaic kingdom. As Josephus says, Alexander placed Jews in many of his garrisons, and gave them rights equal to the Macedonians in Alexandria, and later many other Jews, "of their own accord, went into Egypt, as invited by the goodness of the soil, and by the liberality of Ptolemy" (12.8–9).

# Notes to Chapter 5

Primary sources: 1 Maccabees 1–4; 2 Maccabees 1–11; *Jewish Antiquities* 12.154–326. The sources do not give a uniform chronology, and there is some dispute on whether the temple was rededicated in December of 165 or 164 B.C.E., on which, see Lester L. Grabbe, *Judaism from Cyrus to Hadrian* (2 vols.; Minneapolis: Fortress, 1992), 1:264–66. The interpretation of the conflict follows Elias J. Bickerman's seminal studies, *The God of the Maccabees: Studies on the Meaning and Origin of the Maccabean Revolt* (trans. H. R. Moerhring; Leiden: E. J. Brill, 1979); and *From Ezra to the Last of the Maccabees: Foundations of Postbiblical Judaism* (New York: Schocken Books, 1962). Also very useful are Martin Hengel, *Judaism and Hellenism: Studies in their Encounter in Palestine During the Early Hellenistic Period* (2 vols.; trans. J. Bowden; Philadelphia: Fortress Press, 1974); Peter Green, *Alexander to Actium: the Historical Evolution of the Hellenistic Age* (Berkeley: University of California Press, 1990), 497–524; and Frederick J.

Murphy, *Early Judaism: the Exile to the Time of Jesus* (Peabody, Mass.: Hendrickson, 2002), 91–126. Story is set around 165 B.C.E. Quote is from 1 Maccabees 1:11–15 (Revised Standard Version).

1. Plutarch, *On the Tranquility of the Mind* (*Morals* 466 D).

2. The story is first told in the *Letter of Aristeas* 301–311 (*Old Testament Pseudepigrapha,* vol. 2); recounted by Philo (*On the Life of Moses* 2.31–40) and Josephus (*Jewish Antiquities* 12.101–109). Philo also praises the Ptolemaic dynasty as "exceedingly eminent . . . above other royal families," and Ptolemy Philadelphus as a "most excellent sovereign" (*Moses* 2.28–30).

3. The geographical name Palestine is the Greek designation of territory occupied by the Philistines, the southern coastal lands of modern Israel, primarily from Joppa through Gaza to Egypt, and is used somewhat loosely by Herodotus for the area south of Syria (*History* 2.104), as Josephus notes (*Against Apion* 1.169–171; cf. *Jewish Antiquities* 1.136). Josephus also uses Palestine to describe the land of Israel in the conclusion of his *Jewish Antiquities* (20.259), but more often he uses the older description of the land of the Philistines alongside Judaea (*Jewish Antiquities* 13.180; cf. *Jewish War* 5.384). It was only after the failed revolt of Bar Kokhba that Rome officially named the land of the Jews as Palestine, so that the reference of Josephus in book twenty is unusual.

4. 1 Maccabees 2:44.

5. The Greek *Makkabaios* (Μακκαβαιος) is widely interpreted as the Greek transliteration of the Hebrew (or Aramaic) *maqqabah,* (מקבה) "hammer," therefore Judah the Hammer, or Hammerer. This etymology, however, is uncertain.

6. 2 Maccabees 11:16–33 records three letters concerning the negotiations for peace, and the edict by King Antiochus IV rescinding the ban on Jewish practices, apparently at the request of Menelaus.

7. The Hasidaeans is the English equivalent of the Greek transliteration (*Asidaioi*) of the Hebrew *Hasidim,* meaning Pious Ones. They were a group of Jews who strictly obeyed the law, distinct from Mattathias and his initial supporters. The term *hasid* (plural *hasidim*) is used in the biblical text, translated faithful ones (1 Samuel 2:9; Psalm 149:1), or saints (Proverbs 2:8; 2 Chronicles 6:41), but never as a distinct group of people among Israel. Their origins as an identifiable group is unknown, but likely developed in response to the shift toward Hellenism after Alexander, and certainly before Antiochus.

8. 1 Maccabees 2:33–41. Ancient Near Eastern texts suggest that it was apparently a well known tactic to attack Jews on the sabbath day, and in the first battle of the war, Apollonius took advantage of the sabbath to enter Jerusalem (2 Maccabees 5:24–26); see G. F. Hasel, "Sabbath" in the *Anchor Bible Dictionary* 5:853.

9. The Samaritans had no radical Hellenist party seeking to do away with the laws, and they petitioned the king that if left alone, their crops would be full and their tribute greater. Antiochus agreed and excluded them from the ban (*Jewish Antiquities* 12.257–264). The ban on Jewish customs was certainly restricted to Judaea, and possibly intended to be enforced primarily in Jerusalem, although some effort was made to include the larger towns and villages in the

vicinity of Jerusalem. There is no evidence that it extended to the Jewish communities beyond the Euphrates. See Hengel, *Judaism and Hellenism*, 292–94.

10. Phylacteries (Aramaic *tefillin*) are derived from Exodus 13:9, 16; Deuteronomy 6:8; 11:18. Although we cannot be certain that the original intent of the passages was meant in a figurative sense (since ancient marks and amulets were used for divine protection, e.g., the mark on the forehead of Cain), it is likely that the command to "bind them as a sign on your hand, and they shall be as frontlets between your eyes" (Deuteronomy 6:8) was meant figuratively, since it refers to "these words" (v. 6) that Moses commanded them on that day, which refer at least to chapters 5–11, if not the entire book of Deuteronomy. The passage is similar to other commands such as "The Law of the Lord shall be in your mouth" (Exodus 13:9). In any case, the Torah gives no instruction on how the command should be fulfilled literally, as would be expected with a literal command. The earliest reference to a literal interpretation comes from the *Letter of Aristeas* 159, (*Old Testament Pseudepigrapha* 2:23) which speaks of a sign worn on the hand. Scholars generally date this text between 150–100 B.C.E., and that supports the gradual development of phylacteries, beginning sometime in the early second or late third century B.C.E.

11. The prohibition against boiling a kid in its mothers milk is found in Exodus 23:19; 34:26; Deuteronomy 14:21. We do not know when it was first interpreted as a prohibition against eating any meat with any milk, since the textual evidence is nearly two centuries later, but the origins may be laid to the Hasidaeans in the second, possibly third century, B.C.E., within the general movement to widen the biblical prohibitions. See below in chapter 7.

12. Circumcision of the heart means that the person is receptive to God, and this applies to women as well as men (Leviticus 26:41; Deuteronomy 10:16; Jeremiah 4:4; 9:25–26). Later, Philo (ca. 20 B.C.E.–50 C.E.) explains the meaning of circumcision to a Greek audience, noting that circumcision symbolizes the excision of the passions of the heart (*Special Laws* 1.1–11). Philo also complains that many Jews, the "extreme allegorists," accept only the allegorical meaning of circumcision, and not the literal (*On the Migration of Abraham* 89–93); on the other hand, Philo argues that the true proselyte to the God of the Jews is one who excises the passions of his heart, not one who circumcises his uncircumcision (*Questions on Exodus* 2.2). Not only is there circumcision of the heart, but Scripture applies circumcision to ears, lips, and trees. Moses complains of uncircumcised lips, because the Israelites do not heed his words (Exodus 6:12. 30); Jeremiah accused the Israelites of having uncircumcised ears (Jeremiah 6:10); fruit trees (Leviticus 19:23–25). The word for uncircumcised (adj. *arel*), meaning to have a foreskin, (or n. *orlah* = foreskin) is used figuratively to mean obstructed or unreceptive, or in the case of fruit trees, forbidden, all of which go back to the ancient notion of taboo.

13. The dispute over circumcision, and what degree of foreskin removal constituted fulfilling the command of circumcision, was apparently widespread. Antiochus would not have supported a ban on circumcision had not a sufficient number of influential Jews urged it. We are told in *Jubilees* 15:33,

written around the middle of the second century B.C.E., that many Jews rejected circumcision, either by removing too little of the skin, or by removing nothing at all. Even in the second century C.E., the rabbis felt the need to stipulate what constituted a valid circumcision (Mishnah *Shabbat* 19:6; cf. Babylonian Talmud *Shabbat* 137a–b). *Jubilees* further says that the angels closest to the throne of God are circumcised (15:27).

14. Aulus Cornelius Celsus (fl. under Tiberius 14–37 C.E.), wrote an encyclopedia *On Medicine,* in which he describes the surgical practice of epispasm, cutting and re-extending the skin of the penis (Celsus, *On Medicine* 7.25.1). There is also an obscure reference to such a procedure, possibly forced on some Jews, in the *Testament of Moses* 8.3 (*Old Testament Pseudepigrapha* 1:931).

15. 2 Maccabees 4:12; the hat was traditionally worn by Hermes, the patron god of athletic games, and regular headdress for the youths of the gymnasium.

16. Josephus (*Jewish Antiquities* 12.160–241), recounts the history of Joseph son of Tobias (or the Tobiad) and his sons up to their support of Menelaus. For an evaluation of the account, as well as the chronological difficulties in Josephus, see Goldstein, "The Tales of the Tobiads," in Jacob Neusner, ed., *Christianity, Judaism, and Other Greco-Roman Cults* (4 vols.; Leiden: E. J. Brill, 1975) 3:85–123.

17. It is likely that the name YHWH was no longer generally pronounced by this time; as evidenced by the Septuagint Greek translation of the tetragram by *Kurios,* "Lord." However, equating Zeus with the God of the Jews is an opinion already expressed by the Alexandrian Jew, Aristeas (*Letter of Aristeas* 16). We do not know how widespread the view was, but it represents an effort of the Jews to make worship of their god acceptable in the Hellenistic world. Aristobulus (second century B.C.E.), probably a fellow Jewish Alexandrian, in quoting a few lines from a Greek poem (see chapter 13) which begins by praising Zeus, simply changes the name Zeus to *theos,* God, and tells us that the Greeks are really praising the creator God, therefore, the change is appropriate (frag. 4.6–7; *Old Testament Pseudepigrapha* 2:841).

18. 2 Kings 11 and the expanded account of 2 Chronicles 22–23.

19. Ezekiel the Tragedian, *Exagōgē* 243–253 (translation by R. G. Robertson, *Old Testament Pseudepigrapha* 2.803–19). The drama is dated to the late third century, or early second century B.C.E., most probably written in Alexandria, Egypt. The author of the *Letter of Aristeas* (312–316) is familiar with such drama of the Jewish community, in which portions of Torah were adapted to poetry, although it was deemed against the will of God, at least, until the official and divinely inspired Greek translation was given.

20. Judges 6–7.

21. The battle of Beth-Zur is described in 1 Maccabees 4:26–35 and 2 Maccabees 11:6–12. The sources differ on a number of details, including whether the battle took place before or after the rededication of the temple, but 1 Maccabees is probably correct in making it the key battle that permitted Judah and his men to enter Jerusalem.

22. According to 1 Maccabees 2:46, Mattathias and his men "forcibly circumcised all the uncircumcised boys that they found within the borders of Israel," but it is uncertain how widespread this could have been since the Maccabees had not control of all of Israel, only parts of the land from time to time. In any case, it must have been vigilante justice.

23. The procedure for circumcision is described in Mishnah *Shabbat* 19:2, though it assumes it is done on a child. In antiquity, knives of flint were used (Exodus 4:25; Joshua 5:4–6), but later metal knives were used (Mishnah *Shabbat* 19:1).

24. Blessings for circumcision are given in the Babylonian Talmud *Shabbat* 137b; even allowing for several centuries between the sources, this must reflect a longstanding tradition.

25. Belial, the angel of wickedness, is a personification of evil based upon the biblical Hebrew *beliyya'al,* often translated as "perdition." Deuteronomy 13:13 (Hebrew 13:14) contains the expression "sons of *beliyya'al,*" which the Revised Standard Version translates as "base fellows," those who call on the Israelites to "go and serve other gods." *Jubilees* 15:33 (*Old Testament Pseudepigrapha,* vol. 2) specifically calls those who leave their sons uncircumcised, "sons of Belial" (cf. 1:20). Belial is often mentioned in the Dead Sea Scrolls, and found throughout the Pseudepigraphic literature.

26. Sirach 41:7–9.

27. Deuteronomy 6:4. The longer passage, 6:4–9, became known by the first word, Shema, "Hear, O Israel." Although the formal prayer "Shema" is found only in rabbinic literature (with the addition of Deuteronomy 11:13–21; Numbers 15:37–41), sometime after the exile it became the central creed of Judaism.

# Notes to Chapter 6

Primary Sources: Josephus, *Jewish Antiquities* 13.398–432; *Jewish War* 2.119–166; Dead Sea Scroll *Pesher Nahum* (4Q169). The *pesher,* which means "interpretation," is a commentary of sorts on the book of Nahum, though it takes on the nature of ancient divination; that is, understanding the present and, like an oracle, predicting the future in nebulous language. It is among the most important documents of the Dead Sea Scrolls library because it names historical persons (Antiochus and Demetrius) and, therefore, is datable to the first century B.C.E., and the script of the manuscripts suggests a writing no later than the second half of the first century B.C.E. Modern attempts to understand the historical allusions are entirely dependent on the history of Josephus. Despite a general agreement on the historical setting, interpretations of specific allusions to historical persons differ among scholars—as always—and in the case of *Pesher Nahum,* the debate is alive and well in recent dissertations and publications, such as Gregory L. Doudna, *4Q Pesher Nahum: A Critical Edition* (Sheffield: Sheffield Academic Press, 2001), which I have consulted. The extant fragments of the scroll only cover Nahum 1:3–6; 2:12–14; 3:1–14. Various translations are available: Géza Vermès, *The Complete Dead Sea Scrolls in English* (New York: Allen Lane/Penguin Press, 1997); Florentino García Martínez, *The Dead Sea Scrolls Translated: The Qumran Texts in English* (trans. W. G. E. Watson; Leiden: E. J. Brill, 1994); Michael Wise, Martin Abegg Jr., and Edward Cook, *The Dead Sea Scrolls: A New Translation* (New York: HarperSanFrancisco, 1996). Here I follow the translation of Vermès, with slight modification and smoothing over one lacuna. Among the significant secondary literature on the Qumran community, see Hartmut Stegemann, *The Library of Qumran: On the Essenes, Qumran, John the Baptist, and Jesus* (Grand Rapids: Eerdmans, 1998), and the various groups within Judaism, a most valuable treatment is that of E. P. Sanders, *Judaism: Practice and Belief 63 B.C.E.–66 C.E.* (Philadelphia: Trinity Press International, 1992). The story is set in 67 B.C.E. I choose this date because it allows for the general relevance of the interpretation of Nahum to an important transition in Jewish history, while allowing for a substantial anticipation of the future, but I acknowledge the uncertainty for this date of composition. Because the commentary appears to predict the fall of Aristobulus II by the hand of Pompey (63 B.C.E.), it may have been written shortly before or after 63. On the other hand, we have no hint that the temple had been desecrated by Pompey; therefore I incline to treat this as a genuine attempt to read the signs of the times (the looming presence of Rome), and see the destruction of the Hasmonaeans and their supporters in vague allusions. The quote is from Pesher Nahum 3:7b.

1. 1 Maccabees 2:51. Hasmonaean, or Asmonaean, appears to have been an ancestral name, and became the dynastic title of the descendants of Mattathias. It is not given in 1 Maccabees, but Josephus gives the lineage as Mattathias, son of Joannes, son of Symeon, son of Asamonaios (*Jewish Antiquities* 12.265); and rabbinic tradition refers to the sons of the Hashmonai (e.g., Mishnah *Middot* 1:6; Babylonian Talmud *Shabbat* 21a). The dynastic chronology from the death of Judas is as follows: Jonathan (ca. 161–143 B.C.E.); Simon (ca. 143–134 B.C.E.); John Hyrcanus, son of Simon (134–104 B.C.E.); Aristobulus, son of Hyrcanus (104–103 B.C.E.); Alexander Jannaeus, son of Hyrcanus (103–76 B.C.E.); Alexandra Salome, wife of Jannaeus (76–67 B.C.E.); Aristobulus II and Hyrcanus II, sons of Jannaeus (67–63 B.C.E.).

2. The surnames of the Hasmonaean sons are give in 1 Maccabees 2:2–5, repeated in *Jewish Antiquities* 12.266, and the etymologies are briefly discussed by R. Marcus in the Loeb Classical Library edition of *Jewish Antiquities* (vol. 7.138–39). As noted previously, the standard interpretation of the Greek *Makkabaios* is a transliteration of the Hebrew (or Aramaic) *maqqabah,* "hammer," therefore Judah the Hammerer. Neither this etymology, however, nor any of the others are certain.

3. 1 Maccabees 13:41–42.

4. Josephus describes the Sadducees, Pharisees, and Essenes in *Jewish War* 2.119–166 and briefly in *Jewish Antiquities* 13.171–173; 18.11–22. Josephus

presents them as philosophical schools of thought for his Greek audience, whereas the political origins of the groups have been reconstructed by scholars, using what Josephus says about their political involvement with the Hasmonaean rulers, and clues found in the Qumran scrolls. For a succinct review of the standard reconstructed history of the sectarian origins, see E. P. Sanders, *Judaism,* chapter 2, "The Issues that Generated Parties"; many scholars, however, are revising this model, and in particular, extending the origins of the Essenes further back than the start of the Hasmonaean Dynasty.

5. The etymology of the Greek "Essenes" is uncertain, but the two best candidates are Aramaic words for "doers" or "healers"; on which see Stephen Goranson, "Others and Intra-Jewish Polemic as Reflected in Qumran Texts," in Peter W. Flint and James C. Vanderkam, eds., *The Dead Sea Scrolls After Fifty Years* (Leiden: E. J. Brill, 1999) 534–51.

6. Because the Torah states that the sacred festivals were to be observed on specific days of specific months, the correct start of the month was deemed crucial. There is no firm biblical evidence for an official calendar in Israelite history, whether the Israelites observed festivals according to a solar year or a lunar month. The Essenes, the Qumran community, and the authors of various works, such as the *Book of Enoch* 72–82 and *Jubilees* (*Old Testament Pseudepigrapha*) followed a solar calendar with twelve number months, while the majority of Jews, including the priests who controlled the temple, followed a lunar calendar, intercalated to conform roughly to the solar year, and used the names of months borrowed from the ancient Babylonian calendar (Palestinian Talmud, *Rosh HaShanah* 1.56d).

7. Besides the sources from Josephus mentioned above, Philo speaks about the Essenes in *Every Good Man is Free* 75–91, and *Hypothetica* 11.1–18. In some details, Philo conflicts with Josephus, and the association of Essenes with the Qumran writings remains somewhat controversial, although in the absence of a better solution or more evidence, we are justified in retaining the traditional composite picture. Philo hints that Essenes prefer to honor God by a state of holiness rather than animal sacrifice (*Good Man* 75); Josephus suggests they did not sacrifice in the Temple (*Jewish Antiquities* 18.19).

8. *Jewish War* 2.148, literally "rays of the Deity"; cf. 2.128, and morning worship below.

9. *Jewish War* 2.139–142. The secrets of the Essenes as described by Josephus are supported by the Dead Sea Scrolls, particularly the prominence of angels. Although "messengers" (Hebrew *mal'akh,* Greek *aggelos*) of God appear in biblical texts, it refers to both human or divine beings (Judges 2:1; 13:6; Malachi 3:1), even when they are called sons of God (Genesis 6:2; Deuteronomy 32:8; Job 1:6), and are not clearly related to the "heavenly hosts" (Genesis 28:12; 33:1–3; Psalms 29:1; 89:6–9; 103:20–21). According to the literary evidence (though such evidence assumes earlier popular thought) the hierarchy of angels, the names of chief angels (Michael, Gabriel, Raphael, Uriel), and the appearance of the Satan (Accuser) and evil angels only becomes a part of popular religion during the post-exilic period. Our information comes mostly from

the Pseudepigrapha and Dead Sea Scrolls, and therefore belong to the more es-
oteric elements of Judaism, of whom the Essenes were apparently the primary
keepers of the traditions.

10. A *mikveh* is an immersion pool for removing ritual uncleanness, according to the prescription of Leviticus 15 (specifically nocturnal emissions,
verses 16–18). Archaeologists have located numerous ritual baths (pl. *mikvaot*),
often with two sets of steps for entry and exit, and often set beside a cistern.
One tractate of the Mishnah is devoted to the regulations surrounding the construction and use of the ritual bath. On the complex topic of ritual purity, see
E. P. Sanders, *Judaism,* 214–230.

11. The head of a community was called *mebaqqer* (*Damascus Document;*
[4Q266–272]) or *maskil* (*Community Rule* [1QS]), which may be translated as
Overseer or Guardian, Master, Instructor, Inspector. The hierarchical authority
of the Covenanters was formal and strictly observed.

12. According to Josephus, Alexander Jannaeus took vengeance upon his
political opponents by crucifying eight hundred and butchered their wives and
children before their eyes, while he caroused with his mistresses (*Jewish War*
1.96–98; *Jewish Antiquities* 13.379–383). Although Josephus does not state the
eight hundred were, or included, Pharisees, he does say elsewhere that Pharisees were among the leading opponents of Jannaeus, and that on his deathbed
Jannaeus urged his wife Alexandra Salome to make peace with them, and enlist
their support (*Jewish Antiquities* 13.400–404).

13. Most scholars identify the community at Qumran with the Essenes, for
a number of sound reasons, including the reference of Pliny the Elder (*Natural
History* 5.15.73), the Roman historian who visited Judaea in the first century
C.E. and mentions the Essenes who live on the west bank of the Dead Sea between Jericho and Ein-gedi to the south. On the other hand, assuming that
most of the documents found at Qumran reflect the history and beliefs of the
community, there are significant differences between them and the description
of the Essenes by Josephus; for example, the dualistic theology and the emphasis on apocalypticism in the Dead Sea Scrolls. For this reason we distinguish
between the Essenes at Qumran, whom we may call Covenanters, and those
found elsewhere around the land. On this, see Jodi Magness, *The Archaeology of
Qumran and the Dead Sea Scrolls* (Grand Rapids, Mich.: Eerdmans, 2002).

14. *Jewish War* 2.128. Josephus calls this ritual peculiar, but claims they recite prayers handed down from their forefathers. Reverence for the sun as representative of God has deep roots in Israelite history, including worship of the
sun itself (2 Kings 23:11–12; Ezekiel 8:16; Mishnah *Sukkah* 5:4) and may
account for the east-west orientation of the temple (e.g., Psalms 19:1–6;
85:10–11).

15. 4QMMT (4Q394–399) Text C, lines 7–9. This fragmented document
is variously known as a Halakhic Letter, or Sectarian Manifesto, but commonly
by the designation 4QMMT (Cave 4 of Qumran, *Miqsat Ma'aseh ha-Torah,*
"some of the works of the Torah"). The document is widely regarded as a letter
outlining reasons for the original separation of the early Essenes from a larger

group of Jews dedicated to upholding the law (perhaps the Pharisees), or a split among the Essenes (or earlier Hasidaeans?) themselves. The rules of Torah that are listed mostly concern the mixing of pure and impure, the sacred with the profane. Most scholars date the document to the late second century B.C.E., and while most of the interpretations of Essenes origins based on the scrolls are tentative, the interpretation of this reconstructed document is all the more so.

16. On the sabbath limit, Torah restricts travel on the sabbath in Exodus 16:29, without specifying a distance. This distances of one thousand and two thousand cubits are given in Numbers 35:4–5 for defining the pasture land belonging to a Levite city, and the Essenes chose the shorter distance for a sabbath limit (*Damascus Document* col.10, line 21), while most Jews, including the Pharisees, chose the greater (e.g., Mishnah *Rosh HaShanah* 2:5; *Sotah* 5:3). On marriage with Moabites, see 4QMMT sec. B, lines 39–49; Mishnah *Yevamot* 8:2–3. While the Mishnah ruling, and the later rabbinic grammatical explanation on Moabitess (Babylonian Talmud, *Yevamot* 76b) may be anachronistic to the legal matters of 4QMMT, the issues are listed among the concerns over the law found in the Qumran document, so we know that it was a dispute at the time.

17. The suggestion has been proposed that the Hebrew *Dorshe-ha-Khalakot,* "Seekers of Smooth Things," is a pun on the word *halakha* (plural *halakhot*), which is the rabbinic word for a binding law, based on the verb *halakh,* "to walk," and *halakha* is understood to be the way that Israel should walk. The theory is that the Pharisees are known for their legal interpretations called *halakhot,* and the Essenes considered these interpretations to be easier rulings, or tenuously derived from the biblical texts, and therefore smooth or slippery interpretations, so that they ridiculed the Pharisees as "seekers of smooth things." On the other hand, the word *halakha* is otherwise unattested in pre-rabbinic literature, and the phrase may be an allusion to Isaiah 30:10, which says "speak to us smooth things (*khalakot*)" in the context of false prophecies, and therefore refers to a more general criticism, not specifically to Pharisees. The pun, however, is an enticing suggestion and in the absence of certainty, it has generally been accepted.

18. *Jewish War* 2.147.

19. Daniel 11:30. Kittim are listed as descendants of Javan (later designation for Greece) in the table of nations (Genesis 10:4). The Kittim became a catchword for a distant people from the west, whose ships will come as part of divine judgment (Numbers 24:24; Isaiah 23:12; Jeremiah 2:10; Ezekiel 27:6; cf. *Jewish Antiquities* 1.128). Kittim is equated with Macedonia as the birthplace of Alexander the Great (1 Maccabees 1:1; 5:8), while in Daniel 11:30 to Rome, as may be seen from the Old Greek translation (ca. 150 B.C.E.) of Kittim as "Rome," on which see John J. Collins, *Daniel* (Hermeneia; Minneapolis: Fortress Press, 1993) 384. Within the Qumran library, the use of Kittim for impending domination of Rome is taken up by the *Habakkuk Pesher* and the *War Scroll* (e.g. 1QpHab 3.10–11; 1QM 1.1–2).

20. Philo claims all Essenes eschew marriage because it is a danger to continence and the communal life (*Hypothetica* 11.14–17), whereas Josephus says

that although most Essenes were celibate, some groups did marry for the purpose of procreation (*Jewish War* 2.120–121, 160–161). In all such statements about a group that survived for over a century, we must allow for developments within the group, as well as inadequate information to outsiders who write about them.

21. *Jewish War* 1.78–81; *Jewish Antiquities* 13.311–313; Josephus says the Essenes have knowledge of divine things because of their virtue (*Jewish Antiquities* 15.373–379).

22. The Dead Sea Scrolls emphasize the *eschaton* (last events), and in general hold a strong apocalyptic worldview. Josephus does not attribute a strong eschatological fervor to the Essenes, but that may be due to his Greek and Roman audience who would not understand it, or would find such views dangerous to the peace of the Roman Empire. On the other hand, it is quite possible that many Essenes were devoted to simple meditation and a life of purity, as Josephus and Philo present them, while holding a vague hope in future divine intervention, such as we might expect among the general population.

23. Josephus claims to have seen the pillar (*Jewish Antiquities* 1.203).

24. The excavated site of Qumran may be identified with the City of Salt, *Ir-ha-melach,* one of the six settlements in the wilderness described in Joshua 15:61–62.

25. Isaiah 40:3.

26. 1 Maccabees 8. The independence and internal politics of Judaea must always be viewed within the context of the ideology of empire. This worldview of dominant empires formed the basis for apocalyptic visions, for example, of Daniel 7–12, as well as the Pesher Nahum.

27. Josephus tells us of the struggle that led up to the civil war following the death of Queen Alexandra Salome, which was largely between Pharisees and Sadducees with their respective supporters (*Jewish War* 1.107–119; *Jewish Antiquities* 13.422–432). How the Essenes, as well as the community behind the Dead Sea Scrolls, fit into this conflict is a matter of reconstruction based on other documents, in this case the Pesher Nahum, and we are reminded that all such reconstructions are subject to change as evidence warrants. What is apparent in this commentary is the great hostility between the group behind the *pesher,* and the group behind the code name "Seekers of Smooth Things / Flattery Seekers."

28. For discussion supporting this interpretation, see Tal Ilan, "Shelamzion in Qumran," in *Historical Perspectives: From the Hasmoneans to Bar Kokhba in Light of the Dead Sea Scrolls* (Leiden: E. J. Brill, 2000) 57–68.

## Notes to Chapter 7

Primary sources: Josephus, *Jewish War* 1.358–371, and *Antiquities* 15.121–126. The story is set in the early spring of 31 B.C.E., shortly after the hostility between Octavian and Antony began in October of 32 B.C.E. Quote is from Ecclesiastes 8:14.

1. The "months" of pregnancy were reckoned as its own calendar (Babylonian Talmud *Nidah* 30b).

2. Gehenna, the Latin transliteration of the Greek *Geenna,* itself transliterated from *ge hinnom,* Hebrew for Valley of Hinnom. The valley ran southwest outside Jerusalem, and was associated with the ancient Canaanite child sacrifice by burning, sometimes practiced in ancient Israel, and as a place of refuse, filled with dung, worms, and smoldering fires. Jeremiah placed a curse on the site, calling it the Valley of Slaughter, because of the many bodies thrown into it during the Babylonian conquest (7:30–33). In due course, Gehenna became the Jewish equivalent of Hades or Hell, a metaphorical place of torment for the wicked, with worms and fire (e.g., Sirach 7:17; *Judith* 16:17; Mark 9:48) though in the New Testament Gehenna (Matthew 5:22, 29–30; 18:9; 23:15) is usually distinct from Hades (Matthew 11:23; Revelation 20:10–14). In rabbinic tradition, a stay in Gehenna was temporary (up to twelve months) for all but the most wicked Jews (Mishnah *Eduyyot* 2:10).

3. A *ketubah* is a marriage contract, designed to protect a divorced woman, and may also contain conditions for the marriage. According to second-century B.C.E. rabbinic views, a tanner is among those men compelled to give a divorce if his wife demands one, whether or not a stipulation concerning his "defect" was written in the *ketubah* (Mishnah *Ketubbot,* 7:10). Although the details of the rabbinic traditions on the *ketubah* are later, marriage contracts go back into antiquity, as we have a contract in the fifth-century B.C.E. Elephantiné documents between a Jewess and an Egyptian, and reference to the *ketubah* ("instrument of cohabitation" = RSV "contract") in the second-century B.C.E. book of Tobit (7:14).

4. Genesis 3:16.

5. Babylonian Talmud, *Pesahim* 65a; *Bava Batra* 16a.

6. Tanneries had to be located outside of town at least fifty cubits (twenty-five yards) distance (Mishnah *Bava Batra* 2:9); and they were exempted (like a privy or bathhouse) from having a *mezuzah,* the small box containing verses of Torah placed on the doorpost of every Jewish building (Babylonian Talmud *Yoma* 11a–b). According to rabbinic tradition, tanners, along with fullers and coppersmiths, were exempted from appearing at the Temple on a pilgrimage festival, and forming a separate guild group was forbidden (Babylonian Talmud *Hagigah* 7b).

7. On the production of leather in antiquity, see R. J. Forbes, *Studies in Ancient Technology,* (9 vols.; Leiden: E. J. Brill, 1955–64) vol. 5. The Babylonian Talmud notes many of steps in the tanning process; for example, placing hides in a trough of flour (Babylonian Talmud *Pesahim* 45b).

8. Psalm 126:4.

9. Jacob, Genesis 27:15–16; Tabernacle, Exodus 25:5; 26:14; Elisha, 2 Kings 1:8; Adam and Eve, Genesis 3:21.

10. *Jewish Antiquities* 13.257; however, on the difficulties concerning Josephus' account of the forced conversion of the Idumaeans, see S. J. D. Cohen, *The Beginnings of Jewishness: Boundaries, Varieties, Uncertainties* (Berkeley: University of California Press, 1999) 110–19.

11. *Pesher Nahum* (4QpNah) col. 1, line 3; see Géza Vermès, *The Complete Dead Sea Scrolls in English* (New York: Allen Lane/Penguin Press, 1997).

12. *Jewish Antiquities* 14. 381–385; Tacitus, *Histories* 5.9. Mark Antony brought Herod before the Roman Senate and explained that it was to Rome's advantage, primarily against the threat of Parthia, to install Herod as king of Judaea, which the Senate promptly voted to do. Herod still had to secure the throne by war against the Hasmonaean Antigonus.

13. *Jewish Antiquities* 15.96–103. Josephus, in keeping with Roman sentiment, expressed a very dim view of Cleopatra, and he tells us that Herod even considered killing Cleopatra while she was in his power, but that his counselors prevailed upon him to send her back to Egypt with gifts.

14. These ingredients are listed for several ailments, but for a woman in childbirth they are to be ground up and drunk with beer or wine (Babylonian Talmud *Avodah Zarah* 29a).

15. The belief in demons was widespread and virtually unanimous in antiquity. For example, "It has been taught: Abba Benjamin says, If the eye had the power to see them, no creature could endure the demons. Abaye says: They are more numerous than we are and they surround us like the ridge round a field. R. Huna says: Every one among us has a thousand on his left hand and ten thousand on his right hand . . . If one wants to discover their footprints, let him take sifted ashes and sprinkle around his bed, and in the morning he will see something like the footprints of a cock" (Babylonian Talmud *Berakhot* 6b). The traditions also list numerous amulets, talismans, and ointments that ward off demons.

16. According to one tradition, if a child doesn't breath easily, rub the afterbirth over it (Babylonian Talmud *Shabbat* 134a).

17. The procedure of birth is given by Ezekiel 16:4 (by way of condemnation): "As for your birth, on the day you were born your navel cord was not cut, nor were you washed with water to cleanse you, nor rubbed with salt, nor wrapped in cloths." The four acts are often affirmed, e.g., Babylonian Talmud *Shabbat* 129b.

18. According to one tradition, when a daughter was born to the son of a rabbi, his father said to him: "Increase has come to the world." The tradition goes on to quote the maxim: "The world cannot do without either males or females. Yet happy is he whose children are males, and alas for him whose children are females. The world cannot do without either a spice-seller or a tanner. Yet happy is he whose occupation is that of a spice-seller, and alas for him whose occupation is that of a tanner" (Babylonian Talmud *Bava Batra* 16a; *Pesahim* 65a).

19. Leviticus 12 gives the rules of ritual impurity after childbirth. If a woman gives birth to a son, she remains impure to her husband and all others

for seven days, the boy is circumcised on the eighth day, and the mother must remain outside the temple for thirty-three days; if a girl, the mother is impure for fourteen days, and remains outside the temple for sixty-six days, and may not touch any "holy thing" (12:4). When the days are complete, she brings an offering to the temple, and becomes clean for temple worship. The implementation of this simple purity law became complex, and there is much confusion over it when applying the rabbinic traditions to the daily life of peasants. See E. P. Sanders, *Judaism: Practice and Belief 63 B.C.E.–66 C.E.* (Philadelphia: Trinity Press International, 1992) 217–30.

20. Euphemisms for bodily functions, sex acts, and genitalia were common and habitual in the preserved traditions of Judaism, from the Bible through the rabbis. Mouth was a common euphemism for womb (e.g., Babylonian Talmud *Sanhedrin* 100a; *Menahot* 98a; *Nidah* 16b).

21. In the two accounts of the earthquake, Josephus gives both numbers; ten thousand in *Jewish War,* thirty thousand in *Jewish Antiquities.*

## Notes to Chapter 8

Primary sources: *Jewish Antiquities* 15.365–71 and 17.41–45. Although we cannot be certain, it appears that the two accounts of Pharisees escaping an oath of loyalty to Herod are two versions of the same event, which Josephus has separated by over a decade in his history. The discussion on the laws of Torah is based on several rabbinic texts, as cited in the notes. Secondary literature: Jacob Neusner, *From Politics to Piety: The Emergence of Pharisaic Judaism* (New York: Ktav Pub. House, 1983), and J. Neusner, *The Rabbinic Traditions about the Pharisees before 70,* (3 vols.; Leiden: E. J. Brill, 1971); E. P. Sanders, *Judaism: Practice and Belief 63 B.C.E.–66 C.E.* (Philadelphia: Trinity Press International, 1992). Story is set around 20 B.C.E. Quote is from Mishnah, *Avot* 1:1, which most certainly was a more ancient oral tradition than the point of first writing, around 200 C.E., though probably not as far back as it claims, to the men of the Great Assembly surrounding the time of Ezra. Rabbi Akiva, who flourished 100–135 C.E. said, "Tradition (*masoret*) is a fence around Torah" (*Avot* 3:14), and we have a number of earlier statements on the importance of customs and oral traditions not found specifically in the Torah of Moses: Paul speaks of having been zealous for the "traditions of my fathers" (Galations 1:14); Jesus disputes specific points of the "tradition of the elders" (Matthew 15:1–9; Mark 7:1–8); Josephus notes that the Pharisees introduced to the people customs handed down from their ancestors that are not recorded in the Torah of Moses (*Jewish Antiquities* 13.297; 408); and we have seen the Covenanters criticized the customs of their opponents as Seekers of Smooth Things in the interpretation of Torah, which probably refers to oral traditions called *halakha,* the way Israel should walk. The biblical mandate to preserve the ways of the ancestors may be found in the command "you shall not remove your neighbor's landmark, which the men of

old have set" (Deuteronomy 19:14; cf. Proverbs 22:28), which was often interpreted as preserving ancient customs, as Josephus expands on the law of Moses,
"for those that remove boundaries are not far off an attempt to subvert the
laws" (*Jewish Antiquities* 4.225); and Philo, in commenting on the commandment says, "And this injunction is given, as it seems, not only with respect to in-
heritances, and to the boundaries of the land, in order to prohibit covetousness
respecting them, but also as a guard to ancient customs; for customs are un-
written laws, being the doctrines of men of old, not engraved on pillars or written on paper which may be eaten by moths, but impressed in the souls of those
living under the same constitution" (*Special Laws* 4.149; translation by Yonge).
In general, these customs must be placed in the broad category of the wisdom
of the ancients, revered by all in antiquity, even if the details were constantly
disputed.

1. Tyropoeon Valley, a name known only from Josephus, ran roughly north
to south through the city, to the west side of the temple (*Jewish War* 2.140).

2. Exodus 23:19; 34:26; Deuteronomy 14:21. The rabbinic discussion begins with Mishnah *Hullin* 8:1, the substance of which Jacob Neusner places in
the first rabbinic period at Yavneh (Jamnia) ca. 70–140 C.E. See Neusner, *The
Rabbinic Traditions about the Pharisees before 70*, 3.212. Although it is doubtful the
distinction was first invented then, we do not know how far back this interpretation of the biblical text goes.

3. Adapted from discussion on blessings related to the privies and the ne-
cessities of the human body in Babylonian Talmud *Berakhot* 60b.

4. Babylonian Talmud *Pesahim* 44b; the reasoning principle of *qal vehomer*
(argument *a fortiori*) is traced back to the time of Hillel, but the developed rabbinic tradition relied on here may be anachronistic, it is difficult to know.

5. This verdict is given in a Baraita, an anonymous tradition preserved in
Hebrew, in the Babylonian Talmud *Pesahim* 76b.

6. Rabbi Jose the Galilean (fl. ca. 120–140 C.E.) taught that fowl did not fall
under the prohibition, precisely because Moses mentioned mother's milk,
thereby excluding fowl (Babylonian Talmud *Shabbat* 130a). Philo, writing in
the first century C.E., appears to be unaware of a general prohibition against
milk and meat; while he explains the biblical prohibition on humanitarian
grounds (*On the Virtues* 142–144). It would appear that at this point in the development of Pharisaic observance of the law, the prohibition against meat and
milk must have been still quite uncertain.

7. A list of alternatives to forbidden food is given in a tradition ascribed to
Yalta, wife of Rabbi Nahum, in Babylonian Talmud *Hullin* 109b–110a. In the
passage, the rule on eating roast udder is debated, but the debate, occurring
much later, suggests that such practices had been common at an earlier time.

8. According to Mishnah *Hullin* 8:1, this distinction between lenient and
strict rulings is attributed to the Houses (commonly called Schools) of Shammai and Hillel, not the sages themselves. The Mishnah contains many legal arguments between the School of Hillel and the School of Shammai, and
represent two preferences of Torah interpretation among Pharisees in the first

century and the continued legal discussions of the first generation of rabbis after 70 C.E. The rulings of the School of Shammai were generally more stringent than the rulings of Hillel, so that the occasions in which the School of Hillel was more stringent were noteworthy. Mishnah *Eduyyot* 4–5 collects these exceptions. Mishnah *Avot* 5:17 tells us that the controversies between Hillel and Shammai were for the glory of God and of lasting worth. This particular controversy over fowl and cheese may be anachronistic here, but it reflects sound traditions of controversy.

9. Herod honored Pollion and his disciple Samaias because they urged Jerusalem to admit Herod after he had defeated Antigonus for the kingship in 37 B.C.E. (*Jewish Antiquities* 14.172–76; 15.3–4). These two Pharisees should probably be identified with Shemaiah and Avtalion of rabbinic traditions; on which, see Schürer, *The History of the Jewish People in the Age of Jesus Christ,* revised edition, (4 vols.; Géza Vermès et al., eds.; London: T&T Clark. 1973–1986), 1:296, 313–14; 2:362–3.

10. The number of Pharisees at this particular point Josephus gives at over six thousand (*Jewish Antiquities* 17.42).

11. The age for leadership position was generally considered thirty years, based on the minimum age for Levites to enter into temple service (Numbers 4:47); see Mishnah *Avot* 5:21 for a general dictum on the qualification ages for a male from five to one hundred years, in which thirty is the age for authority. Josephus tells us that Pharisees were renowned as expert interpreters of the Law (*Jewish War* 2.162), and the Gospel of Matthew confirms their authority by the statement of Jesus that the Pharisees sit in the seat of Moses (Matthew 23:2).

12. Among the many legends about Hillel the Elder, one says that a disciple named Jonathan ben Uzziel was the greatest (possibly the eldest, or first), and Johanan ben Zakkai was the least (or last). The legend states: "They said of Jonathan ben Uzziel that when he used to sit and occupy himself with the study of the Torah, every bird that flew above him was immediately burnt." This tradition is of little use historically, but in reconstructing times past and the disciples of Hillel, an unverifiable tradition is better than no tradition at all; at any rate, the name of Jonathan ben Uzziel is not likely to be fictitious (Babylonian Talmud *Sukkah* 28a; *Bava Batra* 134a).

13. During the reign of the Hasmonaean John Hyrcanus, the Idumaeans were incorporated into Judaea by coerced conversion (*Jewish Antiquities* 13.257–258), and Herod's Jewish lineage was always a point of skepticism. Although rabbinic tradition treats the descendent of Herod, Agrippa, favorably, and calls him "our brother" (Mishnah *Sotah* 7:8), it never legitimates Herod the Great.

14. The Boethusians were a small sect or group of priestly aristocracy who, like the Sadducees, were known as opponents of the Pharisees on the question of a resurrection to life after death and other matters. The evidence for this group is found exclusively in rabbinic tradition, and according to one late tradition, they took their name from Boethus, a pupil of Antigonus of Sokho, a sage

in the early third century B.C.E. (Mishnah *Avot* 1:3; and *Avot d'Rabbi Natan* 5; cf. Mishnah *Menahot* 10:3, and *Rosh Hashanah* 2:1, where the Mishnah calls them heretics, but the Babylonian Talmud identifies them as Boethusians).

15. 2 Chronicles 36:13. Although Ezekiel uses the form of Nebuchad-rezzar exclusively and Jeremiah predominantly, other books and later tradition use the variant form Nebuchadnezzar.

16. Ezekiel 17:13–16.

17. Judah Maccabee (Judas Maccabeus) sent an envoy to make a treaty of friendship with Rome in 161 B.C.E., essentially an alliance placing Judaea within the growing hegemony of Rome (1 Maccabees 8), and his brother Jonathan re-newed the friendship around 146 B.C.E. (12:1–4); see also *Jewish Antiquities* 12.414–419; 13.163–165, and according to Josephus, John Hyrcanus renewed the treaty during his reign, around 105 B.C.E. (13.259).

18. Mishnah *Avot* 1:12; cf. Malachi 2:6.

19. The Mosaic "paragraph of the king" (Deuteronomy 17:14–20) sets the requirements for a king, and warns the king against having many wives.

20. Josephus tells us that Herod did execute a number of Pharisees who endorsed a prophecy that Herod's rule would be taken from him (*Jewish Antiquities* 17.44). Concerning the execution by King Alexander Jannaeus of eight hundred political opponents (*Jewish War* 1.96–98; *Jewish Antiquities* 13.379–383), we may infer that many of the slain were Pharisees because they were among the leading opponents of Jannaeus, and upon his death the Pharisees took ven-geance on many who had favored the crucifixion of the eight hundred (*Jewish War* 1.113–114).

21. Proverbs 21:1.

22. As noted earlier, *tefillin,* commonly called phylacteries, are the leather straps and boxes containing portions of Scripture that to be placed as a frontlet or memorial between the eyes, and on the hand (Exodus 13:9, 16; Deuteron-omy 6:8; 11:18). Because the injunction in does not say how to do this, *tefillin* are a prime example of the sanctification of tradition in the oral law (Mishnah *Sanhedrin* 11:3).

23. Deuteronomy 6:4–9; a prayer recitation called the *Shema,* from the first word, "Hear." This passage along with three others (Exodus 13:1–10, 11–16; Deuteronomy 11:13–21), are the Scriptures contained in the leather boxes of the *tefillin.*

24. Exodus 20:8–10.

25. Mishnah *Shabbat* 7:2.

26. Mishnah *Hagigah* 1:8.

# Notes to Chapter 9

Primary sources are Josephus, *Jewish Antiquities* 18.29–30 (temple inci-dent); the Mishnah tractates on the Daily Sacrifice, *Tamid,* and the Passover,

*Pesach.* Secondary literature: on the temple cult, see E. P. Sanders, *Judaism: Practice and Belief 63 B.C.E.–66 C.E.* (Philadelphia: Trinity Press International, 1992); on the Samaritans, see Robert T. Anderson and Terry Giles, *The Keepers: An Introduction to the History and Culture of the Samaritans* (Peabody, Mass.: Hendrickson, 2002); J. A. Montgomery, *The Samaritans* (Philadelphia: John C. Winston Co., 1907); Richard J. Coggins, *Samaritans and Jews: The Origins of Samaritanism Reconsidered* (Atlanta: John Knox, 1975). Story is set in 8 C.E. For the quotation, Josephus gives a paraphrase of the inscription (Josephus, *Jewish War,* 5.194; *Jewish Antiquities* 15.417), but a complete plaque with the warning engraved was discovered in 1871 by Clermont-Ganneau (see Marcus and Wikgren, Loeb Classical Library, *Jewish Antiquities* 15.417 note *d,* for text, translation, and bibliography).

1. The phrase "holy city" as a designation of Jerusalem arose in the post-exilic period, attested in biblical books and other literature: Nehemiah 11:1,18; Isaiah 28:2; Daniel 9:24; 1 Maccabees 2:7; and used by Philo (*Flaccus* 46; *Embassy* 225, 281, 288, 299, 346) and Josephus (*Jewish War* 2.397; *Jewish Antiquities* 4.70, 209, 218, 227; and 20.118 in reference to a conflict with the Samaritans).

2. Josephus' description of Herod's temple differs from that found in the Mishnah tractate *Middot* on various measurements, and the location of the Nicanor Gate of Corinthian bronze. The description of Josephus is preferred because he was a priest, saw the temple throughout his life, and wrote only a few years after the destruction; whereas the Mishnah description was written down over a hundred years later, and appears constrained by the temple of Solomon or Ezekiel's temple at various points. Archaeology also supports Josephus. For an analysis of the differences and a description of the measurements, see E. P. Sanders, *Judaism* 54–76.

3. Our ancient sources, including Josephus, are not consistent on the use of Samaritan, which could mean a group defined by geography, ethnicity, or religious beliefs. The only Hebrew Bible reference is 2 Kings 17:29, *hashomeronim,* where it refers to inhabitants of Samaria, and would be properly translated by the ethno-geographic term Samarians. The self-designation of Samaritans comes from the Hebrew word *shomerim,* the "keepers," meaning those who keep the law. Josephus also uses the name Shechemites (*Jewish Antiquities* 11.342–347), and notes that they called themselves Hebrews (11.344). Josephus also calls them Cutheans, in reference to the people from Cuthea brought to replace the exiled Israelites by Sargon II, thereby emphasizing their Gentile ancestry (2 Kings 17:24); so also exclusively in the Mishnah (e.g. *Berakhot* 7:1; 8:8). For a lucid discussion of the Samaritan origins and development up to the Roman period, see Anderson and Giles, *The Keepers,* 9–49.

4. The Hebrew Bible states that the king of Assyria carried away the Israelites to Assyria, and repopulated the cities with people from Assyria (2 Kings 17:6, 24), but according to the Assyrian annals of Sargon II, only 27,290 Israelites were deported (James B. Pritchard, ed., *Ancient Near Eastern Texts Relating to the Old Testament* [3d ed.; Princeton: Princeton University Press, 1969] 284–85),

no doubt the principle citizens among the aristocracy and artisans, so that many Israelites remained and Samaritans could rightly claim descent from them.

5. Josephus recounts, in disparaging terms and probably a confused chronology, the incident concerning the Samaritan temple and priesthood of Manasseh in *Jewish Antiquities* 11.306–345.

6. According to the Samaritan history, the original center of worship was at Shechem, where Joshua gathered the tribes to re-establish the covenant (Joshua 24:1–28), but under the leadership of Eli, and the corruption of the sacrificial cult, the center of worship moved from Shechem to Shiloh (cf. 1 Samuel 2:12–17, 22–25), and then under David to Jerusalem (2 Samuel 6:1–20), all part of one long regress from the orthodox worship established by Moses.

7. Story related in a Samaritan tradition (*Chronicle of Abu'l Fath,* 113), cited in Montgomery, *Samaritans,* 85. We need not suppose it to be historical, rather representative of the pranks and animosity.

8. Twenty-four courses for temple service, each course serves one week, four times a year; courses were divided into father's houses which served one day; but at the three pilgrim feasts, all twenty-four courses officiated, and shared in the bounty (1 Chronicles 24:4; *Jewish Antiquities* 7.365; Mishnah *Sukkah* 5:6–8).

9. According to rabbinic tradition, which may reflect an earlier reality, it was a serious transgression for singers to perform the duty of gatekeepers (Babylonian Talmud *Arakhin* 11b); but Josephus also tells of the inferior status of the Levite singers who petitioned King Agrippa to wear linen, and were permitted to do so, much to the displeasure of the priest Josephus (*Jewish Antiquities* 20.216–218).

10. Numbers 4:47.

11. Mishnah *Sanhedrin* 9:6, speaks of young priests taking a priest in an impure state outside the temple court for summary execution, in which they "split open his skull with clubs." E. P. Sanders, *Judaism* 61, citing Peretz Segal, "The Penalty of the Warning Inscription from the Temple of Jerusalem" in *Israel Exploration Journal* 39 (1989) 79–84, argues that priests probably had the authority to execute offenders immediately. Certainly, transgression of sacred space was serious. According to Acts 21:26–30, Paul was accused of bringing Greeks into the temple, and a crowd dragged him out of the temple, shut the gates, and tried to kill him.

12. Marcus Licinius Crassus on his way to campaign against Parthia, entered the temple, stole the golden furnishings, and soon after perished in battle in 53 B.C.E. (*Jewish Antiquities* 14.105–119; *Jewish War* 1.179); Pompey, after intervening in the Hasmonaean civil war, entered the Holy of Holies in 63 B.C.E. (*Antiquities* 14.71–72; *War* 1.152–153; Tacitus, *Histories* 5.9), and was later assassinated in Egypt in advance of Julius Caesar's arrival in 48 B.C.E.

13. I follow the conclusions of Leen Ritmeyer, *Secrets of Jerusalem's Temple Mount.* (Washington, DC: Biblical Archaeology Review Society, 1998 [reprint from *Biblical Archaeology Review,* November/December 1989; March/April 1992;

January/February 1996]), 53–56, concerning the use of the Double Gate and Triple Gate in the south wall.

14. The commandment with a promise, and a prescription for social stability: Exodus 20:12; Deuteronomy 5:18.

15. Ananus (Annas) son of Sethi (Seth), was appointed high priest by the governor of Syria, Quirinius after the banishment of Archelaus (*Jewish Antiquities* 18.26). Ananus was high priest until removed by the Prefect Valerius Gratus in 15 C.E., but remained influential, and five of his sons became high priest, and a son-in-law, Joseph surnamed Caiaphas. He is known also from New Testament sources (Luke 3:2; John 18:13–24; Acts 4:6) and rabbinic tradition speaks disparagingly of the family (the "House of Hanin"), among other high priestly families, because of their greed (Mishnah *Keritot* 1:7; Tosefta *Menahot* 13:18; Babylonian Talmud *Pesahim* 57a).

16. The Hebrew *bein ha-arbaim* is usually translated "in the evening," or "at twilight," but literally means "between the two evenings"(Exodus 29:39; Numbers 28:4; cf. Exodus 30:8). The Passover sacrifices also occurs between the evenings (Exodus 12:6), and in the "place which the Lord will choose" (Deuteronomy 16:2, 5). This period was defined from after midday and after sunset before dark (Mishnah *Pesahim* 5:3; Babylonian Talmud *Pesahim* 58a).

17. The entire procedure, which is greatly abbreviated here, is described in the Mishnah tractate *Tamid,* "Daily Whole-offering."

18. Mishnah *Tamid* 5:1; the liturgy was comprised of various set blessings, prayers, and portions of Scripture.

19. The magrefa is a mysterious musical instrument in the shape of a shovel, described in the Babylonian Talmud *Arakhin* 10b–11a: "There was a magrefa in the Sanctuary; it had ten holes, each of which produced ten different kinds of sounds, with the result that the whole amounted to one hundred kinds of sounds." Mishnah *Tamid* 3:8 tells us that the noise could be heard from Jericho.

20. Josephus calls Malthace a Samaritan, but she was most likely of Syrian aristocracy in Samaria, not an adherent of the Samaritan religion or claiming descent from Israel (*Jewish War* 1.562). Whether or not Samaritans ever officially requested rebuilding of their temple, according to Josephus they continued to make the case that Gerizim was the place Moses chose for sacrifices (*Jewish Antiquities* 12.10; 13.74).

21. As with the dimensions and floor plan of the temple, our ancient evidence for the Passover slaughter gives varied and conflicting accounts, difficult if not impossible to reconcile (Josephus, *Jewish War* 6.423–425; Mishnah *Pesahim* 5). Estimates of the number of lambs, and handling the amount of blood that flowed, are particularly difficult. I tend to follow, with modifications, the realistic attempt of E. P. Sanders (*Judaism,* 136–38) to outline the Passover sacrifice. I think the sacrifice had to occur within the Court of Priests so that the blood could be contained, and that the number of sacrificial lambs was probably far fewer than ancient estimates. Josephus gives the impossible to believe number of 255,600 lambs, and says each lamb fed no fewer than ten and

as many as twenty individuals. He then calculates the number of pilgrims at Passover as over 2.5 million, based on an average of ten people per lamb, whereas a realistic average would be closer to fifteen, and this may refer only to male adults, as in a minyan, so that one sacrifice may have provided the ritual portion of lamb for more than thirty men, women, and children. The Mishnah (*Pesahim* 8:3) says "an olive's bulk" of Passover lamb is a sufficient portion to have fulfilled the ritual, which tells us that small portions were an issue. A realistic three hundred thousand people at Passover could have sacrificed fifteen to twenty thousand lambs, and probably, as Sanders suggests, in a continual procession, not in three distinct groups, as the Mishnah says.

22. The egg and olive were used as a standard of measurement by the rabbis for portions that fulfilled a ritual requirement. The symbolic nature of the Passover meal allowed for small portions if required, while one feasted on other food. According to the available tradition, a olive's bulk was the minimum required to fulfill the ritual, and allowed for additional guests to join a company if necessary (Mishnah *Pesahim* 8:3).

23. Numbers 12:1; *Jewish Antiquities* 2.238–253; Artapanus 27.7–8 (*Old Testament Pseudepigrapha* 2:899).

24. Exodus 7:1; Artapanus 27.6 (*Old Testament Pseudepigrapha* 2:899); cf. Philo, *Life of Moses* 1.158.

25. Josephus only says the gates were opened on Passover night (*Jewish Antiquities* 18.29), whereas the Mishnah says the gates were opened at some point in the night for each of the three pilgrim festivals of Passover, Shavuot (Pentecost), and Sukkot (Booths), so that by cock's crow the temple was filled with people (*Yoma* 1:8).

26. Corpse impurity is defined in Numbers 19:11–22. This impurity is contracted by touching a dead body, a human bone, or a grave, and lasts for seven days. While in a state of impurity, the person must remain outside the temple. The impure person must be sprinkled with the water of purification, mixed with ashes from the red heifer, on the third and seventh days, then wash his clothes, immerse, and he becomes pure again. Corpse impurity is the most serious of all impurities, and defiling the temple by corpse impurity is a capital offense. See E. P. Sanders, *Judaism,* 217–19.

27. Besides the act of defilement, the suggestion has been made that the Samaritans chose the bones as a mockery of Ezekiel's vision of the valley of dry bones in Ezekiel 37:1–14. This vision found its fulfillment in the return of the exiles from Babylon, which became the point of departure for conflict between Jews and Samaritans.

28. Deuteronomy 11:29.

29. Deuteronomy 27:6.

30. Samaritans kept their own Torah tradition, called the Samaritan Pentateuch, which may have roots to the time between Ezra and Alexander the Great, although the extent manuscript tradition reflects much development over the centuries. The passage (Deuteronomy 27:4–8) in the Hebrew text says Mount Ebal, one of the two mountains overlooking Shechem, but the

Samaritan Pentateuch reads Gerizim for Ebal. However, there is no sound evidence, textual or historical, for preferring the Samaritan reading; on which see Montgomery, *Samaritans,* 234–39. The basic argument for Mount Gerizim comes from its designation as the mount of blessing (Deuteronomy 11:29), after which, Moses tells them to "seek the place which the Lord your God will choose" to make sacrifices (12:5–7). For a survey of the Samaritan Pentateuch, see Anderson and Giles, *Keepers,* 107–16.

31. Josephus tells of a certain man who convinced a large throng of Samaritans to follow him to Mount Gerazim where he would reveal the sacred vessels of the tabernacle which Moses had buried there. The prefect, Pontius Pilate, fearing an uprising, possibly messianic, prevented the throng from going up the mountain, killing many, both in battle and later crucified. The Samaritans in turn appealed to the governor of Syria, and Pilate was recalled to Rome because of the incident (*Jewish Antiquities* 18.85–89).

32. The Samaritan messianic hope was based largely on the promise of a prophet like Moses to speak for God (Deuteronomy 18:15, 18). While there is little evidence from the first century C.E. for Samaritan theology, such a position is supported in the Samaritan woman's expectation of the Messiah as a prophet who can tell her all things (John 4:19–42). See Anderson and Giles, *Keepers,* 123–25; Montgomery, *Samaritans,* 239–50.

# Notes to Chapter 10

Primary sources: Scandal of Fulvia: Josephus, *Antiquities* 18.81–84; Tacitus, *Annals* 2.85; Suetonius, *Life of Tiberius* 36. Secondary sources: Harry J. Leon, *The Jews of Ancient Rome* (2d ed. Peabody, Mass.: Hendrickson, 1995); John M. G. Barclay, *Jews in the Mediterranean Diaspora: From Alexander to Trajan (323 B.C.E.–117 C.E.)* (Berkeley: University of California Press, 1996); Jo-Ann Shelton, *As the Romans Did* (2d ed. Oxford: Oxford University Press, 1998). Story is set in 19 C.E. Quote: Seneca the Younger (ca. 4 B.C.E.–65 C.E.) cited by St. Augustine in *City of God* 6.11.

1. Formal treaties of friendship in 161 B.C.E. and later (1 Maccabees 8; 14:24; 15:15–24) will have eased the ability of Jews to settle in Rome. See Barclay, *Jews in the Mediterranean Diaspora,* 285–92.

2. *Jewish Antiquities* 14.185–216.

3. Various historians have attempted to estimate the number of Jews in Rome in the early Empire based on a few extant references. According to Josephus, eight thousand Jews of Rome supported a petition of Judaea to Augustus (*Jewish War* 2.80; *Jewish Antiquities* 17.300), all of whom would have been citizens and heads of households, and Philo tells of a large community settled in the Transtiberine quarter of the city (*Embassy* 155). The estimates range from forty thousand to thousand, with fifty thousand being the commonly accepted number for the Jewish population in the city of Rome, and a

population of about six to seven million throughout the Empire; that is, Jews comprised roughly ten percent of the entire population of the Roman Empire. See Leon, *Jews of Ancient Rome,* 135, note 1, and sources cited.

4. The Transtiberine quarter lay outside the walls of first-century C.E. Rome, on the west bank of the Tiber, where unrestricted growth drew foreigners, and according to Philo, was populated mostly by former Jewish slaves, emancipated and now Roman citizens (*Embassy* 155).

5. Juvenal (ca. 60–130 C.E.) recounts the progression of sympathizers of Judaism to complete conversion, beginning with sabbath reverence, to worship of "nothing but the clouds," to abstention from pork, to circumcision and the observance of the Jewish law (*Satires* 14.96–106).

6. Although Philo mentions the "houses of prayer" in the Jewish community of Rome (*Embassy* 156), the archaeological evidence for significant synagogue buildings in Rome during the first century C.E. is disputed. Leon (*Jews,* 140–159) has identified eleven synagogues from ancient inscriptions; one was the Synagogue of the Augustesians, probably founded and dedicated during the reign of Caesar Augustus (27 B.C.E.–14 C.E.); see also Peter Richardson, "Augustan-Era Synagogues in Rome," in Karl P. Donfried and Peter Richardson, eds., *Judaism and Christianity in First-Century Rome* (Grand Rapids: Eerdmans, 1998). In the first century C.E., however, most Jewish congregations would likely have met in private residences, or the courtyards of multi-family dwellings, except for festivals.

7. According to Dio Cassius (*Roman History* 51.21.3), before the battle of Actium in 31 B.C.E. annual interest rates in Rome were about twelve percent, but after Octavian came to power, rates stabilized to around four percent, and no doubt remained between four and six percent under Tiberius.

8. On the crush of traffic in ancient Rome, Juvenal (ca. 60–130 C.E.) says, "We are blocked by a wave of people in front of us. And the great crowd behind crushes us. One man hits me with his elbow, another with a hard pole . . . then, on all sides, big feet step on me, and a nail from a soldier's boot pierces my toe. . . ." (*Satires* 3.232–248, cited in Sheldon, *As the Romans Did,* 69). Sheldon also notes that Julius Caesar prohibited wheeled vehicles on the streets of Rome during daylight hours, so the rich got around in litters.

9. Strabo, *Geography* 5.162; Tacitus, *Annals* 15.43; cf. Suetonius, *Life of Augustus* 89.

10. In the absence of a proper conversion ceremony at this stage of Judaism, Jewish definitions of proselyte, and social acceptance of a God-Fearer remained fluid. Philo (*Life of Moses* 2.17–24) and Josephus (*Against Apion* 1.162–167; 2.281–284) speak of the many Gentiles who are enamored of the Jewish way of life, laws, and customs, and worship of the one God. Josephus takes the Mosaic doctrine of equitable treatment of Gentiles (e.g., the "stranger within your gates" of Exodus 20:10; 22:21) and extends the invitation to all "to come and live under the same laws with us," because relationship is more than bloodline, it is "agreement in the principles of conduct" (*Against Apion* 2.210). Similarly, Philo explains the "stranger within your gates" as not one who

circumcises the flesh, but circumcises the desires and sensual pleasures and passions of the soul, and who rejects other gods (*Questions and Answers on Exodus* 2.2). For an overview of the varieties of Gentile attachment to Judaism, see the analysis of Shaye J. D. Cohen, *The Beginnings of Jewishness: Boundaries, Varieties, Uncertainties* (Berkeley: University of California Press, 1999), 140–74.

11. Pliny (*Natural History* 33.12) describes an iron ring without any stone in it is sent as a gift to a woman when betrothed (known as the *anulus pronubus*); Gellius (*Attic Nights* 10.10) says the standard practice of Greeks and Romans to place it on the left hand finger next to the smallest comes from the Egyptians, who through their practice of dissection of corpses, found that a nerve from the heart goes to that finger only, where it entwines with the other nerves; Macrobius (*Saturnalia* 7.13.7–9) quotes Gellius, and adds that Egyptian priests anoint with perfume that finger on statues in their temples because of the nerve to the heart.

12. There was a widespread belief and slander that Jews worshiped the head of an ass. Josephus recounts two published claims that a golden statue of the head of an ass lay within the Holy of Holies *(Against Apion* 2.80–81, 112–114); Tacitus also mentions a shrine sheltering a statue of an ass (*History* 4.4.2).

13. The official religion of Rome was the state cult, the worship of the Pantheon as the means of ensuring the blessings of the gods upon Rome. But this collective worship was always supplemented by personal devotion for personal gain, and certain religions, like Judaism, also offered eternal life of some sort. The Isis Mystery religion came from Egypt and promised the opportunity to adore Isis after death, as Apuleius tells us in *The Metamorphoses (= The Golden Ass)* 11.5–7. Another mystery religion popular among soldiers was Mithraism, the devotion to Mithras, an ancient god of Zoroastrianism, which taught the immortality of the soul and its journey after death. Bacchanalia was the Latin version of the Dionysiac orgies. See John Ferguson, *The Religions of the Roman Empire* (Ithaca: Cornell University Press, 1970) 99–131.

14. The removal of Herod's son Archelaus, *Jewish War* 2.80–100; *Jewish Antiquities* 18.342–344.

15. Because Diaspora Jews could not express their loyalty to Rome by the religious ceremonies and worship of the gods of Rome, they went to great lengths to demonstrate their loyalty in formal prayers in the synagogues, as Philo attests (*Flaccus* 48–50).

16. We learn numerous details about cosmetics and toiletry from ancient sources. For example, hair pluckers hawked their services in the streets, and Seneca laments that they were silent only when their customers were screaming (Seneca the Younger, *Letters* 56.1, 2). Women spent a great deal of time and money keeping themselves attractive and alluring with facial pastes, oils, creams, depilatories, and hair dyes were common, as well as cosmetics, especially eye paint. Jewish women were no exception (e.g., Mishnah *Shabbat* 8:3, 4; 10:6; *Kelim* 13:2; 16:8). It was customary for women to shave body hair from armpits and private parts, but some Jewish men apparently shaved their armpits

according to Hellenistic fashion, because the rabbis condemn it on the basis of the prohibition of men dressing like a woman (Deuteronomy 22:5), not because Torah forbids it (Babylonian Talmud *Nazir* 59a). On the other hand, women were permitted to keep themselves attractive even when work is to be curtailed during festivals (Mishnah *Moed Qatan* 2:7). Mothers taught their daughters how to preen, and besides shaving or plucking, various depilatories were known, from lime, flour paste, and oil of myrrh (Babylonian Talmud *Moed Qatan* 9b).

17. There are a number of examples from ancient love poetry that portray erotic passion, but in the tradition of Judaism it is sufficient to point to the biblical Songs of Songs, which may originally have been a collection of wedding songs, describing "the way of a man with a maiden" (Proverbs 30:19). Within it we find a longing for the beloved (1:2–4; 2:4–6), reflection on the beauty and charm of the beloved (4:1–7; 7:1–9), and teasing (1:7–8; 2:14–15).

18. Psalm 45:9.

19. Babylonian Talmud *Ketubbot* 56a, which gives a partial confirmation that this formula was used in antiquity.

20. Adapted from the marriage ceremony in *Joseph and Aseneth* (21:2, 7), a Hellenistic Jewish novella, dated between the first century B.C.E. and the second century C.E.; translation by C. Burchard, in *Old Testament Pseudepigrapha,* 2:235.

21. Adapted from Babylonian Talmud *Ketubbot* 7b–8a (Soncino translation). Some form of these blessings, alluding to Genesis 1–3, may well go back to the third century B.C.E., as claimed by the tradition in Babylonian Talmud *Berakhot* 33a: "It was the Men of the Great Synagogue (Mishnah *Avot* 1:1) who instituted for Israel blessings and prayers, sanctifications and *havdalahs."* The reference to the first wedding of Adam and Eve is early, found as a prayer in the marriage of Tobias and Sarah (Tobit 8:5–6). The present form of the blessing is clearly later, and I have altered parts that suggest Jerusalem has been destroyed.

22. Songs of Songs 7:12; 8:14.

## Notes to Chapter 11

Primary sources: parables from the Gospels. Story is set around 29 C.E. Quote: Luke 14:16–21.

1. This is the doctrine of reciprocity as the definition of justice, similar to the *lex talionis,* "an eye for an eye" (Exodus 21:23–25; Leviticus 24:19–20; Deuteronomy 19:21; Matthew 5:38). Aristotle attributes it to the Pythagoreans in *Nicomachean Ethics,* 5.5–8, but I obtain the phrase "justice is a square number . . ." from Will Durant, *The Life of Greece. The Story of Civilization* (vol. 2; New York: Simon & Schuster, 1939), 166.

2. Diogenes Laertius, *Lives of Eminent Philosophers* 1.36 (Hicks, Loeb Classical Library). Thales lived in the sixth century B.C.E.

3. Leviticus 19:18.

4. Babylonian Talmud *Shabbat* 31a. According to the tradition, the Gentile first asked Shammai to teach him while he stood on one foot, but Shammai drove him away with a measuring rod.

5. Matthew 7:12.

6. Deuteronomy 32:35 "Vengeance is mine and recompense," cited in the New Testament as "Vengeance is mine, I will repay" (Romans 12:19; Hebrews 10:30), which follows closely the Aramaic Targums and the Greek Septuagint.

7. Ecclesiastes 1:15; 7:13; and 3:21; 12:7. The spirit (*ruach*) is not the soul (*nefesh*), rather the life breath that animates humans and animals, but if the spirit of man returns to God, the author perhaps meant to leave open the door for continued self-existence. At any rate, the book of Ecclesiastes, along with Job, represents the best effort in Jewish tradition for the quest for meaning in life.

8. Deuteronomy 27:18.

9. Deuteronomy 6:4–9.

10. Proverbs 2:2–5.

11. The superstition known as the "evil eye" may be described as a malicious look based upon envy, and may even be a metonymy for the spirit of envy, but a glance that by itself can bring harm. The quip "if looks could kill" was believed to be possible. An evil eye is among the list of evil things that come from within (Mark 7:22; Matthew 6:23; 22:15; cf. Mishnah *Avot* 2:9). See further in chapter 14.

12. Our knowledge of the beliefs of Sadducees comes primarily from Josephus (*Jewish War* 2.164–66, *Jewish Antiquities* 13.173); with relevant comments in the Gospels (e.g., Matthew 22:23–33) and Acts 23:6–10, which confirm Josephus, and a few rabbinic traditions. The views of the Sadducees follow logically from their appeal to the written law of Moses exclusively for all matters of Jewish belief and practice. All three groups of sources agree that Sadducees rejected the immortality of the soul and a world to come (Matthew 22:23; *Jewish War* 2.165; Mishnah *Berakhot* 9:5; *Avot d'Rabbi Natan* A5), although manuscript variations in the rabbinic tradition may refer to heretics in general, cf. Babylonian Talmud *Berakhot* 54a). For a survey of the Sadducees, see E. P. Sanders, *Judaism: Practice and Belief 63 B.C.E.–66 C.E.* (Philadelphia: Trinity Press International, 1992) 317–40, and Frederick J. Murphy, *Early Judaism: The Exile to the Time of Jesus* (Peabody, Mass.: Hendrickson, 2002) 237–41.

13. See Matthew 13:44, and a slightly different version in the Coptic Gospel of Thomas 109, in which the man who finds the treasure begins lending money at interest, though he did not know about the treasure when he bought the field.

14. Matthew 5:42. Lending money at interest was an ancient practice, but generally frowned upon by the philosophers, since money had little, if any, intrinsic value (Plato, *Laws* 11.921 c-d; Aristotle, *Politics* 1.10). The Torah forbids a Jew lending money at interest to one of his brethren, but permits charging interest to Gentiles (Exodus 22:25 [Hebrew 22:24]; Deuteronomy 23:19–20

[Hebrew 23:20–21]). Jesus does not condemn lending money at interest, indeed, he assumes its value in the parable of the talents (Matthew 25:14–30; Luke 19:11–27), but early patristic writers do condemn it based on the Old Testament prohibition (Clement of Alexandria, *Stromata* 2.18; Tertullian, *Against Marcion* 4.17).

15. Matthew 13:4–9; Mark 4:4–9; Luke 8:5–8; Gospel of Thomas 9.

16. Genesis 26:12–14.

17. Matthew 13:24–30; Gospel of Thomas 57.

18. Luke 12:16–21; Gospel of Thomas 63.

19. This teaching is based primarily on Luke 14:12–24; but see the different versions in Matthew 22:1–10; Gospel of Thomas 64.

20. Luke 14:12–14; cf. Mishnah *Avot* 1:5, "Jose ben Johanan of Jerusalem said: Let thy house be opened wide and let the needy be members of thy household" (translation, Danby).

21. See Ecclesiastes 9:8; 12:7; for a condemnation of the view that all blessings and enjoyment must be found in this life, even at the expense of the poor, see Wisdom of Solomon 2, which may well represent a "Pharisee" critique of a "Sadducee" position.

22. Isaiah 26:19.

23. The story of the Medium of Endor is found in 1 Samuel 28. The Torah condemns sorcery and necromancy, the practice of communicating with the dead (Exodus 22:18; Leviticus 19:26, 31; 20:27; Deuteronomy 18:9–11), thereby confirming a belief that the dead continued in something like a state of sleep from which one can be disturbed (1 Samuel 28:15; Isaiah 14:9), but nothing that may be construed as a life of punishment or bliss.

24. Job 19:25–27.

25. Ezekiel (14:14, 20) sets Job beside the legendary Gentile sages Noah and Daniel (not the Jew of the book of Daniel). The *Testament of Job* (ca. first century B.C.E.–first century C.E. [*Old Testament Pseudepigrapha*, 1:829–68]) identifies Job as Jobab (2:1), the second king of Edom (Genesis 36:33–34), before God changed his name to Job; therefore, a descendant of Esau. Septuagint on Genesis 42:17 also identifies Job as Jobab, a descendant of Abraham (cf. *Aristeas the Exegete* 1 [*Old Testament Pseudepigrapha*, 2:859]). The *Testament* also says that Job married Dinah, daughter of Jacob and Leah, by whom he fathered his second set of children after God restored his fortunes (1:6; cf. Pseudo-Philo 8:7–8 [*Old Testament Pseudepigrapha*, 2:314]; Babylonian Talmud *Bava Batra* 15b; *Genesis Rabbah* 57:4). The later rabbinic opinion is divided on whether Job may be called an Israelite or not, depending on when Job lived (see the extended discussion in Babylonian Talmud *Bava Batra* 15b–16b, which also ascribes the authorship of the book of Job to Moses).

26. Daniel 12:2–3. Most scholars recognize this passage as the first certain reference to bodily resurrection in the Hebrew Bible, written in the mid second century B.C.E., although the development of the concept may be traced back earlier, for example Isaiah 65–66.

27. In the Hebrew tripartite canon of Scripture, Torah, Prophets, and Writings, the book of Daniel is placed among the Writings, and this group of books was not yet widely defined or considered authoritative in the early first century C.E. Other writings of the time, which were not canonized, also speak of resurrection and final judgment, e.g., *1 Enoch* 22–27, 90–104; 2 Maccabees 7:22–23, 27–29.

28. Matthew 22:32; Mark 12:26; Luke 20:37, citing Exodus 3:6.

29. Luke 16:19–30.

30. The story of the reversal of roles in the afterlife has parallels in ancient literature, suggesting the nature of a popular folktale, so that the motif would likely have been familiar, even if the version in Luke is an original composition attributed to Jesus. On what makes Luke's version unique, see Richard Bauckham, "The Rich Man and Lazarus: The Parable and the Parallels." *New Testament Studies* 37 (1991) 225–46.

31. Mishnah, *Sanhedrin* 10:1. See also the commentary in Babylonian Talmud *Sanhedrin* 72a.

32. Sheol, the traditional Hebrew abode of the dead without distinction between good and bad person, had, by the first century C.E., blended with the Hellenistic traditions of Hades. The Greek Septuagint (LXX) consistently translates Sheol as Hades, who is the Greek god of the underworld, into whose house the dead went, but it came to mean the entire abode of the dead. The parable in Luke 16:19–30 refers to Hades (v. 23), but we must assume the original context used the Hebrew Sheol, and that the imagery of Hades is already part of the imagery of Sheol. Within this Greek tradition, the river Styx, located in Arcadia, became a river of the underworld, over which one must cross in a boat rowed by Charon, whose fee was one obol.

# Notes to Chapter 12

Primary sources: Philo of Alexandria's book *On the Embassy to Gaius,* especially sections 351–367; and his other historical book, *Against Flaccus.* Josephus, *Jewish Antiquities* 18.257–309; and selections from *Against Apion* 2.21–81. Secondary literature: John M. G. Barclay, *Jews in the Mediterranean Diaspora: From Alexander to Trajan (323 B.C.E.–117 C.E.)* (Berkeley: University of California Press, 1996). Story is set in 40 C.E. Quote: Philo, *On Dreams* 2.290–291, (Loeb Classical Library, translation by F. H. Colson and G. H. Whitaker).

1. According to Dio Cassius (*Roman History* 66.35), Lucius Annaeus Seneca (ca. 4 B.C.E.–65 C.E.), a tutor and later political adviser to Nero, wrote a satire on Claudius' death, called the *Apocolocyntosis,* in which he likened the deification of Claudius to becoming a gourd or a pumpkin. The coined word *Apocolocyntosis,* built upon the noun *Kolokynte,* "gourd," or "pumpkin," and playing on the word *Apathanatisis* (immortalization), may be translated "pumpkinification." Besides its clever wit, it contains serious political criticism and personal invec-

tive against Claudius. Seneca eventually withdrew from political life and was forced to commit suicide.

2. Isaiah 42:6; 49:6. The mission goes back to the divine promise that all the nations of the earth shall bless themselves because of the descendants of Abraham (Genesis 22:18).

3. On Providence, only two fragments of the work are preserved in Greek from the *Praeparatio Evangelica* of Eusebius, although there is extant an Armenian version. The treatise is roughly in the form of a dialogue, in which a certain Alexander questions the notion of Providence, because of the evil and injustice in the world, and Philo responds that God is not a tyrant, but benevolent king with no better name than father. It is generally agreed that Alexander is none other than Tiberius Julius Alexander, the nephew of Philo.

4. Like holy city, the term holy land, or its equivalent such as sacred territory, occurs in the possibly pre-exilic Psalm 78:54, and in Zechariah 2:12, and later Greek Jewish literature (Wisdom of Solomon 12:3; 2 Maccabees 1:8). Philo uses a similar phrase when contrasting those Jews who dwell in Israel with those in the Diaspora: "[not only] those who were dwelling in the holy land, but over all the Jews in every part of the world" (*Embassy* 330).

5. Aulus Avillius Flaccus was governor of Egypt from 32–38 C.E. All the details of his administration and the pogrom of Alexandria are taken from Philo's book, *Against Flaccus*.

6. At the founding of the city, Alexander, or a later Ptolemy, gave the Jews their own quarter, Delta, with a local political organization similar to that of the Macedonians (*Jewish War* 2.487–488, 495; *Against Apion* 2.35); according to Philo, the Jews filled two of the five quarters, and had spilled out substantially into other sections fo the city (*Against Flaccus* 55).

7. We might assume that Gaius arrested Flaccus for some plot against the throne, not for maladministration against the Jews, but Philo portrays Flaccus as knowing that divine justice brought about his demise, and places a prayer of repentance in the mouth of Flaccus before his execution (*Against Flaccus* 170–175).

8. So the opinion of Josephus, who most likely relied on Philo for much of his own philosophical thought (*Jewish Antiquities* 18.259–60).

9. *Oy* is the ancient onomatopoetic expression of woe, usually with the dative *li* "to me"and *lanu* "to us" (e.g., Isaiah 6:5; Jeremiah 4:13).

10. Herod placed the golden eagle above the Nicanor Gate. Toward the end of Herod's life, when it was known that his disease was incurable, a few Jews, probably Pharisees ("unrivaled interpreters of the law"), tore down the golden eagle, declaring it to be an offense against the law (*Jewish Antiquities* 17.149–163; *Jewish War* 1.650). Insofar as the eagle was not in the temple, nor was it an object of veneration, it is not clear why it was against Mosaic law, but Josephus voices a common view that it was, and even declares the oxen supporting the bronze basin in the temple built by Solomon, and the lions around the king's throne, to have been against the law, or at least against common piety (*Jewish Antiquities* 8.195–196).

11. The standard silver coin, the denarius, usually bore the likeness of a Caesar on the obverse, and because of the imperial cult, at the very least, such coins were considered idolatrous and excluded from the temple precinct (hence the need for money-changers in Jerusalem).

12. On the incident of the iconic military standards in Jerusalem, see *Jewish War* 2.169–174; *Jewish Antiquities* 18.55. Again, what made the images offensive in Jerusalem was probably the fact that the soldiers revered the images as objects of worship, although Josephus says that no image was permitted within the city (*Jewish War* 2.170). The Maccabaean revolt was, of course, over a much more serious desecration of the temple, and very similar to the erection of the statue of Zeus.

13. *Embassy* 157, 317; cf. *Jewish Antiquities* 16.163.

14. *Letter of Aristeas* 16 (*Old Testament Pseudepigrapha* 2:13).

15. Philo, *Special Laws* 1.9 (on circumcision); 4.100–102 (on the prohibition against eating swine); the point of which is teaching moderation, although Philo never suggests Jews should not be circumcised or that they may eat swine; indeed he condemns those who do away with the literal circumcision and other fulfillment of the law (*On the Migration of Abraham* 89–92).

16. Plutarch, *Moralia* 219e; Aelian, *Varia Historia* 2.19; and like most of the stories about Alexander, it is deemed wholly unhistorical that he demanded the Greeks proclaim him as a god, but the story was told.

17. Philo, *Embassy* 194. The phrase is unique to Philo, and somewhat difficult to interpret, but clearly he felt that the universal (i.e., catholic) Jewish way of life; that is, the following of the ancestral customs, the laws of Moses, and the temple worship as the central cult, all of which had been recognized by Rome as the right of the Jews everywhere, was now in danger of being undermined, and this would leave Jews throughout the Diaspora without the protection of Roman law, considered as aliens and foreigners. See also *Against Flaccus* 53.

18. Dio Cassius, *Roman History* 56.30.

19. Following the description of Caligula by Suetonius, *Life of Caligula*.

20. *Embassy* 353; Philo says only that Gaius "uttered an ejaculation which it was impious to hear, much more would it be so to repeat it literally," but the pronunciation of the name of Yahweh seems the most likely interpretation. Caligula may have claimed to be the Jewish God, but simply claiming to be a god himself, would hardly have been unusual, or forbidden to hear by Jews. As may be seen from the Greek magical papyri, the general pronunciation of the name was all vowels, and we learn from Clement of Alexandria (ca. 215 C.E.), that the tetragram is pronounced *Iaoué* ('Ιαουε), which is similar to Yahweh (*Stromata* 5.6.34.5). For additional sources, see the *Universal Jewish Encyclopedia* 10:584–86.

21. Second-century C.E. inscription cited in S. R. F. Price, "Gods and Emperors: The Greek Language of the Roman Imperial Cult," in *Journal of Hellenic Studies* 104 (1984) 95.

22. *Embassy* 357; if Gaius actually said this, it would have been intentionally provocative, since "for me" (*huper*) implies the humanity of Caesar, as against "to me" (*emoi*), which implies divinity. The custom of offering sacrifices for a king was longstanding, as Aristeas notes that the high priest of Jerusalem offered sacrifices on behalf of (*huper*) Ptolemy (*Letter of Aristeas* 45 [*Old Testament Pseudepigrapha* 2:16]); and as Philo says just prior to this, the priests in Jerusalem had sacrificed on behalf of Caesar three times (*Embassy* 356).

23. Josephus, *Against Apion* 2.140–141; Josephus quotes Herodotus (*Against Apion* 1.169; *Jewish Antiquities* 8.262; Herodotus, *History* 2.110, cf. 37, 104) on the ancient practice of circumcision, and Herodotus says that the custom of the Jews (Syrians of Palestine) is borrowed from the Egyptians, and that either Egyptians or Ethiopians began the custom. Herodotus also says the Egyptians abstain from swine (*History* 2.47).

24. Josephus, *Against Apion* 2.80–81; Apion recounts a rumor that Antiochus Epiphanes discovered a golden head of an ass in the Holy of Holies when he entered the Temple (cf. 2.112–114 for another rumor to the same effect).

25. Josephus, *Against Apion* 2.237. Although there is no specific command in the Bible, according to Cohn (Loeb Classical Library, *Against Apion* 237 note *a*), the reasoning is based upon the Septuagint translation of Exodus 22:28, "You shall not revile God." See also *Jewish Antiquities* 4.207; Philo, *Life of Moses* 2. 205; *Special Laws* 1.53.

26. *Against Apion* 2.15–27; this is apparently an Egyptian version of the exodus of Jews from Egypt, and provides an etymology for the word "sabbath," in commemoration of the tumors called *sabbo*.

27. Under the first emperors, windows were contrived of a certain transparent stone, called *lapis specularis* (probably selenite), first found in Spain (later in Cyprus, Cappadocia, Sicily, and Africa), which might be split into thin leaves like slate, but not above five feet long (Seneca, *Letters* 90.25; Pliny, *Natural History* 36.160–162). This incident, however, is fictitious.

28. Josephus, *Jewish War* 2.203; *Jewish Antiquities* 18.305–309.

# Notes to Chapter 13

Primary sources: Acts 17:16–34; Paul's letters and various Greek works. Secondary literature: Ben Witherington, III. *The Acts of the Apostles: A Socio-Rhetorical Commentary* (Grand Rapids: Eerdmans, 1998); Troels Engberg-Pedersen, *Paul and the Stoics* (Louisville: Westminster John Knox, 2000). The story is set in about 51 C.E. Quote: Acts 14:29–31.

1. Josephus makes the case, primarily in book 2 of *Against Apion,* that since Moses lived long before the great Greek philosophers, they must have been influenced by Moses; for example: "Plato principally imitated our legislator in this point, that he enjoined his citizens to have the main regard to this precept, 'That every one of them should learn their laws accurately'" (2.257). Similarly,

Aristobulus (second century B.C.E.) says, "And it seems to me that Pythagoras, Socrates, and Plato with great care follow him [Moses] in all respects," (*Old Testament Pseudepigrapha,* 2:835–42, translated by A. Yarbro Collins). The extant writings of Demetrius the Chronographer (third century B.C.E.), Eupolemus (before the first century B.C.E.), and Artapanus (third to second centuries B.C.E.) are also found in *Old Testament Pseudepigrapha* volume 2.

2. Qohelet (Kohelet) is the pen-name for the author of Ecclesiastes, which contains the reflections of a Jewish Hellenistic philosopher from around the third century B.C.E. Although Ecclesiastes is traditionally ascribed to Solomon, based on the superscription "son of David, king in Jerusalem" (1:1), the internal evidence refutes the claim, and it was among the disputed works in the final canonization process by the early rabbis (Mishnah *Yadaim* 3:5). Ben Sira (Joshua ben Sira) wrote a collection of wisdom sayings around 180 B.C.E., called variously Wisdom of Ben Sira, Sirach, or Ecclesiasticus, and although popular, Rabbi Akiba declared it a forbidden book (Tosefta *Yadaim* 2.13), by which he may have meant for use in public readings and exposition, since Ben Sira is often quoted in the Talmuds. The *Letter of Aristeas,* besides telling the story of the official Greek translation of Torah, contains a lengthy symposium during which the seventy-two sages offer their wisdom to King Ptolemy in the tradition of numerous Hellenistic "On Kingship" treatises in antiquity (*Old Testament Pseudepigrapha,* 2:7–34).

3. Socrates (469–399 B.C.E.); Plato (429–347 B.C.E.); Aristotle (384–322 B.C.E.), Diogenes of Sinope, the Cynic (404–323 B.C.E.); Epicurus of Samos (341–271 B.C.E.); and Zeno of Citium, the Stoic (335–263 B.C.E.).

4. The word cynic comes from the Greek word *kyon,* dog, and is traditionally explained by the crude manners of cynics, in that they despised social convention, slept on the street, went barefoot, and engaged in sex in pubic, among other canine habits. The essence of the philosophy is that virtue is the only good, which requires simplicity, self control, and independence; therefore, the threadbare cloak, the staff, and begging bag were characteristic of Cynics.

5. The foundation of Epicurean thought is that all existence is comprised of atoms, in different combinations; even the gods are made of atoms, and simply dwell in a different sphere, doing neither good nor ill to humanity, serving only as examples of how to live in perfect happiness.

6. Acts 17:22; "cautiously pious" is one way to translate *deisidaimonesterous,* a subtly ambiguous word that means "fear of the daemons (gods)," and can be meant as a negative, "excessively superstitious," or positive, "very religious." Luke uses the word again in Acts 25:19, where it has a more obvious negative tone, but is commonly used by Josephus to mean "religion" (e.g., *Jewish Antiquities* 19.290); see G. Kittle and G. Friedrich, eds., *Theological Dictionary of the New Testament* (trans. G. W. Bromiley; 10 vols.; Grand Rapids: Eerdmans, 1964–1976) 2:20.

7. We have no solid evidence, archaeological or literary, of an altar with the inscription "To an unknown god" (Acts 17:23) during or prior to the first century C.E.; therefore, Luke or Paul may have lumped a variety of altars and dedi-

catory plaques to ancient heroes and foreign deities into the phrase. See the discussion of Witheringtion, *A Socio-Rhetorical Commentary,* 521–23.

8. Aratus of Soli in Cicilia (ca. 315–240 B.C.E.); translation by G. R. Mair in the Loeb Classical Library volume of Calimachus, Hymns; Lycophron; Aratus. This poem on astronomical wonders, *Phaenomena,* was widely read in antiquity, and begins with a proem to Zeus (lines 1–18), of which Luke quotes line five, "for we are also his offspring" (Acts 17:28). Aristobulus had already paved the way for the Jewish use of Hellenistic poetry in support of Judaism by quoting the first nine lines, although he changes the name of Zeus to *theos,* God, throughout, which he defends by saying that is what the Greeks really meant (frag. 4.6–7; *Old Testament Pseudepigrapha* 2:841).

9. On the equation of Zeus with Yahweh, as noted previously, Aristobulus finds it a natural one, Aristeas is likewise explicit (*Letter of Aristeas* 16), and Josephus quotes Aristeas approvingly (*Jewish Antiquities* 12.17–23); moreover, the identification was facilitated by the common title "Most High." As we have seen, the desire to see some glimmer of universal truth in all cultures was probably very strong among the Jews, and this desire may lie behind Paul's statement that the truth about the Creator God has been known all along, but corrupted by the imaginations of mankind, worshiping idols rather than the creator of all; that is, what can be known of God (which is very little) is abundantly evident in creation, a natural theology sufficient for all humanity to make the correct decisions (Romans 1:19–20; cf. Wisdom of Solomon 13:1–9; Philo, *Allegorical Interpretation* 3.97–99, on his version of the arguments of First Cause and Design).

10. Adapted from Martial, *Epigrams* 7.82, who does refer to a Jew.

11. Quoting lines attributed to Epimenides the Cretan (ca. 600 B.C.E.), although Epimenides predates the Stoics, for whom the line "in thee we live and move and have our being" would support their philosophy. The author of Titus seems to know of this poem (1:12), though we do not have the original. Similar lines are found in the *Hymn to Zeus* by Callimachus of Cyrene (ca. 305–240 B.C.E.). See F. F. Bruce, *Commentary on the Book of the Acts* (Grand Rapids: Eerdmans. 1954), 359, especially note 49.

12. According to Acts 17:18, Anastasia, the Greek word for resurrection, was apparently understood as a foreign goddess: "He seems to be a preacher of foreign divinities—because he preached Jesus and the resurrection" (i.e., *anastasis*).

13. Based on advice on drinking wine attributed to the Middle Comedy poet Eubulus (fourth century B.C.E.): "Three bowls only do I mix for the temperate—one to health, which they empty first, the second to love and pleasure, the third to sleep. When this is drunk up wise guests go home. The fourth bowl is ours no longer, but belongs to violence; the fifth to uproar, the sixth to drunken revel, the seventh to black eyes. The eighth is the policeman's, the ninth belongs to biliousness, and the tenth to madness and hurling furniture"; cited in Athenaeus (fl. ca. 200 C.E.), *Deipnosophistae* (The Learned Banquet) 2.36 (translation, Gulick, Loeb Classical Library).

14. Sophocles, *Ajax,* lines 292–293, describe the phrase as well-worn, and is more literally translated, "Woman, silence makes a woman beautiful" (translation, Lloyd-Jones, Loeb Classical Library). The well known quote "A woman should be seen, not heard" is from the translation of Sir George Young.

15. Adapted from Aristophanes, *The Ecclesiazusae* 956–80.

16. Aristotle, *Fragments* 106.

17. The Elysian fields (Homer, *Odyssey* 4.561–69); the Islands of the Blessed (Hesiod, *Works and Days* 161–73; *Theogony* 215–16). Pliny *Natural History* 6.203–205, describes the Fortunate Isles (most probably the Islas Canarias, Canary Islands); see also Plutarch, *Sertorius* 106–107, whose description better fits Madeira; for discussion see Christoph F. Konrad, *Plutarch's Sertorius: A Historical Commentary* (Chapel Hill: University of North Carolina Press, 1994).

18. Acts 23:6; Philippians 3:5.

19. Isaiah 42: 6–7; Luke may have based his Areopagus speech on Isaiah 42:5; compare Acts 17:24–27 with Isaiah 42:5–7. Paul describes his call and obligations in Romans 1:14; 11:13.

20. 1 Thessalonians 1:9–10.

21. Micah 6:8.

22. Paul speaks of becoming adopted sons and daughters of God (Galatians 4:4–7), because they are in Christ, the Son of God (Romans 8:1; 1 Corinthians 15:20–22). Baptism became the symbol of being in Christ and the new life (Romans 6:1–14; cf. 1 Corinthians 6:11), and Paul later expounds on this identification (Colossians 2:11–15).

23. Philippians 2:5–11 (Revised Standard Version), a hymn which is among the earliest evidence of the oral tradition of the gospel of Jesus.

24. Romans 1:19–21, 26; no distinction between Jew and Greek (Romans 10:12; Galatians 3:28).

25. The dilemma would have been simply between the *laissez faire* sexual mores of the Greeks and the Jewish restriction of sex to marriage, which was probably well known, along with the restriction against marrying outside the faith or ethnic boundary (cf. Tacitus, *Histories* 5.5.2). Although the reputation of the Essenes for celibacy was publicized by Philo (*Hypothetica* 11.14–18), Josephus (*Jewish War* 2.120–121), and was known to Pliny the Elder (*Natural History* 5.73), it is difficult to know if this advocacy of celibacy was associated with early Christianity at this stage, and the aspirations of Paul reflected in his teachings in 1 Corinthians 7:7, 29, 32–34, or the saying of Jesus in Matthew 19:12.

# Notes to Chapter 14

Primary source: Acts 19:11–19. Secondary literature: Ben Witherington, III, *The Acts of the Apostles: A Socio-Rhetorical Commentary* (Grand Rapids: Eerdmans, 1998). The story is set around 55 C.E. Quote is Acts 19:17–19a.

1. Exodus 20:7; prohibits the use of the name Yahweh for any empty purpose ("in vain") not in keeping with the honor it deserves, and specifically against magical incantations, for the God of Israel is not subject to manipulation.

2. The name Iao is the most common, since it is the Greek transliteration of YHW (Yaho), as found in the Elephantiné documents; for example, "Great [god] in heaven revolving the world, the true god IAŌ! ruler of all" (*PGM* LXXI.3–4), which is similar to Revelation 1:8, and a magical prayer addressed to "Master, IAŌ, light-bearer" (*PGM* V. 209–10); also "I conjure you by IAŌ SABATH ADO-NAI ABRASAX, and by the great god, IAEŌ" (*PGM* III 76–78). See Hans D. Betz, ed., *The Greek Magical Papyri in Translation Including the Demotic Spells* (2d ed.; Chicago: University of Chicago Press, 1992), 20, 104, 298.

3. Abram to Abraham (Genesis 17:5); Jacob to Israel (32:28).

4. As noted previously, the "evil eye" is a malicious look based upon envy, but a glance that by itself can bring harm. The quip "if looks could kill" was believed to be possible. An evil eye is among the list of evil things that come from within (Mark 7:22; Matthew 6:23; 22:15; cf. Deuteronomy 15:9; Proverbs 23:6; 28:22 (King James Version gives a literal translation); Sirach 14:8–10; 31:13); and is listed by the Sages among the dangers faced by humans (Mishnah *Avot* 2:9, 11; 5:19; Babylonian Talmud *Berakhot* 55b). Besides wearing an amulet for protection against the evil eye, in which the painted eye reflected the malicious envy back upon the person whence it comes, the most common practice was to spit. See G. Kittle and G. Friedrich, eds., *Theological Dictionary of the New Testament* (trans. G. W. Bromiley; 10 vols.; Grand Rapids: Eerdmans, 1964–1976), 6.555–56; Bruce J. Malina, *The New Testament World: Insights from Cultural Anthropology* (3d ed.; Louisville: Westminster John Knox Press, 2001) chapter 4, especially pages 121–25.

5. Hesiod, *Theogony* 270.

6. The great burning of magical texts in Rome occurred in 13 B.C.E. (Suetonius, *Augustus* 31).

7. Deuteronomy 18:9–13; Leviticus 19:31; Isaiah 8:19; cf. Judges 9:37 "Diviner's Oak"; Proverbs 17:8 "magic stone"; Isaiah 2:6; 3:2–3; 44:24–25; Jeremiah 27:9–10; Mica 3:6–7; Zechariah 10:1–2.

8. The many legends of Solomon probably all stem from the single passage, 1 Kings 4:29–34 [Hebrew 5:9–14], which speaks of his wisdom and knowledge of plants, hence the knowledge of cures; see Wisdom of Solomon 7:15–22; Targum Sheni to Esther on 1 Kings 5:13 [English 4:33]; *Jewish Antiquities* 8.45–49; *Testament of Solomon* (*Old Testament Pseudepigrapha*, 1:933–87).

9. Mishnah *Shabbat* 6:10, and commentary in Babylonian Talmud *Shabbat* 67a. Sages disagree on whether such actions should be permitted, but it is evidence of the practice. The smoke of the liver and heart of a fish is noted in Tobit 6:6–8; liver and gall in *Testament of Solomon* 5:9–10.

10. The scheme and defense are adapted from the speech of Auplieus, in *Apologia* (*Pro se de Magia*).

11. Josephus tells of the mysterious *baaras* root in *Jewish War* 7.178–185, and of its use in *Jewish Antiquities* 8.45–49.

12. Aquila, a Jew from Pontus, and his wife Prisca, became Christians in Rome, where they created sufficient controversy with the Jews of Rome to be included in the expulsion of Christians by Claudius in 49 C.E. (Acts 18:2–3; Suetonius, *Claudius* 25.4). Their precise social status and wealth is debated, but they were able to have a home sufficient for a church group, and employed Paul (1 Corinthians 16:19; cf. 2 Timothy 4:19; Acts 18:18). Paul says they "risked their necks" for him, probably at Ephesus (Romans 16:3–4).

13. Babylonian Talmud *Sanhedrin* 65b, recounts a tradition of two sages, Hanina and Oshaia, who spent every sabbath eve in studying the "Book of Creation," a thaumaturgical work that dealt with the laws of creation, which included mystic combinations of the Divine Name. By means of these combinations, the two sages created a calf one third the size of a grown cow, and ate it. Such power, though rarely used, was benign if used only for good.

14. Be'elzebul, Be'elzebub, (Mark 3:22–27; Matthew 12:24–28; Luke 11:15–20). The etymological origin of Ba'al Zevuv (Be'elzebub) is uncertain, possibly a euphemistic alteration for Ba'alzebul, "Lord of heaven"; but in Jewish tradition it came to be a name for the devil. Claims that Jesus was a sorcerer began quite early, perhaps even during his lifetime, although the earliest extant charge of being a "magician" is in the mid-second century (Justin Martyr, *First Apology* 30.1; *Dialogue with Trypho* 69.7); and Celsus, a critic of Christianity (ca. 178–180 C.E.), accused Jesus of performing "miracles" by sorcery (Origen, *Contra Celsus* 1.6; 2.9, 14, etc.). Jesus was apparently accused of being in league with the devil, "He is possessed by Be'elzebul, and by the prince of demons he casts out the demons" (Mark 3:22). John the Baptist was also accused of having a demon (Luke 7:33). Josephus describes Jesus as one who performed "incredible" (*paradoxos*) deeds (*Jewish Antiquities* 18.63), which parallels with Luke's description of the crowd's response to the works of Jesus, "We have seen strange things (*paradoxos*) today" (Luke 5:26). Several Talmudic traditions lay the charge of sorcery to Jesus, most notably: "On the eve of the Passover Yeshu [Jesus] was hanged. For forty days before the execution took place, a herald went forth and cried, 'He is going forth to be stoned because he has practiced sorcery and enticed Israel to apostasy. Any one who can say anything in his favor, let him come forward and plead on his behalf.' But since nothing was brought forward in his favor he was hanged on the eve of the Passover!" (Babylonian Talmud *Sanhedrin* 43a). For a sober and thorough analysis of Jesus and his "miracles," see John P. Meier, *A Marginal Jew: Rethinking the Historical Jesus* (vol. 2; New York: Doubleday, 1994), 507–1038.

15. The story of Simon Magus (i.e., the Sorcerer) in Acts 8:9–24 is an example of the interest in the name of Jesus for the sake of power and money.

16. The name Belial (Greek, Beliar) comes from the biblical Hebrew *beliyya'al,* often translated as "perdition," or "worthlessness," but the etymology is uncertain and it may be connected to being swallowed up, hence associated with the netherworld. Gradually, the descriptive evil became personified into

the archdemon, the angel of wickedness. Found throughout the Qumran literature and the Pseudepigrapha, Belial is the great antagonist of God. Belial ensnares people into sin, particularly into sexual promiscuity, "the plague of Belial" (*Jubilees* 1:20; *Testament of Reuben* 4:7–11; 6:3; *Testament of Simeon* 5:3). Belial accuses people before God and, therefore, is closely linked to Ha-Satan, the Accuser. Satan is a synonym for Belial in the *Testament of the Twelve Patriarchs* (*T.Dan* 3:6; 5:6; 6:1; *T.Gad* 4:7; *T.Asher* 6:4). The name Belial is used once in the New Testament explicitly for Satan as the antithesis of Christ (2 Corinthians 6:15). Belial is often described as the ruler of this world (*Martyrdom and Ascension of Isaiah* 2:4; 4:2). All the above mentioned works are found in the *Old Testament Pseudepigrapha.*

17. The vocabulary for describing evil spirits, fallen angels, and beings of the underworld in post-biblical Jewish literature is diverse, and derived from the merging of Hellenistic and Semitic traditions, and sources that cover centuries of development of demonology. Demon (= daimon) is Hellenistic, with classifications "of the home" or "of the woodlands," while evil spirit, unclean spirit, or spirit of evil in Hebrew is the Semitic *ruach,* spirit or wind, with a Greek equivalent, *pneuma.* Our sources often merge the two in a single phrase, as if they were different types, yet synonymous. For example, Josephus says David cast out "an evil spirit and demons" (*Jewish Antiquities* 6.211), though perhaps he adds demons for his Hellenistic audience, where the Hebrew has "evil spirit from the Lord" (1 Samuel 8:19); or, "they brought to him many who were demon possessed and he drove out the evil spirits" (Matthew 8.16); or, "a man who had the spirit of an unclean demon" (Luke 4:33).

18. Harpies are winged beings, wind-spirits, who carry off persons and things, named Aello, Ocypete, and Celaeno (Hesiod, *Theogony* 267).

19. The chief of the demonic world, called the Prince of Demons (Mark 3:22; *Testament of Solomon* 2:9; 3:5; 6:1), or the Angel of Darkness (Manual of Discipline [1QS] 3.20–21), is known by names other than Belial and Be'elzebul, and rank or origin differ among the sources. Among the most prominent are: Asmodeus (Tobit 3:8, 17; *Testament of Solomon* 5:1–8; Babylonian Talmud *Gittin* 68a–b; *Pesahim* 110a, where he is called "the king of demons"); Mastema (1 Enoch 6–16; *Jubilees* 10:8; 17:16; 19:28; 49:9, 15; 49:2); Azazel (1 Enoch 8:1; 9:6; 10:4–8; 13:1; *Apocalypse of Abraham* 13:6–14;14:4–6; 20:5–7; etc.).

# Notes to Chapter 15

Primary sources: on the legend of the flight of Johanan ben Zakkai, we have four accounts, representing two distinct traditions: 1) Babylonian Talmud *Gittin* 56a–b and *Lamentations Rabbah* 1.31; 2) *Avot d'Rabbi Nathan A,* chapter 4, and *Avot d'Rabbi Nathan B,* chapter 6; on the war we follow Josephus, *Jewish War,* primarily Books 3–5. Secondary literature: on the development of the tradition, see Anthony J. Saldarini, "Johanan Ben Zakkai's Escape from Jerusalem:

Origin and Development of a Rabbinic Legend," *Journal for the Study of Judaism* 6 (1975): 189–204; for the possible historical kernel and dating of a meeting between Johanan and Vespasian, see J. W. Doeve, "The Flight of Rabban Johanan Ben Zakkai from Jerusalem—When and Why?" in *Übersetzung und Deutung. Studien zu dem Alten Testament und seiner Umwelt, Festschrift Alexander Reinard Hulst* (Nijkerk: Uitgeuerijg F. Callenback B.V., 1977), 50–65. I favor Doeve's argument on the chronology, and follow it; also Jonathan Price provides keen observations on the historical potential for the tradition, in *Jerusalem Under Siege: The Collapse of the Jewish State* (Leiden: E. J. Brill, 1992), 264–70. While all legends embellish, they are often embellishments of some kernel of history, and the encounter of a Roman general with a revered sage of Jerusalem no more strains credulity than Josephus's account of a similar encounter which led to his freedom and life of luxury. No one seriously questions the tradition that Johanan ben Zakkai founded rabbinic Judaism at Jamnia (Yavneh). How he got there is the stuff of legends. The year is 69 C.E. Quote: *Jewish War* 6.312–15, possibly referring to the oracle of Daniel 2:44–45.

1. Such sacrifices were part of the diplomatic protocol and guarantees of political loyalty, and in the case of the Jews, served as their alternative to formal emperor worship. Philo, *Embassy to Gaius* 157, 317; Josephus, *Jewish War* 2.197, and his account of the cessation of the sacrifices in 2.409–417. Josephus notes that the sacrifice was "payment of homage of another sort, secondary to that paid to God, to worthy men; such honors we do confer upon the emperors and the people of Rome" (*Against Apion* 2.77 [translation, Thackeray, Loeb Classical Library]).

2. *Jewish War* 2.450–56; probably early September, 66 C.E. A possible rabbinic reference is found in *Megillat Ta'anit:* "On the 17th of Elul the Romans withdrew from Judah and Jerusalem" (H. Lichtenstein, "Megilat Ta'anit," *Hebrew Union College Annual* 8–9 (1931–32): 257–352, specifically pages 304–5, 320).

3. *Jewish War* 2.45–56.

4. *Jewish War* 2.515; 533–55.

5. Josephus records a number of omens, which, in his estimation, some people read falsely as signs of victory, but were properly seen as portents of doom (*Jewish War* 6.288–309, the three mentioned here are found in 289–93).

6. *Jewish War* 3.64–69; 340–408.

7. Eusebius, *Ecclesiastical History* 3.5; although he does not give a precise date, so it may have occurred somewhat earlier.

8. Nero committed suicide on 9 June, 68 C.E.

9. *Jewish War* 4.550, Josephus uses Macedonian months (Daesius = Sivan), but uses dates according to the Jewish months; this date would have been 15 June, or later.

10. Babylonian Talmud *Gittin* 56a.

11. Mishnah *Avot* 2:8.

12. That he was a Levite cantor, and therefore over the age of thirty by the start of the war, is found in Babylonian Talmud *Arakhin* 11b. Various traditions

about Joshua are found throughout the rabbinic corpus, and have been collected in Joshua Podro, *The Last Pharisee: The Life and Times of Rabbi Joshua
ben Hananyah a First-Century Idealist* (London: Vallentine, Mitchell & Co.
Ltd., 1959).

13. Deuteronomy 28:56; Babylonian Talmud *Gittin* 56a.

14. The great patriarch of Zealots was Phinehas, grandson of Aaron, whom
God commends for his zeal in keeping the land pure (Numbers 25:6–10). An
important element of the zeal of Phinehas was the willingness to slay a fellow
Israelite for the glory of God, and Zealots did not cower at the prospect of as-
sassinating Jews.

15. Isaiah 6:1.

16. Daniel 2:44.

17. Daniel 7:13.

18. This statement sums up the Zealot attitude, and is taken from the
speech composed by Josephus for Eliezer ben Jair, the Zealot leader at Masada
before the mass suicide. The arguments made here for the Zealot cause are distilled from that speech (*Jewish War* 7.323–336, 341–388).

19. According to the tradition in *Lamentations Rabbah*, Vespasian used the
baths at Gophna while Johanan ben Zakkai was with him. Gophna is located
fifteen miles northwest of Jerusalem. This tends to corroborate Josephus, who
says that Vespasian subdued Gophna before he rode up to the walls of Jerusalem in June of 69 C.E. (*Jewish War* 4.551).

20. The grumbling of the troops is given voice by Josephus, *Jewish War*
4.592–600.

21. Isaiah 10:34.

22. *Jewish War* 3.400–402.

23. The prophecy of Isaiah is common to both traditions and all texts. This
suggests that the passage is central to the historical kernel of the legends, and
we may accept that this was the proof-text for accepting the destruction of the
temple and the divine sanction on the rule of Rome for the sages. What the
sources do not do, is to develop the remainder of the oracle for the establishment of the Gamaliel Dynasty, but it may have been implied; I have simply
drawn the logical conclusions. If this goes back to an historical kernel, we may
assume Isaiah 10:32–34 was believed, since the quest was to find a suitable
prophecy that was believable.

24. Isaiah 10:32–34.

25. Zechariah 11:1; cf. the legendary statement by Johanan ben Zakkai in
response to the temple gates opening of their own accord a symbolic "forty
years" before the destruction (Babylonian Talmud *Yoma* 39b; Palestinian Talmud *Yoma* 6.3). Its usefulness is only in support of the interpretation of cedars
of Lebanon for the temple, ascribed to Ben Zakkai.

26. It has been argued that Rome, finding itself at war with Judaea, intended to destroy the temple because of its importance to all Jews as a political-
religious symbol for the rule of God ideology, and therefore resistence to the
rule of Rome. In support of this view, scholars cite the fourth century C.E.

Christian historian, Sulpicius Severus, who may have been dependent on lost work by Tacitus, that Titus hoped to wipe out the religion of Jews and Christians by destroying its root (*Chronicle* 2.30.6–7). Roman policy, however, was one of religious tolerance, and Rome was well aware that Jews constituted a substantial portion of their empire, as well as those in Persia. Josephus is at pains to place the blame on the Zealots, not on Rome (*Jewish War* 6.328–350), and describes Titus as trying to spare the temple; but he had good reasons to do so, for the stimulus for writing the Jewish War was to take blame away from Rome and to help pacify the Jewish Diaspora. In any case, the final siege of Jerusalem and the destruction of the temple fell to Titus, not Vespasian, and it is doubtful that Vespasian's goal was destruction of the temple. See Schürer, *The History of the Jewish People in the Age of Jesus Christ,* revised edition, (4 vols.; Géza Vermès et al., eds.; London: T&T Clark. 1973–1986), 1:506–7.

27. Isaiah 45:1.

28. Suetonius, *Life of Vespasian* 1–4.

29. Leather trade is entirely speculative, based on a tradition that he spent a symbolic "forty years in commerce" (Babylonian Talmud *Rosh Hashanah* 31b; *Sanhedrin* 41a). The clan of Zakkai is mentioned in Ezra 2:9; Nehemiah 7:14, but there is no known connection beyond the name.

30. Isaiah 11:1–2.

31. According to later rabbinic tradition, Gamaliel son of Simeon son of Gamaliel the Elder (Acts 5:34–40; 22:40; Babylonian Talmud *Shabbat* 15a), was the direct descendant of Hillel. There are reasons to doubt that Gamaliel the Elder was a grandson of Hillel, as well as the claim that Hillel was descended from David (Palestinian Talmud *Ta'anit* 4.2.68d), albeit, through the maternal line (Palestinian Talmud *Kilaim* 9.32b). However, genealogies were kept, used, and believed, and if the tradition was as old as the Gamaliel here in question, and not invented after the destruction of Jerusalem, then Johanan ben Zakkai would likely have believed it and used it in making his case.

## Notes to Epilogue

1. Genesis 32:28 [Hebrew 32:29].

2. Philo *Embassy* 4.

3. Psalm 24:1.

4. Although documents dating through the Byzantine era have been found at Elephantiné, the latest dated Jewish document is 399 B.C.E. The slow migration of Jews to Ethiopia, or the far earlier presence of Israelites in Ethiopia is debated, though it seems likely that Israelites who got as far as Elephantiné would continue the Jewish diaspora to the south as easily as westward to Spain. The story of the Ethiopian Eunuch in Acts 8:26–40, even if fictitious, represents a group of Ethiopians who worship in Jerusalem, and would appear no more strange to the contemporary reader than Babylonian Jews who made pilgrim-

age to Jerusalem. Modern Falashas have been accepted as fully Jewish by the State of Israel, and Falasha traditions claim great antiquity.

5. Matthew 23:2.

6. Genesis 26:4–5.

7. Psalm 22:27.

8. Isaiah 45:22.

9. Isaiah 52:10.

10. Isaiah 49:6.

11. Isaiah 45:1.

12. On Paul's analogy of grafting converts into the olive tree, see Romans 11:17–24.

13. Josephus, *Jewish Antiquities* 18.63–64. The famous *Testimonium Flavianum,* as it comes down to us has been altered by Christian scribes, but most scholars accept a revised form to have been original with Josephus.

14. Ephesians 6:12.

15. Mishnah *Eduyot* 7:7. While it is not certain Gamaliel's mission was to receive authority for the calendar, that is the likely reason, based on the context of the discussion; see also Babylonian Talmud *Sanhedrin* 11a.

16. *Sibylline Oracles* 3.271; Josephus, *Jewish War* 2.398 in a speech attributed to Agrippa; cf. *Against Apion* 2.282; Philo, *Against Flaccus* 45–46; cf. *Special Laws* 2.163.

# Chronology of Early Judaism

The purpose of this chronology is to give a reasonably full outline of events in the ancient world that form the background to the development of Judaism and the stories. Personal names that appear in the book (excluding footnotes and Josephus) are in bold on first occurrence, and principle fictional names in bold italics. Many dates are uncertain or controversial by a year or two but do not affect the general flow of a chronology. Events preceded by a question mark are particularly uncertain.

## B.C.E.

640 **Josiah** king of Judah (640–609)

622 Josiah begins temple reform, discovery of the Book of the Law

610 Pharaoh **Necho** II (610–595)

609 Josiah killed in battle against Egypt at Megiddo; Josiah's son, Jehoahaz, is made king in Jerusalem; reigns three months; Necho deposes Jehoahaz and exiles him to Egypt, makes his brother Jehoiakim king (609–598)

605 **Nebuchadrezzar** (605–562) defeats Necho at Carchemish

601 Jehoiakim rebels against Nebuchadrezzar

598 Nebuchadrezzar besieges Jerusalem, Jehoiakim dies or is exiled

597 **Jehoiachin** succeeds his father, reigns three months and surrenders to Nebuchadrezzar

First Deportation: thousands exiled to Babylon; men of valor, craftsmen and smiths, and the temple gold; according to Josephus, also **Ezekiel**; Nebuchadrezzar installs **Zedekiah**, third son of Josiah, as vice-regent (597–587)

595 Psammetichus II (595–589) Pharaoh of Egypt

594 **Zedekiah** forms anti-Babylonian coalition but it fails and he sends delegation to Babylon

591 Psammetichus promises support for Judah in rebellion against Babylon and invades Phoenicia

590 (?) Jewish mercenaries fight for Pharaoh Psammetichus in a campaign against Ethiopia, which may be the origin of the Jewish garrison stationed at Elephantiné

589 Zedekiah's second attempt at a coalition, including Egypt and Tyre

Jeremiah counsels submission to Babylon

588 **Hophra** (=Apries, 588–569) Pharaoh of Egypt

587 Nebuchadrezzar begins eighteen-month siege of Jerusalem

586 Jerusalem captured, Babylonians destroy the temple (ninth of Av = August)

Second Deportation: Zedekiah flees Jerusalem; captured near Jericho, blinded and sent into exile along with small group of exiles

**Nebuchadrezzar** sets Gedaliah as administrator of remaining people in Judah

582 Ultra-nationalist and member of royalty, Ishmael assassinates Gedaliah; many Jews in Jerusalem flee to Egypt, taking Jeremiah with them

Third Deportation: according to **Jeremiah,** 745 people

569 General Ahmosis II (= **Amasis**) assassinates Pharaoh Hophra Egyptian army mutinies against Babylon

568 Incident between **Ezekiel,** *Eliakim, Marah, Hattil, Menachem* Nebuchadrezzar puts down rebellion in Egypt against Amasis

562 Amel-Marduk (562–560) king of Babylon, releases Jehoiachin from prison in the thirty-seventh year of his captivity

560 Nergal-shar-usur (Nergilissar, 560–556) king of Babylon

559 **Cyrus,** son of Cambyses, becomes king of the Persian tribe Anshan

556 Death of Nergal-shar-usur; succession by his son Labash-Marduk in May, but deposed by rebels, who establish their own leader, Nabunaid (= Nabonidus)

555 Nabonidus king of Babylon (555–539)

550 Cyrus allies with Nabonidus, revolts against Astyages, king of Medes, becomes king of Medes and Persians

547 Cyrus conquers Mesopotamia and Syria

540 Cyrus controls all land east to Indus River

539 Cyrus welcomed into Babylon by subjects of Nabonidus

538 Cyrus allows Jews to return to the province of Yehud

(?) First return under Sheshbazzar with "heads of father's houses," priests, and Levites

530 Cyrus dies while at war in western Persia

Cambyses (530–522) king of Persia

525 Cambyses conquers Egypt, confirms the status of the Jews at Elephantiné and their temple of Yahu

522 Cambyses dies on his return from Egypt; power struggle in Persia, his general Darius gains the throne

Darius (522–486) reorganizes the Persian kingdom into 120 satrapies

522 Second return of Jews under **Zerubbabel,** and high priest Joshua

Haggai addresses Zerubbabel and Joshua, urging them to finish the Temple

518 Zechariah delivers apocalyptic vision oracles (1–8)

515 Temple in Jerusalem completed

509 First year of the Roman Republic

490 Battle of Marathon: Darius defeated in his attempt to invade Greece

486 Xerxes king of Persia (486–465/4) founds new capital, Persepolis

480 Battle of Salamis: Xerxes defeats Greeks at Thermopylae, burns Athens, but loses his entire navy in battle and returns to Persia

465 Artaxerxes I (465–423), Xerxes assassinated

458 (?) **Ezra,** in the seventh year of Artaxerxes, comes to Jerusalem; orders mixed marriages to be dissolved

*Uriah, Ophrah, Elam*

445 Nehemiah, cupbearer of Artazerxes, persuades king to make Judah an independent province and name him as governor

444 Nehemiah begins rebuilding the walls of Jerusalem, opposed by the governor Sanballat

433 Nehemiah returns to Susa

430 (?) Nehemiah takes up second appointment as governor of Judah, initiates drastic measures, including forced divorce

424 Darius II Ochus, king of Persia (424–404)

419   Arsham (=**Arsames**), Persian governor of Egypt, instructs Jews at Elephantiné to celebrate Passover according to Jerusalem practice

410   Egyptians burn the temple of Yahu (Yahweh) on island of Elephantiné

Jews write to **Bagavahia** (Bagohi/Bagoas), governor of Judaea, asking him to persuade Arsames, governor of Egypt, to rebuild the temple of Yahu

407   Jerusalem reply concerning the temple of Yahu: **Jedaniah, *Rami, Natan, Hekhamet, Hor***

404   Artaxerxes II Arsaces, king of Persia (404–360/59)

Egypt gains independence under king Amyrtaios

401   Artaxerxes defeats rebellion led by his brother, Cyrus the Younger

400   (?) Temple of Jerusalem sacked by Bagoses after Johanan and Joshua fight for high priesthood

399   Death of Socrates (b. 469)

398   (?) Return of Ezra (in seventh year of Artaxerxes II Arsaces)

386   Artaxerxes II Arsaces's control of Ionian cities; confirmed by "King's Peace"

360   Artaxerxes III, king of Persia (360–338)

338   Arses, king of Persia (338–336)

**Philip** of Macedon defeats Athens and Thebes in the Battle of Chaeronea

336   **Alexander** the Great (336–323), upon assassination of Philip, becomes king of Macedon

335   **Darius** III Condomannus, king of Persia (336/5–331/0)

334   Alexander crosses Hellespont and conquers western Asia Minor, battle of Granicus.

333   Alexander wins Battle of Issus in Syria; Darius flees back to Persia

332   Alexander besieges Tyre and Gaza; Jerusalem submits: **Jaddua, *Tobiah, Theokeles***

331   Alexander enters Egypt, founds city of Alexandria

331   Alexander defeats Darius III at Battle of Arbela (Gaugamela)

326   Alexander forced by mutinous troops to turn back from conquering India

323   Alexander dies of fever in Babylon

Successors (Diadochoi) to Alexander struggle for control of the empire

312 Ptolemy invades Coele-Syria (Battle of Gaza), (?) takes Jerusalem on a sabbath, brings many captive Jews to Egypt

305 **Ptolemy** Soter (305–283) recognized as king of Egypt

304 **Seleucus** Nicator (304–280) recognized as king of Syria

301 Battle of Ipsus settles the division of Alexander's Empire: Lysimachus (Thrace, Asia Minor); Cassander, son of Antipater (Macedon, Europe); Seleucus (Syria, Persia); Ptolemy (Egypt, Coele-Syria, Judaea), though control of Coele-Syria remains in dispute between the Ptolemies and Seleucids in the Syrian Wars

285 Erection of the Pharos lighthouse in Alexandria harbor

283 Ptolemy II Philadelphus (283–246)

281 **Seleucus** takes dissolved kingdom of Lysimachus, controls all Asia Minor

280 Antiochus I Soter (280–261) Seleucid king

274 First Syrian War, Ptolemy II versus Antiochus I (274–271)

264 First Punic War, Rome versus Carthage (264–241)

261 Antiochus II Theos (261–246) Seleucid king

259 Second Syrian War, Ptolemy II versus Antiochus II (259–253)

250 (?) Ptolemaic translation of Hebrew Torah into Greek (Septuagint)

249 Arsaces I founds Kingdom of Parthia between Seleucid kingdom and Bactria

246 Ptolemy III Euergetes (246–221), king of Egypt

Third Syrian War, Ptolemy III versus Seleucus II (246–241)

239 War of the Brothers, Seleucus II versus Antiochus Hierax (239–236)

227 Earthquake destroys the Colossus of Rhodes

223 Antiochus III (223–187), king of Syria

221 Ptolemy IV Philopater (221–204), king of Egypt

Fourth Syrian War (221–217) Antiochus III attempts to take Coele-Syria

218 Second Punic War, Rome versus Carthage (218–202), Hannibal attacks Italy

215 First Macedonian War, Rome versus Philip V of Macedon (215–205)

211 Hannibal marches on Rome

204 Ptolemy V Epiphanes (204–180), king of Egypt

Scipio Africanus reaches Africa with Roman army

203 Hannibal recalled to Carthage

202 Fifth Syrian War (202–195) Antiochus III takes Coele-Syria

Simon II, son of Onias, high priest of Jerusalem repairs the temple

Scipio Africanus defeats Hannibal, Carthage becomes client state of Rome

200 Second Macedonian War, Rome invades Greece (200–196).

199 Antiochus III wins control of Judaea

196 Greek States come under the hegemony of Rome

190 Onias III high priest in Jerusalem (190–175)

189 Antiochus III defeated by Rome at Magnesia, surrenders territory west of Mount Taurus

187 Seleucus IV (187–175), Seleucid king

180 Ptolemy VI Epiphanes (180–145)

175 **Antiochus** IV Epiphanes (brother of Seleucus IV) Seleucid king

**Jason** makes Jerusalem a polis, serves as high priest (175–172)

172 **Menelaus** serves as high priest in Jerusalem (172–163)

Roman embassy in Antioch, Antiochus visits Jerusalem

170 Sixth Syrian War, Antiochus IV versus Ptolemy VI (170–168)

Onias III murdered by Menelaus

169 Antiochus IV defeats Ptolemy VI, becomes "protector" of Ptolemy VII; enters Jerusalem, takes temple treasure

168 Antiochus renews attack on Egypt, withdraws under Roman ultimatum in July

Suppression of Judaism and temple pollution

167 **Mattathias** of Modein rebels, joined by Hasidaeans

166 Antiochus IV begins eastern campaign

**Lysias** takes control, besieges Jerusalem, then offers terms

Mattathias dies; **Judah Maccabee** (Judas Maccabaeus) takes leadership of revolt

165 Judas Maccabaeus defeats Lysias at Beth-zur (fall), Jerusalem under his leadership

(?) Book of Daniel, chapters 7–12 composed

164 Antiochus rescinds edict of persecution

Jerusalem temple cleansed and rededicated on the twenty-fifth of Kislev

***Rhodocus, Glaphyra, Hannah, Jacob***

Antiochus V king of Syria (164–162) at age nine

163 Menelaus executed by order of General Lysias

Antiochus V Eupator enthroned as a minor under protection of Lysias, restores Jerusalem temple

162 Demetrius I Soter (162–150) cousin of Antiochus V, claims throne

Alcimus high priest, Hasidaeans make peace with Syria, (some executed?)

161 Demetrius executes Lysias and Antiochus V

Judas Maccabeus makes friendship treaty with Rome, dies in battle with Bacchides

**Jonathan Maccabee** (161–143), leader of Jewish Revolt

160 Alcimus dies; no high priest appointed (or perhaps "Teacher of Righteousness"?)

152 Jonathan becomes high priest with support of Demetrius

150 Alexander Balas (150–145) king of Syria; Jonathan governor of Judaea

147 Jonathan defeats Apollonius and Demetrius II, gains control of Gaza region

146 Rome establishes the province of Macedon, as part of Roman Empire

Rome destroys Carthage, establishes province of Africa

145 Demetrius II takes Seleucid throne (145–140), but struggles with rivals continue

Jonathan receives more territory

143 Jonathan betrayed and executed by Seleucid general Diodotus Tryphon

**Simon Maccabaeus** (143–135), high priest and ruler of Judaea, negotiates with Demetrius for independence

142   Simon gains tribute exemption, Judaea becomes independent state

Simon renews friendship treaties with Rome and Sparta

140   Mithridates, Parthian king, annexes Babylonia from Seleucids

138   Antiochus VII Sidetes (138–129), secures Seleucid throne

134   Simon assassinated by Jewish/Egyptian general Ptolemy

**John Hyrcanus** (134–104) high priest and ruler of Judaea

Seleucid hegemony restored in Judaea in treaty with Antiochus VII, John Hyrcanus opens David's tomb for silver

130   Antiochus VII begins campaign against Parthia (dies in 129)

129   Demetrius II, second reign (129–126)

John Hyrcanus stops Judaean tribute

128   John Hyrcanus captures Shechem and Idumaea, conversion of Idumaeans to Judaism

126   Antiochus VIII Grypus (126–113), Seleucid king

Rome coverts kingdom of Pergamum into province of Asia

113   Antiochus IX (113–95) Seleucid king

104   Aristobulus (104–103), first Hasmonaean to call himself "king"

103   **Alexander Jannaeus** (103–76) high priest and king of Judaea; some fifty thousand Jews slain

93    Civil war in Judaea, Demetrius III attacks Alexander Jannaeus, but leaves when Jews change sides, and Jannaeus executes eight hundred opponents

92    Mithridates II makes peace treaty with Rome

88    First Mithridatic War, Rome versus Mithridates IV Eupator (88–84)

84    Antiochus XII dies in campaign against Nabataean Arabs

83    Second Mithridatic War, Rome gains victory over Cappadocia and Pontus (83–81)

81    **Pompey** campaigns in Africa

76    **Alexandra Salome** (76–67), appoints her son, **Hyrcanus II,** as high priest (76–67)

Pharisees gain power in court

74    Third Mithridatic War, Rome gains control of Asia Minor and Syria (74–64)

67   **Aristobulus II** assumes diadem against brother Hyrcanus II, civil war in Judah

*Seth, Ananias, Guardian Joshaphat*

Pompey sweeps Mediterranean of pirates

66   Pompey defeats Mithridates VI, Rome controls all Syria

64   Seleucid Dynasty ends

63   Pompey invited to settle Jewish rule, takes Jerusalem, enters Holy of Holies, deposes Aristobulus II

Direct Roman rule begins: Hyrcanus II high priest and ethnarch

62   Syria made a province of Roman Empire

58   Gabinius: Roman governor of Syria and Judaea

57   Aristobulus II and son Alexander revolt, defeated by Gabinius

54   Roman general **Crassus** raids wealth of temple before attacking Parthia

53   Cassius governor of Judaea

49   **Julius Caesar** crosses Rubicon, engages Pompey in Roman civil war

48   Caesar defeats Pompey, secures Egypt

Herod governor of Galilee

47   **Herod** kills Galilean bandit Hezekias, appears before Sanhedrin

Caesar establishes Cleopatra VII and Ptolemy XIV as joint rulers of Egypt

44   Caesar assassinated

42   **Antony** takes rule of the east

40   Parthians establish Antigonus II king and high priest

Herod escapes to Rome

39   Herod declared king of Judaea by Roman Senate

37   Jerusalem falls to Herod; Antigonus II executed by Antony in Antioch

Antony marries Cleopatra

High priest Ananel (37–36) a Babylonian appointed by Herod

35   Aristobulus the last Hasmonaean high priest, age seventeen, later drowned by Herod's order

34   High priest Ananel, second appointment (34–?)

31   Great earthquake in Judaea: *Jose, Leah, Mother Miriam, Balsam*

Battle of Actium: **Octavian** defeats Antony

30    Antony and Cleopatra commit suicide, Ptolemaic Dynasty ends

29    Octavian's triumph, administers Rome; legions reduced from sixty to twenty-eight

Marcus Agrippa made heir apparent; Miriamme executed by Herod

27    Octavian receives title **Augustus** (27 B.C.E.–14 C.E.); Samaria/Sebaste rebuilt by Herod

23    Augustus gives Herod Trachonitis, Banatea, Auranitis

20    Augustus gives Herod the northern Galilee (Paneas)

Herod rebuilds Strato's Tower/Caesarea, begins rebuilding of temple

Herod requires oath of loyalty, Pharisees refuse: **Jonathan, Zoma, Hillel, Shammai, Pollion,** *Hanina, Assi*

10    Herod invades Nabataea against Galilean raiders, censured by Augustus

4     Herod dies (March/April)

**Archelaus** king of Judaea, Jerusalem riot at Passover, slays three thousand

High priest Eleazar son of Boethus (4–?), appointed by Archelaus

Varus sacks Sepphoris; crucifies two thousand rebels around Jerusalem

Augustus divides kingdom: Archelaus (–6), **Philip** (–34), **Antipas** (–39)

## C.E.

6     Archelaus banished and Judaea becomes Roman province, Prefect **Coponius** (6–9)

Judas the Galilean leads minor revolt, suppressed by Coponius

High priest **Ananus** (Annas) son of Sethi (6–15), appointed by Quirinius

8     Incident of the Samaritan temple desecration: *Levi, Phinehas, Simeon, Jacob, Manasseh*

9     Prefect Marcus Ambivulus (9–12)

12    Prefect Annius Rufus (12–15)

14    **Tiberius Caesar** (14–37)

15 Prefect Valerius Gratus (15–26)

Germanicus invades lower Germany

18 Building of city of Tiberias begun

High priest Joseph surnamed Caiaphas (18–36), appointed by Gratus

19 Jewish incident in Rome and banishment of four thousand Jewish proselytes under Tiberius

*Marcus, Domitia, Vitalis, Domitius, Petronius, Regina, Severus*

Death of Germanicus at Antioch

26 Prefect **Pontius Pilate** (26–36)

27 Tiberius withdraws to Capris, Sejanus gains power in Rome

29 Mission of **Jeshua of Nazareth**

*Jokim, Bilhah, Dosethius, Rufus*

31 Sejanus exposed in Senate of Rome and executed

33 Jeshua of Nazareth crucified (or ca. 30)

34 Philip dies, his tetrarchy added to Syria

36 Antipas defeated by Aretas IV in dispute over land and marriage

Pilate recalled; Marcellus (36–37) temporary Prefect

37 **Gaius Caligula** emperor (37–41), gives **Agrippa I** a kingdom in Syria

Prefect Marullus (37–41)

38 Prefect Avillius **Flaccus** permits Alexandrian riots against Jews

39 Antipas seeks kingship of all Israel in Rome; exiled to Spain or Gaul

Agrippa I made king by Caligula over territory of Philip and Antipas

40 Caligula attempts to install statue in temple, **Petronius** delays; **Jewish** delegation to Rome: *Agathon, Philip,* **Tiberius Alexander, Apion, Isidorus, Lampo**

41 **Claudius** emperor (41–54), after Gaius Caligula's assassination

Agrippa I made king of Judaea and Samaria

44 Judaea again becomes a province of Rome at death of King Agrippa

Procurator Cuspius Fadus (44–46?)

46    Procurator Tiberius Alexander (46?–48); crucifies the sons of
      Judas the Galilean

48    **Agrippa II** receives kingdom of Herod of Chalcis

      Procurator Ventidius Cumanus (48–52)

51    **Paul of Tarsus** in Athens: **Dionysius the Areopagite,
      Damaris,** *Demetrius, Daphne, Lucian*

52    Procurator Antonius Felix (52–59?)

54    **Nero Caesar** (54–68)

55    Paul's mission in Ephesus: **Aquilla, Prisca, Sceva,** *Eutychus,
      Asteria, Thalassa, Balas*

59    Procurator Procius Festus (59?–62)

61    Josephus leads embassy to Rome on behalf of priests

62    Procurator Lucceius Albinus (62–64)

      High priest Ananus son of Ananus executes certain prominent
      Jews, including James, brother of Jesus, and is deposed by King
      Agrippa II

64    Procurator **Gessius Florus** (64–66)

      Rome burns, and Christians persecuted

      Tiberius Alexander becomes Prefect of Egypt

66    Judaean revolt begins and Josephus takes command of the Galilee

      Tiberius Alexander quells riots in Jewish Quarter in Alexandria

67    **Vespasian** appointed legate to carry on war in Judaea

      Phannias son of Samuel, a lowly priest appointed as high priest by
      the people

68    Josephus surrenders to Vespasian

      Nero dies; **Galba, Otho, Vitellius**

69    **Johanan ben Zakkai** flees Jerusalem and meets with General
      Vespasian: **Ben Battiah, Eliezer, Joshua,** *Shammuah*

      Vespasian emperor (69–79)

70    Jerusalem falls to Titus; destruction of the temple

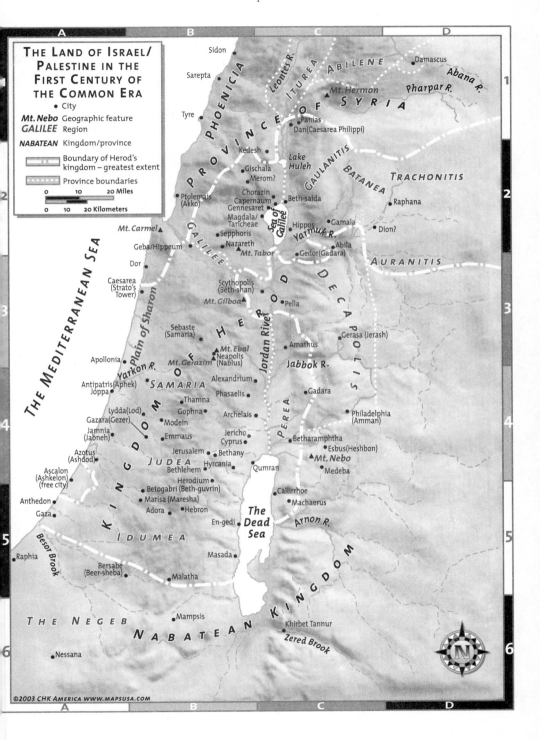

**THE LAND OF ISRAEL/ PALESTINE IN THE FIRST CENTURY OF THE COMMON ERA**

- • City
- **Mt. Nebo** Geographic feature
- **GALILEE** Region
- **NABATEAN** Kingdom/province
- ▦ Boundary of Herod's kingdom – greatest extent
- ┄ Province boundaries

0      10      20 Miles
0   10   20 Kilometers

THE MEDITERRANEAN SEA

PROVINCE OF PHOENICIA

Sidon
Sarepta
Tyre
Kedesh
Gischala
Merom?
Ptolemais (Akko)
Mt. Carmel
Geba/Hippeum
Dor
Caesarea (Strato's Tower)
Apollonia
Antipatris (Aphek)
Joppa
Lydda (Lod)
Gazara (Gezer)
Jamnia (Jabneh)
Azotus (Ashdod)
Ascalon (Ashkelon) (free city)
Anthedon
Gaza
Raphia

Leontes R.
ITUREA
ABILENE
Damascus
Abana R.
Pharpar R.
Mt. Hermon
PROVINCE OF SYRIA
Panias
Dan (Caesarea Philippi)
Lake Huleh
GAULANITIS
BATANEA
TRACHONITIS
Chorazin
Capernaum
Gennesaret
Magdala/ Taricheae
Sepphoris
Nazareth
Beth-saida
Raphana
Sea of Galilee
Hippos
Gamala
Dion?
Yarmuk R.
Mt. Tabor
Abila
Gedor (Gadara)
AURANITIS

GALILEE
Plain of Sharon
Yarkon R.

KINGDOM OF HEROD

Scythopolis (Beth-shan)
Mt. Gilboa
Pella
Sebaste (Samaria)
Mt. Ebal
Mt. Gerazim
Neapolis (Nablus)
Amathus
Gerasa (Jerash)
DECAPOLIS
Jabbok R.
SAMARIA
Alexandrium
Phasaelis
Gadara
Antipatris
Thamna
Gophna
Archelais
Philadelphia (Amman)
Modein
Emmaus
Jericho
Cyprus
PEREA
Jerusalem
Bethany
Betharamphtha
Esbus (Heshbon)
Hyrcania
Mt. Nebo
JUDEA
Bethlehem
Qumran
Medeba
Herodium
Betogabri (Beth-guvrin)
Marisa (Maresha)
Callirrhoe
Machaerus
Adora
Hebron
En-gedi
The Dead Sea
IDUMEA
Masada
Bersabe (Beer-sheba)
Malatha
Arnon R.
NABATEAN KINGDOM
THE NEGEB
Mampsis
Khirbet Tannur
Zered Brook
Nessana
Besor Brook
Jordan River

N

©2003 CHK AMERICA WWW.MAPSUSA.COM

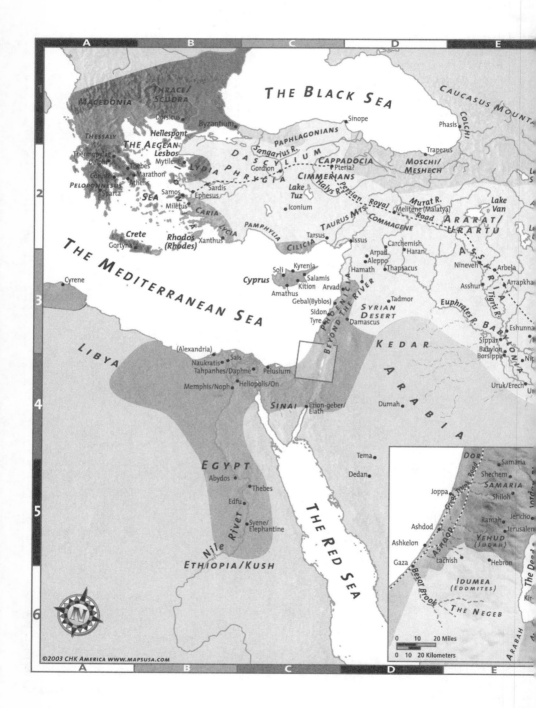

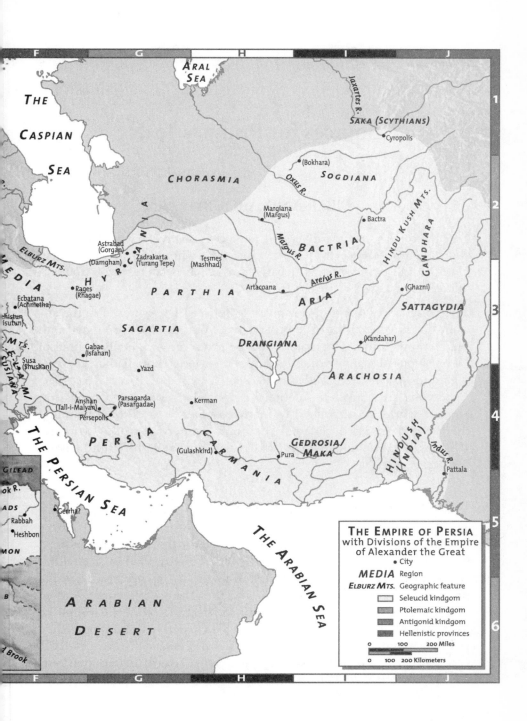

THE CASPIAN SEA

THE

ARAL SEA

SAKA (SCYTHIANS)

Jaxartes R.

Cyropolis

CHORASMIA

(Bokhara)

SOGDIANA

Oxus R.

ELBURZ MTS.

HYRCANIA

Margiana (Margus)

Bactra

HINDU KUSH MTS.

GANDHARA

Astrabad (Gorgan)

(Damghan)

Zadrakarta (Turang Tepe)

Tesmes (Mashhad)

BACTRIA

MEDIA

Rages (Rhagae)

PARTHIA

Artacoana

Areius R.

ARIA

(Ghazni)

SATTAGYDIA

Ecbatana (Achmetha)

histun isutun)

Margus R.

SAGARTIA

DRANGIANA

(Kandahar)

MTS.

USIANA

Gabae (Isfahan)

Yazd

ARACHOSIA

Susa (Shushan)

ELAM/

Anshan (Tall-i-Malyan)

Parsagarda (Pasargadae)

Persepolis

Kerman

PERSIA

CARMANIA

(Gulashkird)

GEDROSIA/ MAKA

Pura

HINDUSH (INDIA)

Indus R.

Pattala

GILEAD

ok R.

ADS

Rabbah

Heshbon

MON

Gerrha?

THE PERSIAN SEA

THE ARABIAN SEA

B

d Brook

ARABIAN

DESERT

THE EMPIRE OF PERSIA
with Divisions of the Empire
of Alexander the Great

• City

MEDIA Region

ELBURZ MTS. Geographic feature

☐ Seleucid kindgom

Ptolemaic kindgom

Antigonid kindgom

Hellenistic provinces

0     100     200 Miles

0   100   200 Kilometers

# Sources for Primary Texts

## BIBLE AND APOCRYPHA

I use the Revised Standard Version, and occasionally the King James Version. I also reference the Coptic Gospel of Thomas, part of the Nag Hammadi Library, which is an early gnostic Christian text from the second century C.E.

The designation Apocrypha is given to thirteen books found in the ancient Greek collections of Jewish writings but never incorporated into the Hebrew canon. The majority of the texts were originally written in Hebrew or Aramaic or other Semitic languages, though they are preserved mostly in Greek and are dated between 300 B.C.E. and 70 C.E. The Apocrypha are considered deutero-canonical by Roman Catholicism, and the works are appended to many editions of the Bible, including the Revised Standard Version. The books referenced in this work are 1 Esdras (3 Ezra), Sirach (Ben Sira, Ecclesiasticus), Tobit, Judith, 1 and 2 Maccabees.

## ARAMAIC PAPYRI OF ELEPHANTINÉ

A number of ancient papyri scrolls written in the fifth century B.C.E. were discovered by accident and excavated over a period of several decades in the late nineteenth century on the island of Elephantiné in the upper Nile near Aswan. Among them is the group of ten papyri known as the Jedaniah Archive, which tell of the destruction of the temple of Yahu and the attempts to have it rebuilt. The papyri have been published in English translation by Arthur Ernest Cowley, *Aramaic Papyri of the Fifth Century B.C., Edited, with Translation and Notes* (Oxford: Clarendon Press, 1923), and by Bezalel Porten, *The Elephantine Papyri in English: Three Millennia of Cross-cultural Continuity and Change* (Leiden and New York: E. J. Brill, 1996).

# DEAD SEA SCROLLS

The collection of ancient papyri texts found at Qumran in 1947 and subsequently. The scrolls contain biblical texts and sectarian documents believed to be associated with the Essenes, but more specifically a separate community similar to the Essenes, commonly called the Covenanters. The texts are mostly dated to the Hasmonaean dynasty (ca. 160–140 B.C.E.) All the texts have now been published and translated. The most popular edition is *The Complete Dead Sea Scrolls in English: Translated from the Hebrew and Aramaic* by Géza Vermès (New York: Allen Lane/Penguin Press, 1997). The following works are referenced: *Pesher Nahum* (4Q169); *Damascus Document* (4Q266–272); *Community Rule* (1QS); 4QMMT (4Q394–399); *Pesher Habakkuk* (1QpHab); *War Scroll* (1QM).

# PHILO

Philo of Alexandria (ca. 20 B.C.E.–50 C.E.) wrote numerous philosophical treatises on allegorical interpretations of the Torah, and two short histories of important events in his life, *Against Flaccus* and *The Embassy to Gaius*. All of his writings are available in *The Works of Philo Complete and Unabridged*, translated by C. D. Yonge, (Peabody, Mass.: Hendrickson Publishers, 1995). The standard academic edition is in the Loeb Classical Library, translated by F. H. Colson, G. H. Whitaker, J. W. Earp, and R. Marcus. Other books referenced: *Special Laws, On the Life of Moses, On the Migration of Abraham, Questions and Answers on Exodus, Every Good Man is Free, Hypothetica, On the Virtues, On Dreams*.

# JOSEPHUS

Flavius Josephus (ca. 37–100 C.E.) wrote four books between 73 and 95 C.E.: *The Jewish War, Jewish Antiquities, Life, Against Apion*. His writings are easily accessible in the single volume, *The Works of Josephus Complete and Unabridged*, translated by William Whiston (Peabody, Mass.: Hendrickson Publishers, 1987). The standard academic edition is in the Loeb Classical Library, translated by A. St. J. Thackeray, R. Marcus, A. Wikgren, and L. H. Feldman.

# MISHNAH

The Mishnah is the earliest document of rabbinic literature, essentially the codification of oral law and traditions into six divisions and sixty-three tractates. The earliest stratum of laws will have likely been the rulings of the Pharisees, but the final corpus contains the development of the laws up to the time of codification, when it was written down under the direction of the Patriarch Judah the Prince around 200 C.E. The standard English translation is *The Mishnah, Translated from the Hebrew with Introduction and Brief Explanatory Notes* by Herbert Danby, (Oxford: Oxford University Press, 1938). Also very useful and accessible is the analytic translation of Jacob Neusner, *The Mishnah: A New Translation* (New Haven: Yale University Press, 1988).

## TOSEFTA

The Tosefta, which means "addition," is a collection of early rabbinic opinions similar to the Mishnah, and is generally viewed as the views that supplement the views contained in the Mishnah. The collection was finalized sometime between the period of the Mishnah and the Palestinian Talmud, generally assigned to the second half of the third century C.E. The only English translation is by Jacob Neusner et al., recently republished as *The Tosefta, Translated from the Hebrew with a New Introduction* (2 vols.; Peabody, Mass.: Hendrickson Publishers, 2002).

## BABYLONIAN TALMUD

The Babylonian Talmud is the commentary, called the Gemara, on the Mishnah by the sages of the Babylonian Jewish community, essentially completed around the year 600 C.E. The standard English translation is the Soncino edition, (general ed. I. Epstein, 35 vols., 1935–1952, reprint in 18 vols., London, 1961).

## PALESTINIAN TALMUD

The Palestinian Talmud, also called the Jerusalem Talmud, contains the commentary of the rabbis of Palestine upon the Mishnah. The sages involved lived during the third and fourth centuries C.E., with a few names associated with the early fifth century C.E., so that the final redaction of the Talmud was around 430 C.E. The only complete English translation is by Jacob Neusner, *Talmud Yerushalmi* (Chicago: University of Chicago Press, 1982–).

## OTHER RABBINIC TEXTS

Reference is made to additional rabbinic texts from the Midrashim, exegetical commentaries on the Torah (Pentateuch) and the Five Scrolls,

Lamentations, Ruth, Esther, Song of Songs, and Qohelet (Ecclesiastes). These works are found in the Soncino edition of the Midrash Rabbah (London: Soncino Press, 1939). Also, note was made to *Avot d'Rabbi Natan,* (Fathers According to Rabbi Nathan), which is an amplification of the Mishnah tractate Avot, compiled during the fifth to seventh centuries C.E.; and *Megillat Ta'anit* (Scroll of Fasting), a listing of the fast days, which probably was compiled in the second century C.E., though its present form is later.

## PSEUDEPIGRAPHA

The designation Pseudepigrapha includes a vast array of Jewish literature in antiquity, mostly written between 250 B.C.E. and 200 C.E. The vast majority of these works were written in Greek, though some are Greek translations from Hebrew and Aramaic originals, and a few were found among the Dead Sea Scrolls. All the texts have been collected and translated in *The Old Testament Pseudepigrapha,* (2 vols., ed. James H. Charlesworth; New York: Doubleday, 1983). Books referenced: *Apocalypse of Abraham; Aristeas the Exegete;* Artapanus Fragments; *1 Enoch;* Ezekiel the Tragedian, *Exagōgē; Joseph and Aseneth; Jubilees; Letter of Aristeas; Martyrdom and Ascension of Isaiah; Testament of Job; Testament of Moses; Testament of Solomon; Testament of the Twelve Patriarchs (Reuben, Simeon, Dan, Gad, Asher).*

## GREEK AND ROMAN CLASSICS

All the works from ancient Greek and Latin classics used in this book are found numerous translations. Generally, I refer to the Loeb Classical Library (Cambridge: Mass.: Harvard University Press). Books referenced:

Aelian (ca. 170–235 C.E.), *Varia Historia*

Apuleius (ca. 123–? C.E.), *The Metamorphoses (The Golden Ass), Apologia* (*Pro se de Magia*)

Aratus of Soli (ca. 315–240 B.C.E.), *Phaenomena*

Aristophanes (ca. 450–385 B.C.E.), *The Ecclesiazusae*

Aristotle (384–322 B.C.E.), *Nicomachean Ethics, Politics*

Arrian (fl. second century C.E. ), *History of Alexander*

Athenaeus (fl. early third century C.E.), *Deipnosophistae*

Callimachus of Cyrene (ca. 305–240 B.C.E.), *Hymn to Zeus*

Celsus (fl. first century C.E.), *On Medicine*

Dio Cassius (fl. ca. 200–230 C.E.), *Roman History*

Diodorus (fl. ca. 60–30 B.C.E.), *Library of History*

Diogenes Laertius (fl. early third century C.E.), *Lives of Eminent Philosophers*

Gellius (ca. 130–180 C.E.), *Attic Nights*

Herodotus (ca. 484–420 B.C.E.), *History*

Hesiod (fl. ca. 700 B.C.E.), *Works and Days, Theogony*

Juvenal (ca. 50–130 C.E.), *Satires*

Macrobius (fl. early fifth century C.E.), *Saturnalia*

Martial (ca. 40–104 C.E.), *Epigrams*

Plato (ca. 429–347 B.C.E.), *Laws*

Pliny the Elder (ca. 23–79 C.E.), *Natural History*

Plutarch (ca. 50–120 C.E.), *Life of Alexander, Moralia*

Sophocles (ca. 496–406 B.C.E.), *Ajax*

Strabo (ca. 64 B.C.E.–21 C.E.), *Geography*

Suetonius (ca. 69–130 C.E.), *Lives of the Caesars (Tiberius, Augustus, Caligula, Claudius)*

Tacitus (ca. 56–115 C.E.), *Histories, Annals*

## EARLY CHURCH FATHERS

The works of the early church fathers are all contained in a multi-volume set of the Ante-Nicene Fathers (down to 325 C.E.) and the Nicene and Post-Nicene Fathers, widely reprinted, for example, (Peabody, Mass.: Hendrickson Publishers, 1994). Books referenced:

Clement of Alexandria (ca. 150–215 C.E.), *Stromata*

Eusebius (ca. 260–340 C.E.), *Ecclesiastical History*

Justin Martyr (ca. 100–165 C.E.), *First Apology, Dialogue with Trypho*

Origen (ca. 185–254 C.E.), *Contra Celsus*

Sulpicius Severus (ca. 360–420 C.E.), *Chronicle*

Tertullian (ca. 160–225 C.E.), *Against Marcion*

THE ROMAN EMPIRE

THRACE  Roman province

·········· Boundary of Roman
           Empire 65 C.E.

·········· Roman road

0        100      200 Miles

0    100    200 Kilometers

©2003 CHK America www.mapsusa.com